The Death Penalty

America's Experience with Capital Punishment

Raymond Paternoster
University of Maryland

Robert Brame
University of South Carolina

Sarah Bacon
Florida State University

Foreword by Stephen B. Bright
Southern Center for Human Rights

New York   Oxford
OXFORD UNIVERSITY PRESS
2008

Oxford University Press, Inc., publishes works that further Oxford
University's objective of excellence in research, scholarship, and education.

Oxford New York
Auckland Cape Town Dar es Salaam Hong Kong Karachi
Kuala Lumpur Madrid Melbourne Mexico City Nairobi
New Delhi Shanghai Taipei Toronto

With offices in
Argentina Austria Brazil Chile Czech Republic France Greece
Guatemala Hungary Italy Japan Poland Portugal Singapore
South Korea Switzerland Thailand Turkey Ukraine Vietnam

Copyright © 2008 by Oxford University Press, Inc.

Published by Oxford University Press, Inc.
198 Madison Avenue, New York, New York 10016
http://www.oup.com

ISBN 978-0-19-533242-1

Printing number: 9 8 7 6 5 4 3 2

Printed in the United States of America
on acid-free paper

RP:
To Ronet. You have my love forever.
RB:
To my wife Geni, the love of my life.
SB:
For the students who will read this book, in the hopes that they will benefit from having done so.

Contents

Part I
The Enduring Legacy of
Capital Punishment in the
United States

Part II
Legal History, Constitutional Requirements, and Common Justifications for Capital Punishment in the United States

Part III
The Administration of the Death Penalty: Issues of Race and Human Fallability

Part IV
What's to Come of the
Death Penalty

Preface

A voice was heard in Ramah, sobbing and loud lamentation; Rachel weeping for her children, and she would not be consoled, since they were no more.

Matthew 2:18

If baseball is American as apple pie, capital punishment can't be too far behind as a national pastime. While the game of baseball has been around since the mid-1800s, capital punishment has been practiced on American soil since the 1600s. In this book we try to provide a comprehensive review of many issues that pertain to the death penalty in America. We have attempted to be broad in our treatment, meaning that we cover not just a few topics, but many—the history of the death penalty, an overview of how the death penalty works today, how the death penalty has historically and continues to be intertwined with race, constitutional questions that have been raised about the death penalty, the risk of executing the innocent, justifications and rationales both for and against the death penalty, the financial costs involved, how the international community views capital punishment, and some assessment as to how the death penalty fits into the American future.

In covering a lot of substantive ground in such a short book, our treatment, although we think comprehensive, is not exhaustive. We could have spent much more time on every one of the topics we cover—there is that much material about the death penalty—and some issues we could not do complete justice to. Our purpose in writing this book, however, was not to give in-depth coverage to a few specific topics related to capital punishment (there are ample books out there that do just that). Rather, we wanted to provide survey-depth coverage of what we thought to be the most interesting and relevant issues about the death penalty and provide some historical, legal, cultural, and political context. Our target was the person who is interested in the death penalty but wants to know a lot about it without focusing on any one specific issue. After reading this book, readers can focus their attention on more specific topics, and we hope we have provided them with some guidance on how to do that in our "Student Resources" section at the end of each chapter.

Just as our purpose was not to be exhaustive but to be general, we have avoided being academically "disciplinary." This is not a sociological book about the death penalty, any more than it is a political science, history, psychology, or legal treatment of capital punishment. Each of us is a criminologist with multidisciplinary training, and the approach of this book reflects that. We talk about legal, historical, political, philosophical, cultural/literary, and criminal justice/criminology issues as they pertain to the death penalty. We honestly attempted to be "jacks-of-all-trades" and masters of none. Readers wanting to know the "fill in the discipline" perspective about the death penalty will be disappointed. Those wanting a basic but detailed view of the operation, history, and topical issues with respect to the death penalty will, we hope, be rewarded and also encouraged to do more in-depth examination of the particular topics that fascinate them.

The death penalty has existed in American society for a long, long time, and it shows no sign of disappearing. While America executes many fewer persons today than in decades past, there was still an average of 70 executions per year for each of the past 10 years (1996–2005), and in April 2006 there were more than 3,300 prisoners on state and federal death rows across the United States. While the number of executions fluctuates year to year, at least one execution has occurred every year since 1981.

What is striking about the death penalty in America is that in spite of its historical longevity, it generates such controversy and ambiguity. While we as a society think we want to put people to death for some kinds of crimes, we have always tried to narrow and limit what those kinds of crimes are. Theoretically, we have tried to restrict the death penalty to the "worst of the worst" because that is who we think "deserves" it in some sense. But the death penalty has not in practice had that kind of surgical precision. We execute those whom many would think of as "moral monsters" (those who kill many persons, brutally and seemingly with no remorse), but we also put to death those whose crime consisted of a botched armed robbery by a scared kid that resulted in the death of a store clerk.

Even while thinking we need to put some people to death, we have always been troubled with the method of how to do it. Although we expel murderers from the human community by executing them, we also think they possess enough humanity that we should be concerned that their death is quick and painless. We are also troubled by the possibility that in a system operated by fallible human beings, an innocent person might be put to death. To avoid the conviction and execution of an innocent person we have thick layers of procedural protections and rounds of appellate review—to make sure we "get it right"—but then we are also troubled by the fact that prisoners are not executed quickly enough.

What we have learned in our many years of researching and reading about the death penalty is that no one wins. We are humbled by the tragic loss that many parties feel when they are brought together with capital punishment. An innocent life has been lost; there is incomprehensible grief by family members and loved ones of the murdered victim. If the executioner takes his due, another life will be lost. If the executed person is not innocent, surely the family members of the executed are, and their loss and sense of grief are likely as painful as those of the family members of the victim. Through an event—murder—which in one sense has ripped them and their lives apart, the family members of the victim and offender are brought together by the common bond of inconsolable pain and grief. "Rachel" weeping for her children in Matthew 2:18 could be a mother on either side of this seemingly great divide.

Acknowledgments

The authors wish to thank the following reviewers for their comments and helpful suggestions: John Cochran (University of South Florida), Kimberly J. Cook (University of North Carolina, Wilmington), Tom Durkin (Northwestern University), Judith A. McDonald (Westfield State College), Stephen Morreale (Walden University and Roger Williams University), David Schulberg (Chapman University and California State University, Fullerton), Dennis J. Stevens (University of Southern Mississippi), and Scott Vollum (James Madison University). ✦

Foreword

Stephen B. Bright

A re some people unfit to live? Are the rest of the people in the community qualified to make the momentous decision as to whether another human being—even one guilty of murder—is to be tied down and put down? How does a community make the decision to kill one of its members? It's one thing to decide whether a person is guilty or innocent—the instructions given by the court are clear. But how does one decide whether a fellow human being is fit or unfit to live? These and many other questions addressed in this book have been subjects of debate since the 1600s.

Those issues have not been resolved, but they *have* been joined by many other issues and arguments that are organized and presented by Professors Paternoster, Brame, and Bacon in this book—including racial discrimination, laws that best regulate when death is to be imposed and how, constitutional issues that have repeatedly divided the courts, the risk of executing an innocent person, and related issues of importance to the use of the death penalty in the United States.

Everyone should be concerned about these issues. Winston Churchill said that the "treatment of crime and criminals is one of the most unfailing tests of any country." That test surely includes whether a country includes the death penalty in its "treatment" of criminals. Some countries do, such as China, Iran, Saudi Arabia, and the United States. Some do not. Neither Canada or Mexico has it; the European countries no longer use it; and a majority of other countries in the world have abandoned it. Those without it seem to get along as well as or better than those that have it. Twelve states in the United States do not have capital punishment; other states have it but do not use it.

An informed citizenry is essential in deciding whether to have the death penalty and, if it is instituted, how and when to use it. However, in voting to strike down the death penalty in 1972, Supreme Court Justice Thurgood Marshall observed that Americans know almost nothing about capital punishment. That situation is still true today. Many Americans know one thing about the death penalty: they are for it or against it. But beyond the idea of capital punishment in the abstract, what are they for or against? Do they know how often it is used? Do they know whether racial disparities occur in its use? Or that it is imposed in some parts of the country or their state more than others?

Sixty percent of Americans believe that the death penalty is fairly imposed while only 35 percent think it is unfairly imposed. But how reliable are those opinions? How do they know? Have they been attending trials? Do they know the ethics, competence, and plea bargaining practices of the prosecutors in their state? Do they know what kind of lawyers are appointed to represent the accused? Are the familiar with the other facts and issues examined in this book? Unless people are informed their answers to polling questions are of little or no value.

A society that uses such a unique and extraordinary punishment—one that is enormous, severe, irreversible, and that has played a central role in the nation's history of racial oppression—should know about it. This book will be immensely valuable for those who want to be fully informed about the death penalty in the United States. It examines the issues and provides references to other sources.

Understanding the death penalty begins with understanding the process through which some people are condemned to die. The death penalty is authorized for thousands of people who commit murders each year, but only about 125 were sentenced to death each year from 2004 through 2006. Even fewer—around 60—are actually put to death each year. Most others—some guilty of far more heinous crimes and with worse records of criminal behavior—are punished with life imprisonment without possibility of parole or some other sentence. One example is Gary Ridgeway, known in Seattle as the Green River Killer and believed to have murdered over 70 people, who avoided the death penalty by pleading guilty to 48 counts of murder in November 2003. Others include Charles Cullen, a nurse who killed at least 29 patients in New Jersey and Pennsylvania, and Theodore Kaczynski, the Unabomber, who mailed explosives to people, killing three and injuring others. Few people on death row have committed crimes as heinous as theirs.

These three cases, as well as most of the thousands of other potential capital cases, were resolved by prosecutors, not juries. Prosecutors decide whether a case will be prosecuted as a capital case—a prosecution is never required to ask for the death penalty—and, if it is, whether it will be resolved through a plea bargain or go to trial. Most capital cases, like the overwhelming majority of all cases in the criminal justice system, are resolved not at trials but through plea bargains in which the defendant enters a plea of guilty and the prosecution agrees to imposition of a sentence other than death.

But the practices of prosecutors vary widely. In most states, prosecutors are elected by districts. In Texas, for example, over 100 prosecutors are elected. Prosecutors are completely independent of each other. They may have completely different policies with regard to the death penalty.

Some prosecutors never seek the death penalty, while others seek it at every opportunity. And the rest fall somewhere between these two poles.

The unlimited discretion that prosecutors exercise in deciding whether to seek the death penalty and whether to accept plea bargains largely determines who is sentenced to death and who is not. The prosecutors in Manhattan and the Bronx did not seek the death penalty at all in the ten years that New York had capital punishment before the New York Court of Appeals found the death penalty law unconstitutional. So no one from those jurisdictions went to death row. Prosecutors in Philadelphia and Houston seek the death penalty far more often and send far more people to death row than prosecutors in Pittsburgh, Dallas, and the rest of the country. There are similar differences among prosecutors within every state. This discretion is something to keep in mind when considering the Supreme Court's decisions requiring that the death penalty be imposed consistently.

In some instances, the discretion of prosecutors is influenced by race. This book, appropriately, gives considerable attention to race and the death penalty. The history of racial discrimination in the infliction of the death penalty is a brutal and shameful one. Its impact on the courts can still be felt today. The race of the victims and the defendants influences who is sentenced to death. Far too often, African Americans facing the death penalty have their fate decided by all-white juries because prosecutors use their discretionary jury strikes to remove people of color from juries.

This discrimination is not limited to capital cases. The criminal justice system is the institution that has been least affected by the Civil Rights Movement. African Americans continue to be significantly underrepresented among prosecutors, judges, defense lawyers, and jurors. Some of these members of the legal system have racial attitudes that influence, consciously or subconsciously, their decisions. The criminal courts often treat African Americans more harshly than whites, from stops by law enforcement (such as those for "driving while black"), to more severe sentences for blacks than whites for all types of crimes.

Poverty, like race, has a major influence on who is sentenced to death, as described in several places in this book. The overwhelming majority of the people accused of crimes—whether capital or noncapital—are poor. The major consequence of poverty for the accused is inability to hire a lawyer. Instead, a a judge or an agency assigns a lawyer to represent the accused.

Being represented by a court-appointed lawyer is not necessarily bad, but it usually is. Some states—including Colorado, Connecticut, and New York—have capital defender offices that employ lawyers and investigators who specialize in the defense of capital cases. But in other states—including many in the South that send the most people to death row—the appointed lawyer may be one in private practice who may not even specialize in criminal law. And the lawyer will not be paid much. It may be a flat fee—in Mississippi, it is $1,000—or it may be hourly. Whatever the method, the compensation will be well below what a lawyer could make for any other type of work. And too often, the system gets what it paid for: perfunctory representation from a lawyer who is not fully aware of the procedures and legal issues involved in a capital trial and who lacks the time and resources to conduct an investigation or consult with experts.

Some instances of poor representation are shocking: lawyers slept during three different capital trials in Houston; a lawyer in an Alabama case was so drunk that he was sent to jail for a day midtrial; and lawyers in three Georgia cases referred to their clients with racial slurs. In other cases, inadequate representation is usually less dramatic, but just as fatal. The lawyer may fail to conduct an investigation, consult with an expert, negotiate a plea bargain, raise the applicable legal points in motions and objections, or carry out other basic responsibilities of defending a case.

Poor legal representation is one of the major causes of wrongful convictions. An innocent defendant is more likely to be convicted if he or she is represented by lawyers who fail to investigate the prosecution's case and locate witnesses whose testimony establishes innocence. Dennis Williams was twice sentenced to death in Illinois. He was represented at his first trial by an attorney who was later disbarred and at his second trial by an attorney who was later suspended from the practice of law. Williams was later exonerated by DNA evidence. Gary Drinkard was sentenced to death at a trial in Alabama where he was represented by two lawyers—one who did commercial work and one who handled foreclosures and bankruptcy cases. After five years on death row, he was given a new trial, where he was represented by lawyers who specialize in defending capital cases. At that trial, he was acquitted.

Lawyers are critical during every stage of the process of review of capital cases. Nevertheless, some death-sentenced inmates do not have lawyers at all for these critical proceedings. Alabama and Georgia do not provide lawyers for the stages of review that occur after the first appeal. Other states provide lawyers, but their competence and resources vary greatly. Texas provides lawyers, but many have not helped their clients. Several lawyers in Texas and elsewhere missed deadlines with the result that their clients were denied review procedures in the state and federal courts and executed. Another Texas lawyer filed the same brief in two different cases—word for word and typographical error for typographical error—and missed a deadline for filing in one case so the client was executed without review of the case by the federal courts. Another Texas lawyer filed a brief containing gibberish, incoherent repetitions, and sections lifted from one of his briefs in another case; his client was executed. This quality of representation is one reason that Texas has executed far more people—over 350—than any other state. It is hard to believe that the courts allow people to go to their deaths because of the errors of their lawyers. In a few cases they do not; but usually they do.

Will the death penalty eventually be abandoned, or will the United States still be putting people to death well into the twenty-first century? It is impossible to know what developments will influence what happens with regard to capital punishment, but two may be particularly important.

The first is the extent to which Americans are willing to accept the occasional execution of an innocent person. Supreme Court Justice Sandra Day O'Connor, who regularly voted to uphold death sentences before retiring from the Court, has observed that "Serious questions are being raised about whether the death penalty is being fairly administered" and "the system may well be allowing some innocent defendants to be executed."

Some proponents of the death penalty argue that an innocent person could never be executed. This belief assumes a level of perfection in the criminal courts that simply does exist. Others acknowledge that innocent people will be executed but argue that it is still worthwhile to have the death penalty—innocent people are killed in any war, including the "war on crime." To others, the execution of an innocent person is simply unacceptable.

Many people sentenced to death and to lesser sentences have been found innocent years after they were convicted. Moses Harrison, when Chief Justice of the Illinois Supreme Court, observed that many were found innocent "only because of luck and the dedication of the attorneys, reporters, family members and volunteers who labored to win their release. They survived despite the criminal justice system, not because of it. The truth is that left to the devices of the court system, they would probably have all ended up dead at the hands of the state for crimes they did not commit. One must wonder how many others have not been so fortunate."

Poverty, race, and many other factors discussed in this book contribute to the inability of the criminal justice system to get it right all the time. But no amount of effort or resources will prevent the execution of an innocent person because, as the Canadian Supreme Court has pointed out, courts will always be fallible and reversible, while death will always be final and irreversible.

The second trend influencing the U.S. death penalty is the mounting international pressure on the United States as other nations not only abandon the death penalty but express their disapproval of those who continue the practice. The death penalty is seen as primitive and uncivilized. Felix G. Rohatyn, after serving as U.S. Ambassador to France, stated "no single issue evoked as much passion and as much protest as executions in the United States."

From time to time, Americans reconsider whether the death penalty is still needed, what purpose it serves, and its place in our society. In making this assessment for its country, the Constitutional Court of South Africa observed that its society was in transition from hatred to understanding and from vengeance to reconciliation. Despite the country's high crime rate, the court struck down the death penalty. It decided that there is no place for the death penalty in a society striving for understanding and reconciliation.

America is a different society and has chosen another path. But Americans will continue to debate the wisdom of capital punishment. This book will help readers decide whether there is something about those condemned to die or the crimes they committed that requires their elimination from the human community or whether, despite the enormity of their crimes, they, like thousands of others convicted of the same or worse crimes, can be punished in less drastic, less degrading, and less violent ways that recognize their humanity, their frailties, and the possibility of atonement and redemption. ✦

Part I
The Enduring Legacy of Capital Punishment in the United States

It was a time of great debate about the death penalty. Those who argued in its favor claimed that the death penalty is absolutely necessary to deter future crimes. A failure to get "tough on crime" would only mean additional lawlessness and social breakdown. It was also argued that those who kill another have forfeited their right to live in the human community and that death by execution is the only morally appropriate punishment for murder. It was further argued that the death penalty, if not directly condoned by God, is approved in the Bible. It was also thought that by punishing the worst crime with the worst penalty, capital punishment would strengthen the moral fabric of society. Finally, it was alleged by those in favor of capital punishment that the current method of execution was not barbaric but rather involved a quick and painless death.

Those who argued in favor of abolishing the death penalty countered these points by claiming that society is too civilized to tolerate the death penalty, that capital punishment is a punishment of a more barbaric past, and that society has evolved and progressed to the point that it no longer permits such a seemingly ruthless act on behalf of the state. They also suggested that life imprisonment is enough punishment to dissuade would-be murderers from committing their crime and that death by execution provides no greater deterrent effect. In addition, capital punishment opponents contended that offenders in prison for life could work and that the proceeds of that labor could be used both to reduce the cost of their confinement and to provide some restitution to the survivors of the murdered victim. Finally, those who wished to do away with the death penalty maintained that because decision makers in the criminal justice decision are human beings, they are fallible, and there is a risk that innocent persons will be convicted and executed by mistake.

These arguments both for and against the death penalty have a contemporary ring to them. Those who support the death penalty today often cite its greater deterrent effect and the retributive ("eye for an eye") purpose it serves. They also argue that the death penalty does not involve "cruel and unusual" punishment because, unlike the death of the victim, that of the offender is quick and without pain.[1] Opponents today argue that our society is progressive and enlightened, and for that reason most civilized people are repulsed by the idea of capital punishment still being available in America. They also point to numerous instances of people convicted of capital crimes spending years on death row before being exonerated due to the efforts of new lawyers, journalism students, or new DNA evidence.

While the positions staked out in the first two paragraphs of this book seem to be the very arguments presented today about capital punishment, they were actually those that were raised in debates about the death penalty in the early nineteenth century (Banner 2002). While the death penalty has been part of our culture since colonial days, so has ambiguity about and opposition to it. In fact, the history of the death penalty in America is best characterized as consisting of a series of periods of intense support and use of capital punishment followed by periods of doubt, opposition, and attempts to outright abolish it, restrict its use, or at least make the method of execution less offensive and more humane.

There are, therefore, few topics in the field of criminology or public policy as controversial as capital punishment. It fuels spirited debate among both those who support its use on the most serious criminal offenders as justified punishment or an effective deterrent to murder and those who oppose it and think it is a barbaric remnant of our past. It is a frequent topic of discussion among students, academics, and of course those who work in the criminal justice system, especially lawyers who defend those accused of capital crimes, prosecutors who seek to impose it, and judges who try to ensure the fairness of the system. It is also the subject of political debate among those who vie for national office and those seeking election to statewide or local political office. During a televised 1988 presidential debate, CNN reporter Bernard Shaw asked Democratic nominee Michael Dukakis whether he would support the death penalty for a hypothetical offender who raped and killed Dukakis' wife. Mr. Dukakis stammered and stumbled through an answer in which he stated his opposition to capital punishment for both the fictional murderer of his wife and most if not all capital offenders. Many political commentators thought that his answer started the decline of Dukakis' campaign for the presidency. In the 2000 presidential campaign capital punishment became an issue since candidate George W. Bush had signed numerous death warrants while governor of Texas.

In the first section of this book we will provide a brief history of capital punishment in the United States, starting before it was even a nation. We will describe some basic facts about capital punishment, such as the methods and manner in which death sentences have been carried out and an estimate of the number of executions that have been performed in the United States at various times. We will also provide more recent and accurate data on the characteristics of the death penalty in the United States. There is a lot of ground to cover, as from 1608 until the end of 2006, there were over 19,000 executions on American soil.[2] The death penalty has been with us for a long time, and while some aspects have changed dramatically, it has long been a consistent feature of the American legal, cultural, and political scene.

For organizational purposes, we will divide the history of capital punishment in America into three distinct periods, (1) the Early Period, 1608–1929; (2) the Premodern Period, 1930–1967; and (3) the Modern Period, 1976 to the present. Admittedly, the division of the history of capital punishment in the United States into these three periods is somewhat arbitrary, but we did it for a reason. The distinction between the Early and Premodern periods reflects the fact that by 1930 the movement of the administration of capital punishment from local to state jurisdiction had been completed, as well as the movement from public to private executions. In addition, it was not until 1930 that accurate data on the number of executions could be obtained, because the United States Census Bureau included the category "death by execution" in its compilation of the nation's mortality statistics. We end the Premodern Period in 1967 for a reason. On June 2, 1967 when Luis Jose Monge was hung by the state of Colorado, he was the last person in the United States to be put to death for almost 10 years. During this time no executions occurred anywhere in the country, as state and federal courts were deciding some fundamental issues with respect to the death penalty, including whether capital punishment itself was constitutional.

The Modern Period of capital punishment began in 1976 when the U.S. Supreme Court gave constitutional approval to some new state statutes that offered procedural reforms in administering the death penalty. The 10-year moratorium on the death penalty in the United States officially ended on January 17, 1977 with the execution by firing squad of Gary Gilmore in the state of Utah.

When you read the history of capital punishment in the United States, you will notice two things: (1) history is always changing so that some things we have written about may have already changed by the time you read these chapters, and (2) history has a tendency to repeat itself—issues raised and problems with the death penalty that appear in our early history make their reappearance in sometimes only slightly altered form in later years.

Endnotes

1. In his concurring opinion in *Callins v. Collins,* 510 U.S. 1141, 1143 (1994), Justice Scalia described his view of the fate of the defendant convicted of the murder and rape of an 11-year-old girl: "How enviable a quiet death by lethal injection compared to that!"

2. The best historical record on the number (and some characteristics) of executions in the United States comes from the "Espy file." This data set can be obtained from the Inter-University Consortium on Political and Social Research (ICPSR) at the University of Michigan. See Oberly (2002). For data on executions since 1977, an excellent source are the series of reports, Death Row U.S.A., published by the NAACP Legal Defense and Education Fund. ✦

Chapter 1

Capital Punishment in the Early Period: 1608–1929

Capital punishment has a long history in the United States. The first re-corded execution was of Captain George Kendall, one of the original counselors in Jamestown colony, who was executed by firing squad for treason and mutiny in 1608 (Espy and Smykla 2002). During the 322 years of what we have called the "early period" of capital punishment in the United States (1608–1929), there were an estimated 10,598 executions, an average of approximately 33 per year. Before they even became states, the American colonies permitted the use of the death penalty for a long list of criminal offenses. The types of offenses in the colonies that were capital crimes reflected a combination of the influence of English law in its colonies,[1] the religious foundation of the first new world settlements in New England, and the unique economic arrangement that existed in the Southern colonies.

Capital Crimes and Capital Statutes in the Early Period

As was true under English law, in the northern colonies of North America capital punishment was available for many criminal acts against the person, such as murder, manslaughter, and rape (Fischer 1989). Not all of the New England colonies punished rape with death, however, and even manslaughter was not a capital crime in Pennsylvania (Banner 2002). Few property crimes were capital offenses in New England, contrary to both existing English law and the custom and practices in the Southern colonies. In the first criminal codes of Connecticut, Massachusetts, and Pennsylvania, for example, bur-glary, arson, and robbery were not capital crimes (they were in England), and they were only capital crimes when committed for the third time in New York and New Hampshire (Banner 2002). There was, however, an occasional execu-tion for a property offense. The capital punishment historian Daniel Hearn (1999) noted that in 1623 a man was hung in a colony near Weymouth, Massa-chusetts for stealing corn from the Native Americans.

In addition to serious offenses against the person, and because of their reli-gious origins, capital punishment in the Northern colonies could also be in-flicted for offenses such as witchcraft, idolatry, blasphemy, bestiality, adultery, "man stealing," and other sexual transgressions (Hearn 1999). Although capi-tal punishment was technically available for such offenses against God and morality, there are few recorded actual executions for such violations, leading to the suspicion that such laws existed primarily for symbolic benefit.[2] What may have given this symbol some meaning, however, was that executions for religious offenses did sometimes occur in New England colonies. Hearn (1999) has identified 20 executions in New England over the time period 1623–1688 for offenses including bestiality, adultery, blasphemy, and witchcraft. The majority of these executions were for witchcraft. He records no other executions in New England for witchcraft after 1692, when 20 inhabitants of the Salem, Massachusetts colony were put to death as suspected witches or warlocks. In a recent history of the death penalty, Banner (2002) has argued that in terms of severity, the laws of the Northern colonies were fairly comparable to what existed in England with respect to crimes against the person, more lenient with respect to the punishment of property crimes, and more severe with respect to "religious" offenses.

Box 1.1
'If a Man Lies With a Beast, He Shall Be Put to Death . . .'

Many New England colonists, particularly the Puritans in Massachusetts and Connecticut, viewed themselves as the children of Israel, and as such they embraced a long list of Biblical offenses and punishments. In the 20th chapter of Leviticus it is written that: "If a man lies with a beast he shall be put to death; and you shall kill the beast. If a woman approaches any beast and lies with it, you shall kill the woman and the beast; they shall be put to death, their blood is upon them." This admonition was sometimes taken very seriously. In 1641 William Hackett was hanged on the Boston gallows for the offense of bestiality. Hackett, described as a "very stupid, idle and ill-disposed boy," was reported to authorities by a neighbor for behaving indecently with a cow. Hackett was hung, the cow was killed, and they were buried together. On April 8, 1642, George Spencer was hung for having sexual relations with a pig. The pig was killed with a sword, and both man and animal were buried together (Hearn 1999). ✦

Because of their unique plantation economy, which required the coerced labor of half of their inhabitants, Southern colonies were more aggressive in imposing the death penalty for property crimes than those in the North (Hindus 1980; Schwarz 1988). In this respect, the harshness of Southern property crime law was much like that in England. The laws of Southern colonies included the death penalty for such crimes as embezzling tobacco, stealing hogs, stealing small amounts of money (5 English pounds), and receiving stolen horses. Even more numerous were various capital offenses that were directed only against slaves or in other ways protected the slave-based plantation economy and the rules of racial etiquette. The colony of North Carolina had over 20 capital offenses, including concealing a slave with the intent to free him, slave stealing, inciting slaves to insurrection, and circulating seditious literature among slaves. Other Southern colonies could impose the death penalty on slave or free blacks for destroying foodstuffs, enticing other slaves to run away, striking or injuring whites, or raping a white woman (Banner 2002). Although the Southern colonies had many more property crimes that were capital, unlike those in the North they did not make religious or moral offenses such as idolatry or blasphemy capital crimes. A list of some of the types of offenses for which persons were put to death during the Early Period of capital punishment is provided in Table 1.1. This partial list illustrates several important points: (1) there was a long list of capital offenses during this historical time period, (2) during this period capital punishment was used in response to both secular and religious offenses (owing to the religious nature of New England colonies), and (3) secular offenses included both violent and property crimes.

Table 1.1 Types of Offenses That Resulted in Execution, 1608–1929

Murder
Rape
Housebreaking—burglary
Horse stealing
Forgery
Counterfieting
Piracy
Robbery
Arson
Treason
Spying—espionage
Rioting

Slave revolt
Aiding a runaway slave

Witchcraft
Sodomy/Burglary/Bestiality
Concealing a birth

Source: Oberly (2002).

Box 1.2
Capital Punishment in the Early Period: The Salem Witch Trials

In February of 1692, 9-year-old Betty Parris, the daughter of newly hired village minister Samuel Parris, began to act in an odd way. She seemed unable to concentrate on anything, including her chores, screamed wildly whenever she heard the Lord's Prayer, spoke gibberish, experienced convulsions, and would bark like a dog when her father scolded her. This peculiar behavior also afflicted 11-year-old Abagail Williams, Samuel Parris' niece who was living in the minister's home, and several other village teenage girls who associated together.

In recent months all the girls were frequently in the company of Samuel Parris' Barbadian slave girl Tituba, who had been suspected of dabbling in voodoo and the occult. A physician called to examine the girls suggested that the unusual behavior might have a supernatural or demonic cause. This explanation became more convincing as the number of girls who exhibited similar symptoms began to grow. In late February and early March of that year arrest warrants against Tituba and two other girls, Sarah Good and Sarah Osborn, were issued. At a village meeting Tituba confessed to being a witch and named four other girls in the town, including Good and Osborn, as witches. The girls then began to name other alleged witches and soon a witch-naming orgy began.

Governor Phips of Massachusetts Colony created a new court to hear the witchcraft cases and 59-year-old Bridget Bishop was the first brought to trial. She was convicted of witchcraft and hanged on June 10, 1692. Eighty-year-old Giles Corey was accused by several of the girls of being a wizard and was arrested and brought to trial. When he refused to cooperate, he was "pressed" to death with heavy stones. Other suspected witches were arrested, tried, convicted, sentenced to death, and hung. One of these was George Burroughs, a former minister of the village. Doubts about the authenticity of the accusations grew stronger as Burroughs proclaimed his innocence and flawlessly recited the Lord's Prayer, something wizards were thought to be unable to do. Before the 1693 trials ended, hundreds in Salem were accused of witchcraft, and 20 suspected witches were convicted and executed. See Roach (2004) for an excellent description of the Salem witch trials. ✦

Characteristics of Executions in the Early Period

The information we have available about executions during the early period of American history is incomplete, because good historical records were not kept, or if kept were lost, destroyed, or damaged over the course of several hundred years. In addition, there were likely many executions both under legal authority and vigilante lynchings that are unaccounted for. What we have is at best a partial understanding of what capital punishment was like during this period, both in terms of how many people were executed and who those people were. In fact, it has been only within the past few decades that historians of the death penalty have put together information that sheds some light on capital punishment during these early years.

While admittedly incomplete, this is the best information we currently have. Figure 1.1 shows the estimated number of executions from the 1600s to 1929. There were only 49 recorded executions from 1600 to 1649, and 138 from 1650 to 1699. These historically low numbers of executions reflect both the limited population in the colonies at the time and the absence of a complete historical record on the use of capital punishment. This number increased to approximately 382 executions from 1700 to 1749 and to 1,009 from 1750 to 1799. The nineteenth century witnessed a substantial increase in the number of executions, with 1,496 recorded in the period 1800 to 1849 and a sharp increase to 3,885 from 1850 to 1899 (an annual average of 79 executions).

Figure 1.1   The Number of Executions on American Soil, 1600–1929

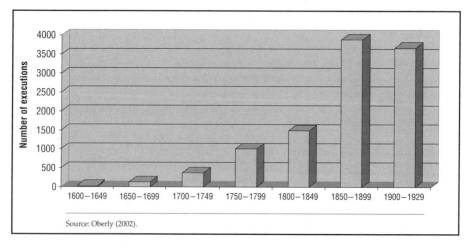

Source: Oberly (2002).

The beginning of the twentieth century continued this trend. There were 3,664 executions from 1900 to 1929, an annual rate of 122 executions. Although these numbers are informative as to the general trend in the use of the death penalty, we would urge caution with respect to the estimates for the time periods before the nineteenth century, where the historical record is incomplete. What Figure 1.1 does clearly show, however, is that the death penalty is not some recent phenomenon, but rather has been around since the earliest history of our nation, and in some historical periods it was frequently used.

We also have some other limited information about executions during the Premodern Period. Figure 1.2 shows that about 43 percent of those executed were white, a slight majority were black (51 percent), and about 6 percent were some other minority group. This shows that almost six out of every ten of those executed were racial/ethnic minorities. Figure 1.3 indicates that the vast majority (96 percent) of those executed were male. Although there is not much information available about the age of the condemned, the youngest known offender to have been executed during this period was 12 years old, the oldest was 83, and the average age at execution was approximately 30 (Oberly 2002).[3]

Changes in the Practice of the Death Penalty in the Early Period

Although they never completely abandoned the practice, colonies that had the death penalty did substantially modify their capital statutes when they became states in the new United States of America. Two of the most important historical trends from colonial times until 1929 were (1) the reduction in the number of potentially capital crimes, and (2) the movement to centralize the imposition of capital punishment from local to state authority. For example, when Massachusetts Bay Colony became the Commonwealth of Massa-

Figure 1.2 Race of Offender Executed, 1608–1929

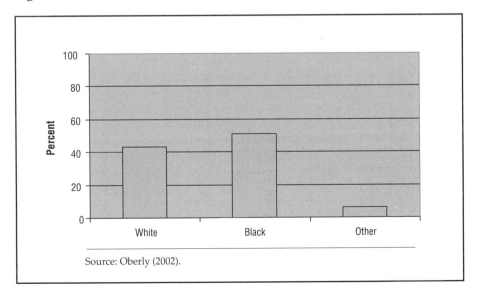

Source: Oberly (2002).

Figure 1.3   Gender of Offender Executed, 1608–1929

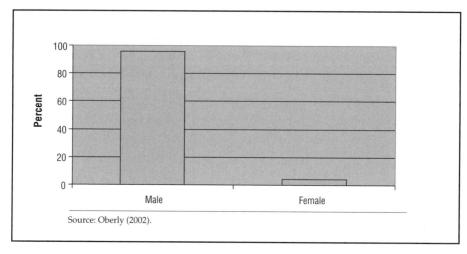

Source: Oberly (2002).

chusetts, the number of capital offenses was reduced, and religious offenses that previously could have been punished by death (such as witchcraft, bestiality, and idolatry) were made noncapital. The reduction in the number of potentially capital offenses characterized the history of virtually every former American colony that became a state. The criminal statute of the new state of Pennsylvania included only eight capital offenses, and by 1870 Virginia's statute had only five capital offenses for whites (but some 70 offenses could result in the death penalty if the offender was black). This decline in the number of capital offenses partly reflected the fact that previously capital crimes that involved religious or morals offenses were made noncapital in the movement from colony to state. In addition, however, there were modifications in other components of the law of the former colonies. These primarily took the form of making noncapital offenses of property crimes that were once subject to the death penalty. For example, when Pennsylvania reformed its criminal statutes in 1786, it abolished capital punishment not only for sodomy and buggery but also for robbery and burglary (Banner 2002).[4]

The reduction in the number of potentially capital crimes came about not only by dropping many religious offenses such as blasphemy and witchcraft and property offenses such as burglary and robbery, but also by the explicit granting of discretion to capital sentencing authorities and the legal development of different degrees of murder. Under English law, and the law as adopted by most of the original American colonies, there was only one degree of murder, and the mandatory penalty for conviction of murder was death. The requirement of a mandatory death sentence for everyone convicted of murder did not sit well with many juries, who believed that some defendants might be guilty of murder but nonetheless not deserving of the death penalty. Rather than convict these defendants of murder, thereby ensuring their execution, juries would simply take the law into their own hands and fail to convict—or, if they could, convict the defendant of a lesser offense that did not carry an automatic death sentence. This problem of "jury nullification" (juries voiding or nullifying their oath to return a guilty verdict if they believed the defendant committed the crime beyond a reasonable doubt) provided the stimulus for some reforms of the law of murder. The problem of jury nullification existed for other capital crimes as well, particularly property crimes, where juries were reluctant to sentence people to death for crimes that involved either no substantial financial loss by the victim or no physical injury. In the cases of less serious instances of murder or property crimes that were capital offenses, many juries felt that a death sentence was disproportionately severe.

In 1794 Pennsylvania became the first state to enact into law the notion of different degrees of murder (Keedy 1949). Under the reformed Pennsylvania statute, only murder in the first degree could be punished by death.[5] The explicit purpose of devising degrees of murder was to legally give juries the discretion they had already been exercising in practice. Now they could render a verdict of guilty of murder in the first degree to those whom they deemed deserving of the death penalty, and find a verdict of guilty of murder in the second degree for those they believed guilty of murder but whose extenuating circumstances did not make them deserving of death. Two other states, Virginia in 1796 and Kentucky in 1798, quickly followed Pennsylvania's lead. By the 1900s most states followed the example of legal reform adopted by Pennsylvania by creating two or three different degrees of murder, with the penalty of death being reserved only for first degree murder.

One way in which the use of capital punishment was restricted, then, was the adoption of degrees of murder. The creation of degrees of murder proved not to be a particularly satisfying solution to the problem of jury nullification, however, since the statute authorizing degrees of murder did not eliminate mandatory capital punishment; it simply narrowed the kinds of murders that would be subject to a mandatory death sentence. Under these reformed statutes, a sentence of death was still mandatory for those convicted of first degree murder. In the eyes of many jurors, however, not even all first degree murderers are equally culpable and deserving of death. There may be some defendants who are technically guilty of first degree murder but whom jurors could nevertheless determine do not deserve to be put to death. In other words, even narrowing the imposition of capital punishment to first degree murder hides the fact that some first degree murderers deserve death while others may not, and under these statutes all convicted first degree murderers would be sentenced to death. Under the Pennsylvania statute, for example, first degree murder included the deliberate and premeditated killing of another or any murder committed in the commission of arson, rape, robbery, or burglary (Keedy 1949). A defendant who intentionally committed an armed robbery but who unintentionally killed his victim would face a mandatory death sentence if convicted of first degree murder. Juries who disagreed with the deservedness of a death sentence could and did get around this dilemma by acquitting the otherwise guilty offender, or, if they could, they convicted him of a lesser degree of murder. Furthermore, the construction of different degrees of murder did nothing to remedy the perceived sense of disproportionality of a death sentence for a property crime such as burglary or robbery. Juries could and did nullify in these instances as well.

To provide jurors with the discretion not to impose a death sentence when they thought it was not deserved, state legislatures began to once again revise their capital statutes, this time explicitly extending to jurors sentencing discretion. Under the 1838 Tennessee statute, for example, jurors had the option of imposing death or some noncapital penalty for convicted first degree murderers (Bedau 1982). By 1930 most states had abandoned mandatory death penalty statutes in favor of those that gave jurors the discretion to impose a capital or noncapital sentence upon conviction of a capital crime. In addition to restricting the use of capital punishment by reducing the number of potentially capital crimes, devising degrees of murder, and extending sentencing discretion to juries in all capital offenses, two other important historical developments occurred in the administration of capital punishment during this period. These had to do with the method and location of executions.

Methods of Execution in the Early Period

In colonial times and after the American Revolution, a capital sentence was carried out under local legal authority, usually the sheriff of the county, and executions were highly public and symbol-laden events. Typically, the condemned, sometimes dressed in special clothes, would be taken from the place of confinement and transported to the location of the execution. This transport was usually by horse-drawn carriage, the procession to the execution site was deliberate, and the way was generally lined with throngs of spectators. At the execution site, religious leaders would deliver homilies about the "life of crime" led by the defendant and exhort the crowd to follow the "right path" (Halttunen 1998). These sermons would be great opportunities not only to condemn the actions of the defendant but to demonstrate the oratorical skills of the minister. They were also an important vehicle for teaching the assembled crowd about the need for their own repentance and the importance of salvation. Execution sermons were often published. The sheriff or other legal authority would then either read an execution warrant or make a speech of his own. Then the condemned would be allowed to give his final words, which frequently consisted of an act of remorse and contrition. This was followed by a final hymn or prayer, and then execution. The entire event from jail to gallows would often take several hours and was typically a heavily symbolic public ceremony (Banner 2002).

Not only were these executions public events, they were well attended; it was not unusual for thousands of onlookers to appear, including women and children. In large measure the large crowds were due to the fact that executions were relatively rare, particularly in rural areas, and people traveled great distances to attend one. That executions were public was, of course, deliberate, as was each component of the entire ceremony from jail to gallows. One of the understood purposes of the death penalty was deterrence. The person hanging from the gallows was a vivid lesson about the potential costs of crime and the seriousness of the law in dealing with it. The best way to communicate this lesson was to make the execution pubic, thereby visible to all. The public nature of the death penalty also had more symbolic importance. The crowd was expressing its moral cohesion in rejecting the behavior of the criminal, thus strengthening its own resolve in the face of criminal temptation. While perhaps sympathetic to the plight of the one about to be hanged, the crowd nevertheless was speaking with one voice in condemning his behavior (Halttunen 1998; Masur 1989).

Up until the mid-nineteenth century in the North and the early twentieth century in the South, executions were entirely local and public ceremonies (a point we will return to later). Inherited from the English, the method of capital punishment up to the end of the nineteenth century was virtually always hanging. The domination of this method of execution during this early period is shown in Figure 1.4. Of the over 10,000 executions that took place from 1608 until 1929, approximately 83 percent were conducted by hanging, 14 percent by electrocution, and less than 3 percent by other means.[6] Furthermore, all electrocutions occurred after 1889; prior to that time the overwhelming majority of executions were by hanging, with the most frequent alternative being death by burning. From 1608 to 1890 there were some 5,900 executions, 96 percent of which were carried out by hanging (Oberly 2002).

This is not to say that all hangings were alike. Just as there were less severe versions of hanging, so there were more severe gradations, and there was experimentation with different forms of hanging.[7] One form of capital punishment more severe than the "usual" hanging was to display the corpse in a public place, often in an iron cage or gibbet. Those who committed the most severe offenses against existing authorities were dismembered after execution or turned over to medical authorities for dissection.[8] These latter two types of post-mortem abuse were perceived as particularly dreadful forms of punish-

Figure 1.4   Method of Execution, 1608–1929

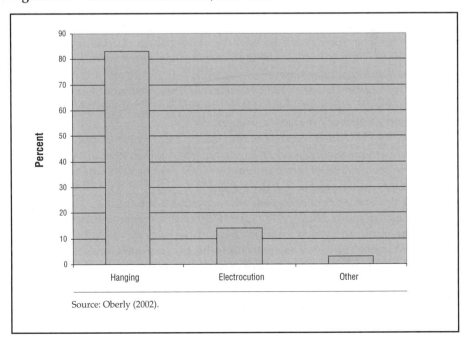

Source: Oberly (2002).

ment because of the dishonor brought by a mutilation of the body and the absence of a "proper burial" (Masur 1989; Banner 2002).

Traditionally, in a hanging the condemned stood on a trap door with a rope around his neck until the door was sprung. The body then dropped a given distance until the slack in the rope was taken up. It was expected that the combination of the careful location of the knot, the distance dropped, and the force applied to the neck, which was proportional to the weight of the body, would create a sharp jerk that would sever the condemned's spinal cord, resulting in a quick and painless death (Duff 2001). This method of hanging was referred to as a "drop down" hanging, for obvious reasons.

Unfortunately, things did not always go well for the condemned (Duff 2001). The hanging was usually done by a local sheriff who lacked the skill and the experience (hangings were for most a rare event) to locate the knot in the optimal spot, as well as the ability to finesse the many other variables (the weight of the condemned, the elasticity of the knot, the tension in the neck, the distance dropped) that went into the "painless" hanging. The "botched" hanging was not a pretty sight. If the drop was too short or the knot misplaced, the condemned hung suspended in the air for 20 to 30 minutes gasping and choking until he was slowly strangled. And if the drop was too long or the condemned was too heavy, the velocity of the fall and the weight of the body could snap the head completely off (Teeters 1963; Moran 2002).

By the nineteenth century, legal authorities began to express some concern both about the public nature of executions and the most common method of performing them, hanging. It was not that authorities were bothered by the behavior of the public at executions. For the most part, the historical record seems to indicate that public hangings were somber and orderly affairs. Rather, there was concern that the condemned was experiencing unnecessary pain as a result of the "drop down" hanging, and botched hangings were unpleasant for the spectators to endure. The combination of these two events—the recognition that hangings were unnecessarily painful and were frequently grotesque to witness—led to public outcries to abolish capital punishment (Teeters 1963; Banner 2002; Moran 2002), and it was perhaps this fear of fueling the abolition movement that lead to attempts to "reform" the method of execution in a spirit of "reform to preserve."

While the sometime excesses of the "drop down" method of hanging did not result in any state abolishing it, the criticisms did lead to additional experimentation (Teeters 1963; Duff 2001; Banner 2002; Moran 2002). Reasoning that the force that could be applied to the neck of the condemned was limited by the weight of the body being dropped, a new method of hanging—the "upright jerker" method—was initiated. In this method, the condemned was literally lifted off the ground by a concoction of weights and pulleys. At the execution of Charles Gibbs in New York City in 1831, the rope around Gibbs' neck was attached to two other ropes, and each of those two was attached to five 56-pound weights, for a total of 560 pounds (far more weight than that of any person being dropped through a trap door: Banner 2002). The upright jerker not only promised the exertion of greater force on the neck of the condemned, it also promised a swifter application of that force, since the weights could be applied suddenly (with the cutting of a rope, the weights would drop and the body would be instantly lifted off the ground), and it was expected with greater confidence that the neck would quickly and painlessly be broken.

The upright jerker method of hanging did not, however, eliminate the problems of unsightly executions and the resulting shock and revulsion felt by witnesses to it. The primary problem with the upright jerker was the same as that for the drop down method of hanging. The persons in charge of operating the machinery were generally inexperienced, since they handled so few executions during their career. Further, if anything, the upright jerker method of execution was more complicated and required more expertise than the simple method of "drop them down a trap door." As a result, upright jerker hangings were often gruesome events for spectators to witness (Teeters 1963). Banner (2002) recounts the 1860 execution of James Stephens, who, because of the failure of the local deputy to cut the support rope for the weights, was yanked some 4 feet off the ground, where he died "after eight minutes of gurgling and contortions" (p. 172). The appeal of the upright jerker method was that it promised to quickly break the neck of the condemned, thus leading to a swift and painless death. Unfortunately, even when there were no malfunctions it frequently failed to break the spinal cord, leading to death by strangulation.

By the late 1800s, then, vocal opposition to hanging by either method came from both those who opposed capital punishment generally and those who, while they supported the death penalty, were shocked and repulsed at the brutality of these methods. Numerous and lurid newspaper accounts of the horrors of botched executions only fueled the public's concern over the use of hanging as a method of capital punishment. Proponents of the death penalty were keenly afraid that revulsion toward hanging in general and distasteful hangings in particular would provide the momentum for the abolitionist movement, which had gone through several periods of public support and decline.

The concern about the usefulness of hanging as a method of execution reached a peak in the late 1800s, and the most important expression of this concern took place in New York State. For several decades in the 1800s New York authorities had been engaged in debates about the efficacy and humaneness of execution by hanging. The call for reform of capital punishment in the state was at a high point in the mid 1800s, fueled in large measure by an anti-capital punishment abolition movement, particularly the New York State Society for the Abolition of Capital Punishment (Denno 1994). This reform effort was stalled when the nation was thrown into civil war but was revitalized thereafter.

In 1886 New York Governor David Bennett Hill appointed a commission of three prominent citizens to investigate the possibility of a more "humane and practical" method of execution. The commission was named the Gerry Commission after its chair, Elbridge T. Gerry, a New York attorney and a founder of the New York Society for the Prevention of Cruelty to Children (Moran 2002). The other commissioners were Matthew Hale, an attorney from Albany who was the grandson of Revolutionary War hero Nathanial Hale, and Buffalo dentist Dr. Alfred Southwick. As part of its work, the Gerry Commission sent a survey to judicial and law enforcement officials in the state of New York and to a number of medical and electrical experts asking them, among other things, what they thought the method of execution for New York should be. About half of the re-turned surveys recommended a method of capital punishment other than hang-ing—and most of these were in favor of death by electricity.[9]

The idea that death could be imposed by the application of electricity was not new. There were two editorials in the prestigious journal *Scientific American* about the issue. The first appeared in 1883 and concerned the electrocution of cows for providing a painless death for animals to be slaughtered (Moran 2002). The second appeared two years later and directly suggested that elec-tricity (coming from a streetlight) could and should be used to painlessly exe-cute criminals. Commissioner Southwick was a vocal advocate of death by electrocution. In 1881 he witnessed the accidental electrocution of a Buffalo, New York man who made contact with a live wire and who appeared to Southwick to have suffered a relatively painless and quick death (Denno 1994; Moran 2002). Southwick also performed experiments on animals that further convinced him that electricity could be used to put convicted offenders to death in a humane fashion. Southwick's enthusiasm for death by electricity was not, however, shared by the Commission's chair, Elbridge Gerry.

The Gerry Commission's mandate was to suggest to the legislature what the most humane and practical method of execution should be for New York. The Commission studied several alternatives to the gallows (34 different alter-natives in fact—see Moran 2002), including death by the lethal injection of a drug or poison. Although death by lethal injection seemed to promise a quick and painless alternative to the rope, the medical profession of New York was strongly opposed to the idea of using a medical instrument, the hypodermic needle, to deliberately kill someone.[10] Apparently sensing the fact that Com-missioner Gerry himself was lukewarm to the idea of death by electrocution, Dr. Southwick asked the internationally known scientist, inventor, and electri-cal expert Thomas Edison his views on the subject of death by electricity and his advice as to how best it could be administered. At first, Edison rejected Southwick's plea for help, writing that he was an opponent of the death pen-alty and preferred life imprisonment as an alternative to hanging or any other form of capital punishment. Undaunted, Southwick sent a second letter to Edi-son making two points: (1) capital punishment was a fact in the state of New York that could not be ignored, so the civilized thing to do would be to deter-mine the most humane and painless way to inflict death; and (2) appealing to Edison's ego, Southwick argued that the Commission would greatly benefit from the suggestions of so great a scientist and thinker (Moran 2002; Ressig 2003). Edison's initial reluctance to get involved in the work of the Gerry Com-mission's work softened, and he remarked in his response to Southwick that while he would like to see capital punishment abolished, the most humane method of execution would be death by electricity—more specifically, death by the application of an *alternating* current of electricity. Edison's second letter to Southwick eventually turned Elbridge Gerry into an advocate of death by electrocution.

The reasons at least partly behind Edison's change of heart make for fasci-nating reading, and they have as much to do with good business as being a good humanitarian.[11] Edison's clear reference to alternating current (AC) as the preferred way to execute by electricity was made to distinguish it from Edison's own electrical generating system, which was based on direct current (DC). The system of alternating current electricity was developed by Edison's chief rival for the growing business and residential electricity market, George Westinghouse. Edison was the first to provide electric lighting, and for a short time he dominated the small but potentially lucrative electricity market. Although it was considered safe, the major problem with Edison's direct current electricity was that it could not be transmitted over great distances, so an electrical generation station could only send electricity a short distance (about a mile) away. This meant a large number of electrical generation stations were necessary to service a given geographical area. Westinghouse's AC system could transmit electricity over greater distances than DC electricity and was, therefore, much cheaper to generate. During the later part of the 1800s, Westinghouse and Edison battled over control of the growing commercial and residential electricity market, and by 1888 it clearly appeared that Westinghouse was dominating (Denno 1994; Resig 2003).

In staking out his position that Westinghouse's AC current should be used to execute criminals, Edison sought to highlight the dangerousness and lethality of AC current. If potential or existing electricity customers could associate AC current with the power to kill, they may be less inclined to adopt it and, of course, more inclined to adopt Edison's own DC electricity. In addition to using the association between Westinghouse's AC electricity and the proposed notion of the electrocution of criminals as a way to drive his own market share up, Edison himself likely believed that AC current was more lethal and dangerous than his own DC current (Denno 1994; Moran 2002). Naturally enough, Westinghouse would not take this characterization of his electricity silently, and there ensued a "war of the currents" between these two electrical giants over the use of AC current as a method of capital punishment. What was clear is that Edison's throwing his weight and reputation behind the use of electricity as the preferred new method of executing New York's condemned had a profound impact on the Gerry Commission. The "genius of Menlo Park," as Edison was referred to, was a scientific celebrity, and in matters of electricity, his word was exceedingly influential.

In 1888 the Gerry Commission presented its report to the New York legislature. Concluding that electocution would produce a death that was quick and painless, the commission recommended the use of electricity over hanging or any other method as the way to execute criminals in New York State. It was silent, however, with respect to the question of whether Westinghouse's AC or Edison's DC should be applied, stating only that "a current of electricity, of sufficient intensity to destroy life instantaneously, be passed through the body of the convict" (Report 1888, 80). The commission also suggested the procedure by which execution should take place, with all executions being conducted privately behind the walls of a state penitentiary rather than in the town or county where the crime and trial had occurred. The New York legislature then went to work crafting legislation that would legally authorize electrocution as the state's method of capital punishment. In 1888 the legislature passed the Electrical Execution Act, under which anyone convicted of a capital crime after January 1, 1889 would be put to death by electrocution rather than by hanging. New York thus became the first state to abandon hanging in favor of electrocution.[12] Like the Gerry Commission, the Electrical Execution Act of the legislature did not define which type of current should be used, instead turning over responsibility for deciding that to the Medico-Legal Society of New York (Denno 1994).

In the fall of 1888 the Medico-Legal Society began its work to decide exactly how criminals should be executed. The chair of the committee assigned to do the work was Dr. Frederick Peterson. He, together with a little-known and self-trained electrician, Harold Brown, performed experiments with animals using AC and DC of different amperes and voltage. Brown had been experimenting on the execution of animals for a while before the Peterson Committee was formed, at the laboratories and using the equipment of Thomas Edison (Moran 2002). Among the many witnesses called to testify before the Peterson Committee were Harold Brown and Thomas Edison. In December 1888, the New York State Medico-Legal Society recommended that its capital offenders be put to death with Westinghouse's alternating current. Although a battle in the press (and eventually the courts) ensued between Westinghouse and Edison, Edison had succeeded in making his business opponent's AC current the executioner's own brand.

The first person to be put to death under New York's new Electrical Execution Act was William Kemmler, a self-employed fruit-peddler who lived in Buffalo. Kemmler had what today would be described as a "drinking problem," and on the morning of March 29, 1889, woozy from a drinking spell the night before, he brutally killed his live-in girlfriend, Tillie Ziegler, with a hatchet. Kemmler turned himself in to police and confessed to the crime. After a four-day trial, Kemmler was convicted on May 10, 1889, and sentenced to death on Tuesday, May 14. Although he was the first person to be sentenced to death by electrocution, Kemmler would not go to the newly built electric chair for over a year. A new set of lawyers, allegedly backed financially by George Westinghouse, appealed his sentence under the grounds that electrocution constituted "cruel and unusual" punishment under New York law (Moran 2002; Ressig 2003).[13] Westinghouse's interest in the case was obvious—Kemmler was sentenced to die by an electrical generator that would produce his alternating current, and his rival Edison would surely take that opportunity to highlight its dangerousness.

After losing several rounds of appeals in New York state courts, Kemmler's lawyers filed a writ of habeas corpus to the United States Supreme Court alleging that his death sentence was in violation of the Fourteenth Amendment to the United States Constitution. It its ruling in *In re Kemmler,* the U.S. Supreme Court made no determination as to whether death by electrocution itself constituted cruel and unusual punishment. The Court did rule that the Eighth Amendment to the Constitution, which prohibits cruel and unusual punishments, was not applicable to the states[14] and that, therefore, the Supreme Court of the United States could not interfere with a legitimate act of the New York Legislature. In making its decision, the Court provided a definition of what constitutes a "cruel and unusual" punishment:

Punishments are cruel and unusual when they involved torture or a lingering death; but the punishment of death is not cruel, within the meaning of that word as used in the Constitution. It implies there is something inhuman and barbarous, something more than the mere extinguishment of life.[15]

This was the standard that the Court used in evaluating the actions of New York State's Court of Appeals and its state legislature and found that neither had acted unlawfully. The Court argued that the legislature had the responsibility for deciding which method of capital punishment the state could adopt; the legislature had reviewed the available evidence and believed that death by electrocution was more humane than the previous method (hanging). The courts of New York agreed that death by electrocution was not inhumane under the state standard of cruel and unusual punishment, and the Supreme Court in deferring to the state's judgment concluded that the Fourteenth Amendment "was not designed to interfere with the power of the state to protect the lives, liberties and properties of its citizens."[16] Essentially, the *Kemmler* court concluded that the state of New York did nothing unlawful in changing its method of execution from hanging to electrocution.

After having exhausted all possible appeals, William Kemmler on August 6, 1890 was the first person to have his death sentence carried on by the lethal application of electricity. Kemmler's execution by electrocution, however, was not as quick, easy, and obviously painless as proponents would have liked. After the first surge of electricity, which lasted some 17 seconds, one of the attending officials, Dr. Spitzka, pronounced Kemmler dead (Ressig 2003; Moran 2002). The officials and witness' self-congratulations soon turned to horror, however, when it was noticed that Kemmler's body was still twitching. One witness yelled that Kemmler was still alive, while another screamed to turn the current back on (Moran 2002). Doctors attending the execution found a pulse and felt a heartbeat and recommended that the electric current be turned back on. The electric generator came to life and sent 2000 more volts into Kemmler's body, and the smell of burnt flesh filled the execution room. After this second application of electricity, Kemmler finally lay dead. Rather than quell any questions about a quick and painless death, the execution of William Kemmler only sparked further debate both about the penalty of death generally, and the new "civilized" method of death by electrocution.

New York was not the only, but simply the first, state to abandon the use of hanging as a method of capital punishment at the beginning of the twentieth century. Other state legislatures, equally concerned about the sometimes horrible sight that hangings produced and the effect they had on unsettling proponents and energizing opponents of capital punishment alike, were quick to switch to the new "modern" method of electrocution. In 1896 Ohio became the second state to switch from hanging to the electric chair, Massachusetts did so in 1898, New Jersey in 1906, Virginia in 1908, North Carolina in 1909, Kentucky in 1910, South Carolina in 1912, and seven other states in 1913. The quick ascendancy of electrocution as the preferred method in death penalty states can be seen in Table 1.2, which reports the percentage of executions by method in death penalty states in 1889 (the year before Kemmler's execution by electrocution), 25 years later in 1914, 35 years later in 1924, and 40 years later in 1929. There were 93 known executions in the United States in 1889, all by hanging. In 1914, the majority of executions were still conducted by hanging (57 percent versus 43 percent for electrocution). By 1924, however, the majority of the executions were by electrocution (56 percent versus 44 percent for hanging). By 1929 over two-thirds of all executions were being conducted by electrocution (68 percent).

Table 1.2 Percentage of Executions by Method in the United States, 1889–1929

Death by:	1889	1914	1924	1929
Hanging	100%	57%	44%	32%
Electrocution	NA	43	56	68
Lethal gas	NA	NA	0	>1

Source: Oberly (2002).

Box 1.3
Facts About the Electric Chair

· The Philippines is the only other country in the world to use the electric chair as a method of execution.

· Martha Place was the first woman to die in the electric chair. She was put to death on March 20, 1899 in New York's Sing Sing prison.

· Since 1977, 151 men and 2 women have been executed with the electric chair. Most modern executions are performed by lethal injection.

· On January 12, 1928, *New York Daily News* photographer Tom Howard took a picture of the electrocution of Ruth Snyder. Howard smuggled the camera in to the execution by strapping a small one-shot camera to his ankle. ✦

Location of the Death Penalty in the Early Period

From the earliest executions in the United States until the middle of the nineteenth century, executions were a local affair, conducted by local (city or county) judicial and religious authorities in or at least near the town where the crime occurred. We have already alluded to the fact that these ceremonies were highly symbolic and public events and that hangings were generally well attended and the crowd was generally well behaved. One of the troubling features of these public executions was that it was not unusual for the crowd to develop feelings of sympathy and pity for the condemned (Banner 2002). Further, there was concern about the moral quality of the crowds thought to attend executions among those who saw themselves as morally superior. Opponents of public executions were critical that the "wrong kinds of persons" were in attendance and that the execution only served as some kind of prurient entertainment. When the Pennsylvania legislature became the first to argue for the abolition of *public* executions, they argued that the audience at a hanging was composed generally of "the thoughtless; the profligate; the idle; the intemperate; the profane; and the abandoned" (quoted in Banner 2002, 151).

Box 1.4
Executions as a 'Spectator Sport'

When they were public events, executions were generally well attended. The execution of Daniel Wilson in Providence, Rhode Island in 1774 was attended by more than 12,000 spectators, more than three times the population of the city (Banner 2002). Some 50,000 came to see the hanging of John Johnson in New York City in 1824. In July of 1841 a crowd estimated at between 20,000 and 35,000 came to see the hanging of four black men in St. Louis. Two enterprising men in Alton, Illinois, across the Mississippi from St. Louis, chartered a steamboat and sold tickets for people to see the execution (Banner 2002). ✦

By the first quarter of the nineteenth century, state legislatures had begun to require that capital punishment be administered beyond the gazing eye of the public. At first, executions were conducted within the local jail, then increasingly they came under state supervision, and the condemned were to put to death within the walls of a state penitentiary. Connecticut started this trend in 1830 when it became the first state to abolish public executions, and by 1836 six other states (all Northern) had joined in (Banner 2002). The movement to executions under state supervision within a state penitentiary went hand in hand with a state's replacement of hanging with the electric chair as the method of execution. While it was fairly easy and economically feasible (though as we have seen from the frequency and notoriety of gruesome executions, not always effective) for each county to have a gallows, this was far less the case for an electric chair, which required a relatively expensive electrical generator and complex electrical equipment, including the "chair."[17]

Figure 1.5 shows the place of execution from 1801 to the end of the early modern period in 1929. Prior to 1801, all executions were conducted by local authorities, and in the period 1801–1820 there was only one recorded execution in a state prison (less than 1 percent of the total). By 1880–1899 this increased to nearly 8 percent. Then from 1900 to 1919 slightly over 40 percent of all executions were conducted within a state prison (recall that in 1890 William Kemmler was the first person electrocuted). Finally, from 1920 to 1929 a majority of all executions in the United States were conducted by state rather than local authorities. Although there was a general trend away from public executions, this movement took place much sooner in Northern than Southern states. Southern states were slower to abandon public executions and frequently used the gallows as the preferred punishment for the offense of rape, particularly in cross-racial crimes with a black offender and white victim. The last public execution in the United States was the hanging of Rainey Bethea for rape in Kentucky in 1936, an execution that was attended by a crowd estimated at between 10,000 and 20,000 (Banner 2002).

Figure 1.5   Percentage of Executions Conducted Under Local and State Supervision, 1801–1929

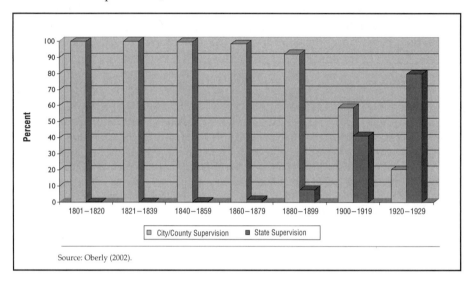

Source: Oberly (2002).

Chapter Summary

Capital punishment has been a part of American society from the very beginning. The first recorded execution in America was of George Kendall in 1608. Although the specific kinds of offenses eligible to be punished by death varied somewhat from colony to colony, there were some general patterns. In virtually all of the colonies the death penalty could be imposed for serious breaches of community order such as murder and rape. In the Northern colonies, crimes against the church such as blasphemy, witchcraft, bestiality, and adultery were death-eligible offenses, reflecting the religious foundation of these communities. Further to the South, the death penalty for religious offenses was less likely while crimes against property were more likely to be punished by death.

Over time, there was a reduction in the number of crimes that could be punished by death. Religious and minor property offenses were the first to be removed as death-eligible crimes. Gradually, legal authorities began to make distinctions among different types or degrees of murder, punishing only the most serious and blameworthy with death. The attempt of legal authorities, which continues to the present day, was to make some kind of moral distinction between those crimes "deserving" death and others, with the death penalty being reserved for both the worst offenses and the worst offenders. In addition, there were legal reforms to change death penalty laws that made capital punishment mandatory upon conviction and to provide juries with discretion to impose or not impose a sentence of death. Although the historical record is incomplete, the information we have indicates that the majority of executions during this period were of racial minorities, and the overwhelming majority were male.

Reflecting a technologically primitive society, the death penalty in the early period was usually conducted by hanging the condemned. As it turned out, hanging someone is not as easy as it seems—the location of the knot had to be precise, as well as the distance the offender dropped. Although we do not know how frequently it occurred, the historical record does show that hanging often resulted in the condemned painfully and fitfully choking to death. The "inefficient" hanging was gruesome to watch and motivated a search for other ways to impose death. After a fairly exhaustive investigation by a panel of "experts," New York State eventually decided to abandon hanging in favor of death by electrocution, and the electric chair was born. The emergence of the electric chair was part of a business battle between two notable figures in American history: George Westinghouse and Thomas Edison. The discomfort presented by hanging and the search for a more humane and "quick and painless" method of execution is symbolic of society's ambiguous feelings about the death penalty.

Early executions were also different from those performed today in that they were frequently public events. Hangings were announced well in advance and attracted large crowds. The attraction of spectators provided the opportunity for ministers and preachers to maximize any deterrence message or moral message provided by the hanging. Over time, public executions performed by local officials were replaced by private executions under state authority. The shift from death by hanging to death by electrocution hastened the movement to private and state-run executions, as local authorities could not afford their own electric chairs.

Discussion Questions

1. In the past, executions were public events. Do you think executions today should be open to the public to attend or be televised? What would be the arguments in favor of and against such a practice?

2. One of the "reforms" of the death penalty during the Early Period was the narrowing of what a capital murder is. What arguments favor the position that all murders should be capital crimes, and what arguments would argue against that position? What arguments favor the position that capital punishment should be restricted to only first degree murders or only the "worst of the worst" offenders? How would you determine what constitutes the "worst of the worst," and do you think there would be general society agreement about this?

3. New York State wanted to replace death by hanging with death by electrocution on the grounds that it was a more humane death. What does a more humane death mean? Do you think the desire to have a more humane method of execution is done out of consideration for the condemned or because inhumane deaths might cause the public to turn against the death penalty? Do you think that considerations of being humane and wanting to inflict a "quick and painless" death should have a large role in determining what method of execution a state should employ?

4. Although the historical record is sketchy, the data indicate that executions were overwhelmingly administered to men more often than women, and disproportionately to racial minorities compared with whites. What do you think accounts for this pattern, and do you think it will have changed over time? Why or why not?

Student Resources

Historians of the death penalty continue to research the history of capital punishment in the United States and continue to publish their findings in new books and journal articles. A good way to keep up with this scholarship is to use Internet search resources to find new work in the area. One simple way to stay current is to go to online booksellers such as Amazon.com or Overstock.com and search for books on capital punishment. You can find the most recent books published in the area that way. You can also use bibliographic search resources in your college library to identify the most recently published books.

Another good technique is to use legal research databases, such as LexisNexis, to locate law review articles that pertain to the death penalty generally or historical issues in particular. In addition, several very good websites offer information about the death penalty in the United States. An informative website for legal information is maintained by the Cornell Law School's Legal Information Institute. From this website you can locate information about the U.S. Constitution, Supreme Court and lower federal court cases, and state law and opinions. You can find this information at <www.law.cornell.edu>.

Another informative site is maintained by the Death Penalty Information Center, a nonprofit organization that collects and disseminates information about the death penalty in America. It also maintains a database on the number of executions and some characteristics. They can be found at <www.deathpenaltyinfo.org>.

A website that contains valuable information about arguments in support of the death and links to other sites is <www.prodeathpenalty.com>.

In many chapters of this book the "Student Resources" section will provide you with what we think are helpful websites in finding information about the death penalty. You do need to be careful in using any website, as many are maintained by organizations that either oppose or support the death penalty; the information they provide should be read carefully and with a critical eye.

Endnotes

1. It should not be too surprising that the American colonies used capital punishment for what they believed to be serious crimes. Although established distinct from the mother-country, and sometimes in opposition to it, the founders of the original American settlements were after all English and were heavily influenced by English legal traditions, including capital punishment. Radzinowicz (1948) reported that there were an estimated 3,780 executions in England from 1509 to 1547, an average of 140 annually. From 1548 to 1553, there were 3,360 executions in England, an average of 560 per year. From this high point the number of both capital offenses and executions began to steadily decline. From 1625 to 1649, 2,160 people were put to death, an annual average of 90, and 990 executions took place from 1650 to 1658. In the mid–1700s, there were almost 200 potentially

capital offenses in England, many for minor property offenses such as poaching game or petty theft. Capital punishment in England existed well into the 1900s.

2. Like today, the pronouncement of a death sentence did not mean that an execution would take place for any capital offense in colonial times. One way in which a pending execution could be avoided was if mercy was extended by some form of executive clemency by a colonial governor. Unlike today, when governors rarely conduct an independent review of the death sentences that cross their desks via clemency petitions and even more rarely grant a reprieve, the extension of executive clemency was much more prominent during the seventeenth and eighteenth centuries. It was a common way for the governing authority to correct legal errors that occurred during the trial, to avoid the execution of what would appear to be an innocent person or one whose punishment should be mitigated because of unique factors (the offender's youth or lack of a previous criminal record), or just to grant a favor to someone who was "well-connected" (Banner 2002). There were other ways in which a death sentence would not be carried out. Adapted from English law, offenders could avoid being executed by claiming the "benefit of clergy." Originally, clergy charged with a criminal offense could escape prosecution by the state because they would claim that they were under the jurisdiction of church courts. Over time, the benefit of clergy was extended to anyone who could read (under the notion at the time that only the clergy would have enough formal education to be able to read). In colonial America, a benefit of clergy could be extended to the literate making the claim, but it would be granted only once a burn mark was placed on the offender's thumb (Banner 2002). Finally, some death sentences in colonial America were only symbolic, in the sense that the offender was never actually put to death but had to stand on the gallows with the hangman's noose around his or her neck for a specified length of time (Banner 2002).

3. The Espy file data set includes information on the age of the person executed for only 30 percent of the cases during the years 1608–1929.

4. Pennsylvanians could still sentence to death defendants convicted of murder, treason, manslaughter, rape, arson, and counterfeiting.

5. At this time Pennsylvania also abolished the death penalty for treason, manslaughter, rape, arson, and counterfeiting (Banner 2002).

6. Other methods of execution during this time period included burning, breaking on the wheel, pressing, hanging in chains, and gibbeting (Oberly 2002).

7. We noted earlier than one form of capital punishment was the "symbolic" hanging. In some instances the defendant would be sentenced to stand on the gallows with a rope around his neck for some specified period of time. In other instances, the condemned actually thought they were going to be hung; the full ceremony was performed until at the last moment the condemned was informed either that there really was no death sentence imposed or that there was a reprieve granted (Banner 2002).

8. Virtually all executions in the United States during this period were hangings. There were instances of death by firing squad, and death by burning—the latter being most typically reserved for Native Americans and slaves or those assisting in slave revolts.

9. There are several excellent histories of the rise of electrocution as the primary method of punishment in the United States. Three of the best are Denno (1994), Moran (2002), and Ressig (2003).

10. The Gerry Commission also noted that death by the injection of the pain killer morphine was "too painless" and rejected it as an alternative to hanging (Moran 2002).

11. See Denno (1994), Moran (2002), and Ressig (2003) for detailed accounts of this history.

12. The Electrocution Act also imposed a "gag order" on the press, preventing the reporting of any details of an execution. As will be discussed in later sections, this (and the imposition of the death penalty within the walls of a state penitentiary, rather than in an open, and public arena) further removed the view of executions away from the public and into a more private domain.

13. Denno (1994) reports that Westinghouse hired one of the country's leading criminal defense lawyers, W. Bourke Cochran, and spent more than $100,000 on Kemmler's appeal, an amount equal to approximately $2 million today.

14. This holding was later overturned by the Supreme Court, but not until 1962 in *Robinson v. California*, 370 U.S. 660 (1962).

15. *In re Kemmler*, 136 U.S. 436 (1890) at 447.

16. *In re Kemmler*, 136 U.S. 436 (1890) at 497.

17. Both Mississippi and Louisiana briefly experimented with a mobile electric chair that could be moved around from jurisdiction to jurisdiction. ✦

Chapter 2

Capital Punishment in the Premodern Period: 1930–1967

As we tried to make clear in the first chapter, there is a long history of capital punishment in the United States. Although its use began when the country consisted of nothing more than small and isolated colonies, capital punishment began to take on a decidedly different character by 1930. Without taking anything away from the important historical data that have been collected on earlier executions, it was not until the 1930s that we began to get truly accurate data on the annual number of executions in the United States. By the 1930s almost all executions were conducted by state rather than local authorities; in addition, it was in the 1930s that official data began to be regularly collected on the frequency of executions. Starting in 1930 The National Bureau of the Census included in its official record keeping the category of "death by execution" in its annual publication, *Mortality Statistics*. It is with this publication that we begin to get a really accurate assessment of the annual number of executions in America.

We end what we call the Premodern Period of capital punishment in 1967. On June 2, 1967 Luis Jose Monge was hung by the state of Colorado. Monge was the last person in the United States to be put to death for almost 10 years. During this time there were no executions anywhere in the United States, as state and federal courts were deciding some fundamental issues with respect to the death penalty, including whether or not capital punishment itself was constitutional. This 10-year moratorium on executions ended on January 17, 1977, with the execution by firing squad of Gary Gilmore in the state of Utah. We will examine in detail the legal and constitutional reasons behind this moratorium on executions in a later chapter.

Capital Crimes and Capital Statutes in the Premodern Period

During the period 1930–1967 several crimes were defined by state statute as carrying a capital sentence. Besides murder, a sentence of death could be imposed in some states for rape, armed robbery, kidnapping, burglary, and aggravated assault (and for espionage at the federal level). Most of the executions that occurred in this period, however, were for two offenses. Approximately 98 percent of the defendants executed from 1930 to 1967 committed either murder or rape.

In Chapter 1 we learned that when death penalty laws were first created after the Revolutionary War, they took the English common law form of mandatory statutes. Under these statutes a sentence of death was automatically imposed when a defendant was found guilty of a particular crime. The sentencing authority had no discretion under theses laws: Once a defendant was convicted of a capital crime, the death penalty was required by law. As we learned, it became clear that juries often circumvented what they perceived to be the harshness of mandatory death statutes by refusing to convict or, where they could, by convicting for a lesser offense those defendants not believed to be deserving of a death sentence. The practice of what became known as "jury nullification" was recognized as a real problem with mandatory capital statutes, and states began to reform their laws. Tennessee was the first state to do away with a mandatory death statute in 1848 in favor of a discretionary statute. Alabama followed in 1841, and Louisiana in 1876. By the 1920s, all but eight death penalty states had adopted a discretionary statute, and by 1963 all states had done so (Bedau 1982).

Under a discretionary capital statute, the authority deciding the convicted capital offender's sentence (jury or judge) is provided with two general options: a capital sentence (death) or a noncapital sentence (life imprisonment). Although the specific form of the statute varied from state to state, all discretionary statutes gave the sentencing authority the opportunity to return a sentence less than death for any potentially capital crime. If a jury had the authority to sentence, the usual procedure was that before deliberating on the sentence they were given a set of instructions by the court. These instructions generally informed the jury that they should consider all of the factors that would argue for a sentence of death and all extenuating circumstances that would argue for a sentence less than death. There did not have to be any established findings of fact, and with a few limitations described in the law (for example, sometimes the jury was told they could not be affected by considerations of prejudice or emotion), they were left free to decide the appropriate sentence. In California, a death penalty state during this time, the jury was given the following set of instructions, which were fairly typical:

> . . . in arriving at this [penalty] determination you should consider all of the evidence received in court here presented by the People and defendants throughout the trial before this jury. You may also consider all of the evidence of the circumstances surrounding the crime, of each defendant's background and history, and of the facts in aggravation and mitigation of the penalty which have been received here in court. . . . Notwithstanding facts, if any, proved in mitigation or aggravation, in determining which punishment shall be inflicted, you are entirely free to act according to your own judgment, conscience, and absolute discretion. (*McGautha v. California*, 402 U.S. 183 [1971])

It is clear from this language that California juries, and juries in other states with comparable statutes, had great latitude in imposing a death sentence. There was nothing in the law that required them to impose a death sentence in even the most heinous capital crime, and nothing that prevented them from imposing it in the least heinous one either.

The fact that capital juries had virtually unlimited sentencing discretion was thought by opponents of capital punishment to lead to death sentences that were arbitrary and capricious. Critics argued that a sentence of death should be reserved for only the worst and most deserving offenders (a belief largely held by supporters of the penalty as well). When critics looked at how death sentences were actually being imposed by juries, however, they claimed that the discretion given to the jury was being abused. There seemed to be no rational or meaningful basis for determining who received a sentence of death and who did not. Moreover, some of the factors that did appear to matter (race and social class, for example) were troubling. The alleged abuse of sentencing discretion in the hands of capital juries formed the basis for a series of legal challenges in state and federal courts in the middle to late 1960s and early 1970s. It was these legal challenges against the death penalty that led to the 10-year moratorium on the use of the death penalty that began in 1967. As we will discuss in more detail in a later chapter, these legal challenges were at first successful. In *Furman v. Georgia* (1972), the U.S. Supreme Court held that as it was currently being administered under state statutes that granted juries considerable discretion, capital punishment was unconstitutional because it violated the Eighth Amendment's prohibition against cruel and unusual punishments.[1] Just four years later, the Supreme Court would hold in *Gregg v. Georgia* and its companion cases that procedurally reformed death penalty statutes created by many of the states in response to *Furman* were constitutional.[2] Once these new statutes were given constitutional approval, the way was cleared for the end of the moratorium on the death penalty and the resumption of executions.

Characteristics of Executions in the Premodern Period

Figure 2.1 shows the annual number of executions in the United States from 1930 until 1967. During this period 3,891 executions were performed under both state and federal authority. The number of executions averaged over the 38 years is approximately 102 per year (about one execution every three days). Figure 2.1 clearly shows that the frequency of executions was substantially higher at the beginning of this period than toward the end. Capital punishment was much more frequently imposed during the mid-1930s, with an annual average of over 160 executions, or slightly less than one every other day. From this high point, the number of executions declines to an annual average of about 130 executions in the 1940s, then to an average of around 70 executions per year in the 1950s, finally to an average of fewer than 20 annual executions in the 1960s. While the imposition of capital punishment was a fairly frequent occurrence during the 1930s and 1940s, by the beginning of the 1960s it became a relatively rare event until it temporarily disappeared by the end of 1967.

One of the facts about capital punishment during the time period 1930–1967, then, is its consistently declining use over time. Figure 2.1 obscures an important characteristic of capital punishment in the Premodern Period, however. Although a majority of states had capital punishment statutes "on their books," there was great state-to-state variation in the extent to which it was put to use, and this variation produced a consistent pattern: Executions were much more likely to be a Southern phenomenon. Figure 2.2 reports the annual number of executions in different regions of the country from 1930 to

Figure 2.1   Number of Executions in the United States During the
Premodern Period, 1930–1967

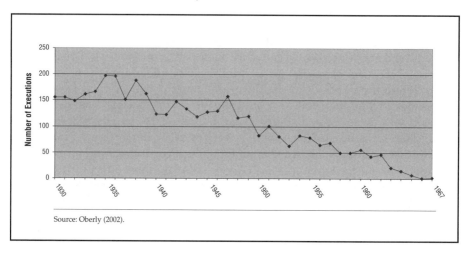

Source: Oberly (2002).

1967. It can be seen that while the number of executions in Northeastern states,
North Central states, and the West track very close to one another, those for
Southern states are substantially higher. Nearly half of the total executions from
1930 to 1967 occurred in nine Southern states: Georgia, Texas, North Carolina,
Florida, South Carolina, Mississippi, Louisiana, Alabama, and Arkansas, and
60 percent occurred in 17 Southern states—an average of 135 executions per
death penalty state. In fact, the number of executions performed in the South
from 1930 to 1967 was more than that in all other regions of the United States
combined.

Figure 2.2   Number of Executions 1930–1967 by Region

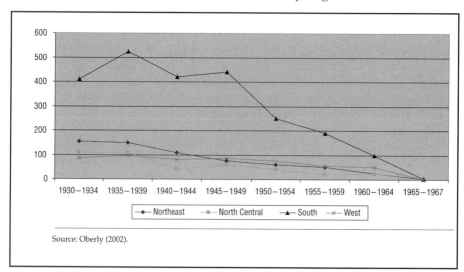

Source: Oberly (2002).

Related to the fact that executions during the Premodern Period were largely occurring in the South, a second consistent feature of executions during this period was that they were disproportionately imposed on racial minorities. Although African Americans made up about 10–12 percent of the total U.S. population, slightly over 50 percent of the total number of executions involved black defendants (See Figure 2.3). This disparate racial impact was more pronounced for some kinds of offenses. Figure 2.4 reports the percentage of executions of whites and nonwhites separately for murder and rape. About half of those executed for murder were nonwhite, but nearly 90 percent of those executed for the crime of rape were nonwhite (97 percent of the executions for the offense of rape occurred in Southern states). Although not definitive proof, these data suggest the possibility that for the offense of murder and more convincingly for the crime of rape the imposition of the death penalty may have been influenced by the race of the offender (especially in the South). We will examine the issue of racial disparity in the administration of the death penalty in greater detail in Chapters 7–8 of this book. As was true of the early period of capital punishment in America, Figure 2.5 shows that virtually all of those executed were male (99 percent).

Methods of Execution in the Premodern Period

During what we are calling the Premodern Period, the preferred method of capital punishment was death by electrocution. We have alluded to the fact that there was swift movement among the states to adopt the electric chair after 1890 when William Kemmler in New York became the first person to be put to death by electricity. After New York, the electric chair was quickly adopted as the method of execution by Ohio (1897), Massachusetts (1900), New Jersey (1906), and Virginia (1908). There were, however, both remnants of older methods of capital punishment and at least one attempt to experiment with a technologically newer method—lethal gas. Figure 2.6

Figure 2.3   Race of Offender Executed, 1930–1967

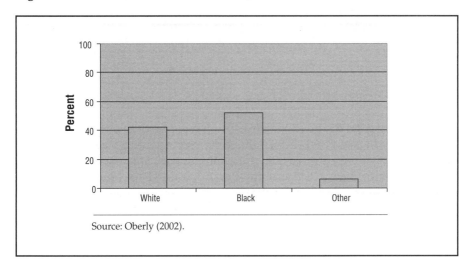

Source: Oberly (2002).

Figure 2.4 Racial Distribution of Those Executed for Murder and Rape, 1930–1967

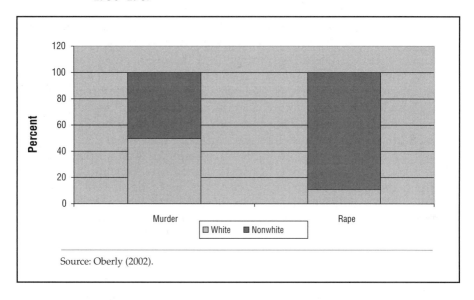

Source: Oberly (2002).

Figure 2.5 Gender of Offender Executed, 1930–1967

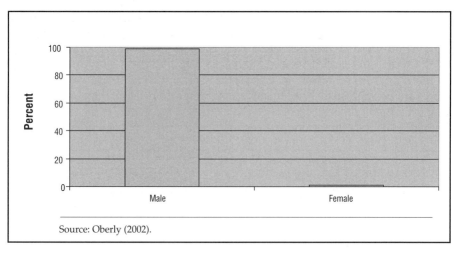

Source: Oberly (2002).

shows the trends in the method of execution over the time period 1930–1967. It can clearly be seen that during this time electrocution was the most frequent method of imposing capital punishment, with at least 60 percent of all executions being conducted with the electric chair. The proportion of executions by hanging drops over this period from about 20 percent to about 6 percent. What we also see in Figure 2.6 is the number of executions by lethal gas increasing considerably, from about 8 percent in the 1930s to about 30 percent by the middle to late 1960s.

Box 2.1
The Celebrated Case of Caryl Chessman

In 1948 someone was driving on scarcely traveled roads in the city of Los Angeles victimizing couples. Occasionally, the offender would use a red light on his car to impersonate a police officer to pull the victims' cars over. He would then rob the couple and sometimes take the woman in his car to another spot and sexually assault her. The offender became known as the "red light bandit." Caryl Chessman, a 27-year-old paroled ex-convict who had spent much of his adult life behind bars, was questioned about the crimes. He ultimately confessed to many. Chessman later recanted his confession saying it was coerced by harsh police tactics. He nevertheless was convicted of kidnapping under California's "Little Lindbergh" law (which provided for the death penalty in the case of rape involving "bodily harm") and was sentenced to death. For 12 years while on death row Chessman appealed his own case to the U.S. Supreme Court several times and wrote four books. His first book, *Cell 2455 Death Row*, named after his prison home, sold a half million copies and was translated into 18 different languages. As his execution approached, it was protested by such notables as Billy Graham, Eleanor Roosevelt, Robert Frost, and Pablo Casals. Chessman was put to death in California's gas chamber on May 2, 1960. ✦

In 1921 Nevada was the first state to adopt lethal gas as its method of execution. The Nevada legislature perceived death by electrocution as too inhumane and opted for the gas chamber. The original plan was to surprise the condemned prisoner by gassing him in his cell while he slept, but this method proved unworkable. A gas chamber was then constructed on a permanent site. The first person to die in Nevada's gas chamber was Gee Jon, a member of a Chinese gang who killed a rival gang member. Jon was put to death on Febru-

Figure 2.6   Method of Execution, 1930–1967

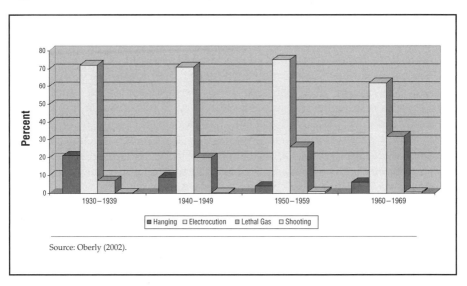

Source: Oberly (2002).

Box 2.2
'Old Sparky,' 'Gruesome Gertie,' and Some of the Others

In an odd sort of ritual, some states have given names to their electric chairs. Florida's electric chair was nicknamed "Old Sparky." The Old Sparky that was first used to electrocute Frank Johnson in 1924 was the same chair used to execute Allen "Tiny" Davis in 1999. Other nicknames for the chair have included "Sizzlin' Sally," "Old Smokey," "Yellow Mama," and "Gruesome Gertie." Condemned inmates going to die in the electric chair were said to be "riding the lightning." Both Louisiana and Mississippi had portable electric chairs that were mounted on trucks and driven to the jurisdiction of the electrocution.

Louisiana abandoned its portable electric chair in 1957 when it built a permanent chair, "Gruesome Gertie," at the Louisiana State Penitentiary in Angola. Gruesome Gertie was used to execute 87 prisoners, the last being Andrew Lee Jones on July 22, 1991. In 1991 Louisiana adopted lethal injection as its method of execution. Gruesome Gertie was used for the execution scene in the 2001 movie *Monster's Ball*. She sits now in the Louisiana Prison Museum in Angola.

In 1954 Mississippi dropped its portable chair in favor of a permanent gas chamber at the Mississippi State Penitentiary in Parchman. Notables to have been electrocuted include Sacco and Vanzetti, Bruno Hauptmann, Julius and Ethel Rosenberg, and Ted Bundy.

James Neil Tucker of South Carolina was the last person (as of June 2006) to be electrocuted (he refused to make a choice between the electric chair or lethal injection, and under South Carolina law the electric chair is used in the absence of a inmate's choice). ✦

---

ary 8, 1924. His lawyers sought to have the Nevada gas chamber declared cruel and unusual punishment under the Eighth Amendment to the Constitution but were unsuccessful. The Nevada "experiment" seemed to be working well, as there were no startling news stories about "botched executions" in the gas chamber to match those from death by electrocution. For about 10 years, however, Nevada stood alone in its use of lethal gas. Finally, in 1933 Colorado and Arizona also adopted the gas chamber. Eight other states, all in the West or South, switched to lethal gas, with New Mexico being the last in 1955 (Banner 2002). Most of these states had used hanging prior to the adoption of gas. California executed the most by lethal gas, sending 142 men and 4 women to death.

The gas chamber in California's San Quentin prison was like those in other states. It was housed in a basement and consisted of a sealed, small metal eight-sided box (6 feet across and 8 feet high) with windows on five sides so witnesses can view the execution. The chamber contains a chair for the condemned to be strapped into (California's gas chamber had two chairs for joint executions) and under the chair is a bowl of sulfuric acid and distilled water. Suspended above the bowl of acid is a bag of sodium cyanide pellets. When the door to the gas chamber is sealed and a signal from the warden is given, an executioner operates a lever that drops the cyanide pellets into the sulfuric acid, releasing hydrogen cyanide gas. The condemned dies because oxygen is shut-off from the brain. Witnesses to gas executions have reported that the person turns purple and has seizures or body spasms. The gassed prisoner generally loses consciousness after a minute or two. As of 2006, German citizen Walter

LeGrand was the last person in the United States to suffer death by lethal gas. He was put to death in Arizona's gas chamber on March 4, 1999. He chose to die by gas rather than lethal injection, an option under Arizona law. San Quentin still conducts California's executions in its gas chamber, only now the two chairs have been removed and replaced with a hospital gurney, where lethal injections are conducted.

In addition to death by electrocution and gas, the only other method used during this period was the firing squad. Only Utah and Nevada allowed the option of death by shooting, a method traced to the significant Mormon influence in both states. The doctrine of "blood atonement" in Mormon theology teaches that some sins are so egregious that they can only be cleansed by literally shedding the offender's own blood (Banner 2002). Death by shooting was the only method that promised the direct and obvious shedding of blood.

Location of the Death Penalty in the Premodern Period

In our discussion of capital punishment in the Early Period we stated that for a long time executions were performed by local authorities, but by the early 1900s they had begun to be transferred to state control. Executions during the Premodern Period were securely under state supervision, but in a limited sense. By the 1930s most states were performing their executions in state-operated penitentiaries, and executions were certainly conducted under state authority in that the capital punishment statute was an act of the state legislature and the act had statewide authority. This trend in conducting executions within state prison walls was completed by the 1960s.

Figure 2.7 shows the trend from 1930 to 1967 in the location of executions. It can be seen that capital punishment became less a local and more a state affair. However, in spite of the statewide jurisdiction of any given state's capital punishment statute, there is no uniformity *within* a state in the imposition of capital punishment. That is, just as there is substantial variation *across states* in the use of capital punishment, there is just as much variation *within a state* in the use of capital punishment. Some jurisdictions within a state use the death penalty much more frequently than others. In this important sense, then, the imposition of capital punishment is still very much a local rather than a state affair.

The source of the fact that the death penalty remains a local affair is that the conduct of criminal trials is a local (county/city) duty. It is local (usually county/city) prosecutors who must decide to seek the death penalty for a defendant who is eligible to receive a death sentence because of the crime he or she committed. Not every crime that *could* be punished by death is charged as a capital crime by the local prosecutor. Because of factors such as the quality of the evidence and financial limitations, local prosecutors must "pick and choose" among which "death-eligible" cases they will seek a death sentence for. In some jurisdictions the local prosecutors may select a high proportion, while in others they may select only half; in still others they may select only a very few. Juries act similarly, with juries in some jurisdictions sentencing to death a high proportion of cases, while others sentence a much lower proportion of cases. This discretion in the hands of both prosecutors and juries pro-

Figure 2.7   Percentage of Executions Conducted Under Local and State Supervision, 1930–1969

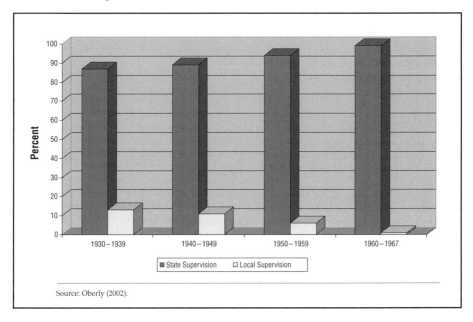

Source: Oberly (2002).

duces substantial jurisdiction-to-jurisdiction variation in the imposition of the death penalty within the same state. The fact that initial decisions in a death-eligible case are made at the local level by local criminal justice officials means that from 1930 to 1967 the death penalty remained very much a local affair, even though regulated by a state statute that is supposed to have statewide authority.

There is evidence that shows how decidedly local the administration of the death penalty was during the Premodern Period even when it was seemingly under unified state authority. Table 2.1 reports the findings from a study of pre-*Furman* (before 1972) capital sentencing in the state of Georgia. These data show that the likelihood of a death sentence was almost twice as high in urban areas of the state as it was in more rural areas. It also indicates that a death sentence was three times more likely in the southeast portion of Georgia compared with the north, and both Fulton County (Atlanta) and the north central part of the state had death sentencing rates that were about twice that in the north. In addition to these broad rural/urban and regional differences, substantial variability occurred by individual judicial circuits in Georgia both in terms of the likelihood that the local prosecutor would seek a death sentence and the likelihood that a jury would impose a death sentenced (Baldus, Woodworth, and Pulaski 1990). For example, in some judicial circuits fewer than 10 percent of the juries imposed a sentence of death in a capital case, while in other circuits it was over 50 percent. Even though Georgia had one death penalty law at the time that was in force throughout the state, the death penalty was more a local phenomena.

Table 2.1 Death Sentencing Rates in Different Places in Georgia During the Pre-*Furman* Period

Location	Death Sentencing Rates
Urban/Rural Areas	
Urban	.20
Rural	.11
Region	
North	.07
North Central	.14
Fulton County	.16
Southwest	.12
Southeast	.21

Source: Baldus et al. (1990), Table 22, p. 121.

Chapter Summary

In this chapter we examined the operation of the death penalty in the United States during what we call the Premodern Period. In the period from 1930 to the late 1940s, there were about 140 executions each year or about one every other day. Starting around 1948, however, the frequency of executions gradually and steadily declined until there were only a handful each year in the 1960s. Executions stopped completely in 1967 and were not resumed again until nearly 10 years later. This 10-year moratorium on capital punishment occurred because state and federal courts were dealing with important and troubling constitutional issues. These issues included both the procedures that states used in administering the death penalty and the central issues as to whether the death penalty constituted "cruel and unusual" punishment under the Eighth Amendment. The U.S. Supreme Court decided in the *Furman* case (1972) that while capital punishment itself was not unconstitutional, the legal procedures states were using gave juries too much discretion in affixing the appropriate penalty. The Court's decision emptied death rows across the country, and states that wanted to retain the death penalty scrambled to pass new legislation that would meet the Court's requirements of a constitutionally acceptable set of procedures.

Continuing the trend of reducing the number of capital crimes started in the Early Period, death-eligible offenses during the Premodern Period included murder, rape, kidnapping, armed robbery, and a few other offenses. The vast majority (over 95 percent) of the executions during this period were for the offenses of murder and rape. Most of the executions during these years occurred in Southern states. If the Early Period of capital punishment was the period of hanging, the Premodern Period was the time of the electric chair. While hanging remained a possible method in a few states, by the 1940s most states used electrocution as the preferred way to impose the death penalty. Although some states experimented with the use of lethal gas to execute prisoners, the vast majority of executions were performed by electrocution.

The historical trend of removing capital punishment from local authority in favor of state control continued during the Premodern Period, such that by the end of the 1960s all executions were performed under state authority. In part this reflected the economics of the death penalty and the change in the method of executions. While hangings and shootings could easily be conducted by local authorities, the movement toward the electric chair and the gas chamber virtually required more centralized financing and a permanent facility to house the death chamber.

As in the past, executions during the Premodern Period were conducted disproportionately against male offenders. In large part this reflected the fact that males are overwhelmingly more likely than females to commit the kinds of crimes that are capital offenses (murder, rape, kidnapping). A majority of the executions during this period were imposed on black offenders. This was because the vast majority of the executions for rape (over 90 percent) were of blacks, while about half of the executions for murder were of black offenders. The Premodern Period of capital punishment ended in 1967 with the execution of Luis Jose Monge in Colorado. No more executions took place in America until January 1977. It is to this moratorium period, and to the Modern Period of capital punishment, that we now turn our attention.

Discussion Questions

1. During what we have called the Premodern Period of capital punishment, the death penalty was imposed for offenses other than murder, such as rape, kidnapping, and even armed robbery. Since the argument of "an eye for an eye" cannot be made in the case of these other offenses, what justification do you think exists for this practice of capital punishment for nonmurder offenses?

2. During the first few decades of the Premodern Period, executions occurred with great frequency. Do you think we will ever return to having 200 or more executions per year? Why or why not?

3. Under capital statutes during this time, juries were given great discretion in terms of what factors they could consider in deciding whether or not a convicted capital offender should be sentenced to death. What factors do you think *should* go into making that decision, and how would you ensure that the jury consider those factors?

4. Since a capital jury had the discretion to impose or not impose a death sentence, do you think it is fair that two juries could come to an entirely different sentencing decision on the same case, with one jury imposing death and one a life sentence? Think about what you mean by "fair" and how you would ensure that capital sentencing procedures were "fair" under that standard.

5. Suppose you had the job of deciding what procedures should be in place for offenders accused of a capital crime. In creating these procedures you were aware that it would be possible that you could be accused of a capital offense and that you too would be subject to such procedures.

What kinds of procedures would you put in place, and why would you include them?

6. Why do you think that some states have adopted capital punishment while others have decided to punish their capital offenders with some other penalty, such as life imprisonment or life imprisonment without parole?

7. Do you think you would be safer from being murdered in a state that had the death penalty as a possible punishment for murder? Why or why not?

Student Resources

An interesting way to learn about the death penalty is to read fiction that portrays capital punishment. In his book *A Lesson Before Dying*, the celebrated American novelist Ernest J. Gaines tells the story of a young black field worker in 1940s Louisiana wrongfully convicted of the murder of a white man and sentenced to death. It is a fascinating portrayal of human dignity under extreme hardship. Another spellbinding book that illuminates capital punishment during this period is Truman Capote's *In Cold Blood*. The book is a fictionalized account of a true murder. Perry Smith and Dick Hickock killed four members of a Kansas farm family in 1959. They were eventually convicted of murder, sentenced to death, and hung. You might also want to watch the movie *The Green Mile*, which is about a death row prison guard, Paul Edgecomb, in the 1930s and his dealings with eight-foot tall inmate John Coffey who is awaiting execution.

Endnotes

1. *Furman v. Georgia*, 408 U.S. 238 (1972).

2. *Gregg v. Georgia*, 428 U.S. 153 (1976); *Proffitt v. Florida*, 428 U.S. 242 (1976); *Jurek v. Texas*, 428 U.S. 262 (1976); *Woodson v. North Carolina*, 428 U.S. 280 (1976); *Roberts v. Louisiana*, 428 U.S. 325 (1976). ✦

Chapter 3
Capital Punishment in the Modern Period: 1976–Present

The Modern Period of capital punishment began in 1976 when the U.S. Supreme Court gave constitutional approval to revised state death penalty statutes. These statutes were recrafted by the states in response to the Court's *Furman* decision and were approved in *Gregg v. Georgia*, *Proffitt v. Florida*, and *Jurek v. Texas*. So what we have called the Premodern Period ended in 1967 and the Modern Period started in 1976. Why is there a nearly 10-year gap in our timeline?

In the years following the execution of Luis José Monge in Colorado in 1967, state governors voluntarily imposed a moratorium on executions until the federal courts could address several critical issues about the death penalty (Meltsner 1973). Among these issues was the central one of whether capital punishment is constitutional under the Eighth Amendment to the Constitution or is one of the "cruel and unusual" punishments forbidden by that amendment. We will provide a detailed history of these issues and others in the next chapter, but some context is in order as we begin this one.

In 1972, the Supreme Court ruled in *Furman v. Georgia* that *as currently practiced* the death penalty in the United States was unconstitutional, in violation of the Eighth Amendment. The Court was clear to say that the death penalty was not per se unconstitutional (in fact, only two justices took that position), just that the procedures that were in place did not sufficiently reduce the risk that death sentences could be applied with capricious, random, or discriminatory results. It clearly held out the possibility that states could construct new death penalty statutes that would meet with a majority of the Court's approval. *Furman* did, however, both empty all death rows and officially continue the moratorium on future executions. In response, some states put themselves to the task of drafting new death penalty statutes that they believed adequately dealt with the risks identified by the *Furman* decision.

This effort ultimately proved successful. New statutes were created, offenders were sentenced to death, and states waited for the Court to approve of what they had done before executions could resume. The Court gave that approval in *Gregg v. Georgia* and its companion cases. Then, after a 10-year moratorium, executions in the United States resumed with the death of Gary Gilmore on January 17, 1977 in the state of Utah. Gilmore's execution was memorable for a number of reasons: (1) it was the first execution in the United States in a decade, (2) it was conducted by firing squad rather than by electrocution or lethal gas, (3) it became the basis for a bestselling book by Norman

Mailer (*The Executioner's Song*), and (4) Gilmore gave up his legal appeals and essentially "volunteered" for the death penalty.

While Gilmore's was the first execution after the moratorium, and the only one that took place in the United States for two more years, it ushered in a new, Modern Period of America's experience with the death penalty. Table 3.1 indicates that as of the end of the year 2005, most states and the federal government had death penalty statutes. A total of 38 states have the death penalty, along with the federal government and U.S. military, while only 12 states (and the District of Columbia) do not have the death penalty. Among the states with death penalty laws, five have not executed anyone during the Modern Period, and only New Hampshire has not even sentenced anyone to death during this period, even though it has the statutory authority to.

Table 3.1 States With and Without the Death Penalty, 1977–2005

States With the Death Penalty (38)

Alabama	Illinois	Nevada	South Carolina
Arizona	Indiana	New Hampshire[2]	South Dakota[1]
Arkansas	Kansas[1]	New Jersey[1]	Tennessee
California	Kentucky	New Mexico	Texas
Colorado	Louisiana	New York[1]	Utah
Connecticut	Maryland	North Carolina	Virginia
Delaware	Mississippi	Ohio	Washington
Florida	Missouri	Oklahoma	Wyoming
Georgia	Montana	Oregon	
Idaho	Nebraska	Pennsylvania	
Plus:	U.S. Military	U.S. Government	

States Without the Death Penalty (12)

Alaska	Massachusetts	Rhode Island
Hawaii	Michigan	Vermont
Iowa	Minnesota	West Virginia
Maine	North Dakota	Wisconsin
Plus	Washington, D. C.	

[1] States with the death penalty by law but no executions conducted since 1977.
[2] New Hampshire has the death penalty on its books but has not imposed a death sentence since 1977.

Capital Crimes and Capital Statutes in the Modern Period

In the early years of the Modern Period, there were numerous capital crimes listed in state statutes—murder, armed robbery, rape, and kidnapping, to name only a few. In addition to first degree murder, then, capital defendants could have been and were sentenced to death for such crimes as armed robbery and rape that did not involve the taking of another life. One of the legal trends that continued during the Modern Period was the limiting of capital crimes to offenses involving a killing (excluding crimes such as rape, kidnapping, or armed robbery). Just as there were legislative reforms in the Early and Premodern Periods that narrowed the number of potentially capital crimes, then, over time the number of capital crimes was reduced during the Modern Period as well. During this era, however, the restriction of what was to constitute a capital offense was done by the judiciary more than the legislature, most notably by the U.S. Supreme Court.

Not long after the initial Georgia capital statute was approved by the Supreme Court in its 1976 *Gregg* decision, another case came to the Court's attention from Georgia. In this case the defendant was sentenced to death for the crime of rape. Under the Georgia statute that was approved by the Supreme Court in *Gregg v. Georgia*, the death penalty could have been imposed for five other offenses in addition to murder: armed robbery, kidnapping, rape, treason, and aircraft hijacking. Other states besides Georgia included crimes other than murder as capital crimes, most generally kidnapping, rape, and armed robbery. The Supreme Court, however, would soon begin to reduce the range of possibly capital crimes.

It reviewed the constitutionality of the death penalty for the rape of an adult woman in the 1977 case of *Coker v. Georgia* (433 U.S. 584, 1977). While not depreciating the seriousness of a rape, the Court held nonetheless that a death sentence was not permissible under the Eighth Amendment for the crime of the rape of an adult woman where there was no life taken, because the punishment was excessive. While the Court explicitly held in *Gregg* that one who murders is deserving of the death penalty, in *Coker* it concluded that one who commits rape does not. It wrote that "[t]he murderer kills; the rapist, if not more than that, does not" (p. 598). It used the same rationale that year in deciding in *Eberheart v. Georgia* (433 U.S. 917, 1977) that the death penalty was also an excessive punishment for the crime of kidnapping of an adult where there was no loss of life. Although the constitutionality of the death penalty for the rape or kidnapping of a child has not been directly challenged, for the most part a capital offense during the Modern Period has now been restricted to instances where there was a murder.

Box 3.1
The Death Penalty for a Crime Not Involving a Murder?

In March 2006 a bill was introduced into the South Carolina Senate that called for the death penalty for those convicted for a second time of raping a child under the age of 11. The event that triggered this change in the South Carolina law was the arrest of a man who had been released early from an 18-year sentence for raping an 11-year-old girl. The man was arrested for holding two teenage girls captive in an underground "dungeon" behind his house and raping them. State prosecutors had argued against the early release of the man because they thought he would likely rape again. The state legislature passed the bill, which was signed into law by Governor Mark Sanford.

Florida, Louisiana, and Montana already had laws that allowed the death penalty for the sexual assault of a child, and Oklahoma passed a similar law after South Carolina. The Oklahoma measure makes the death penalty an option for anyone convicted of a second or subsequent conviction for rape, sodomy, or lewd molestation involving a child under 14. In 2003, Patrick O. Kennedy of Louisiana was sentenced to death under its law permitting capital punishment for the rape of a child under the age of 12. The U.S. Supreme Court has not determined whether such laws are constitutional. There has not been an execution for rape in the United States since 1964. ✦

One of the questions raised during the Modern Period has been how involved an offender must be in a killing before the death penalty becomes an appropriate penalty. Many state statutes allowed the death penalty for accomplices to murder—those who did not directly do the killing ("nontriggermen") but were implicated and involved in the crime. Florida was one such state, and in 1975 it sentenced to death Earl Enmund for a death that occurred during the course of an armed robbery. The prosecutor was aware that one of Enmund's accomplices, Sampson Armstrong, had been the one who actually killed the victim. Enmund's intention was only to commit a robbery, and at the time of the killings he was sitting in the getaway car about 200 yards from the crime scene. Despite the fact that he was not directly involved in the killing, Enmund had been charged and convicted of capital murder and sentenced to death. In his appeal to the Supreme Court, Enmund argued that his death sentence was disproportionate, since he did not take a life nor did he intend to take a life. The Court agreed, and in *Enmund v. Florida* (458 U.S. 782, 1982) it held that a sentence of death was unconstitutionally excessive for someone like Enmund who did not take a life, attempt to take a life, or intend to take a life.

A few years later the Court revisited the issue of the necessary complicity in a homicide before the death penalty may be imposed in *Tison v. Arizona* (107 S.Ct. 1676, 1987). In this case, Ricky, Raymond, and Donald Tison smuggled guns into the Arizona State Penitentiary to assist in the escape of their father, Gary, who was serving a life sentence for killing a prison guard during a previous escape attempt. The Tison boys and their father successfully made their escape from the prison, but their getaway car got a flat tire while driving through the Arizona desert. A passing motorist, his wife, their 2-year-old son, and a 15-year-old niece stopped to give them assistance. After asking his sons to go find water, Gary Tison killed all four people. Taking the victims' car, the Tisons continued their escape, which ended at a police road block. One of the sons, Donald, was killed at the road block; Gary ran off into the desert but later died of exposure; and Raymond and Ricky Tison (and one other escapee) were captured. Although they were not the triggerman and were not even at the scene when their father killed the four victims, both Raymond and Ricky Tison were sentenced to death under Arizona's felony murder statute.

It may seem that since the testimony in the case clearly showed that Ray and Ricky Tison did not actually kill the victims, nor did they intend to kill them (in fact, before the shooting they were instructed to get water, which the Tison brothers thought would be left for the victims when they were stranded in the desert), they could not be sentenced to death under the *Enmund* standard. However, the Court made great pains to distinguish Enmund's relatively minor participation in the armed robbery with that of Raymond and Ricky Tison. A majority of the Court argued that in carrying weapons into the prison to assist in the escape of their father, who had already murdered in a previous prison break, and in failing to protect or assist the victims in any conceivable way, they demonstrated a reckless disregard for human life. This, a majority of the Court stated, was sufficient to establish their culpability as fundamentally different from the defendant in *Enmund* and as deserving of a death sentence. The Court in *Tison* held, then, that although the death penalty cannot be imposed on defendants whose participation in a felony murder is minor and who do not take, attempt to take, or intend to take a life, it is constitutionally permissible to impose it for that group of felony murderers whose participation in the crime is major and who demonstrate by their actions a reckless disregard for human life. There are some non-triggermen who deserve to die, the *Tison* Court declared, and those states that choose to do so may put such criminals to death.

Table 3.2 shows the crimes that are punishable by death for the 38 states that had the death penalty at the end of 2005. Notice that with but a few minor exceptions (for example, capital sexual battery in Florida, aggravated kidnapping in Idaho, aggravated rape of victim under age 12), a capital offense must involve some form of first degree murder, and usually first degree murder plus at least one aggravating or special circumstance described by the state statute.

Table 3.2 Capital Crimes in the Modern Period

State	Crime(s) Punishable by Death
Alabama	Intentional murder with 18 aggravating factors
Arizona	First degree murder accompanied by at least 1 of 10 aggravating factors
Arkansas	Capital murder with a finding of at least 1 of 10 aggravating circumstances; treason
California	First degree murder with special circumstances; train wrecking; treason; perjury causing execution
Colorado	First degree murder with at least 1 of 17 aggravating factors; treason
Connecticut	Capital felony with 8 forms of aggravated homicide
Delaware	First degree murder with aggravating circumstances
Florida	First degree murder; felony murder; capital drug trafficking; capital sexual battery
Georgia	Murder; kidnapping with bodily injury or ransom when the victim dies; aircraft hijacking; treason
Idaho	First degree murder with aggravating factors; aggravated kidnapping
Illinois	First degree murder with 1 of 21 aggravating circumstances
Indiana	Murder with 16 aggravating circumstances
Kansas	Capital murder with 8 aggravating circumstances
Kentucky	Murder with aggravating factors; kidnapping with aggravating factors
Louisiana	First degree murder; aggravated rape of victim under age 12; treason
Maryland	First degree murder, either premeditated or during the commission of a felony, provided that certain death-eligibility requirements are satisfied
Mississippi	Capital murder; aircraft piracy
Missouri	First degree murder
Montana	Capital murder with 1 of 9 aggravating circumstances; capital sexual assault
Nebraska	First degree murder with a finding of at least 1 statutorily defined aggravating circumstance

Table 3.2 Capital Crimes in the Modern Period (Cont.)

State	Crime(s) Punishable by Death
Nevada	First degree murder with at least 1 of 14 aggravating circumstances
New Hampshire	Six categories of capital murder
New Jersey	Knowing/purposeful murder by one's own conduct; contract murder; solicitation by command or threat in furtherance of a narcotics conspiracy; murder committed during a crime of terrorism
New Mexico	First degree murder with at least 1 of 7 statutorily defined aggravating circumstances
New York	First degree murder with 1 of 13 aggravating factors
North Carolina	First degree murder
Ohio	Aggravated murder with at least 1 of 10 aggravating circumstances
Oklahoma	First degree murder in conjunction with a finding of at least 1 of 8 statutorily defined aggravating circumstances
Oregon	Aggravated murder
Pennsylvania	First degree murder with 1 of 18 aggravating circumstances
South Carolina	Murder with 1 of 10 aggravating circumstances
South Dakota	First degree murder with 1 of 10 aggravating circumstances; aggravated kidnapping
Tennessee	First degree murder with 1 of 15 aggravating circumstances
Texas	Criminal homicide with 1 of 8 aggravating circumstances
Utah	Aggravated murder
Virginia	First degree murder with 1 of 13 aggravating circumstances
Washington	Aggravated first degree murder
Wyoming	First degree murder

Characteristics of Executions in the Modern Period

Figure 3.1 shows the number of executions in the United States from January 1977 to the end of 2005. During this time there were 1,004 executions, with 1001 people put to death under state authority and three by the federal government. As can be seen, the pace of executions was extremely slow during the late 1970s and early 1980s, which in part reflected the fact that it was not until 1976 (with the decision in *Gregg v. Georgia* and its companion cases) that the Supreme Court had given constitutional approval to guided-discretion capital statutes. States that had valid death penalty statutes at the time of *Gregg* were being confronted with numerous constitutional challenges by lawyers for those sentenced to death. These challenges needed time to filter through state and federal courts of appeal.

Beginning in 1992, however, the annual number of executions in the United States began to slowly though erratically inch up, until there were 98 executions in the year 1999. There had not been that many executions in any one year since 1951, when there were 101. Since then, however, the annual number of executions has dropped by about one-third to approximately 60 per year, close to the annual number of executions during the middle to late 1950s.

Figure 3.1   Number of Executions in the United States, 1977–2005

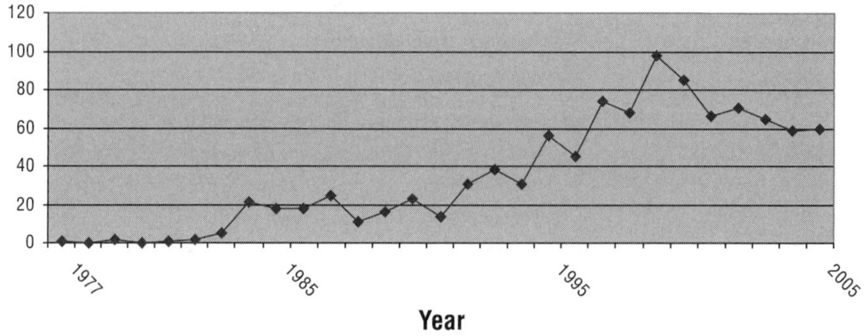

Source: Death Penalty Information Center (2005).

In fact, in recent years there have been signs of a declining use of the death penalty. This trend is reflected not only by the sharp drop in the number of executions but in the lower number of new death sentences being imposed by state (and federal) courts.

Figure 3.2 reports the annual number of death sentences in the United States during the Modern Period. There was at first a sudden and sharp increase in the number of death sentences imposed as states began to sentence defendants to death under their newly constructed post-*Furman* statutes. In the year of the *Gregg* decision (1976) there were nearly 300 new death sentences. At the same time it decided *Gregg* and approved of the procedures adopted by the state of Georgia, however, the Supreme Court also disapproved of the manner in which other states responded to *Furman*. These states adopted mandatory death penalty statutes hoping that they would comply with *Furman* by completely taking away the capital jury's sentencing discretion. Among the several states that adopted such mandatory capital statutes were North Carolina and Louisiana, and the Court struck down these statutes in *Woodson v. North Carolina* and *Roberts v. Louisiana*. Immediately after these decisions struck down mandatory death statutes, the number of new death sentences sharply declined to around 150–160 per year during the late 1970s. As those states that had mandatory statutes subsequently revised their death penalty laws by the early 1980s, the number of new death sentences climbed again to nearly 300 per year, and it stayed between 250 and 300 until the end of the 1990s. Since 2000, however, there has been over a 50 percent decline in the number of death sentences. By the early 2000s there were approximately only 150 new death sentences handed down by state (predominantly) and federal courts and 128 in 2005. In a subsequent section of this chapter we will provide some speculation as to why both the number of executions and new death sentences has declined so dramatically.

Figure 3.2 Number of Death Sentences in the United States, 1973–2005

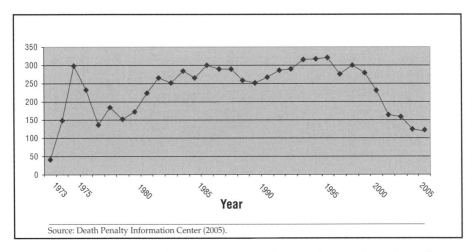

Source: Death Penalty Information Center (2005).

The demographics of those executed during the Modern Period very much mirror those of the Premodern Period. Figure 3.3 reports that as in the past, virtually all (99 percent) of those put to death during the Modern Period have been male. Only 11 women (out of over 1000 executions) have been executed since 1977 (about 50 are currently on death row). Although women are rarely executed, they do make up a sizable share of those killed by condemned offenders. In Figure 3.4 it can be seen that approximately half of the victims of executed defendants were females. In terms of race, a slight majority of those executed have been white (58 percent, see Figure 3.5), while a little more than one-third (34 percent) have been black. The percentage of white defendants executed during the Modern Period is slightly greater than the percentage during the Premodern Period (42 percent, see Figure 1.8). Figure 3.6 reveals an interesting fact about the death penalty during the Modern Period about which we will have much to say in later chapters: Since executions were resumed in 1977, a substantial majority (80 percent) of capital defendants have been put to death for killing at least one white victim. In terms of the combination of offender's and victim's race, Figure 3.7 (on page 50) indicates that the majority of those executed since 1977 have been white defendants who killed white victims (54 percent); the next most likely racial combination has been nonwhite offenders killing white victims (25 percent), while only 3 percent of all executions have involved white offenders who killed nonwhite victims. We can now see that a likely reason that white offenders are more often executed (Figure 3.5) is that they are more likely to kill white victims, and those who kill white victims are more likely to be executed than those who kill nonwhites (Figure 3.6). Most killings are intraracial, with whites generally kill whites and nonwhites kill nonwhites, and the observed racial pattern is due to the fact that killers of white victims are more likely to be executed than killers of nonwhite victims.

In both the Early and Premodern periods of American capital punishment, considerable regionalization occurred in the number of executions, with the

Figure 3.3   Gender of Those Executed, 1977–2005

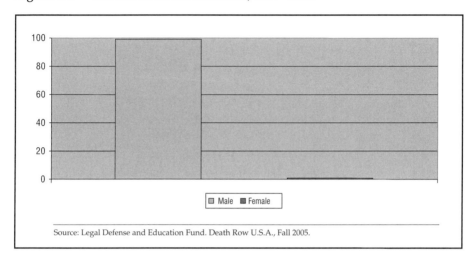

Source: Legal Defense and Education Fund. Death Row U.S.A., Fall 2005.

Figure 3.4   Gender of Victims for Those Executed, 1977–2005

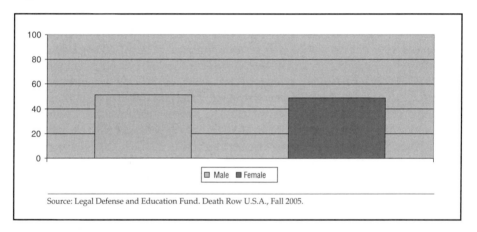

Source: Legal Defense and Education Fund. Death Row U.S.A., Fall 2005.

South responsible for a disproportionately large number. This trend continues into the Modern Period. Figure 3.8 (on page 50) shows the distribution of execution by region for the years 1977–2005. It can be seen that over 80 percent of the executions in the Modern Period have been conducted in Southern states. In fact, one Southern state, Texas, accounts for 35 percent of all executions during this period, and three Southern states combined (Texas, Virginia, and Oklahoma) account for over half. All Southern states have the death penalty, and all have executed at least one person since 1977, while the block of states in the Northeast United States either are abolitionist jurisdictions (Maine, Massachusetts, Rhode Island, Vermont, the District of Columbia) or have death penalty laws but have not executed anyone (New Hampshire, New Jersey, and New York). Clearly, then, in terms of capital punishment, Southern states dominate the rest of the United States, and a very few Southern states dominate within that region.

Figure 3.5   Race of Those Executed in United States, 1977–2005

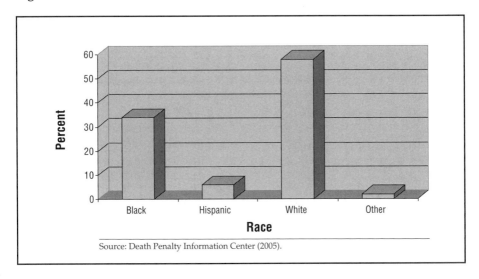

Source: Death Penalty Information Center (2005).

Figure 3.6   Race of Victims Among Those Executed in United States, 1977–2005

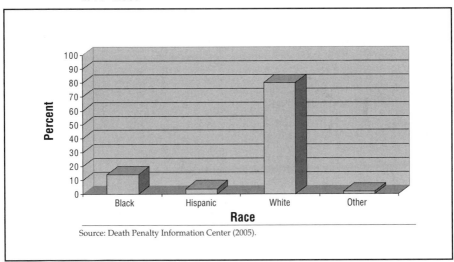

Source: Death Penalty Information Center (2005).

This regionalization of capital punishment has become more pronounced in the Modern Period. Figure 3.9 (on page 51) reports the percentage of executions in each region of the country during both the Premodern and Modern periods. Although the Southern states have more executions than any part of the country in both periods, their dominance is even greater in recent history. While not exclusively a Southern phenomenon, clearly the executioner is substantially more active in the South than any other place in the country. The number of executions in each state from 1977 to the end of 2005 is given in Table 3.3.

Figure 3.7   Race of Offenders and Victims Among Those Executed in
United States, 1977–2005

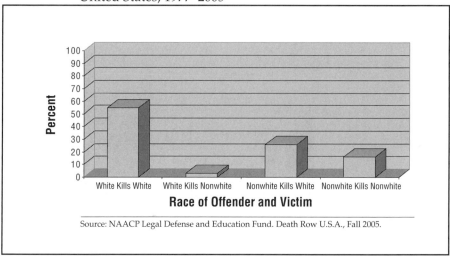

Race of Offender and Victim

Source: NAACP Legal Defense and Education Fund. Death Row U.S.A., Fall 2005.

Figure 3.8   Executions in the United States by Region, 1977–2005

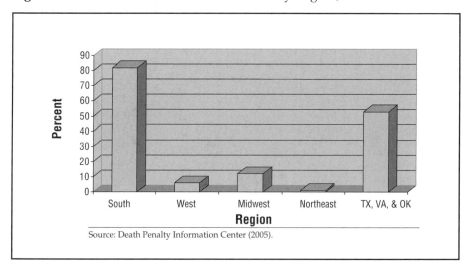

Region

Source: Death Penalty Information Center (2005).

Overlaid on this regional variation is substantial variability across the
United States in the rate at which each death penalty state executes its convicted offenders. Although Texas by far has the most executions than any
other state, this is because it is a populous state that vigorously seeks the death
penalty (well, some jurisdictions in Texas do, such as Harris County—Houston). When each state's population is taken into account, Texas does not have
the highest rate of execution. Figure 3.10 (on page 51) reports the execution
rate per 10,000 population for each death penalty state. When looking at this
figure it is important to keep in mind that all these are death penalty states and
all have executed at least one person since 1977. The clear sense you get is that

Figure 3.9   Percent of Executions by Region in Both Premodern and Modern Periods

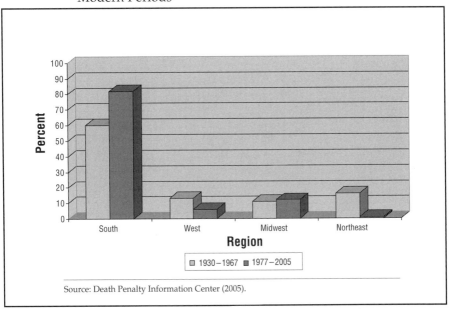

Source: Death Penalty Information Center (2005).

Figure 3.10   Rate of Executions per 10,000 Population for States With at Least One Execution Since 1977

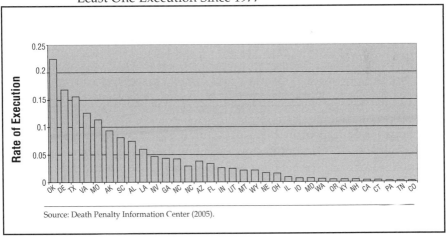

Source: Death Penalty Information Center (2005).

some states are substantially more aggressive in imposing capital punishment than others. Not surprisingly, given our previous figure, many of the states with the highest execution rates are in the South, but not all. The state with the highest execution rate is Oklahoma, with .224 executions per 10,000 people. As an indication of just how much state-to-state variability there is, the risk of execution in Oklahoma (.224) is more than twice the rate in Arkansas (.094) and South Carolina (.081), more than six times greater than that for Florida (.034),

Table 3.3 Number of Executions by State, 1977–2005

State	Number of Executions
Texas	355
Virginia	94
Oklahoma	79
Missouri	66
Florida	60
Georgia	39
North Carolina	39
South Carolina	35
Alabama	34
Louisiana	27
Arkansas	27
Arizona	22
Ohio	19
Indiana	16
Delaware	14
Illinois	12
California	12
Nevada	11
Mississippi	7
Utah	6
Maryland	5
Washington	4
Nebraska	3
Pennsylvania	3
Kentucky	2
Montana	2
Oregon	2
Colorado	1
Connecticut	1
Idaho	1
New Mexico	1
Tennessee	1
Wyoming	1
Federal government	3

Source: Death Penalty Information Center (2005).

32 times greater than for Maryland (.007), and nearly 75 times greater than for California (.003). California is the most populous state and imposes a lot of death sentences but has not performed many executions in the Modern Period.

What we know about the death penalty in the modern era then, is that there are some states without the death penalty (Alaska, Hawaii, Iowa, Maine, Massachusetts, Michigan, Minnesota, North Dakota, Rhode Island, Vermont, West Virginia, and Wisconsin), some states that have the death penalty as a possible sanction but have not executed anyone since 1977 (Kansas, New Hampshire, New Jersey, New York, and South Dakota), many death penalty states that do execute but that have a low rate of execution (Oregon, California, Connecticut, and Pennsylvania), and only a handful of states that aggressively impose the death penalty (Oklahoma, Delaware, Texas, Virginia and Missouri). As we will seen in a later section of this chapter, there is not only substantial variation across states in the use of the death penalty but also substantial variation *within* a state from jurisdiction to jurisdiction.

Methods of Execution in the Modern Period

Whereas hanging was the method of choice during the Early Period and the electric chair during the Premodern Period, lethal injection has been the main method during the Modern Period. Figure 3.11 shows that from 1977 to 2005 over 80 percent of all executions in the United States were done with lethal injection. Further, Table 3.4 reveals that all but one death penalty state has death by lethal injection as either the sole method or an alternative method of execution. Nebraska is the only state which has electrocution as its sole method of capital punishment.

Figure 3.11   Method of Execution for Those Put to Death in United States, 1977–2005

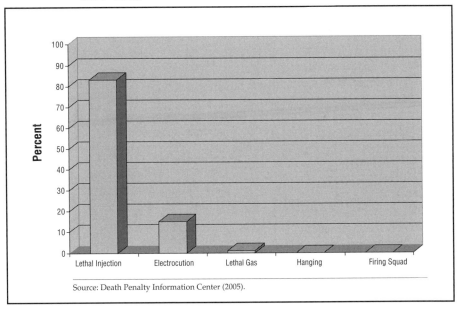

Source: Death Penalty Information Center (2005).

The notion of giving condemned offenders a lethal dose of some toxic substance is not entirely new. You may remember that Socrates was put to death by Athenian authorities with a cup of poison. Further, when the Gerry Commission of New York investigated alternatives to hanging in 1888, one of the methods it considered was the injection of morphine of sufficient dosage to kill a person. They thought that the lethal injection could be administered while the condemned was lying on a bed and that such a death would be relatively quick and painless. Even in the late 1880s criminal justice reformers were well aware of the common practice of putting unwanted or dangerous dogs and cats "to sleep" with a lethal injection of poison. However, in spite of what appeared to be the method's obvious benefits, the Gerry Commission rejected the adoption of lethal injection to replace hanging primarily because of stiff opposition by the medical community, and ironically because they believed that such a death would be "too painless" (Moran 2002, 79).

Table 3.4 Method of Execution, by State, 2005

Lethal Injection	Electrocution	Lethal Gas	Hanging	Firing Squad
Alabama	Alabama[13]	Arizona[1]	Delaware[2]	Idaho[3]
Arizona[1]	Arkansas[4]	California[5]	New Hampshire[6]	Oklahoma7
Arkansas[5]	Florida[8]	Missouri[5]	Washington[9]	Utah[3]
California[5]	Kentucky[10]	Wyoming[11]		
Colorado	Nebraska			
Connecticut	Oklahoma[7]			
Delaware[2]	South Carolina[8]			
Florida[8]	Tennessee[8]			
Georgia	Virginia[8]			
Idaho[3]				
Illinois				
Indiana				
Kansas				
Kentucky[10]				
Louisiana				
Maryland				
Mississippi				
Missouri[5]				
Montana				
Nevada				
New Hampshire[6]				
New Jersey				
New Mexico				
New York				
North Carolina				
Ohio				
Oklahoma[7]				
Oregon				
Pennsylvania				
South Carolina[8]				
South Dakota				
Tennessee[12]				
Texas				
Utah[3]				
Virginia[8]				
Washington[9]				
Wyoming				

Source: Death Penalty Information Center (2005).

[1] Arizona authorizes lethal injection for those who were sentenced to death after November 15, 1992; for those sentenced to death before that date the defendant may select lethal injection or gas.

[2] Delaware authorizes lethal injection for those whose capital offense occurred after June 13, 1986; for those whose capital crime occurred before that date the defendant may select lethal injection or hanging. As of July 2003 no one on death row was eligible to choose hanging, so lethal injection is the sole method of execution.

[3] These states authorize either lethal injection or firing squad as the method of execution.

[4] Arkansas authorizes lethal injection for those whose capital offense occurred on or after July 4, 1983; for those whose capital crime occurred before that date the defendant may select lethal injection or electrocution.

[5] These states authorize either lethal injection or gas as their method of execution. In California death is by lethal injection unless the inmate requests gas. In Missouri it is unclear who decides what method to use.

[6] For New Hampshire lethal injection is the authorized method of execution. Hanging is provided by law only if the defendant cannot be given lethal injection.

[7] Oklahoma authorizes electrocution if lethal injection is ever held to be unconstitutional, and firing squad if both lethal injection and electrocution are held unconstitutional.

[8] These states authorize either lethal injection or electrocution as their method of execution.

[9] Washington authorizes either lethal injection or hanging (at the inmate's request) as its method of execution.

[10] Kentucky authorizes lethal injection for defendants who were sentenced to death on or after March 31, 1998. For those sentenced to death before that date, the defendant may choose either lethal injection or electrocution.

[11] Wyoming authorizes lethal gas as its method of execution if lethal injection is ever held to be unconstitutional.

[12] Tennessee authorizes lethal injection for those whose capital crime occurred after 12/31/98. For those defendants committing their offense on or before that date, the defendant may choose between lethal injection or electrocution.

[13] As of July 1, 2002 Alabama authorizes lethal injection unless the inmate requests electrocution.

There are a number of reasons that many states switched from electrocution to lethal injection as the preferred method of execution during the modern era. One is economic. After the 10-year moratorium on executions while the Supreme Court ruled on lingering issues about the death penalty, the pace of executions did not reach more than 10 per year until 1984. In the mid-1980s, therefore, it would have been 15 or 20 years since many states had last executed someone. For many of these states, the passing of so much time meant that their electric chairs were technologically obsolete at best, and were rusted, rotten, and incapable of being used at worst. A large number of death penalty states had the choice of buying new electric chairs, repairing the old one, or investing in a new cheaper technology—lethal injection. Over time virtually all states chose the latter.

A second reason that many states moved from the electric chair to lethal injection was the growing number of what might be characterized as unsightly or gruesome-appearing electrocutions. Just as there were hangings that malfunctioned, causing what appeared to be great physical torment to the condemned, there were also well-publicized problems in administering a fatal jolt of electricity, which dramatized the debate about both electrocutions specifically and the death penalty in general. John Spenkelink, the first person electrocuted after the *Gregg* decision, was not killed by the first jolt of electricity from Florida's electric chair (nicknamed "Old Sparky"), it merely opened a 3-inch wound on his leg and filled the death chamber with smoke and the smell of burning flesh. It took five more minutes and two additional jolts of electricity for Spenkelink to finally be pronounced dead. One of the witnesses to the execution remarked that "we saw a man sizzled and sizzled again" (Denno 1997, 412).

The Spenkelink execution was not the last or the worst time that "Old Sparky" was to produce a gruesome death for the condemned offender. In 1990 convicted cop killer Jessie Tafero's head caught fire during his electrocution, and smoke and 6- to 12-inch flames poured out of the hood that covered his head during the process (Denno 1997). It took four minutes and three separate surges of electricity to kill Tafero. According to witnesses at the execution of Pedro Medina in 1997, as soon as the first jolt of electricity hit his body, blue and orange flames about a foot high shot up the side of his head that lasted approximately 10 seconds. Smoke and the stench of burnt flesh quickly filled the room, and a Florida Department of Corrections spokesperson said that a maintenance supervisor wearing electrical gloves had to pat the flames out on Medina's head and another state official had to open a window to let the odor and smoke out of the death chamber. When asked whether this latest malfunction of the electric chair might compel Florida to change its method of execution, Bob Butterworth, the state's attorney general, replied that in fact it might serve a greater deterrent effect: "People who wish to commit murder, they'd better not do it in the state of Florida because we may have a problem with our electric chair" (Denno 1997, 424). Florida's electric chair malfunctioned once again on July 8, 1999 with the execution of Allen Lee "Tiny" Davis. Photographs of the execution showed that Davis had burns on his head and face, and his leather face strap was so large and pulled so tight that there is evidence that he was suffocating before his execution (Denno 2003).

Florida's electric chair is not the only one that has malfunctioned resulting in what can only be described as a gruesome death for the condemned (Radelet 2003; Borg and Radelet 2004). With flames flying from an electrode attached to his leg, it took the state of Alabama 14 minutes to electrocute John Louis Evans in 1983. It took Indiana 17 minutes and five surges of electricity to pronounce William Vandiver dead. Vandiver's attorney, who witnessed the execution, described his client's death as "outrageous," while an Indiana Department of Corrections official admitted that the execution "did not go according to plan" (Radelet 2003; Borg and Radelet 2004). It took 19 minutes and two jolts for Alabama to kill mildly retarded prisoner Horace Dunkins. After the first administration of electricity failed to kill Dunkins, a corrections officer opened the door to the witness room and admitted, "I believe we got the jacks on wrong" (Denno 1997; Radelet 2003; Borg and Radelet 2004). After the cables were correctly connected, the second, lethal dose of electricity was applied. Flames also erupted from the head and body of Robert Williams in Louisiana in 1983, and blood poured out of the hood of Wilbert Evans in Virginia. At the execution of Alpha Otis Stephens in Georgia it took two surges of electricity to kill him; the second jolt could not be administered until some six minutes after the first one because Stephens' body was too hot for physicians to examine him to determine if he was dead. He was not, and the second jolt finally killed him. A Georgia official explained that Stephens was "just not a conductor of electricity" (Radelet 2003; Borg and Radelet 2004).

At the beginning of the Modern Period, the only viable alternative to the electric chair was death by lethal gas (death by firing squad or hanging was an option in only a few states). Lethal gas, however, also involved an expensive piece of machinery and produced some grisly executions of its own. In 1983 the state of Mississippi put Jimmy Lee Gray to death by lethal gas. After eight minutes of Gray's gasping for air and moaning, state officials cleared the witness room because they did not want them to see the end of Gray's life. While convulsing, Gray was banging his head against a pole in the gas chamber. One witness reported that "he looked like he was being strangled to death . . . [i]t was obvious that Mr. Gray was in excruciating pain" (Denno 1997). The Mississippi State Commissioner of Corrections later stated that its method of death by lethal gas had to be "refined" so that witnesses would have to see "as little gore as possible." At the Nevada execution by lethal gas of Jesse Walter Bishop in 1979 a witness reported that he appeared to be in great pain and was convulsing for more than 10 minutes (Denno 1997).

In addition to the cost, therefore, grisly executions with both the electric chair and gas chamber fueled the motivation for death penalty states to come up with a more humane form of execution. A logical choice was death by the injection of lethal drugs. As we noted, this method was considered by the Gerry Commission in the late 1800s, it was familiar to most Americans, many of whom had used it to "put down" their pets painlessly, and it was relatively cheap. In 1977 Texas and Oklahoma were the first states to adopt death by lethal injection, and other states quickly followed.

While the substitution of electrocution and gas for hanging was gradual, the adoption of lethal injection as a method of execution spread rapidly. The first person to be put to death by lethal injection was Texas inmate Charlie Brooks in 1982. Since that time the vast majority of executions in the United States (over 80 percent since 1976, and an even higher percentage since 1990) have been carried out by the injection of lethal drugs. As of 2005, Nebraska is the only state that has electrocution as its sole method of execution. In all other states lethal injection is either the sole method of execution or an alternative method.[1]

Although adopted for the supposedly humane manner in which it kills the condemned, death by lethal injection has not been immune from charges that it too involves nontrivial pain. Sometimes executioners cannot find a good vein in which to insert the needle because of the condemned's previous extensive intravenous drug use; other times the condemned seems to have had a severe allergic reaction to the drugs. For example, it took the state of Georgia an hour and nine minutes to put Jose High to death. The medical technicians searched some 39 minutes to find a usable vein. Eventually one needle was stuck in High's hand and a second was placed between his shoulder and neck (Cook 2001). On June 8, 2000 the execution of Bennie Demps took 33 minutes, again because medical technicians could not find a second good vein. In his final statements before his death, Demps exclaimed that "they butchered me back there. I was in a lot of pain. They cut me in the groin; they cut me in the leg. I was bleeding profusely. This is not an execution, it is murder" (Bragg 2000).

In addition, recent medical evidence has suggested that because of the types of drugs that are administered in state executions, death by lethal injection may not be painless. A Research Letter written by a University of Miami School of Medicine research team that appeared in the British medical journal *The Lancet*

Box 3.2
A Comfortable Death . . . for the Witnesses?

The person believed to have devised the current procedure for death by lethal injection is forensic pathologist Dr. Jay Chapman, Jr., a medical examiner with no experience in pharmacology. Dr. Chapman developed the three-drug "cocktail" now currently in use without much research into the matter. His method calls for the use of three drugs:

1. Sodium thiopental: a barbiturate that causes unconsciousness.
2. Pancuronium bromide: to cause paralysis and cease breathing.
3. Potassium chloride: to stop the heart.

Potassium chloride is known to be so painful that U.S. veterinarian guidelines prohibit its use on domestic animals unless the vet first ensures they are deeply unconscious. There are no such safeguards for the execution of humans. Further, the pancuronium bromide which causes paralysis may prevent the person who is experiencing even excruciating pain from crying out.

Dr. Mark Dershwitz, a professor of anesthesiology at the University of Massachusetts, has argued that there are other drugs available that would promise a much more painless death. The "down side" of these drugs, however, is that they would take substantially longer to kill the prisoner (30–45 minutes rather than the usual 2–10 minutes) and could cause spasmodic jerking motions that might startle those witnessing the execution. (See Death Penalty Information Center, 2005) ✦

has argued that the drugs used do not properly sedate the condemned. As a result, the medical team argued that prisoners are fully conscious when they die, quite painfully, and usually by suffocation (Koniaris et al. 2005). The researchers studied toxicology reports from 49 prisoners and found that in 43 instances the blood concentrations of the anesthesia sodium thiopental, a short-acting barbiturate, were lower than that required by surgery. In 21 cases it was low enough that the prisoner was likely aware during his execution. In spite of being conscious and slowly suffocating, prisoners undergoing execution like this are unable to move, cry out, or even speak because of the effects of a second drug used during executions, pancuronium bromide, which produces paralysis. The third typical drug is potassium chloride, which stops the heart and can cause excruciating pain if the person is conscious. The three-drug combination, then, may create an execution scene that appears to be serene and humane, but only because the prisoner who is paralyzed by the pancuronium bromide is unable to cry out (Tofte 2006).

Professional ethics of the American Medical Association prevent physicians from participating in lethal injections. The "Code of Ethics" of the American Medical Association states, "A physician, as a member of a profession dedicated to preserving life when there is hope of doing so, should not be a participant in a legally authorized execution" (American Medical Association 2006). The AMA defines the prohibited participation to include monitoring vital signs; attending or observing as a physician; rendering technical advice regarding executions; selecting injection sites; starting intravenous lines; prescribing, preparing, administering or supervising the injection of drugs; inspecting or testing lethal injection devices; and consulting with or supervising lethal injection personnel. Under the AMA Code, the only permissible participation by a physician in an execution is to provide a sedative to a prisoner upon his request prior to his execution and to certify the prisoner's death after another person has pronounced it. For the most part, doctors have strictly adhered to this ethical code of conduct, refraining from participating in executions. In 1990, however, three physicians administered a lethal injection to Charles Walker, the first Illinois prisoner to be executed in the Modern Period.

In June 2006, the Supreme Court unanimously ruled that state inmates may make legal claims that death by lethal injection may cause unnecessary

---

Box 3.3
'I Will ... Abstain From Whatever Is Harmful or Mischevious'

This phrase appears in the Hippocratic oath, the oath taken by many physicians before entering practice. Does this requirement to "do no harm" conflict with the role any physician may take with respect to execution by lethal injection? The American Medical Association's position is that any physician's opinion on the death penalty is entirely personal but that physicians should not be a participant in an execution, other than to provide a sedative to comfort the anxiety of a prisoner before the execution and to certify death. In February 2006 two California anesthesiologists refused to monitor the execution by lethal injection of Michael Morales. The execution was postponed. Upon hearing the news of the postponement, the mother of the victim said, "Here our beautiful daughter lies murdered, and there they worry about the way this monster feels and if he'll feel any pain." ✦

pain and suffering in violation of the Eighth Amendment. In *Hill v. McDonough* (547 U.S., 2006) Clarence Hill, a Florida prisoner, claimed that there were other mixes of drugs that could be used to conduct executions but that the currently used three-drug "cocktail" resulted in gratuitous suffering. The Court agreed with the narrow issue that inmates have the right to argue that there may be better ways to conduct lethal injections, acknowledging, however, the state's right to put prisoners to death through lethal injection. Writing for the Court, Justice Kennedy said, "Hill's challenge appears to leave the state free to use an alternative lethal injection procedure." In July 2006 U.S. District Court Judge Fernando J. Gaitan, Jr. barred all executions in Missouri until the state hired a board-certified anesthesiologist to oversee executions in the state and provide detailed procedures for executions, including assurances that the condemned receive a sufficient dose of anesthetic drugs. In sworn testimony, the Missouri doctor who mixed the drugs used in lethal injections stated that he at times did not provide as much anesthesia to inmates as required by state execution policy. Missouri officials tried to comply with the judge's order, sending letters to nearly 300 certified anesthesiologists asking for someone to provide the medical assistance for its executions but were turned down by all of them. The attorney general of Missouri reported to the federal judge that the state could not comply with his order for a board-certified anesthesiologist but countered that it could provide the assistance of "medical personnel in roles appropriate" such as a physician, nurse, or pharmacist. Judge Gaitan has not yet ruled whether the state's plan was sufficient, but certainly in view of *Hill* there will be intense litigation over the constitutionality of lethal injections.

Location of the Death Penalty in the Modern Period

In addition to the considerable variability across states in the imposition of the death penalty, research has shown that there is substantial variation *within* single states as well. This situation may at first seem odd, as one might expect that a law would be uniformly applied within the state, but this is decidedly not the case with capital punishment. We have noted how in previous historical periods the administration of the death penalty was a local affair, with hangings being carried out by local judicial and law enforcement authorities. Even during the modern era, however, the actual day-to-day process of the administration of capital punishment is primarily in the hands of local rather than state officials. It is local prosecutors who investigate cases and decide whether a case is a capital crime. If a case is not charged as a capital offense, the death penalty cannot subsequently be imposed by the sentencing authority. Thus, even though a capital punishment law has statewide jurisdiction, we should not be too surprised to learn that the defendants' risk of being sentenced to death varies substantially within every capital punishment state.

Take as one example the state of Maryland. Maryland has been a capital punishment state since 1978, when the state legislature modified its state statute to bring it into compliance with the U.S. Supreme Court's *Gregg* decision. To be considered a capital crime or "death eligible," a crime must include at least one of 10 statutory aggravating circumstances, such as the killing of more than one victim or killing during the course of a specified felony such as armed robbery or rape. However, even if a crime does include one or more of these statutory aggravating circumstances, it will not result in a death sentence if the local prosecutor does not charge the crime as a capital crime. The prosecutor must first serve a notification to defense counsel that it intends to seek a death sentence. However, even if a prosecutor files such a notification it can be withdrawn, and even if it is not withdrawn he or she may decide not to advance a case to a penalty trial after conviction. Each of these decisions in the death penalty process is in the hands of the local prosecutor, although all are guided by the state statute. Essentially, then, although there is a law with statewide jurisdiction in Maryland granting the authority for capital punishment, this power is in the hands of 24 local prosecutors who have a substantial amount of discretion. As a result, the imposition of the death penalty in practice is very local, varying considerably from county to county within the same state.

Table 3.5 shows the number of death-eligible crimes committed in each of six of Maryland's largest legal jurisdictions and the remaining 18 smaller jurisdictions combined (Maryland has 24 judicial jurisdictions—23 counties and Baltimore City) from August 1978, when the state's new death penalty law took effect, until December 31, 1999. It also reports for each jurisdiction the probability that a case was charged by the local prosecutor as a capital crime and the probability that a death sentence was imposed given that it was death eligible. For the state as a whole, the probability that the prosecutor would seek a death sentence in a death-eligible crime was .269, or about 27 percent of the time. This means that prosecutors in Maryland are seeking a death sentence 27 percent of the time when they can and that they opt not to seek a death sentence even though they could by law 73 percent of the time. The probability that a death sentence will be imposed by a sentencing authority (judge or jury) in a death-eligible homicide is .058 for the entire state. This means that a death sentence is imposed in about 6 percent of all death-eligible crimes.

The probability that the prosecutor will seek a death sentence is not uniform throughout the state, however. Although across the state a death sentence is sought in 27 percent of all death eligible cases, it is as high as 65 percent

Table 3.5 Probability That the Prosecutor Will Seek a Death Sentence and That a Death Sentence Will Be Imposed in a Death-Eligible Case in Maryland, 1978–1999

	Number of	Probability of:	
Jurisdiction	Death-Eligible Crimes	Death Sought	Death Sentence
Anne Arundel County	79	.201	.047
Baltimore City	567	.046	.006
Baltimore County	152	.651	.137
Harford County	35	.500	.045
Montgomery County	59	.117	.010
Prince George's County	30	.381	.017
Remainder of state	383	.481	.055
Maryland as a whole	1305	.269	.058

Source: Paternoster et al. (2004).

in one jurisdiction (Baltimore County, .651) and as low as 5 percent in another jurisdiction (Baltimore City, .046). In other words, the probability that a prosecutor will seek a death sentence in a death-eligible case is over 14 times higher in Baltimore County than in Baltimore City. This difference is all the more remarkable because Baltimore County borders Baltimore City. When individuals who commit a death-eligible crime simply cross the county line from Baltimore City to Baltimore County, they increase their risk of having the prosecutor's office seek a death sentence against them by a factor of 14. The likelihood that the prosecutor will see a death sentence in Baltimore County is also more than five times higher than that in Montgomery County and three times higher than in Anne Arundel County. The implication from the second column of Table 3.5 is that even though they all operate under the same state law, some prosecutors in Maryland are substantially more aggressive in seeking the death penalty than others.

This differential likelihood that Maryland's local prosecutors will seek the death penalty carries over into the imposition of the death penalty. Table 3.5 indicates that some jurisdictions are far more likely to sentence defendants to death than others. Someone who commits a death-eligible crime in Baltimore County, for example, is about three times more likely to be sentenced to death than one who commits a crime in Anne Arundel County, eight times more likely than someone from Prince George's County, 14 times more likely than one from Montgomery County, and 23 times more likely than a defendant from Baltimore City. Again, despite a capital punishment statute with statewide authority, the death penalty in Maryland is decidedly local.

Table 3.6 Death Sentencing Rates in Different Places in Georgia During the Pre-*Furman* Period

Location	Death Sentencing Rates
Urban/Rural Areas	
Urban	.19
Rural	.27
Region	
North	.09
North Central	.33
Fulton County	.13
Southwest	.23
Southeast	.22

Source: Baldus et al. (1990), Table 22, p. 121.

Evidence that the death penalty is applied differently within the same state has been found in other studies as well. Table 3.6 reports data from a study of capital sentencing in Georgia conducted by law professor David Baldus and his colleagues (1990). They reported their results by a rural/urban distinction and by distinct geographic areas of the state. The data in the table show that in Georgia the likelihood of a death sentence is about one and a half times higher in rural than in urban areas. In terms of geographic region, a death sentence is most likely in the north central part of Georgia, where a death sentence is almost four times higher than in the northern area of the state and two and a half times more likely than in Fulton County (Atlanta). In addition to these broad differences, the researchers also reported substantial variability by individual judicial circuits in Georgia, in terms of both the likelihood that the local prosecutor would seek a death sentence and the likelihood that a jury would impose a death sentence (Baldus et al., 1990).

In a study of the death penalty in Georgia and Florida, Bowers and Pierce (1980a) found that the percentage of cases that were death eligible that actually resulted in a death sentence was markedly different in different parts of the state. Table 3.7 shows that in Georgia, death-eligible defendants who were tried in the central or southwest portion of the state were almost eight times more likely to be sentenced to death than those from Fulton County (23 percent and 22 percent versus 3 percent) and about four times more likely than those from the northern area of the state. In Florida, death-eligible defendants who were convicted in the panhandle area of the state were more than four times more likely to be sentenced to death than those from either northern or southern Florida (58 percent versus 13 percent and 14 percent).

Table 3.7 Percentage of Death-Eligible Defendants Who Are Sentenced to Death

State and Region	Percentages of Death Sentences
Georgia	
North	6%
Central	23
Fulton County (Atlanta)	3
Southwest	22
Southeast	17
Florida	
Panhandle	58
North	14
Central	27
South	13

Source: Bowers and Pierce (1980a), p. 694, Table 5.

In his study of capital sentencing in South Carolina, Paternoster (1983) found substantial differences in the rate at which local prosecutors sought the death penalty across the state. Although one death penalty statute applied in every judicial circuit of the state, some prosecutors were more aggressive in seeking the death penalty than others. Table 3.8 clearly shows the circuit-to-circuit variability in the decision to seek a death sentence in South Carolina. Prosecutors in the 10th, 11th, and 15th judicial circuits were about four times more likely to charge a death-eligible crime as a capital offense than were prosecutors in the 4th, 5th, or 9th judicial circuits. Again, even though each prosecutor was guided by the same state capital punishment law, how it was interpreted and how that law was implemented differed depending on local practice.

Table 3.8 Number of Death-Eligible Cases, Number of Death Penalty Requests, and Percent of Cases Resulting in a Death Penalty Request in South Carolina

Judicial Circuit	Number of Death-Eligible Murders	Number of Death Penalty Requests	Percent of Cases With a Death Request
1st	9	4	44%
2nd	15	4	27
3rd	14	6	43
4th	12	2	17
5th	30	6	20
6th	5	2	40
7th	10	7	70
8th	9	4	44
9th	45	11	24
10th	5	4	80
11th	15	12	80
12th	14	4	29
13th	30	7	23
14th	17	10	59
15th	15	13	87
16th	16	9	56

Source: Paternoster (1983).

Comparable results for New Jersey indicating substantial within-state variation in both capital charging and sentencing were reported by Leigh Bienen and her colleagues (1988). They found that local prosecutors in two New Jersey counties were particularly aggressive in charging death-eligible defendants with a capital crime. Murder defendants in Mercer County, for example, were almost 50 times more likely to go to trial than comparable defendants in Camden County. Defendants charged with a crime in Monmouth County were 13 times more likely to be charged with a capital offense than those in Camden County. The researchers also found that in some New Jersey counties approximately two-thirds or more of all death-eligible defendants were sentenced to death, while in other counties fewer than one-third were. As with other states, it makes a difference where in New Jersey you commit your crime.

This variation by legal jurisdiction within a state is also characteristic of the state of Washington. The prosecutor in Washington's largest county (King) has historically sought a death sentence in 25 percent of the death-eligible crimes, while the rate at which death sentences are sought in the second largest county (Pierce) is double that (52 percent) (Larranaga 2003). In some counties a death sentence has never been sought even though there were death-eligible crimes, while in others a sentence of death is sought in two-thirds or more of the death-eligible cases. Even in the death penalty capital of the United States, Texas, not all jurisdictions are equally aggressive in pursuing capital punishment. Harris County (Houston) prosecutors are responsible for one-third of the executions in Texas, and at the end of 2005 they had sent more people to death row than all of Virginia's prosecutors combined.

In Illinois, the likelihood that someone will be sentenced to death also varies greatly by where in the state the crime was committed. Pierce and Radelet (2002) reported that even after taking into account differences in the characteristics of the homicides committed, the risk of getting sentenced to death in Cook County (Chicago) was substantially lower (84 percent lower) compared with the risk in rural areas of the state. Once again, one of the factors that determines who is sentenced to death is where in the state a crime was committed. Finally, Hindson et al. (2006) found that averaged across the state, prosecutors in Colorado sought a sentence of death in about 3 percent of the homicides. There was great variation, however, with some counties seeking death in nearly 8 percent of the homicides and other counties seek death in only 1 percent.

Collectively, this body of evidence clearly suggests that substantial variation exists within any death penalty state in the likelihood that a crime will be considered and treated as a capital offense. Although laws that define what a capital crime is and how it should be punished have statewide jurisdiction, they are applied very differently in different jurisdictions within any state. Just as there is no national policy about the death penalty, there is no real state policy. In one important way, then, the death penalty in America today is as local an institution as it was in the 1700s.

Changes in the Practice of the Death Penalty in the Modern Period

Figure 3.12 graphs both the annual number of executions and the number of new death sentences imposed during the Modern Period of capital punishment. These two pieces of data track each other very nicely. We see a gradual but consistent rise in both the number of death sentences imposed and carried out by execution from the later 1970s through the early to middle 1980s, when both began to level off. From 1985 to the late 1990s approximately 290 new death sentences were imposed throughout the United States each year, and approximately 25 annual executions. Beginning in 1998, however, the number of death sentences began to decline rather consistently, and the number of executions began to decline about a year later. The drop in the number of annual death sentences was particularly dramatic, from 317 in 1996 to 128 in 2005.

What could possibly account for this dramatic reduction in both the number of death sentences imposed and the number of executions carried out? We already know that historically, despite a general acceptance of the death penalty by Americans, there have been times when its use came into relative disrepute. We have seen how gruesomely performed executions have in the past stirred public sentiment against the death penalty generally as well as against a particular method. So throughout our history of capital punishment there have been times when the nation has seemed to pause and reconsider its use. This national pause has led to the abolition of the death penalty in some states

Figure 3.12 Number of Death Sentences and Executions in the United States During the Modern Period

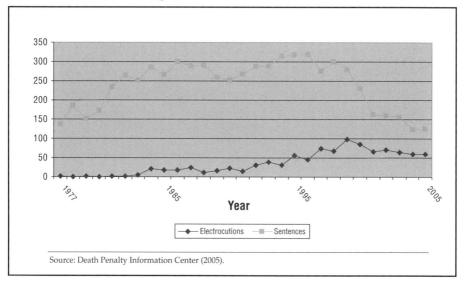

Source: Death Penalty Information Center (2005).

(sometimes just abolition over the short term, in other states over the long term), and at other times it has led to the curtailment of its use.

At the end of the twentieth century and the beginning of the twenty-first, there did seem to be a disturbing problem with the administration of the death penalty in America. Around this time the national media carried stories about a number of condemned inmates who had later been found to be innocent and subsequently released from death row. Because of the stories that began to appear about the "exonerated" and the fear of executing an innocent person, it is possible that public confidence in the death penalty may have weakened (we explore this topic further in Chapter 10). Figure 3.13 shows that from 1973 to 1992 the average number of former death row inmates who were later exonerated averaged 2.75 per year. This number more than doubled over the next 13 years, raising concerns that the risk of executing an innocent person might be higher than previously thought. Moreover, these exonerations received wide coverage in the popular media. In addition to newspaper and television coverage, a play was written and performed throughout the country called *The Exonerated* (from which a movie was made), which told the story of those who wasted years on state death rows before finally being released because they were factually innocent. In addition, conferences and symposia were held throughout the country to discuss the problem of exonerations from death row and were frequently attended by some of those who were released who discussed their story in vivid detail.

The problem of exonerated death row inmates was particularly problematic in some states. For example, from 1977, when its new death penalty law took effect, until 2000, the state of Illinois had sentenced over 200 people to death and had executed 12. By January 2000, however, Illinois had also exonerated and released 13 men from its death row. One of these, Anthony Porter, came within 48 hours of his execution, and his exoneration came about not be-

Figure 3.13 Number of Persons Exonerated and Released From Death Row

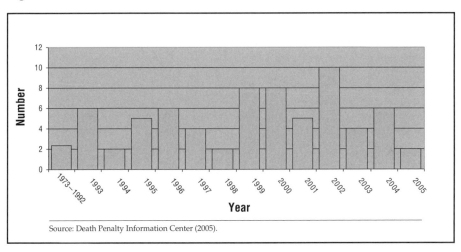

Source: Death Penalty Information Center (2005).

cause of the actions of anyone in the Illinois legal system but because of the investigation undertaken by a group of Northwestern University journalism students and their professor. The problem with the administration of the death penalty in Illinois was horrific, with well-documented evidence of prosecutorial and police negligence and outright misconduct. The problems in Illinois were so startling that its Republican Governor, George Ryan, a long supporter of the death penalty, declared on January 31, 2000 a moratorium on all executions in the state until he could investigate the problems and devise possible reforms. Dissatisfied with the quality of capital justice given to those on Illinois' death row, Governor Ryan took the extraordinary step on January 10, 2003, of issuing pardons for four men on death row because he was convinced of their innocence. On the next day he commuted to life the death sentences of the remaining 167 persons on the state's death row. Although Illinois' case was the most dramatic, other states began investigations of how they administered the death penalty.

It is certainly conceivable that all of the publicity about the possibility of executing an innocent person, along with large numbers of condemned inmates being exonerated and released from death row, shook public confidence in the death penalty (even temporarily). This situation is reflected in public opinion polls. In 1994, approximately 80 percent of the American public stated that they were in favor of the death penalty for those who committed murder. In 2003 this figure had declined to 66 percent (Death Penalty Information Center 2003). More to the point, in a Gallup Poll taken in 2003, 73 percent of those questioned said that they thought that an innocent person had been executed within the past five years (Gallup Organization 2005). As we will see in the final chapter of this book, public skepticism about the death penalty, as well as a belief that an innocent person has been executed, may have "maxed out," and support for capital punishment may be rebounding.

Another reason for the decline in death sentences and executions is the complex, lengthy, and uncertain appeals process. One study found that approximately two-thirds of all death sentences imposed in the United States are

Box 3.4
Governor Ryan Declares a Moratorium: From Death Penalty Supporter to Opponent

When George H. Ryan was elected to the Illinois State Legislature in 1970, he was a conservative law-and-order candidate. In 1977 a bill came before the legislature that would reinstate the death penalty in Illinois, whose previous statute was struck down by the *Furman* decision. Ryan provided both vocal support and a vote for the bill that passed. In February 1998, just one month after being inaugurated as the new governor, Ryan was confronted with the facts of the Anthony Porter case, a mentally retarded Chicago man who came within two days of being executed before being granted a stay. A Northwestern University journalism professor, David Protess, and his students had conducted their own investigation and obtained a confession from the real killer. Two more inmates on death row were then exonerated, bringing the total number of exonerations since the new death penalty law had taken effect in 1977 to 13. On January 21, 2000 Governor Ryan had had enough. He declared a moratorium on all executions in the state until a death penalty commission he appointed could conduct a review of the administration of the death penalty in the state and make recommendations for reform. In April 2002 the death penalty commission delivered its report to Governor Ryan. This report included over 80 recommendations for reforming the Illinois capital punishment system. In May 2002 Governor Ryan introduced legislation to improve the administration of the death penalty in the state based on the committee's recommendations. On January 10, 2003 Governor Ryan pardoned four death row inmates whom he believed were tortured by police into making confessions to crimes they did not commit. The next day, he commuted the death sentences of all 167 Illinois death row inmates. ✦

reversed on appeal, many resulting in new guilty phase trials or new penalty trials (Gelman et al. 2004). These new death sentences then proceed down the long path of state and federal death penalty appeals. This complexity of the capital appeals process has "clogged" death rows. Over the period 1977–1983, the average time from a death sentence to an execution was four years. By the end of 2003, the time on death row before execution was on average over 10 years. The machinery of death penalty justice moves very slowly, and this slowness and uncertainly may certainly be a factor in the reduced number of death sentences and executions.

Whatever the reasons behind the reduced number of death sentences and executions, one thing we should understand from this chapter is that the death penalty has a long and healthy history in the United States, and while there may be periods when it falls out of grace, and while some states may take steps toward abolishing it, it seems to be able to rebound and continue to be a part of both state and federal criminal justice systems.

The Federal and Military Death Penalty

In addition to states, both the federal government and U.S. military currently have a death penalty and have used capital punishment for federal and military crimes for a long time. The first recorded execution of a federal prisoner occurred on June 25, 1790, when Thomas Bird was hung for murder. Since then, 340 persons have been executed under federal authority. The characteristics of those executed mirror the characteristics of those put to death by the states: The overwhelming majority have been male (99 percent), and a majority have been racial minorities (61 percent). From 1927–2003, 37 federal executions took place. Offenses included murder, sabotage, espionage, rape, and kidnapping. Federal methods of imposing the death penalty also reflect developments in the states. In the past, federal authorities have used hanging, the gas chamber, and electrocution to perform executions. There were no federal executions from 1963 to 2001, when Timothy McVeigh was executed for his role in the Oklahoma City bombings. Three federal executions occurred from 2001 until the end of 2005, all by lethal injection. Under the 1994 Federal Death Penalty Act, the method of execution authorized is the one existing in the state where the federal sentence is handed down. If that state does not have a death penalty, the presiding judge may move the execution to a state that does. The U.S. Federal Penitentiary at Terre Haute, Indiana now holds the federal death row and an execution chamber where lethal injections are performed.

Executions under federal authority occurred in both the Early and Premodern periods of capital punishment. Federal statutes authorizing the death penalty were struck down like state statutes with the Supreme Court's *Furman* decision. Before the Modern Period the last federal execution was Victor Feguer, who was hung for kidnapping on March 15, 1963. In the Modern Period, the federal government enacted legislation authorizing the death penalty with the 1988 Anti-Drug Abuse Act (also known as the Drug Kingpin Act). This act permitted the death penalty for murder that was part of an ongoing criminal enterprise and drug trafficking crimes. In 1994 the list of possibly capital federal crimes was greatly expanded with the passage of the Federal Death Penalty Act (FDPA). The FDPA authorized the death penalty for some 60 crimes, including first degree murder; genocide; murder for hire; murder in the aid of racketeering; murder by a federal prisoner; drive-by shooting; foreign murder of U.S. nationals; murder by escaped prisoners; killing of persons assisting a federal investigation; retaliatory killing of witnesses, victims, and informants; kidnapping; hostage taking; destruction of aircraft/motor vehicles or facilities; transportation of explosives; destruction of property by fire or explosives; mailing injurious articles; wrecking trains or railroad property; bank robbery; car jacking; violence against maritime navigation and fixed platforms; and violence at international airports (in each of the nonmurder offenses, a condition of the death penalty is that a death results from the crime of the offender). The federal death penalty was expanded yet again in 1996 with the passage of the Antiterrorism and Effective Death Penalty Act. This act allows for the death penalty for those convicted of a death that is the consequence of an act of terrorism, use of a weapon of mass destruction, an act of terrorism that occurs across national boundaries, and the use of chemical weapons. As of June 2006, there were 44 prisoners on federal death row.

In addition to the federal government, the U.S. military has its own death penalty. As with civilian executions, the number of military executions in the past is difficult to estimate since good records were not kept until recently. There are historical accounts of military executions for mutiny and desertion during the American Revolution (Hughes 1927). Executions for mutiny also occurred during the Creek War and the War of 1812 (Brands 2005). There are estimates that nearly 300 Union soldiers were executed for various military offenses during the Civil War (Alotta 1989; Davis 1988); information about any Confederate executions is nonexistent. In December 2003, a document was found behind a filing cabinet in the Pentagon that listed all military executions that occurred from 1942 to 1961 (Death Penalty Information Center 2005). It showed that 169 members of the U.S. military had been executed, the last being U.S. Army Private John Bennett on April 13, 1961 (for the offense of rape and attempted murder). In the Modern Period, the military death penalty was reestablished in 1984 by an authorized order of President Ronald Reagan. The rules for capital courts-martial include a list of 11 aggravating factors that make an offense eligible for the death penalty. The Uniform Code of Military Justice calls for capital punishment for 15 specific offenses, many of which, such as desertion or disobeying the order of a superior officer, must occur during wartime. As of October 2005, there were nine prisoners on military death row; all are males and six are African American.

Box 3.5
The Execution of Private Eddie Slovik

On January 31, 1945, near the French village of Sainte-Marie-aux-Mines, Army Private Eddie Slovik was executed by firing squad for desertion. He was the first person executed for desertion by the U.S. military since the Civil War. Supreme Allied Commander and future U.S. President General Dwight Eisenhower personally ordered the execution to deter military desertions during the closing days of the war. During World War II, more than 21,000 military personnel were convicted of desertion, 49 of whom (.02 percent) were sentenced to death, and only Private Slovik was actually executed. He was buried in France in a cemetery with 94 other American soldiers executed for crimes such as murder and rape. Their gravestones bore no name, only a number. Slovik's body remained in France until 1987, when it was returned to the United States for burial next to his wife, Antoinette. In spite of repeated requests, Private Slovik was never pardoned for his crime (see Huie 1954). ✦

Chapter Summary

The Modern Period of capital punishment began in 1976 when the U.S. Supreme Court approved procedurally reformed death penalty statutes in the cases of *Gregg, Proffitt*, and *Jurek*. After a 10-year moratorium, executions were resumed the next year, with the firing squad execution of Gary Gilmore in Utah. Gilmore urged his attorneys to stop appealing his case and essentially "volunteered" to die. From Gilmore's death in 1977 until the end of 2005 there have been just over 1,000 executions in the United States. The annual number of executions has been erratic over the years, with nearly 100 executions in 1999 and as few as a handful in some other years. The death penalty did return in 1977 but not with the same energy as in previous periods. While a majority of states have the death penalty on their books as law, the frequency with which capital punishment is actually used differs dramatically from state to state and even from place to place within states. As in the past, far and away the most executions during this time period have occurred in Southern states (and a majority in only a few Southern states). Texas has executed the most offenders of any state, but two others (Oklahoma and Delaware) have higher rates of execution than Texas. The concentration of the death penalty in Southern states has become more pronounced from the Premodern to the Modern period.

We also found substantial variation within a death penalty state in the frequency with which the death penalty is sought by local prosecutors and imposed. Former U.S. Speaker of the House of Representatives Thomas P. "Tip" O'Neill, once said that "all politics is local"; it appears that all capital punishment is local too. While the imposition of the death penalty is under state authority, local authorities essentially determine when that power will be used, and there is little consensus within a state about that important issue. Also consistent with the past, the death penalty falls heavily on nonwhite offenders, those who kill white victims, and males. Out of more than 1,000 executions during the Modern Period, only 11 have been women (about 1 percent).

The range of potentially capital crimes was further narrowed during the Modern Period. With few exceptions, a sentence of death may be imposed only if a crime involved a murder. In terms of the method of execution, if the Premodern Period was the period of the electric chair, the Modern Period will likely be known as the period of lethal injection. Recall that the use of a lethal "cocktail" of drugs was considered by the New York Gerry Commission in the 1890s in favor of death by electrocution. In the early years of the Modern Period most executions were carried out by electricity, but now the vast majority of executions involve lethal injection. From 1977 to 2005, approximately 80 percent of all executions were done by lethal injection. As of 2006 Nebraska is the only state that has the electric chair as its only method of execution. The use of lethal injection to replace the electric chair and gas chamber was based on the fact that it was thought to be a more humane form of death. In recent years, however, concerns have been raised by the medical establishment that current procedures and chemicals used in lethal injections may result in a painful death for prisoners. If the past is any guide, there will be attempts to find a newer, even more humane way to impose the death penalty than the current form of lethal injection.

Although the death penalty returned in 1977 after a 10-year moratorium, starting in about 1998 there has been a consistent and rather dramatic decline in the number of both death sentences handed down and executions performed. This decline in death sentences and executions may have been influenced by growing problems with the administration of the death penalty (issues of possibly innocent people, concerns raised in different states about racial issues) and public dissatisfaction with some aspects of the death penalty (public approval for capital punishment showed signs of decline). Whether this phenomenon is just temporary or is the beginning of a more pronounced decline in the "popularity" of the death penalty as was seen in the mid to late 1960s only time will tell. Finally, in addition to a majority of U.S. states, both the federal government and the U.S. military have had the death penalty as an authorized punishment for some offenses and continue to do so.

Discussion Questions

1. Why do you think there have been repeated attempts to find a method of capital punishment that promises a "quick and painless" death?

2. Gary Gilmore gave up on all his legal appeals and essentially "volunteered" for the death penalty. Do you think condemned offenders should have the right to drop their appeals and let the state execute them? Or should their appeals be followed even if they want to die?

3. What are the arguments for and against having the death penalty as a possible punishment for a crime that does not include the murder of the victim?

4. Do you think that it is fair that substantial variation occurs within a state in terms of the likelihood that a prosecutor seeks the death sentence? Should one factor that determines which convicted capital offender lives and which dies be where in the state the crime was committed?

5. Why do you think that the death penalty has been and continues to be a largely "Southern" phenomenon?

6. What do you think accounts for the fluctuation in the number of both death sentences and executions since 1977?

7. What kind of "proof" or evidence would it take to convince you that the administration of capital punishment in your state was discriminatory? If it was found to discriminate against those who killed white victims, what remedies would you suggest?

8. Why do you think the death penalty would be more likely to be imposed on those who killed a white victim rather than a nonwhite victim?

9. Do you think that evidence of being rehabilitated and reformed while in prison should be a basis for commuting a death sentence to life in prison? Why or why not?

10. Do you think the death penalty will ever be abolished in the United States? If you think yes, what do you think will contribute to its abolition? If you think no, why do you think capital punishment will not be abolished?

11. If you were the governor of a state that had the death penalty with as many problems as Illinois seemed to have, would you have commuted all death sentences as Governor Ryan did? What would you have done? What effect do you think his actions had on other death penalty states?

Student Resources

Many excellent books have been written about the administration of capital punishment in the Modern Period. One of America's greatest writers, Norman Mailer, wrote *The Executioner's Song* about the crimes and execution of Gary Gilmore. A Catholic nun, Sister Helen Prejean, has written eloquently about the horrific murder, prison time, and death of Louisiana killer Patrick Sonnier in the book *Dead Man Walking*. Both books were also made into movies. Other films that portray the death penalty during this time period include *Last Dance, Monster, The Life of David Gale,* and *Monster's Ball.*

The position of the American Medical Association on capital punishment can be found in its ethics statement available at the AMA website, <www.ama-assn.org>. Up-to-date information about the death penalty, numbers, law, practices, and pending constitutional issues can be found at the website of the Death Penalty Information Center, <www. deathpenaltyinfo.org>. The NAACP Legal Defense and Education Fund maintains a website that contains a quarterly report (Death Row U.S.A.) providing an updated list of all those put to death by state since 1977. This website can be found at <www.naacpldf.org>. The Office of the Prosecutor of Clark County, Indiana provides a website rich with links to many other sites that contain both pro and against capital punishment information. It can be found at: <www.clarkprosecutor.org/html/links/dplinks.htm>.

Endnote

1. On October 5, 2001, the Georgia Supreme Court declared that death by electrocution was cruel and unusual punishment under the state's constitution. On April 25, 2002, Governor Donald Siegelman signed legislation passed by the Alabama legislature stating that lethal injection would be the means of execution unless an inmate explicitly expressed a desire to be electrocuted. It is not certain how long Nebraska will be able to retain the electric chair. In October 2003 U.S. District Court Judge Joseph Bataillon declared that Nebraska's use of electrocution was unconstitutional. ✦

Part II
Legal History, Constitutional Requirements, and Common Justifications for Capital Punishment in the United States

W e saw in Chapter 1 that the death penalty has been around for a long time in the United States. In fact, there are two things we can say with some degree of certainty about capital punishment in America: (1) it has been a continuous part of our history, and (2) it has been a controversial practice. In this part of the book we explore three issues about capital punishment.

In Chapter 4 we discuss the legal history of the death penalty in the United States. While the death penalty has been implemented since colonial times, there have always been struggles over whether executing a fellow citizen at all constitutes "cruel and unusual" punishment and whether particular methods of carrying out the death penalty might be so barbaric and inhumane that they constitute "cruel and unusual" punishment. And while the death penalty itself might be constitutional and a particularly method of imposing it might not be offensive and cruel, it is still possible that the death penalty could be unfair in a procedural sense. In Chapter 4 we take up the beginning of this legal history. We start with early U.S. Supreme Court cases that examined whether particular methods of imposing the death penalty constituted cruel and unusual punishment under the Eighth Amendment of the Constitution. In the course of answering a question about a specific method of imposing death, the Court had to struggle with the issue of what exactly constitutes a cruel and unusual punishment. Since the Supreme Court is the ultimate body that decides what criminal justice practices are constitutional for both the states and the federal government, we will limit our attention to challenges that came before this Court and how it decided those challenges. Furthermore, since the body of cases regarding capital punishment issues that the Court has addressed is vast and could easily fill more than one book, our attention has to be selective.

We will then examine a couple of Supreme Court cases that have nothing directly to do with the death penalty but that are important in understanding what principles the Court will subsequently use in trying to determine what a cruel and unusual punishment is under the Eighth Amendment. In these cases the Court fashioned some doctrine or theory of what the Eighth Amendment requires that it continues to apply in death penalty cases. Finally in Chapter 4, we examine two important legal challenges to capital punishment that were decided in the 1970s. These two cases were mostly about procedural issues—what capital trials in state courts must have in order to be procedurally fair—but they had far-ranging implications for the future of the death penalty in America. One of these Court decisions had the practical effect of emptying death rows across the United States, requiring states to virtually rewrite their death penalty laws.

In Chapter 5, we pick up our study of the legal history of capital punishment. In this chapter we review the Supreme Court's examination in the summer of 1976 of attempts by state legislatures to revise their death penalty laws to make them comply with the Court's requirements. In its decisions in five cases announced that summer, the Court found some of these revisions to be acceptable and others not. The effect of these 1976 decisions was to give constitutional approval for properly administered state death penalties and to begin what we call the Modern Period of capital punishment. It also presaged the end of a nearly 10-year moratorium on executions in the United States.

The 1976 decisions of the Supreme Court that approved of some types of state death penalty statutes did not end the legal wrangling over capital punishment. In fact, what these decisions essentially did was to begin the Court's attempt to provide some monitoring and regulation of state death penalties. From 1976 to the present the Supreme Court has been constantly dealing with death penalty issues coming from state courts. These issues concern such matters as who can be put to death, what crimes death can be imposed for, how good the defense lawyers must be in capital cases, what kinds of appeals and reviews are required after trial, what kinds of evidence may or may not be heard at the guilt and penalty phase of a capital trial, and numerous other constitutional questions. We review and discuss many of the most important of these issues in trying to understand the requirements of a constitutional death penalty statute. Death penalty law is, however, one of the most complex and arcane bodies of law, so our coverage of these legal issues cannot be exhaustive (see Streib 2005).

In the last chapter of Part II, Chapter 6, we review several justifications or rationales for the death penalty. Many reasons have been offered as to why the death penalty is an appropriate form of punishment: it is morally justified, it acts as an effective deterrent, it is less of a burden on taxpayers than life imprisonment, and so on. We review what each position argues about the death penalty and what someone with a different point of view might assert. These justifications for and against capital punishment are not only held by members of the public but also inform debate among the Supreme Court's justices about the fairness and constitutionality of the death penalty. ✦

Chapter 4

A Brief Legal History of Capital Punishment in the United States

From reading Chapter 1, you know that the practice of capital punishment existed in colonial and postrevolutionary America. You also know that the constitutionality of the death penalty itself was seldom questioned at that time because the Founding Fathers explicitly assumed it in several amendments to the Constitution.[1] While there may have been some disagreement about the morality of capital punishment and its effectiveness in deterring crime,[2] there was little doubt among either a majority of the public at large or those who wrote the Constitution about the death penalty being a permissible sanction. When the first challenge came about the death penalty, then, it is not too surprising that the issue before the Supreme Court was not whether capital punishment itself was constitutional but whether a particular method of carrying it out was.

Early Constitutional Challenges to the Method of Imposing Death

In *Wilkerson v. Utah* (99 U.S. 130, 1878) the Court was confronted with the issue of whether death by firing squad was an unconstitutional punishment. In 1852 the territory of Utah (it did not become a state until 1896) passed a legislative act providing that a person convicted of a capital crime should be put to death by being shot, hanged, or beheaded. The defendant in this case was convicted of first degree murder and sentenced under that act to be publicly shot to death. In determining that death by shooting was not unconstitutional, the U.S. Supreme Court argued that in the Territory of Utah firing squads were not an uncommon practice. It was, for instance a permissible punishment for soldiers convicted of desertion in the Utah Territory. Although the defendant in the *Wilkerson* case was a civilian, the Court nevertheless held that death by firing squad was not an unusual punishment within the meaning of the Eighth Amendment's prohibition against cruel and unusual punishments. While concluding that the firing squad was not a constitutionally prohibited method of capital punishment, the Court acknowledged the difficulty of defining what would constitute a "cruel and unusual" punishment, but it offered some suggestions as well:

> Difficulty would attend the effort to define with exactness the extent of the constitutional provision which provides that cruel and unusual punishments shall not be inflicted; but it is safe to affirm that punishments of tor-

ture . . . and all others in the same line of unnecessary cruelty, are forbidden by that amendment to the Constitution. (pp. 135–136)

The "punishments of torture" alluded to by the Court were those acts thought to be cruel and unusual by the original framers of the Eighth Amendment: disembowelment, drawing, quartering, burning alive. What the *Wilkerson* Court suggested was that a punishment could be regarded as cruel and unusual under the Eighth Amendment when it involved torture or "unnecessary cruelty," and death by firing squad was neither.

The Supreme Court had another occasion to comment on the meaning of the Eighth Amendment's prohibition against cruel and unusual punishment just 12 years later in *In re Kemmler* (136 U.S. 436, 1890). We already know from Chapter 2 that William Kemmler was the first person in the country to face death by electrocution (see Denno 1994, 1997, 2003; Moran 2002; Essig 2003). In 1888 the New York State Legislature passed a bill that abolished the use of hanging as its method of imposing the death penalty in favor of the newly created electric chair. New York's legislature reasoned that death by electrocution was a more humane way to terminate human life in that it was thought to be both quick and painless. Kemmler was the first person to be sentenced to death under the new method, and he objected to its use on the grounds that to be killed by electricity was cruel and unusual punishment under the Eighth Amendment.

After losing appeals in New York State, Kemmler appealed to the U.S. Supreme Court. The Court in *Kemmler* did not decide whether electrocution constituted cruel and unusual punishment, essentially refusing to make that decision by concluding that the Eighth Amendment did not apply to the states (at that time). It did, however, have something to say about what the Eighth Amendment's cruel and unusual punishment clause may mean and how that related to New York's attempt to execute William Kemmler. In seeming to accept the principle of the death penalty itself, the Court argued, "The punishment of death is not cruel within the meaning of that word as used in the Constitution" (p. 447). It also adopted a variation of the *Wilkerson* Court's position that while capital punishment itself is constitutionally permissible, some methods of imposing a death sentence may violate the Eighth Amendment. The *Kemmler* Court implied that when a method of imposing death is "manifestly cruel and unusual" it likely is unconstitutional and that "punishments are cruel when they involve torture or a lingering death . . . it implies something inhuman and barbarous, something more than the mere extinguishment of life" (p. 447). It also provided some specific examples as to the matter of just what a "manifestly cruel and unusual" punishment might be, noting that ". . . if the punishment prescribed for an offense against the laws of the state were manifestly cruel and unusual, as burning at the stake, crucifixion, breaking on the wheel, or the like, it would be the duty of the courts to adjudge such penalties to be within the constitutional prohibition" (p. 446).

Ultimately, the Court argued that since the intent of the New York legislature was to devise a more humane method than hanging for executing its capital defendants, the Supreme Court had to defer to its judgment. Since several

New York courts (including the New York Court of Appeals) found that the legislature had acted with sound judgment and a humanitarian purpose in replacing death by hanging with electrocution (which proponents argued promised a quick and painless death), absent compelling evidence to the contrary, the Supreme Court would not disagree.

Both *Wilkerson* and *Kemmler* seem to suggest that capital punishment itself was acceptable, as was any method of imposing death that does not involve the deliberate infliction of severe pain. *Kemmler* adds the notion that a punishment provided by a legislature may be unusual in that it has not been previously used but that this feature does not render it unconstitutional as long as the intent of the innovation is humane. His legal appeals exhausted, William Kemmler was executed by New York State's new electric chair on August 6, 1890.[3]

The next occasion for the Court to review a claim that a particular method of imposing the death penalty was cruel and unusual came in the rather bizarre case of *Louisiana ex rel. Francis v. Reweber* (329 U.S. 459, 464, 1947). In this case 15-year-old Willie Francis was sentenced to death by electrocution (see Miller and Bowman 1988). At the time, Louisiana operated a mobile electric chair with the electric generator mounted on the back of a pickup truck. During the course of administering a dose of electricity, the generator failed. Francis felt enough of the electrical jolt to cause his lips to swell and his body to tense and stretch. He was conscious enough, according to one witness, to yell, "Take it off" (p. 480).[4]

The malfunction of the electric chair clearly caused pain but did not kill Francis, who was eventually removed from the chair and returned to his cell to await a second chance at electrocution after the generator was repaired. Francis objected to the attempt of the State of Louisiana to put him to death a second time (six days after the first attempt), claiming that a second visit to the electric chair after a failed first attempt constituted cruel and unusual punishment under the Eighth Amendment and a violation of the Fifth Amendment's protection against double jeopardy. The claim made was not that capital punishment was always cruel and unusual, just that more than one attempt by the state (what Justice Burton in his dissent eloquently characterized as "death by installments," p. 474) to electrocute someone was cruel and unusual because it was comparable to torture and was a punishment degrading to human beings.

A majority of the Court rejected Francis' claim that his second execution was unconstitutional, focusing as it did in the *Kemmler* case on the state's *intent* and not what it actually did. The majority opinion argued that Louisiana did not intend for the electric chair to malfunction and that on the contrary the expectation of the legislature was that death by electrocution would be quick and painless. What happened to Willie Francis was characterized as an "unforeseeable accident" and an "innocent misadventure," rather than the deliberate infliction of pain by the State of Louisiana on one of its citizens. Such an accidental event is not, the majority concluded, a violation of the Eighth Amendment:

The cruelty against which the Constitution protects a convicted man is cruelty inherent in the method of punishment, not the necessary suffering involved in any method employed to extinguish life humanely. . . . There is no purpose to inflict unnecessary pain nor any unnecessary pain in the proposed execution. (p. 464)

In allowing Louisiana a second opportunity to execute Francis, the Court also seemed to agree with the understanding of what constitutes a "cruel and unusual" punishment offered by the *Wilkerson* and *Kemmler* Courts when it observed that "[t]he traditional humanity of modern Anglo-American law forbids the infliction of unnecessary pain in the execution of the death sentence" (p. 462). This continues the Supreme Court's assumption that the death penalty is constitutional on its face, but when imposed in a manner that involves torture or the unnecessary infliction of pain it would become a "cruel and unusual" punishment. As for Willie Francis, about one year after the malfunctioning of its portable electric chair the State of Louisiana successfully executed him.

Constitutional Theories About What the Eighth Amendment Prohibits

There are two things we know about the constitutional status of the death penalty after the *Francis* case: (1) the death penalty is a constitutional punishment, (2) it could become unconstitutional, however, if it was imposed in such a manner that it involves torture or unnecessary cruelty (*Wilkerson v. Utah*), is inhuman and barbarous (*In re Kemmler*), or involves the infliction of intentional or unnecessary pain (*Francis v. Resweber*). States were free to execute, therefore, as long as the method they used did not deliberately involve torture or the infliction of unnecessarily severe pain. Methods such as shooting, hanging, and electrocution did not cross the unnecessary/barbarous pain line, while methods such as disemboweling, crucifixion, burning at the stake, breaking at the wheel, or other forms of execution that involved almost gratuitous suffering did. Death by execution was allowed, but it had to be relatively quick and painless.

The Eighth Amendment assumption that the Supreme Court made in these cases was that what constituted a "cruel and unusual" capital punishment was that which would be seen to be cruel and unusual by the original framers of the Amendment (Berger 1982). At the time the Eighth Amendment was adopted, it was clear that capital punishment was fully accepted by the framers. We know this because capital punishment was implicitly recognized by other amendments such as the Fifth, which provides that "no person shall be held to answer for a *capital* or otherwise infamous crime, unless on a resentment or indictment by a Grand Jury . . . nor shall any person be subject for the same offense to be twice put in jeopardy of *life* or limb . . . nor be deprived of *life*, liberty, or property, without due process of law" (emphasis added). Under this "framer's intent" theory, the Eighth Amendment could not be used to define the death penalty as cruel and unusual punishment, because those who wrote that and other amendments to the Constitution were fully aware of the death penalty and accepted it. In 1950, at least, what the Eighth Amendment prohibited, therefore, were particular ways or methods of imposing the death penalty.

This understanding of the meaning of the cruel and unusual punishment clause of the Eighth Amendment is referred to as a "fixed" meaning because its understanding is fixed at the time of the framers' intention. In other words, under this fixed interpretation, what constitutes a cruel and unusual punishment is any punishment that the framers of the Eighth Amendment might have thought cruel and unusual at the time they wrote the Amendment. The actual meaning of the term "cruel and unusual" is, therefore, fixed in time. As long as this fixed interpretation of the Eighth Amendment stood, legal challenges against particular methods of capital punishment could be raised, but there could be no legally valid argument that the death penalty itself was unconstitutional because it was "cruel and unusual." Over time a new interpretation of the Eighth Amendment's cruel and unusual punishment clause would emerge, one that anchored the meaning of that key phrase not in the original intent of the framers but in something that was more historically fluctuating. In discussing how this new Eighth Amendment theory emerged, we have to briefly digress and discuss two important nondeath penalty cases.

A Definition of 'Cruel and Unusual'

One of these cases, decided by the Supreme Court in 1910, was *Weems v. United States* (217 U.S. 349). In this case the defendant, a U.S. government official in the territory of the Philippines, was convicted of falsifying financial records of the U.S. Coast Guard, resulting in the government being defrauded out of 612 pesos. For this crime he was sentenced to 15 years at hard labor, forced to carry a chain at the ankle hanging from the wrist, surveillance by the government for life, and a loss of his voting rights. Weems complained that such a punishment was grossly disproportionate to the crime he committed and was, therefore, cruel and unusual. In deciding that the defendant's punishment was excessive in comparison to the crime, the Court broke new ground in its understanding of the Eighth Amendment's cruel and unusual punishment clause.

The *Weems* Court argued that what constitutes a cruel and unusual punishment cannot be restricted to only those punishments that the framers of the Eighth Amendment thought at the time to be cruel and unusual (burning at the stake, ear cropping, etc.). The Court reasoned that these specific punishments were no longer in use and not likely ever to be used again. If the definition of cruel and unusual punishment were to be restricted to the framers' intent, therefore, the Eighth Amendment would not offer citizens much protection against excessive governmental power. The Court offered the counterargument that what the framers meant to do was not to forbid particular punishments that it thought intolerable in their day but to offer a much broader protection for cruel and unusual punishments it could not envision at the time but that a citizen might one day need to be protected from:

> Legislation, both statutory and constitutional, is enacted, it is true, from an experience of evils, but its general language should not, therefore, be neces-

sarily confined to the form that evil had heretofore taken. Time works changes, brings into existence new conditions and purposes. Therefore a principle to be vital must be capable of wider application than the mischief which gave it birth. . . . In the application of a constitution, therefore, our contemplation cannot be only of what has been but of what may be. Under any other rule a constitution would indeed be as easy of application as it would be deficient in efficacy and power. Its general principles would have little value and be converted by precedent into impotent and lifeless formulas. Rights declared in words might be lost in reality. (*Weems v. U.S.*, 217 U.S. 349, 1910, at p. 373)

In this view, while the Eighth Amendment grew out of a fear of a particular category of punishment ("an experience of evils") known to and experienced by the framers, they intended that the amendment protect future generations of Americans from unimagined cruel and unusual punishments. Using this flexible definition of what constitutes a cruel and unusual punishment, the Court declared that the punishment given Weems was unconstitutional because it was excessive in comparison to the crime he committed.

The second case occurred more than 40 years later. In *Trop v. Dulles* (356 U.S. 86, 1958), the defendant, a solider, was convicted of desertion during World War II. As part of his punishment for wartime desertion, Trop was stripped of his United States citizenship. After the war when he applied for a passport, Trop was informed that no passport could be issued to him since he was not a citizen of the United States and in fact belonged to no country. He complained to the Supreme Court that his punishment was cruel and unusual, in violation of the Eighth Amendment. In determining whether the taking away of someone's citizenship is a cruel and unusual punishment, the Court could not rely entirely on the *Weems* Court's excessiveness argument. Since Trop could have by law been sentenced to death for desertion of his post during a time of war, the punishment he received could not be considered excessive. The Court did, however, adopt the position in *Weems* that the meaning of "cruel and unusual" in the Eighth Amendment is not fixed in time but evolves with changing social and cultural conditions. The *Trop* Court furthered the theory that what constitutes a cruel and unusual punishment changes over time because society changes over time, and what it may once have found as an acceptable punishment earlier in its history it may later come to see as cruel because society has morally progressed. The Court argued that "[t]he [Eighth] Amendment must draw its meaning from the evolving standards of decency that mark the progress of a maturing society" (p. 101). In other words, as a society evolves and becomes more enlightened, it rejects as morally unacceptable punishments it once tolerated.

The Court further offered the argument that what the Eighth Amendment protects against is the general violation of the human spirit or human dignity by the government: "[T]he basic concept underlying the Eighth Amendment is nothing less than the dignity of man" (p. 100). The *Trop* Court, then, advanced a theory of the Eighth Amendment that it protects American citizens against having their dignity as human beings violated and that what constitutes an indignity changes over time as society evolves and progresses. Using this understanding, it held that the punishment imposed on the defendant Trop, stripping him of his citizenship and making him "a man without a country," did indeed constitute cruel and unusual punishment.

The importance of the *Weems* and *Trop* cases is that they provided the context for a new understanding of the cruel and unusual punishment clause. After these cases an Eighth Amendment theory could be developed to attack the death penalty as a cruel and unusual punishment even though it was explicitly approved of by the original authors of the Constitution. The general content of this theory would be that although the death penalty was a permissible punishment in the late eighteenh century when the Constitution was written, society has evolved and progressed over the years such that a more morally enlightened citizenry no longer finds it tolerable. Eventually such a theory would be crafted and used against capital punishment, but before that occurred, opponents of the death penalty first waged a battle against it on purely procedural rather than substantive grounds. It is to this procedural argument against the death penalty that we must now turn our attention.

The Death Penalty's Decline in Popularity and Challenges to Its Constitutionality—The Prelude to *McGautha v. California*

Traditionally, support for capital punishment for serious crimes (murder, rape, kidnapping) was high in the United States. In the 1930s nearly 60 percent of those asked in national opinion polls whether they supported the death penalty for those convicted of murder replied "yes" (see Figure 4.1). By the early 1950s, this support reached almost 70 percent. For about a decade and a half after that, however, public support for capital punishment began to slide. In 1960 a Gallup Poll indicated that support for the death penalty for murder declined to only 53 percent (Death Penalty Information Center 2005), and in 1966 less than a majority (42 percent) of those polled stated that they supported the death penalty as a punishment for murder. Reflecting this low level of public support, the actual number of executions trickled to only a handful by the mid-1960s before temporarily halting for nearly 10 years in 1967. Beginning in the 1970s, public support for the death penalty began to increase. We will have much to say about public opinion and the death penalty in the final chapter of the book, but what we would like to point out now is that by 1970 support for the death penalty among the public had been in decline for a while, and barely a majority of them said that they approved of the death penalty as a punishment for murder.

In addition to growing public disenchantment with the death penalty, some in the legal community were vocal in expressing their skepticism as well. In 1961, for example, the *University of Southern California Law Review* published an article by legal scholar Gerald Gottlieb (1961) in which he argued that the death penalty is unconstitutional under the Eighth Amendment because it violates contemporary moral standards, an argument only made possible by the Court's decisions in *Weems* and *Trop*. That same year, Professor Walter Oberer (1961) published a paper in the *University of Texas Law Review* that was sharply critical of a common trial court practice in capital cases known as "death quali-

Figure 4.1   Percent of Public Approving of the Death Penalty for Those
Who Commit Murder: 1930s–1970s

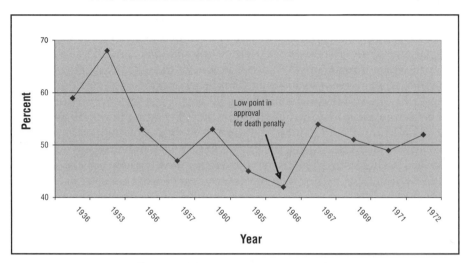

fying" a jury. Under the law of most states, a juror who expressed strong reservations about the death penalty could be removed from serving in a capital case. Professor Oberer argued that the process of death qualifying purged the jury of its more compassionate members and produced a jury that was biased against the defendant in terms of being more likely to convict and more likely to impose a sentence of death.

The community of practicing lawyers, aware of problems with existing death penalty statutes, began to devise procedural reforms. In the early 1960s the American Law Institute drafted something called the Model Penal Code—a theoretical body of principles it thought criminal statutes ought to embody. Part of this Model Penal Code included two reforms of existing death penalty law: (1) requiring two separate hearings in capital cases, an initial hearing on the issue of guilt/innocence and a second hearing on the appropriate penalty upon conviction of a capital crime—known as a bifurcated trial, and (2) a list in the statute of specific factors in aggravation and mitigation that the jury would focus on in determining the appropriate penalty in a given capital case. Factors in aggravation would be those characteristics of a crime or offender that make the offense more egregious (such as killing more than one victim), while factors in mitigation would be those offense or offender characteristics that would tend to make the crime less serious (such as the defendant had no prior criminal history).

By the early 1960s, then, several things were occurring at once: Public support for capital punishment was at an all-time low, as was the actual frequency of executions; legal scholars were arguing both that the death penalty itself may be unconstitutional and that current procedures may be flawed; and legal practitioners were devising workable reforms of existing death penalty statutes. Several events were converging, then, creating a fertile ground for opponents of the death penalty to attack it.

One more event also gave these opponents some optimism that their efforts may not fall on deaf ears. In October 1963 the Supreme Court declined to hear (what is called refused to grant *certiorari*) a case coming from the state of Alabama, *Rudolph v. Alabama* (375 U.S. 889, 1963), in which a defendant convicted of raping a woman was sentenced to death. Usually, when the Supreme Court denies *certiorari* it does not provide any rationale, and the case is likely not to be heard from again. In *Rudolph,* however, three justices who dissented from the denial of *certiorari* wrote and published their views. Justice Goldberg (along with Justices Brennan and Douglas) wrote that the entire Court ought to take the opportunity to answer the question of whether the death penalty is a cruel and unusual punishment under the Eighth Amendment for a rapist who did not take a life during his crime. This was an unusual move not only because dissents from a denial of *certiorari* are rarely written, but also because in their written brief to the Court the defense lawyers never even raised the issue of the constitutionality of the death penalty for the offense of rape where there was not a killing. The Court did not change its mind with respect to Rudolph's case, but the dissent was important in that it gave a small group of activist lawyers working for the NAACP's Legal Defense Fund opposed to the death penalty some hope that the full Court might be interested in a question about the constitutionality of the death penalty under an Eighth Amendment (cruel and unusual punishment) challenge (Meltsner 1973).

The Legal Defense Fund's lawyers did develop a legal argument against the death penalty that became part of an Arkansas capital case that was winding its way through the state and federal court system. William Maxwell was an Arkansas man convicted in 1962 for the rape of a white woman and sentenced to death. In his appeal to the Arkansas Supreme Court, Maxwell's lawyers made the claim that Arkansas juries were discriminatory in the imposition of the death penalty for rape, sentencing black offenders to death (especially when they raped white women) at a substantially higher rate than white offenders. This racial discrimination argument was rejected at the state level by the Arkansas Supreme Court and at the federal level by the U.S. District Court, the U.S. Court of Appeals (for the Eighth Circuit), and the U.S. Supreme Court (which refused to review the case). In a second round of federal appeals, Maxwell's attorneys provided statistical evidence of racial discrimination in the sentencing of Arkansas rape cases (see Wolfgang 1974). This argument too was rejected by both the Federal District Court and Federal Court of Appeals. In 1967, however, Maxwell was granted a stay of execution by the U.S. Supreme Court. After his death sentence was again affirmed by the U.S. Court of Appeals in 1968, the Supreme Court issued a second stay of Maxwell's execution. By this time a number of death penalty cases, raising important constitutional issues, were being pursued by Legal Defense Fund lawyers and others.

While Maxwell's case was being considered by the Supreme Court in its final round of appeals, the Court issued an opinion in another death penalty case, *Witherspoon v. Illinois* (88 S. Ct. 1770, 1968). William Witherspoon was convicted of the murder of a Chicago police officer and sentenced to death in 1960. The jury that convicted Witherspoon and sentenced him to death had been "death qualified," a common practice under death penalty statutes at the time. In death qualification, a juror who indicates opposition to or scruples against the death penalty, however mild, could be removed for cause as a potential juror. In Witherspoon's own case almost half of his potential jurors were eliminated from consideration based on this death qualification process, even though only five of 47 expressed the strong view that their opposition would prevent them from returning a death sentence in any capital case. In its decision, the Court agreed with Witherspoon's claim that the process of death qualification produced a jury that was more likely to impose a death sentence. The Court crafted a new rule that only those jurors who were unalterably opposed to the death penalty (those who would automatically reject a death sentence regardless of the evidence) could be excluded for cause from jury service in a capital case. The *Witherspoon* decision had two important consequences: (1) It led to slightly different procedures in the questioning of potential jurors in capital cases, and (2) it served notice that the Supreme Court was aware of procedural difficulties in how states were conducting death penalty trials and was willing to develop new law that provided extended procedural protections to capital defendants.

We raise the issue of *Witherspoon* both because it is interesting in its own right and because the issue of death-qualified juries appeared in the final appeal of William Maxwell to the Supreme Court. Recall that Maxwell was denied relief by the Eighth Circuit Court of Appeals in 1968. He appealed this denial to the Supreme Court, which granted Maxwell a stay of execution. In their appeal to the Court, Maxwell's Legal Defense Fund lawyers raised two issues: (1) Maxwell's trial was unconstitutional because it combined both the question of his guilt or innocence and whether he should be sentenced to death or some other penalty (what was known as a single-verdict jury), and (2) the jury that sentenced Maxwell to death had no guidance or standards to follow in deciding which punishment he should receive (what was known as the standardless jury).

Rather than decide the case on these two new issues, however, the Court decided the case on more narrow grounds, reversing Maxwell's death sentence on the *Witherspoon* ground that several prospective jurors in his case were impermissibly removed based solely on their general opposition to the death penalty. The Court did, however, serve notice that it would not delay in deciding the other two questions in Maxwell's brief: single-verdict and standardless juries. It announced that it had agreed to grant *certiorari* in two new death penalty cases where these issues were central. These two cases, *Crampton v. Ohio* and *McGautha v. California,* were consolidated as one in *McGautha v. California* (402 U.S. 183, 1971).

The Death Penalty Is Not Procedurally Flawed—The Case of *McGautha v. California*

Under Ohio law at the time, defendant Crampton was tried by a single-verdict jury, meaning that after hearing all of the evidence at trial the jury had to make two decisions: (1) whether the defendant was guilty of a capital crime and, if yes, (2) whether the defendant should be sentenced to death. To be clear, in the single-verdict procedure the defense and the prosecution had one opportunity to present all their information to the jury, and the jury had only one opportunity to review this evidence and make a determination as to both guilt or innocence *and* the appropriate punishment after a single deliberation.

Crampton objected to the single-verdict jury because he stated that it forced him to make a choice between two equally compelling constitutional rights. If he wanted to protect his right to remain silent and not speak to the jury about the issue of his guilt or innocence, he had to surrender his right to speak to the jury about the issue of the appropriate punishment in his case. For example, suppose Crampton wanted to tell the jury that he deserved a penalty less severe than death because basically he had a good character and had committed the murder in part because he had a history of horrific child abuse. If he were to tell the jury this information about himself, however, he would be admitting that he'd committed the murder, and his statement about his basically good character could open the door to the prosecution's cross-examination about such things as his prior criminal history and other issues he might want to keep from a jury determining his fate. This, Crampton argued, is the fundamental constitutional flaw of the single-verdict capital jury, and the solution would be to have a bifurcated capital trial. In a bifurcated trial there are two separate hearings. First there is a hearing in which the issue is only whether the defendant committed the capital crime (the guilt phase), and the only permissible information at this phase is information directly relevant to the question of guilt and innocence. The second hearing (assuming that the defendant is first convicted of a capital crime) is the penalty phase, in which the question is whether the defendant should be sentenced to death or some other punishment. At this hearing the defendant and prosecution may introduce evidence relevant to the appropriate penalty that would not have been permissible or appropriate at the guilt phase. At the time, the state of Ohio had single-verdict capital trials while other states such as California had bifurcated capital trials.

Under the capital statutes of all states, however, the jury was given relatively little guidance in making the determination as to the appropriate penalty in a capital case. In fact, the jury by law had a great deal of discretion in making the sentencing decision as to which convicted capital defendants should live and which should die. Beyond very general statements, the laws of most states did not give juries much guidance as to which pieces of information they could or could not use in making this critical decision. In other words, the jurors were not told things like, "You should focus your attention on how brutal the crime was committed, the number of victims that might have been killed, whether the defendant has an extensive or serious criminal history, the age of the offender, or whether or not they were under the influence of emotional distress, drugs or alcohol." Neither were juries explicitly told that they were forbidden to consider such factors as gender, social class, or race. Instead, they were given virtually unlimited and unrestricted discretion in determining which capital defendants were to die and which were to

live. For example, in instructing its juries in a capital case the law in California said:

> In this part of the trial the law does not forbid you from being influenced by
> pity for the defendants and you may be governed by mere sentiment and
> sympathy for the defendants in arriving at a proper penalty in this case;
> however, the law does forbid you from being governed by mere conjecture,
> prejudice, public opinion or public feeling . . . in determining which punish-
> ment shall be inflicted, you are entirely free to act according to your own
> judgment, conscience, and absolute discretion . . . the law itself provides no
> standard for the guidance of the jury in the selection of the penalty, but,
> rather, commits the whole matter of determining which of the two penalties
> [death or life] shall be fixed to the judgment, conscience, and absolute dis-
> cretion of the jury. (*McGautha v. California*, 402 U.S. 183, 1971, at p. 189)

As you can see, these instructions do not really provide capital juries with specific directions or guidelines to follow in determining what factors they should
use in determining whether to impose a sentence of death or imprisonment.
Since juries were given little guidance or standards, these juries were called
"standardless." Given such vague direction, critics of such capital statutes argued that juries could make their sentencing decision either on whim or caprice or on legally impermissible factors such as race or social status. Under
such a system some people would be sentenced to death while others who committed equally serious crimes would not, and some could be sentenced to death
because they were members of a minority group, were unattractive, or were
poor. As a result, death sentences would not be based on rational considerations (they would not be reserved for the "worst of the worst") but would be
imposed instead on the unlucky or the poor or despised. Such death penalty
procedures, it was argued before the Court, are unconstitutional. Notice, however, that what is being complained about is not the punishment of death per se
but the procedures in place and followed to put people to death. The argument
in the *McGautha* case, therefore, is a *procedural* argument on capital punishment
based upon the Fourteenth Amendment's due process clause, rather than an
argument against the death penalty itself.

The two issues before the Supreme Court in the *McGautha* case, then, were
the acceptability of single-verdict juries and the permissibility of standardless
juries. In a 6–3 decision handed down on May 3, 1971, the Supreme Court rejected the position that the Fourteenth Amendment required either bifurcated
capital trials or that capital juries be provided with explicit sentencing guidelines (*McGautha v. California*, 402 U. S. 183, 1971). In arguing that bifurcated trials were not required, Justice Harlan, writing for a majority of the Court, made
the interesting point that while single-verdict juries may be "cruel" (p. 214)
and that "bifurcated trials . . . are superior means of dealing with capital
cases," it is not the business either of the Constitution or the Supreme Court to
"guarantee trial procedures that are the best of all worlds" (p. 221). What about
the fact that single-verdict juries require defendants on trial for their life to decide on either remaining silent on the issue of their guilt and thereby not inform the jury why their life should be spared, or speaking to the jury with

respect to the issue of guilt, thereby exposing themselves to critical questioning about their character, perhaps condemning them to death? In response to this dilemma, Justice Harlan essentially said that all criminal defendants have to make numerous difficult choices as a matter of trial strategy, and this instance is no different than any other decision that defendants must confront. While Justice Harlan agreed that defendants on trial for their life should be able to provide those deciding their fate with information that they either uniquely possess or may speak most eloquently of, he was also quite clear that the exercise of this right does not come with a guarantee that there will be no adverse consequences.

With respect to the issue of standardless capital juries, Justice Harlan argued that it is likely impossible to know beforehand what factors a sentencing authority should focus on in deciding which convicted capital defendants should live and which should die. It is not the fact that a list of such relevant factors would be difficult to come up with or unwieldy to implement, it is that it is that compiling such a list is simply too morally complex for human beings:

> To identify before the fact those characteristics of criminal homicides and their perpetrators which call for the death penalty, and to express these characteristics in language which can be fairly understood and applied by the sentencing authority, appear to be tasks which are beyond present human ability. (p. 204)

Justice Harlan and the majority of the Court were of the opinion that providing the capital sentencing authority with an understanding of what factors it should consider and which it should not in determining who lives and who dies is beyond human moral knowledge.

What was particularly interesting about this conclusion is that it would seem to fly in the face of the efforts of the American Law Institute's (ALI) Model Penal Code, which at the time did provide a list of factors for a capital sentencing authority to consider—factors that would argue both for (aggravating factors) and against (mitigating factors) a sentence of death. These factors were seemingly intuitive and fairly easy to follow—for example, the number of victims, the criminal history of the defendant, the culpability of the victim in his or her own death. Based on the ALI's efforts, it would perhaps appear that determining beforehand what factors should influence the decision as to a death or life sentence was not a task "beyond present human ability." Justice Harlan rejected such efforts, however, dismissing them as both too limiting and too general to be of any practical value to capital juries and judges, and that any future effort to experiment with other possible aggravating and mitigating factors would most likely produce a list that juries and judges already use:

> It is apparent that such criteria do not purport to provide more than the most minimal control over the sentencing authority's exercise of discretion. . . . For a court to attempt to catalog the appropriate factors in this elusive area could inhibit rather than expand the scope of considerations, for no list of circumstances would ever be really complete. The infinite variety

of cases and facets to each case would make general standards either mean-ingless "boiler-plate" or a statement of the obvious that no jury would need. (pp. 207–208)

To the Court in *McGautha*, then, the "truly awesome responsibility" (p. 208) of taking a human life is a decision that cannot be reduced to legal formulas.[5]

The decision of the Court in *McGautha v. California* was that neither sin-gle-verdict nor standardless juries are unconstitutional under the due process clause of the Fourteenth Amendment. The *McGautha* decision in 1971, there-fore, would seem to have the effect of lifting the moratorium on the death pen-alty that had been in effect since the middle of 1967, thereby clearing the way for states to again begin to put offenders to death. Executions did not immedi-ately resume, however. In fact, on the very day that the *McGautha* decision was announced by the Supreme Court, the governors of Ohio and Maryland an-nounced that there would be no executions in their state until the Court had re-solved the issue as to whether or not the death penalty in 1970s America constituted cruel and unusual punishment prohibited by the Eighth Amend-ment. Recall that the *McGautha* case simply dealt with the procedural issue of single-verdict and standardless juries—i.e., did the due process clause of the Fourteenth Amendment require bifurcated capital trials and some guidelines or standards to structure the discretion of capital juries and judges? The ques-tion remained as to whether the death penalty could exist at all in the 1970s or if American society had morally evolved to the point where it would find such a punishment no longer acceptable. There would not be a long wait for the an-swer to this question. Less than two months after the decision in *McGautha v. California*, the Supreme Court announced an order that it had agreed to hear four death penalty cases with regard to the following question: "Does the im-position and carrying out of the death penalty in [these cases] constitute 'cruel and unusual' punishment in violation of the Eighth and Fourteenth Amend-ments?" (403 U.S. 952, 1971). These cases were *Aikens v. California, Branch v. Texas, Furman v. Georgia*, and *Jackson v. Georgia*.[6] The cases were consolidated for review by the Court in *Furman v. Georgia* (1972).

The Death Penalty as Currently Administered Is So Procedurally Flawed That It Constitutes 'Cruel and Unusual Punishment'—The Case of *Furman v. Georgia*

In slightly different ways, these four cases challenged the constitutionality of the death penalty in each particular state under the principle that it violated the prohibition of the Eighth Amendment to the United States Constitution that states may not inflict cruel and unusual punishments.[7] The legal chal-lenge that these cases presented was also strikingly similar to one of those that the Court seemed to have already ruled on in *McGautha*. The particular issue before the Court in *Furman* was whether capital punishment as administered under existing state law constituted cruel and unusual punishment. We know already that up to the time of the *Furman* decision the Court held to the belief that the death penalty was not by its very nature cruel and unusual. What the Court had to grapple with in *Furman* was whether the way or manner in which the states were imposing the death penalty at the time made it a cruel and unusual punishment. The question, in other words, was, Could a punishment be applied in a way that was so procedurally flawed that it produces a cruel and unusual outcome?

Under existing state capital punishment law, juries who convicted defendants of a capital offense were not required to impose a sentence of death upon every conviction. Rather, juries were given the option or discretion to impose death or some other sentence specified by state law (usually some form of a life sentence). Confronted by a defendant convicted of a capital offense, therefore, the next question the jury had to address was, Should we sentence this defendant to death or allow him to live? The central question before the Court in *Furman* was whether the death penalty was a cruel and unusual punishment when it was imposed under laws that gave juries unguided and unfocused discretion in affixing the penalty. In other words, do so-called standardless juries in capital cases make the death penalty a cruel and unusual punishment?

The Court issued its decision in *Furman* on June 29, 1972, and it was an extremely contentious opinion. It was decided by a bare 5–4 majority; there were nine separate opinions each written by one of the Justices on the Court; and at well over 250 pages it was the longest Supreme Court opinion in its history. Supreme Court scholar Robert Weisberg (1984) appropriately described it as "not so much a case as a badly orchestrated opera, with nine characters taking turns to offer their own arias" (p. 315). The five members of the majority voted to strike down capital statues that included standardless juries as in violation of the Eighth Amendment's prohibition against cruel and unusual punishment.

There were dire consequences predicted to come from the Court's *Furman* decision. Both proponents and opponents of the death penalty argued that as a result of the Court's action the death penalty in America was thereafter likely abolished. This was not going to be the case, however, because as we will soon see, the death penalty was reinstated in many states as early as 1976. The more immediate and practical effect of the *Furman* decision was that slightly over 600 defendants on death row at the time had their death sentences vacated to life imprisonment.

In trying to make sense of the *Furman* case it is important to understand the positions taken by the five justices who make up the majority. Before examining these positions, however, one may well wonder why the Court even decided to review Furman's death sentence, since the issue of standardless juries in capital cases seemed to have been decided just one year earlier in *McGautha v. California*. A six-justice majority in *McGautha* thought then that standardless juries were perfectly constitutional, and the makeup of the Court did not change in the intervening year. One would have thought, therefore, that the legal principle of *stare decisis* (let the precedent stand) would mean that Furman's complaint, that he was sentenced to death by a standardless jury, was moot.[8]

Recall that the legal theory used by the defendants in *McGautha* was that standardless juries (and single-verdict juries) violated the due process clause of the Fourteenth Amendment, while *Furman* raised an Eighth Amendment theory about standardless juries. The only sense to make of the Court's decision to agree to hear the appeal in *Furman* was that some of the justices now came to believe that the Eighth and Fourteenth Amendments had very different things to say about such standardless juries. The argument in *Furman* seemed to be that while the *process* of sentencing defendants to death by standardless juries was permissible under the due process clause of the Fourteenth Amendment (thus remaining faithful to *McGaugtha*), the *product* that it may produce is condemned by the Eighth. In other words, what made standardless juries unconstitutional under *Furman* was that such juries produced unconstitutional death sentences. But what exactly made them unconstitutional under the Eighth Amendment?

Only two of the justices who composed the majority in *Furman*, Justice Brennan and Justice Marshall, saw the death penalty per se as unconstitutional. That is, in their opinion it was not that there was something wrong with the specific state statutes they examined in the *Furman* case, it was that the death penalty was always and under any statute unconstitutional. For slightly different reasons Justices Brennan and Marshall thought that American society had morally evolved to the point where the taking of another life by the state in the form of capital punishment was a cruel and unusual punishment no matter what procedures the state had in place to impose it.

Justice Brennan thought the death penalty was cruel and unusual because it was an affront to human dignity. In his opinion he supplied four principles in determining whether a punishment treated those on whom it was imposed without human dignity: (1) a punishment must not be so severe (disemboweling, drawing and quartering) that by its very nature it degrades human dignity, (2) a punishment must not be inflicted arbitrarily, (3) a punishment must not be in conflict with contemporary standards of decency, and (4) a punishment must not be excessive. Examined within the context of American society in the 1970s, Justice Brennan concluded that the death penalty violated every one of these four principles: (1) it created great pain and suffering on the condemned and it involved the state in the calculated and deliberate killing of another human being; (2) it was imposed so infrequently relative to the number of homicides that one was forced to the conclusion that it was arbitrarily imposed (i.e., not inflicted just on the "worst of the worst"); (3) given the fact that over time virtually all state legislatures had restricted the occasions when it could be imposed and that juries were reluctant to sentence defendants to death, one was forced to conclude that American society had evolved to the point where it no longer saw the death penalty as an acceptable punishment; and (4) death was an excessive punishment because a state could achieve its goals of deterrence and retribution with the punishment of life imprisonment.

Like Justice Brennan, Justice Marshall concluded that the death penalty in any form violates the Eighth Amendment. For Justice Marshall the death penalty was cruel and unusual because it was an excessive punishment, and like Justice Brennan, he thought that the state could achieve its legitimate objective of deterring serious crime with long-term imprisonment. He also believed that American society had morally progressed to the point where it found the death penalty cruel and barbaric. In response to an anticipated objection that Americans did not find the death penalty objectionable because they approved of it in public opinion polls and at least sometimes imposed it, Marshall offered the hypothesis that this "support" was only apparent, due to the fact that citizens were uninformed about how the death penalty actually operates. He thought that if Americans knew that the death penalty was not a more effective deterrent than life imprisonment, that it was frequently imposed in a discriminatory manner, and that innocent persons were sometimes executed, they would conclude, like he did, that it is morally abhorrent.

In the opinions of Justices Brennan and Marshall, then, there was nothing the states could do to improve how they administered the death penalty—capital punishment had become unconstitutional in contemporary America they concluded. The other three Justices of the five-person majority did not believe that the death penalty was per se unconstitutional. Rather, they thought something was specifically wrong with standardless juries in the statutes before them that made them unconstitutional. Standardless juries had too much discretion, and too much discretion produced "bad" death sentences. What made discretion produce "bad" death sentences was slightly different for each of these three justices.

For Justice Douglas, juries with too much discretion in deciding the appropriate sentence in a capital case could easily use factors such as a defendant's race, gender, or social class in making that decision. Justice Douglas was not prepared to conclude that the state statutes were on their face discriminatory (for example, they did not explicitly state that the penalty of death was to be imposed more on black defendants than white). However, he did conclude that by providing capital juries with so little guidance and extending them so much discretion, the statues under which states operated the death penalty provided juries with the opportunity to act in a discriminatory manner:

> Thus, these discretionary statutes are unconstitutional in their operation. They are pregnant with discrimination and discrimination is an ingredient not compatible with the idea of equal protection of the laws that is implicit in the ban on "cruel and unusual" punishments. (at pp. 256–257)

To Justice Douglas, death penalty statutes that provided no sentencing guidance were constitutionally defective because they produced a pattern of death sentences that reflected the more general legal persecution of those at the bottom of the American social heap—political, racial, economic, and cultural outcasts:

> . . . We know that the discretion of judges and juries in imposing the death penalty enables the penalty to be selectively applied, feeding prejudices against the accused if he is poor and despised, and lacking political clout, or if he is a member of a suspect or unpopular minority, and saving those who by social position my be in a more protected position. (at p. 255)

From a constitutional viewpoint, the crucial problem with standardless juries for Justice Douglas, then, was that without guidance and direction provided by a statute as to those legally relevant factors that should inform its decision, jurors might all too often rely on their own fear, prejudices, and bigotry—what he earlier described in his dissent in the *McGautha* case as "man's deepseated sadistic instincts" (p. 242). In his opinion, Justice Douglas argued that there is an implicit equal protection requirement in the Eighth Amendment's ban on cruel and unusual punishment. A punishment could be cruel and unusual in his view, therefore, if it was not applied in a fair and even-handed manner.

Justice Stewart also objected to the fact that juries were given too much sentencing discretion under existing capital statutes. Unlike Justice Douglas, who believed that race and social class may be factors that juries use in deciding who gets sentenced to death, Justice Stewart thought that there was relatively little that explained the pattern or distribution of death sentences. While Justice Douglas thought that one's race or social class might determine who gets sentenced to death, Justice Stewart thought that death sentences were unpredictable. For him, the pattern of death sentences could not be explained by any rational process (and discrimination is a rational process). In fact, Justice Stewart thought that the imposition of death sentences by juries that were not provided sentencing guidance was so irrational and meaningless that he likened it to being struck by lightning: "These death sentences are 'cruel and unusual' in the same way that being struck by lightning is cruel and unusual . . . these petitioners are among a capriciously selected random handful upon whom the sentence of death has in fact been imposed" (at pp. 309–310).

Lightning does not hit those who might in some moral sense deserve it—that is, lightning does not strike the evil or wicked, but rather hits in a random fashion; it is simply a matter of bad luck, of being in the wrong place at the wrong time through no fault of your own. Justice Stewart argued that the death penalty is such a random process, where "random" means characterized by chance, caprice, or luck. Given this process, those who do receive the death penalty are not those who most deserve it (the "worst of the worst") but are simply those who were "unlucky." Unable to rationally distinguish between those who live and those who die, Justice Stewart concludes that capital sentences are "wantonly and freakishly" imposed and therefore cruel and unusual.

The fifth member of the *Furman* majority, Justice White, also objected to the fact that under standardless capital statutes juries are given too much sentencing discretion. For him, however, it was not that capital sentences are imposed in a discriminatory manner (as for Justice Douglas) or that they are imposed in an irrational manner (as for Justice Stewart); rather, it was that they are imposed too infrequently. Justice White adopted a utilitarian position regarding the death penalty. He saw the death penalty as a constitutionally appropriate penalty when it meets legitimate state objectives. The legitimate state objective in putting defendants to death is to deter other would-be offenders from committing capital crimes. However, when the death penalty is not imposed in enough cases, it ceases to be a credible threat to others. When capital punishment ceases to be a credible threat and fails as an effective deterrent, then a legitimate state objective (deterrence) is thwarted, and the death penalty becomes, in Justice White's words, "the pointless and needless extinction of life" and therefore cruel and unusual.

It can clearly be seen from this brief discussion that the majority in *Furman* was a fragile alliance. Two of the justices (Brennan and Marshall) thought that contemporary Americans found the death penalty morally objectionable and therefore unconstitutional no matter how it was administered. Three other justices (Douglas, Stewart, and White) disagreed that the death penalty was per se unconstitutional but concluded that how it was currently being administered under state statutes that permitted standardless juries was in violation of the Eighth Amendment. Add to this mix the fact that four other justices (who make up the dissent in *Furman*) thought there was nothing wrong with existing state capital punishment statutes. The message given to the states by the *Furman* decision was not a clear one, other than that a majority of the Court did not believe that the death penalty for serious crimes, such as murder, was per se unconstitutional.

Since only two justices harbored objections to the death penalty in any form, it was clear that states could fashion constitutionally acceptable death penalty statutes if they could only do something about the fact that juries who made the decision about whether to impose a death sentence had too much discretion in making that decision. Assisting the states in constructing such permissible death penalty statutes, buried in a footnote of Chief Justice Berger's dissenting opinion, is the suggestion that in order to meet the Court's approval, sentencing discretion in capital cases could be either guided and structured or eliminated altogether:

> While I would not undertake to make a definitive statement as to the parameters of the Court's ruling, it is clear that if state legislatures and the Congress wish to maintain the availability of capital punishment, significant statutory changes will have to be made. Since the two pivotal concurring opinions [those of Justices Stewart and White] turn on the assumption that the punishment of death is now meted out in a random and unpredictable manner, legislative bodies may seek to bring their laws into compliance with the Court's ruling by providing standards for juries and judges to follow in determining the sentence in capital cases or by more narrowly defining the crimes for which the penalty is to be imposed. If such standards can be devised, or the crimes more meticulously defined, the result cannot be detrimental. (pp. 400–401)

Chief Justice Burger was informing state legislators that there is nothing to be found in the Court's *Furman* opinion that would prevent them from retaining the death penalty if they wished to keep it. He did correctly point out that existing statutes would have to be substantially modified to deal with the problem of unguided sentencing discretion in capital cases. Chief Justice Burger proposed two possible solutions to the problem of discretion. The first was to encourage legislators to devise standards that would direct and guide the discretion of capital juries. The second was to completely eliminate sentencing discretion in capital cases by requiring a mandatory death sentence upon the conviction of carefully specified capital crimes. As it turns out, state legislators (and the federal government and U.S. military) would take Chief Justice Burger up on his two suggestions.

Chapter Summary

While the history of the death penalty in the United States is a long one, it has also been a controversial one—and the controversy about capital punishment continues today. In a series of early cases, the U.S. Supreme Court held, in approving of both death by firing squad and electrocution, that a method of capital punishment cannot involve torture or the needless infliction of pain. By the 1900s, while there may have been some controversy about the method of imposing death, there was not substantial disagreement that capital punishment was a permissible punishment under the U.S. Constitution. With time, however, a different Eighth Amendment argument would be raised in objection to the death penalty: that American society has progressed and become more civilized so that while citizens may have once found the death penalty acceptable, they no longer do. In the middle to late 1960s, this argument seemed to have some support. Public support for the death penalty had been in decline, reaching an all-time low of only 42 percent in 1966, and written views in opposition to the death penalty began to appear both in law review articles and by Supreme Court justices. A procedural objection to the death penalty was dismissed by the Court in its 1971 decision, *McGautha v. California*. In 1972, however, the Court handed down its opinion in *Furman v. Georgia* in which it declared the death penalty unconstitutional *as currently practiced*. The problem of capital statues identified by the *Furman* Court was unguided discretion. The effect of the *Furman* decision was to empty death rows across the United States; states that wanted to maintain capital punishment now had to rewrite their laws to bring them into compliance with whatever it was that *Furman* required.

Discussion Questions

1. What evidence could you point to today to make an argument that the death penalty is unconstitutional because it is no longer thought to be an acceptable punishment under the "evolving standards of decency" standard of the Eighth Amendment? What evidence would you point to if you had to refute that claim?

2. If you had been a U.S. Supreme Court Justice, what would have been your decision in *Furman*? Why? Which justice's opinion in that case is most like your own? Which is least like your own?

3. At the time of the *Furman* decision, do you think that public sentiment had evolved to the point where it found the death penalty to be a cruel and unusual punishment?

4. What are the arguments in favor of a "fixed" interpretation to the Eighth Amendment, one that says that a "cruel and unusual" punishment is one that the framers of the Constitution had in mind when they wrote that document? What are the arguments against such an interpretation?

5. Justice Stewart's complaint about the death penalty in his *Furman* decision was that being sentenced to death had no more moral rationality to

it that being struck by lightning. Would you have agreed with him then, and do you think it's still true now?

6. In his *McGautha* opinion, Justice Harlan seemed to argue that it was virtually impossible to come up with a set of standards or a list of what factors a jury should use in deciding whether to sentence a defendant to death. Do you agree with this? If you had to, what factors would you come up with that a jury should and should not consider in making the life/death decision?

7. Justice Brennan in his *Furman* decision concluded that the Eighth Amendment precludes the death penalty because execution is an affront to human dignity. What did he mean by that? What other kinds of punishments do you think would meet this test?

8. If the case of Willie Francis happened today, do you think it would rise to the level of cruel and unusual punishment? Why or why not?

Student Resources

Comprehensive discussions of some of the issues in death penalty law as well was legal history can be found in Victor Streib's *Death Penalty in a Nutshell* (2005); Welsh White's series *The Death Penalty in the Eighties* (1987) and *The Death Penalty in the Nineties* (1991); Barry Latzer's *Death Penalty Cases*; and Raoul Berger's *Death Penalties: The Supreme Court's Obstacle Course* (1982).

There are also some very good websites that provide access to Supreme Court, federal court and state court cases. The Legal Information Institute at Cornell Law School is one of the best. You can access it at <www.law.cornell.edu/>. The website maintained by the U.S. Supreme Court is <www.supremecourtus.gov/>.

Endnotes

1. For example, the Fifth Amendment to the Constitution states that "No person shall be held to answer for a *capital,* or otherwise infamous crime, unless on a presentment or indictment of a Grand Jury . . . nor be deprived of *life,* liberty or property without due process of law . . ." (emphasis added).

2. Beginning in the 1760s, some Americans began to question the propriety of imposing the death penalty on property offenders, and by the 1780s its use for any crime was hotly debated (Banner 2002). James Madison was opposed to the death penalty for any crime while both Thomas Jefferson and Benjamin Franklin approved of its use only for murder. In 1764 an Italian nobleman, Cesare Beccaria, published his highly influential *Essay on Crimes and Punishments,* which contained an Enlightenment-inspired comprehensive argument against the death penalty.

3. The first execution by electrocution in the United States may also have been the first "botched" execution. After the first jolt of electricity which lasted approximately 17 seconds, one of the attending physicians to the execution ordered that the flow of current be stopped and pronounced Kemmler dead. But, another physician detected a pulse, and a second, longer, dose of electricity was applied. The second application involved a current either so long or so strong that beads of blood resembling sweat appeared on Kemmler's forehead.

4. One official witness to the execution remarked, "This boy really got a shock when they turned that machine on" *Francis v. Resweber* (329 U.S. 459, at p. 480 note 2).

5. Justice Brennan wrote the dissenting opinion in *McGautha,* joined by two other justices (Justice Douglas and Justice Marshall). In his dissent, Justice Brennan accuses the majority of misunderstanding the essential question before the Court in the case. He argued that the Court was not called upon to review the factors that capital juries and judges in California and Ohio actually used in making the decision as to who lives and who dies, because neither state ever attempted to provide such standards. He stated:

> It is of critical importance in the present cases to emphasize that we are not called upon to determine the adequacy or inadequacy of any particular legislative procedure designed to give rationality to the capital sentencing process. For the plain fact is that the legislatures of California and Ohio, whence come these cases, have sought no solution at all. We are not presented with a State's attempt to provide standards, attacked as impermissible or inadequate. We are not presented with a legislative attempt to draw wisdom from experience through a process looking toward growth in understanding through the accumulation of a variety of experiences. We are not presented with the slightest attempt to bring the power of reason to bear on the considerations relevant to capital sentencing. We are faced with nothing more than stark legislative abdication. (pp. 249–250)

6. The appeal to the U. S. Supreme Court in *Aikens v. California* was dismissed when the California Supreme Court declared in *People v. Anderson* (6 Cal 3d 628, 493 P. 2d 880, 100 Cal. Rptr. 152, 1972) that capital punishment for murder in its state was unconstitutional under the provisions of the state's constitution. However, only nine months after *Anderson* a public referendum was passed which again permitted capital punishment in California.

7. Keep in mind that the Eighth Amendment to the United States Constitution is held applicable to each of the states under the Fourteenth Amendment.

8. Recall also that in his opinion in *McGautha* Justice Harlan seemed to think that it would be humanly impossible to develop standards for juries in capital cases to use effectively: "To identify before the fact those characteristics of criminal homicides and their perpetrators which call for the death penalty, and to express these characteristics in language which can be fairly understood and applied by the sentencing authority, appear to be tasks which are beyond present human ability" *McGautha v. California* (403 U.S. 183, 1971 at 204). Interestingly, since *Furman* stated that one way that unconstitutional state death penalty statutes could be made constitutional would be the development of standards to guide the jury in its sentencing decision, the Court perhaps thought what only one year before was "beyond present human ability" was now possible. ✦

Chapter 5

Constitutional Requirements for Capital Punishment in the United States

Contrary to the predictions of both critics and supporters of the *Furman* decision, it did not lead to the permanent abolition of the death penalty in America (Meltsner 1973). In fact, after the decision was announced some states immediately went to work to draft new death penalty statutes that would meet with the Court's approval. Not surprisingly, these new statutes adopted one of the two solutions to the problem of too much capital sentencing discretion that were proposed by Chief Justice Burger: either guiding the decision making in capital sentencing or attempting to eliminate all capital sentencing discretion.

Just five months after the Supreme Court handed down its decision in the *Furman* case, the state of Florida convened a special session of the state legislature to draft a new death penalty statute. Other states soon followed Florida's lead, so that by 1976, 35 states had enacted new death penalty statutes that allowed for the execution of offenders convicted of serious crimes (generally, these new statutes restricted a capital crime to murder or rape). The federal government also joined this group, passing a law in 1974 that permitted the death penalty for the crime of aircraft piracy that resulted in death. With these new death penalty statutes passed by the states and federal government, defendants soon began to occupy death rows awaiting execution. Only one thing separated these newly condemned inmates and the execution chamber that awaited them: the Supreme Court had yet to decide whether these new, procedurally reformed death penalty statutes adequately met the requirements of *Furman*. Until it declared that these new statutes were different from those reviewed in *Furman*, and therefore did not constitute cruel and unusual punishment, the informal moratorium on executions that had been in place since 1967 would still be in effect, and the actual imposition of the death penalty would be delayed a while longer. Further, since it was not clear exactly what *Furman* did require, no one was really certain whether the reforms put in place in these new death penalty statutes would be sufficient.

It would not take the Court long to decide. On July 2, 1976, just two days before the nation was to celebrate its bicentennial, the Supreme Court handed down its decision in five death penalty cases: *Gregg v. Georgia* (428 U.S. 153, 1976), *Proffitt v. Florida* (428 U.S. 242, 1976), *Jurek v. Texas* (428 U.S. 262, 1976), *Woodson v. Louisiana* (428 U.S. 280, 1976) and *Roberts v. Louisiana* (428 U.S. 325, 1976). In these five cases the Court reviewed several variations of procedurally reformed death penalty statutes. Before reviewing these cases, however, let us briefly discuss the two general reforms of death penalty law—guided discretion statutes and mandatory statutes—that were enacted in response to *Furman*.

The Response to *Furman*: Mandatory and Guided Discretion Capital Statutes

Some states sought to remedy the defect of too much sentencing discretion in previous capital punishment statutes by virtually taking any sentencing discretion away from the jury. That is, if the problem that *Furman* identified was that too much discretion was given to juries in deciding to impose a death sentence, perhaps the best way to solve this problem would be to eliminate all sentencing discretion. This was done by making a sentence of death mandatory upon the conviction of a specified capital crime. Under a mandatory statute state legislatures created new types of capital offenses. Upon the conviction of one of these newly defined capital crimes, a sentence of death was required or mandatory. With a mandatory statute, then, once a defendant was convicted of a capital crime, there was no discretion—a sentence of death automatically followed.

An example of a mandatory death penalty statute was the one passed by the North Carolina legislature in 1974. This statute redefined murder in the first degree and made death the mandatory punishment for the conviction of this crime. The statute read:

> Murder in the first and second degree defined; punishment.—A murder which shall be perpetrated by means of poison, lying in wait, imprisonment, starving, torture, or by any other kind of willful, deliberate and premeditated killing, or which shall be committed in the perpetration or attempt to perpetrate any arson, rape, robbery, kidnapping, burglary or other felony, shall be deemed to be murder in the first degree and shall be punished with death. All other kinds of murder shall be deemed murder in the second degree, and shall be punished by imprisonment for a term of not less than two years nor more than life imprisonment in the State's prison. [N. C. Gen. Statute Sec. 14-17 (Cum. Supp. 1975)]

A defendant in North Carolina who committed an armed robbery during the course of which a person was killed and who was subsequently convicted of first degree murder for this crime by a jury would be automatically sentenced to death (as James Woodson, the defendant in *Woodson v. North Carolina* was). The jury would have no decision to make other than guilt or innocence of the charge of first degree murder. The sentencing discretion to impose a death or a life sentence it had under the North Carolina pre-*Furman* law was eliminated by the mandatory nature of the new statute.

Other states chose not to eliminate the jury's sentencing discretion entirely in capital cases but rather to focus and guide it. These guided discretion statutes sought to remedy the defect of too much sentencing discretion by focusing the attention of the jury on factors about the offense or offender that the legislature thought should be important considerations in deciding who should be sentenced to death. Under these statutes the capital trial actually consisted of two parts or phases and is referred to as a *bifurcated* trial. The first phase of the capital trial is the guilt phase and the second, later phase is the penalty phase. The purpose of each phase is different, and the information presented at the guilt and penalty phases is very different.

The issue during the guilt phase of a capital trial is the traditional question of whether the defendant is guilty of a specified capital crime. The evidence and testimony at this first phase has to be directed solely at the issue of the guilt or innocence of the accused. If the determination in this phase is "guilty of a capital crime," the trial then moves to the penalty phase.[1] The question to be answered at the second phase is whether the convicted defendant should be sentenced to death or some other punishment. Testimony and evidence at this phase focus on what the appropriate penalty should be. The kinds of evidence that can be presented in the penalty phase of a bifurcated capital trial are much broader than those permitted at the guilt phase. The defense and prosecution essentially conduct a morality play in which the defense tries to convince the jury that the defendant's life should be spared because he or she is a redeemable human being in spite of the obviously malignant crime that was committed. The prosecution tries to convince the jury that the defendant is a dangerous, remorseless, and odious being who should be completely cast out of the human community.

While the precise features of a guided discretion statute vary somewhat in each state, they all require the formal consideration of what are called aggravating and mitigating factors. The development of aggravating and mitigating factors is an explicit recognition that not all murders are alike, that some are so serious that they deserve to be punished with death while others are less serious (though still brutal crimes) and do not deserve to be punished with the death of the offender. By focusing the jury on both aggravating and mitigating factors, it is hoped that the worst cases will be culled out and result in a death sentence, leaving the less serious crimes to be punished by a less severe penalty. In this way, there would be a meaningful and rational basis for distinguishing those defendants sentenced to death and those not—the crimes of the former would be much more serious in an objective way.

An *aggravating factor* is a feature or characteristic of an offense or offender that the legislature has deemed makes the crime more serious than others and thereby deserving of death. Aggravating factors vary from state to state, are explicitly listed in the state statute, and include such things as killing more than one victim, killing a police officer, killing in the course of another felony, and killing by an offender with an extensive and violent criminal history. These aggravating factors play two roles. First, to be eligible for the death penalty a defendant must be convicted by a jury of at least one of the aggravating factors listed in the state statute. That is, unless the jury finds one of the aggravating factors listed in the statute and charged by the prosecutor, it may not impose a sentence of death. The finding of a statutory aggravating factor, therefore, serves as a lower threshold for all death-eligible cases. The finding of at least one statutory aggravating factor serves to narrow the range of cases in which death is an appropriate penalty, since it may not be imposed in the absence of one of these factors. This finding of a statutory aggravating factor is made during the guilt phase of a capital trial, and under *Ring v. Arizona* (536 U.S. 584, 2002) this finding must be made by a jury. Unless the jury determines that at least one aggravating factor is present, the case does not advance to the penalty phase. The second purpose of statutory aggravating factors is to serve as the foundation for the prosecutor's case that the appropriate sentence should be death. During the penalty phase of a capital trial the prosecution will enter the fact that the defendant has been found guilty of one or more aggravating factors and will use this as one basis for the argument that the appropriate sentence should be death.

Box 5.1
Jury Participation in Death Sentences Is Required

Traditionally, in the American system of criminal justice, defendants could choose between a "bench" trial by judge or a jury trial. When states revised their capital punishment statutes in response to the *Furman* decision, some of them chose to place the finding of aggravating factors and the sentencing decision in the hands of a judge rather than a jury. Under Florida law at the time, for example, the jury upon a finding of guilty of a capital offense, weighed aggravating and mitigating circumstances and made a recommendation of sentence to the judge. The judge could override that recommendation, however, and could sentence a defendant to death after a jury's recommendation of life or could sentence a defendant to life after a jury's recommendation of death. Under the Arizona statute at the time the judge alone determined the presence of aggravating and mitigating circumstances and imposed the sentence. In 1990, the U.S. Supreme Court held in *Walton v. Arizona* (497 U.S. 639, 1990) that Arizona's procedure of judge sentencing in capital cases was constitutional. The Court later ruled in *Apprendi v. New Jersey* (500 U.S. 466, 2000), a noncapital case, however, that a judge could not make any findings of fact which would have the result of increasing a defendant's sentence beyond that established at conviction. This would seem to call into question the capital sentencing schemes of those states where the judge imposes sentence after making a determination of aggravating circumstances. If a judge finds aggravating circumstances that were either not found by the jury or given lesser weight and on that basis imposes a more severe sentence, the judge is in essence increasing the defendant's penalty in violation of *Apprendi*. In *Ring v. Arizona*, decided in June 2002, the Supreme Court took precisely that view. It held that a death sentence where the necessary finding of aggravating factors is determined by a judge rather than a jury is unconstitutional. Ring called into question the capital sentencing practices of nine states that at the time of the decision used some form of judge sentencing in capital cases (Arizona, Idaho, Montana, Colorado, Nebraska, Alabama, Delaware, Florida, and Indiana). ✦

Table 5.1 provides the list of aggravating factors under the first post-*Furman* death penalty statute developed by the Georgia legislature, which became the subject of review by the U.S. Supreme Court in *Gregg v. Georgia*. The Georgia legislature identified 10 specific factors it believed made a crime more serious than others and deserving of the death penalty. The list of statutory aggravating factors included the commission of murder, rape, armed robbery, or kidnapping by someone with a previous conviction for a capital crime or a history of violent crimes; murder during the commission of another felony; murder for hire; and murder during an escape attempt. If the trier of fact found at least one of these aggravating factors, the case could advance to the penalty phase. If there was no finding of any aggravating factor listed, the defendant was not eligible for the death penalty and a sentence other than death had to be imposed. At the penalty phase, hearing evidence would be presented with respect to both aggravating and mitigating factors.

Table 5.1 Statutory Aggravating Factors in the 1975 Georgia Death Penalty Statute

A1: The offense of murder, rape, armed robbery, or kidnapping was committed by a person with a prior record of conviction for a capital felony, or the offense of murder was committed by a person who has a substantial history of serious assaultive criminal convictions.

A2: The offense of murder, rape, armed robbery, or kidnapping was committed while the offender was engaged in the commission of another capital felony, or aggravated battery or the offense of murder was committed while the offender was engaged in the commission of burglary or arson in the first degree.

A3: The offender by his act of murder, armed robbery or kidnapping knowingly created a great risk of death to more than one person in a public place by means of a weapon or device which would normally be hazardous to the lives of more than one person.

A4: The offender committed the offense of murder for himself or another, for the purpose of receiving money or any other thing of monetary value.

A5: The murder of a judicial officer, former judicial officer, district attorney or solicitor or former district attorney or solicitor during or because of the exercise of his official duty.

A6: The offender caused or directed another to commit murder or committed murder as an agent or employee of another person.

A7: The offense of murder, rape, armed robbery, or kidnapping was outrageously or wantonly vile, horrible or inhuman in that it involved torture, depravity of mind or an aggravated battery to the victim.

A8: The offense of murder was committed against any peace officer, corrections employee or fireman while engaged in the performance of his official duties.

A9: The offense of murder was committed by a person in, or who has escaped from, the lawful custody of a peace officer or place of lawful confinement.

A10: The murder was committed for the purpose of avoiding, interfering with, or preventing a lawful arrest or custody in a place of lawful confinement, or himself or another.

Source: Georgia Code Ann. Sec. 27-2534.1 (b) Supp. 1975.

A mitigating factor is something about the offense or offender that makes the crime less serious or the offender less blameworthy and therefore not deserving of the penalty of death. Such elements are called mitigating factors because they make an offense less harsh or serious and as such argue against the death penalty despite other factors that argue for it. For example, when determining how much to punish a child for a misdeed, a parent will try to determine how blameworthy the child is. A child who is older and should "know better" is thought to be more blameworthy than a younger child and will receive greater punishment. In other words, the young age of the child "mitigates" against a more severe punishment. This is precisely what mitigating factors in a capital statute do. When creating mitigating factors, the state legislature decides that some facts about an offense or an offender arguing against a death sentence and should be considered in affixing the proper penalty. The purpose of mitigating factors, therefore, is to support an argument against a death sentence, and defense counsel's job is to argue for as many mitigating factors as he or she can. The prosecution's job is to argue either that the mitigating factors do not exist or that they do not offset or outweigh the aggravating factors it has argued for in favor of a death sentence.

Table 5.2 provides a list of the mitigating factors under the post-*Furman* capital statute that was passed by the state of Florida. The Florida legislature thought that defendants with no significant prior criminal history, those whose own will to commit the crime was compromised by emotional distress or the stronger will of another, and young defendants were factors that mitigated against a penalty of death. During the penalty phase of a capital trial, defense counsel in Florida would use the presence of one or more of these mitigating factors as a basis for arguing for a sentence other than death (assuming, of course, that the evidence in the case supports the claim of mitigation).

Under a guided discretion statute the jury considers and weighs both aggravating and mitigating factors before imposing a sentence. The purpose of these aggravating and mitigating factors is to focus the attention of the jury on those features of a crime the state legislature thought should be used in deciding which death-eligible defendants should receive the death penalty and which should be given a term of imprisonment. Theoretically at least, by using these factors the process of capital punishment would select only the worst crimes and most deserving or blameworthy offenders for a death sentence.

In its collection of 1976 cases, then, the Supreme Court had before it two general solutions to the problem of too much discretion in the hands of the jury in capital cases: guided discretion and mandatory statutes. In its decision in

---

Table 5.2 Statutory Mitigating Factors Under Florida's Post-*Furman* Capital Statute

M1: The defendant has no significant history of prior criminal activity.

M2: The capital felony was committed while the defendant was under the influence of extreme mental or emotional disturbance.

M3: The victim was a participant in the defendant's conduct or consented to the act.

M4: The defendant was an accomplice in the capital felony committed by another person and his participation was relatively minor.

M5: The defendant acted under extreme duress or under the substantial domination of another person.

M6: The capacity of the defendant to appreciate the criminality of his conduct or to conform his conduct to the requirements of law was substantially impaired.

M7: The age of the defendant at the time of the crime.

Source: Fla. Stat. Ann. Sec. 921.141.

the cases of *Gregg v. Georgia, Proffitt v. Florida*, and *Jurek v. Texas*, the Court by a 7–2 vote in each case approved the use of guided discretion statutes. In its decision in the cases of *Woodson v. North Carolina* and *Roberts v. Louisiana*, both narrowly decided by 5–4 votes, the Court struck down mandatory death penalty statutes as unconstitutional. Since it seems that the best way to handle the problem of sentencing discretion would be to get rid of it entirely, as mandatory statutes did, some review of the Court's reasoning in all of these cases is necessary. The crucial votes in the mandatory cases were cast by Justices Stewart, Powell, and Stevens. They were joined by Justices White, Rehnquist, Blackmun, and Chief Justice Burger in upholding guided discretion statutes, and by Justices Brennan and Marshall in striking down mandatory statutes.

In its decision in *Gregg v. Georgia*, the first order of business for the Court was to determine whether the use of capital punishment for the offense of murder was unconstitutional under the Eighth Amendment's ban on cruel and unusual punishment. After reviewing the legal history of the cruel and unusual punishment clause and noting that "[t]he most marked indication of society's endorsement of the death penalty for murder is the legislative response to *Furman*" (recall that a majority of states passed new death penalty statutes when theirs had been struck down by the *Furman* decision), Justice Stewart concluded that the death penalty for murder does not by itself violate the Eighth Amendment's prohibition against cruel and unusual punishment. In addition to the rapid legislative changes in state death penalty law, the Court could also point to recent public opinion polls, which found that about two-thirds of Americans were in favor of the death penalty for those who committed murder. Clearly, then, American society had not "evolved" to the point where it found capital punishment for the offense of murder morally reprehensible, harsh, or barbaric. But if capital punishment was not unconstitutional per se, the question remained open as to whether the statutes under review contained sufficient procedural reforms to save them from the same fate as that reviewed by the Court in *Furman*. This task of reviewing the adequacy of procedural reforms was made all the more difficult because the Court in *Gregg* and its companion cases did not have any objective, empirical information that the statutes actually worked in the way they were supposed to. In other words, the Court simply had to consider whether the procedural reforms enacted in the statute *would promise* to produce outcomes different from those condemned in *Furman*.

In its review of the Georgia statute in *Gregg v. Georgia* (428 U.S. 153, 1976), the Court argued that three procedural reforms were in place that, while it did not think were all required for the statute to be constitutional, nonetheless thought they would be effective in producing fair death sentences[2]: (1) a bifurcated hearing that separated the issue of guilt from the issue of penalty, (2) statutory factors that focused the attention of the jury on legally important case characteristics, and (3) an automatic appeal of all death sentences to the state supreme court as a further check on consistency and proportionality.[3] Under the new Georgia statute, then, defendants accused of a capital crime would have two phases to their trial, a guilt phase and a penalty phase. The Georgia statute listed 10 specific aggravating circumstances (see Table 5.1). The jury had to find the defendant guilty of at least one of these factors beyond a reasonable doubt before it could consider the death penalty. During the penalty phase of the trial, the jury would consider both aggravating and mitigating factors in determining the appropriate penalty.

The Georgia statute did not explicitly list factors in mitigating, but the law clearly understood that such factors would be argued to and considered by the jury. Finally, the statute required that the Georgia Supreme Court review each death sentence imposed to determine if it was appropriate.[4] In approving the general approach of the Georgia statute, Justice Stewart concluded that "on their face these procedures seem to satisfy the concerns of *Furman*" (p. 198), and Justice White noted that there "is reason to expect that Georgia's current system would escape the infirmities which invalidated its previous system under *Furman*" (p. 222). Notice the very careful language in these two statements of approval for the Georgia statute. Neither justice had any actual evidence that the statute did perform any better than the one struck down only three years earlier in *Furman*. Rather, they thought that enacted procedural reforms would likely perform better—i.e., "on their face" or there "is reason to *expect*" (emphasis added) that the new statute would escape the problems of the earlier Georgia death statute.

The Florida statute that was under review in *Proffitt v. Florida* (428 U.S. 242, 1976) was different in two significant ways from Georgia's guided discretion statute. First, in addition to aggravating factors, the Florida statute explicitly listed factors in mitigation for the trial court to consider (See Table 5.2). Second, the decision of the jury at the penalty phase was only an advisory sentence to the judge. While this advisory sentence was presumed to be correct, the trial judge could under some conditions override a jury's recommendation for either a death or a life sentence. Similar to Georgia law, the Florida statute also required capital trials to be bifurcated and each death sentence to be reviewed by the state supreme court.[5]

The Texas capital statute approved by the Supreme Court in *Jurek v. Texas* (428 U.S. 262, 1976) was an odd, hybrid statute that actually combined elements of both a guided discretion and mandatory statute. The Texas statute may reasonably be considered a "quasi-mandatory" one. As with the Georgia and Florida statutes, the capital trial in Texas was bifurcated, with separate guilt and penalty phases. In addition, as in these other two states, each death sentence imposed in Texas was to be automatically reviewed for "correctness" by a court with statewide jurisdiction, in this case the Texas Court of Criminal Appeals. Under the Texas statute, a defendant found guilty of a capital murder charge during the guilt phase may then pass on to the second or penalty phase. During the penalty hearing both the prosecution and defense present evidence and arguments directed at the appropriate penalty in the case. In its penalty deliberation after these arguments, the jury is required by statute to answer three specific questions:

1. Whether the conduct of the defendant that caused the death of the deceased was committed deliberately and with the reasonable expectation that the death of the deceased or another would result.

2.   Whether there is a probability that the defendant would commit crimi-
     nal acts of violence that would constitute a continuing threat to society.

3.   If raised by the evidence, whether the conduct of the defendant in killing
     the deceased was unreasonable in response to the provocation, if any, by
     the deceased. [Texas Code Crim. Proc. Art. 37.071, Supp. 1975-1976)

If the answer to each of these questions posed to the jury during the penalty
phase hearing is "yes" beyond a reasonable doubt, a sentence of death is mandatory. This component of the Texas statute makes it mandatory. The Texas statute
escaped the same fate as the North Carolina and Louisiana mandatory statutes
reviewed at the same time because the majority of the Court thought that the second question (about the future dangerousness of the defendant) would be interpreted broadly so as to allow the same kind of aggravating and mitigating
evidence heard under the Georgia and Florida laws. By allowing for the consideration of the aggravating and mitigating factors in each specific case, the Court
was of the opinion that the Texas statute would allow for the "individualization" of death sentences—a critical feature of any constitutional capital punishment system, as we will now see.

The Supreme Court reviewed two mandatory capital statutes at the same
time that it reviewed the statutes of Georgia, Florida, and Texas. In response to
Furman, the legislatures of North Carolina and Louisiana decided not to guide
the discretion of the jury in capital cases but to attempt to remove sentencing
discretion entirely. Both state legislatures drafted laws that narrowly defined
capital murder, and made the penalty of death the mandatory punishment for
anyone convicted of that crime. Juries in capital cases had no discretion once a
defendant was convicted of these narrowly drawn types of capital offenses.
For example, in its new death penalty statute passed in 1974 just two years after *Furman* was decided, North Carolina defined both what a capital murder
was and how it was to be punished:

> *Murder in the first and second degree defined; punishment*—A murder which
> shall be perpetrated by means of poison, lying in wait, imprisonment,
> starving, torture, or by any other kind of willful, deliberate and premedi-
> tated killing, or which shall be committed in the perpetration or attempt to
> perpetrate any arson, rape, robbery, kidnapping, burglary or other felony
> shall be deemed to be murder in the first degree and shall be punished with
> death. All other kinds of murder shall be deemed murder in the second de-
> gree, and shall be punished by imprisonment for a term of not less than two
> years nor more than life imprisonment in the State's prison. (N.C. Gen. Stat-
> ute Sec. 14-17, Cum. Supp. 1975)

Under this statute, once a jury convicted a defendant of first degree murder its
task was completed. There was no need for a penalty hearing, because the automatic punishment was death. Most of the post-*Furman* mandatory death penalty statutes were generally similar to this.

The Court found that statutes like those of North Carolina and Louisiana that
made the punishment of death mandatory after conviction of a capital offense

were unconstitutional, in violation of the Eighth Amendment. In invalidating mandatory death penalty schemes, Justice Stewart, writing in *Woodson v. North Carolina*, noted three specific defects of all mandatory schemes:

1. Mandatory statutes do not comply with contemporary standards of decency. Historically, most states have moved away from mandatory criminal penalties in favor of some sentencing discretion and the "individualization" of death sentences. The fact that some state legislatures (like those of North Carolina and Louisiana) had recently crafted mandatory statutes did not mean that society now finds them acceptable. Justice Stewart argued that such legislative efforts merely reflect attempts by the states to bring their laws into compliance with what they thought to be the requirements of *Furman*.

2. Mandatory statutes merely "paper over" the problem of sentencing discretion, since juries that do not wish to see a death sentence imposed on a defendant may simply refuse to convict the person of first degree murder (the problem of *jury nullification*). Juries still exercise considerable unguided discretion under mandatory statutes, but that discretion is now simply "hidden" from view.

3. A mandatory statute by definition does not allow the sentencing jury to consider "the diverse frailties of humankind" that may argue for a sentence of death. The central defect that the Court identified with mandatory statutes was that they failed to give capital defendants any individual consideration of their unique culpability and instead treated them as "members of a faceless, undifferentiated mass to be subjected to the blind infliction of the penalty of death" (p. 305). In striking down mandatory statutes, the Court was saying that not all convicted of a capital crime deserve to die; some are more deserving and blameworthy than others, and there must be some provision within the law to separate those deserving of death and those not deserving. Mandatory statues provide no such provision; they simply ignore moral differences among those convicted of first degree murder by treating them all the same—all deserve to die. The Court objected, therefore, to the defining feature of mandatory statutes: that they treat all persons convicted of a capital crime alike, as if there were no differences among them. To honor human dignity, therefore, capital defendants must be given the opportunity to offer and juries must be given the opportunity to hear and independently consider all of the unique features of each defendant that would argue both for and against a sentence of death. In other words, each death sentence must be individually tailored to the unique moral culpability of each defendant.

In sum, in the five cases of *Gregg, Proffitt, Jurek, Woodson*, and *Roberts*, the United States Supreme Court did several things. First, by declaring that the death penalty does not always violate the Eighth Amendment's prohibition against cruel and unusual punishment, it once again allowed states the opportunity to put some criminal defendants to death. States were back in the death penalty "business." Second, it signaled that there would be procedural rules that had to be followed by the states in deciding which convicted capital defendants were to die and which were to live. State laws had to provide some mechanism by which both the state and the defendant could produce information relevant to the appropriate sentence in each case, and the jury had to formally consider such aggravating and mitigating factors. It also signaled that state capital trials would be subject to scrutiny and review by the U.S. Supreme Court—the Court was now back in the death penalty business. Finally, it put forth two principles that would guide the Supreme Court's review of the death penalty.

The first principle that any constitutional death penalty scheme had to honor was the principle of *consistency*. One of the problems with death sentences noted by the *Furman* Court was that the imposition of a death sentence seemed so irrational. The Court noted that getting sentenced to death was like being struck by lightning or playing a lottery, experiences guided by chance and luck rather than rationality. In *Gregg, Proffitt,* and *Jurek*, the Court argued that to be constitutional, death sentences had to be consistent. An offense that leads to a death sentence for one defendant should lead to a death sentence for another, comparable defendant. One mechanism to ensure this kind of consistency was (a) the bifurcation of a capital trial into guilt and penalty phases where relevant sentencing information could be withheld from the first and dominate the second hearing; (b) the requirement that at least one statutory aggravating factor be found by the trial court before a defendant may be passed to a sentencing hearing, and the consideration of aggravating and mitigating factors at the penalty phase that would serve to focus and guide the sentencing discretion of the sentencing authority; and (c) a provision for the review of each death sentence by a higher court in the state to determine that the death sentence was both factually correct and consistent with other death sentences imposed by juries in that state.[6]

The second principle that a constitutional death penalty system had to adhere to was the principle of the *individualization of death sentences*. To comply with the human dignity requirement of the Eighth Amendment, juries cannot treat all convicted capital offenders alike. They must be able to hear and give independent weight to all the factors that may have led *this particular person* to commit their crime. Before rendering sentence, the jury must have as much information as possible about the unique culpability of the offender, and mandatory statutes preclude that.

The Execution of Special Groups—The Retarded, the Young, and the Mentally Ill

In Chapter 3 we noted that with very few exceptions, the death penalty can currently be imposed only when there is a murder and the defendant was the "trigger-man," hired the "trigger-man" to commit the crime, or was a major participant in a homicide and showed a reckless indifference to human life. While the Supreme Court has explicitly ruled that some particular crimes are ineligible for the death penalty (armed robbery, the rape of an adult woman, kidnapping), what about capital punishment for particular kinds of *people*?

The Death Penalty for the Mentally Retarded

When the death penalty was reinstituted in the United States after the *Gregg* decision, no state expressly prohibited the execution of those who were mentally retarded. Generally, mental retardation was simply considered one of any number of possible mitigating factors that defense counsel could argue for (and prosecutors could argue against) during the penalty phase of a capital trial. The fact that a defendant may have substantially impaired intellectual ability was, therefore, given no special legal status. As a result, there were numerous instances of mentally retarded persons convicted of capital crimes and put to death.

In 1984, James Henry was executed by the state of Florida even though he had an IQ measured in the low 70s (generally, an IQ of 70 or below is taken as evidence of mental retardation). Ivon Stanley was executed in Georgia that same year, and his IQ measured only 61 as an adolescent and 81 at the time of his trial. Since then, some of the mentally retarded offenders who have been executed include Morris Mason (Virginia: IQ of 66), Jerome Bowden (Georgia: IQ between 59 and 65), and James Terry Roach (South Carolina: IQ of 70). Mario Marquez, who was executed in Texas in 1995, had an IQ of 65 and was characterized as having the social skills of a 7-year-old (Death Penalty Information Center 2004). Ricky Ray Rector essentially lobotomized himself when he shot himself in the head in 1981 after first killing an Arkansas police officer. As he was being led to the execution chamber he was said to have asked a guard to save his pie and that he would have it later. Since 1977 there have been some 34 executions where there was evidence of the mental retardation of the condemned. In none of these cases did either the state or the U.S. Supreme Court stop the execution out of concern about the constitutionality of the death penalty for the mentally retarded.

Over time, some 18 states, as a matter of state law, have not allowed the execution of the mentally retarded (Arizona, Arkansas, Colorado, Connecticut, Florida, Georgia, Indiana, Kansas, Kentucky, Maryland, Missouri, Nebraska, New Mexico, New York, North Carolina, South Dakota, Tennessee, and Washington, plus the federal government). The issue of executing the mentally retarded as a violation of the Eighth Amendment to the U.S. Constitution, however, was not formally considered by the Supreme Court until *Penry v. Lynaugh* (109 S. Ct. 2934, 1989).

Johnny Paul Penry was convicted and sentenced to death in Texas for the rape and murder of Pamela Carpenter in 1979. Before his trial, Penry was examined for mental competency by a clinical psychologist, who testified that Penry was mentally retarded, with an IQ that measured in the mid-50s. The psychologist testified that Penry had the mental capacity of a child 6½ years of age and the social maturity of a 9- or 10-year-old. In spite of this, Penry was deemed to be mentally competent to stand trial, was convicted by a Texas jury, and was sentenced to death. The Texas Court of Criminal Appeals reviewed Penry's death sentence and found no fault with it, concluding that his mental retardation did not automatically preclude him from being put to death.

> ## Box 5.2
> ## Executing the Mentally Retarded: The Case of Earl Washington, Jr.
>
> Earl Washington, Jr. was convicted and sentenced to death in Virginia for the 1982 rape and murder of a 19-year-old girl. Before Rebecca Lynn Williams died of multiple stab wounds, she told a neighbor who came to her assistance that she was assaulted by a black male. A year after the still-unsolved murder, Earl Washington, who had an estimated IQ of 69 (with the intelligence of a 10-year-old) was arrested by police on an unrelated charge. While in police custody, Washington "confessed" to five different crimes. In four of the cases Washington's knowledge of the facts were so contrary to actual events that the state viewed them as completely unreliable and the result of Washington's desire to please interrogating police officers. The fifth of these "confessions" was the killing of Rebecca Williams. The problem with the confession, however, was that Washington said that Rebecca Williams was black (she was white), that she was short (Williams was 5'8" tall), and that he stabbed her "once or twice" (Williams was stabbed an estimated 38 times). The verbal confession was written up and was virtually the only evidence used in court to convict Washington of the murder of Rebecca Williams.
>
> Earl Washington was scheduled for execution on September 5, 1985. In their petition to Virginia Governor Douglas Wilder, Washington's lawyers included DNA evidence first compiled by the state which indicated that Washington was likely *not* the one who sexually assaulted Ms. Williams. Rather than pardon Washington, however, Governor Wilder commuted his sentence to life imprisonment. At this point, Washington had already spent more than nine years on Virginia's death row. Washington's lawyers persisted in their plea for his innocence. They petitioned the new Virginia governor, James Gilmore, for more sophisticated DNA testing. After much delay, Governor Gilmore authorized the testing. The DNA tests exonerated Washington, and he was given a full pardon on October 2, 2000. Earl Washington was finally released from prison on February 12, 2001. On May 5, 2006 a federal jury ruled that a Virginia State Police investigator deliberately falsified Earl Washington's confession, and it awarded Washington $2.25 million. Washington spent some 18 years in prison, more than nine on death row, and at one point he'd come within nine days of being executed (see Freedman 2001). ✦

When his case was appealed to the U.S. Supreme Court, the Court decided that the execution of the mentally retarded was not outright forbidden by the Eighth Amendment's prohibition against cruel and unusual punishment.[7] Rather than create a general rule stating that no one who is mentally retarded can be executed, the Court held that the fact of mental retardation and diminished mental capacity in general should be treated as simply one of the mitigating circumstances presented during the sentencing phase of a capital trial. It did overturn Penry's own death sentence, however, because it felt the instructions to the jury in his case did not allow them to give proper weight and consideration to his mental disabilities. Penry was sentenced to death a second time, but this death sentence, too, was overturned by the Supreme Court. A third Texas jury was also not convinced that he was mentally retarded and sentenced Penry to death, but in October 2005 this death sentence was overturned by the Texas Court of Criminal Appeals.

The Court reexamined the issue of the execution of the mentally retarded in 2002 in the case of *Atkins v. Virginia* (536 U.S. 304, 2002). This would be the third case that involved the execution of the mentally retarded, indicating the

Court's desire to reexamine the issue after its initial decision in *Penry*. As stated above, the Court revisited Penry's case but overturned his death sentence on the grounds of faulty jury instructions. The Court also agreed to hear the case of *McCarver v. North Carolina* (533 U.S. 975, 2001). Ernest McCarver was estimated to have an IQ between 70 and 80 and was just hours away from execution before a stay was granted by the Supreme Court. In September 2001, the Court dismissed this case because North Carolina in the interim had passed legislation prohibiting the execution of the retarded, including McCarver. The Court then accepted the Atkins case.

Daryl Renard Atkins was convicted in Virginia of abduction, armed robbery, and capital murder. At his penalty phase hearing, a forensic psychologist testified that Atkins was "mildly" retarded, with a measured IQ of 59. The jury sentenced Atkins to death. In his appeal to the Virginia Supreme Court, Atkins argued that he could not be sentenced to death because of his mental retardation. Relying on *Penry*, the state supreme court rejected this claim and affirmed Atkins' death sentence. Noting that there have been dramatic legislative changes concerning the execution of the mentally retarded since *Penry*, the U.S. Supreme Court agreed to review the case.

The *Atkins* Court noted that since the *Penry* decision 16 state legislatures and the federal government had moved to prohibit the execution of the mentally retarded, while no state had moved in the opposite direction of lifting a ban on the practice. In addition, the Court noted accumulating scientific evidence suggesting that the mentally retarded have difficulty in accumulating, processing, and understanding information and that such cognitive disabilities makes it difficult for them to both control their impulses and understand the possible consequences of their behavior both to themselves and to others. Because of these considerations, the Court concluded that the mentally retarded lack the moral culpability required for criminal responsibility. Finally, the Court added the argument that other countries of the world had appeared to have all but abandoned the practice of executing the mentally retarded. The Court used this evidence to support its conclusion that American society had evolved to the point where it no longer found the execution of the mentally retarded an acceptable practice and that doing so now violated the Eighth Amendment's prohibition against cruel and unusual punishment. In a nutshell, the Court argued that standards of decency in American society had evolved such that it no longer found acceptable the execution of anyone who is mentally retarded. What the Court avoided in *Penry* then, they did in *Atkins*, creating a general rule that prohibited the execution of the mentally retarded.

The issue of executing the mentally retarded was not, however, completely settled with the *Atkins* case, simply because although the Court did rule out the execution of the mentally retarded it left it up to the states to decide who was mentally retarded and what procedures should exist in making that determination. The Court, then, failed to create a general standard for the states to use in deciding what constitutes mental retardation. It only determined that when someone is indeed certified to be mentally retarded that person cannot be put to death. In subsequent hearings Johnny Paul Penry was found not mentally retarded according to Texas' requirements, and Daryl

Atkins too was found not mentally retarded by Virginia's standards. As we noted, the Texas Court of Criminal Appeals overturned Penry's newest death sentence in October 2005, and in June 2006 the Virginia Supreme Court ordered a new mental retardation hearing for Daryl Atkins.

The Death Penalty for Juveniles

The death penalty has never been reserved for adults only. Although the historical records are far from complete, they indicate that from the mid-1600s until 1929, there were executions of youth as young as 12 and 13 years old (Espy and Smykla 2002). While no one that young has been put to death since 1930, there are examples in the recent past of individuals younger than 17 be-

---

Box 5.3
What Consitutes Mental Retardation According to Capital Punishment Law?

Exactly what mental retardation means and how it is established differs somewhat from state to state. Usually there is a minimum IQ requirement (often 70 or below) that indicates below-average mental functioning. Frequently there is also a requirement that the person indicate deficient functioning in one or more life areas, such as effectively communicating with others or the ability to take care of oneself. There is often a lower age boundary when the manifestations of subnormal IQ and/or social functioning must appear by. Here are a few examples:

From Idaho:
Mentally retarded means significantly subaverage general intellectual functioning that is accompanied by significant limitations in adaptive functioning in at least two (2) of the following skill areas: communication, self-care, home living, social or interpersonal skills, use of community resources, self-direction, functional academic skills, work, leisure, health and safety. The onset of significant subaverage general intelligence functioning and significant limitations in adaptive functioning must occur before age eighteen (18) years. (b) "Significantly subaverage general intellectual functioning" means an intelligence quotient of seventy (70) or below. Idaho Code § 19–2515A

From Virginia:
Mentally retarded means a disability, originating before the age of 18 years, characterized concurrently by (i) significantly subaverage intellectual functioning as demonstrated by performance on a standardized measure of intellectual functioning administered in conformity with accepted professional practice, that is at least two standard deviations below the mean and (ii) significant limitations in adaptive behavior as expressed in conceptual, social and practical adaptive skills. Virginia Code § 19.2–264.3

From Maryland:
An individual who has significantly subaverage intellectual functioning as evidenced by an IQ of 70 or below on an individually administered IQ test, and impairment in adaptive behavior. The age of onset is before the age of 22. Md. Code. Ann. art. 27 Sect.412

From Washington:
The individual has (1) significantly subaverage general intellectual functioning; (2) existing concurrently with deficits in adaptive behavior; and (3) both significantly subaverage general intellectual functioning and deficits in adaptive behavior were manifested during the developmental period. The age of onset is 18 years of age. The required IQ level is 70 or below. Was. Rev. Code Ann. Sect. 10.95.030 ✦

ing executed. For example, James Lewis, Jr. was 15 years old when he was executed by the state of Mississippi on July 23, 1947 (Paternoster 1991). His co-defendant, Charles Trudell, was 16 when he was put to death on the same day (Paternoster 1991). The state of South Carolina executed George Junis Stinney, Jr. on June 16, 1944. Stinney was 14 years old, stood 5'1" tall, and weighed less than 100 pounds (Paternoster 1991). Stinney's case is interesting from a number of angles. He was an African American youth who was arrested for the rape and murder of two white girls in rural South Carolina. His trial began on the morning of April 24 before an all-white jury, and he was convicted of first degree murder and sentenced to death early in the evening of the same day.

Although it was more common in the past, the execution of juveniles has continued in the modern era. From when executions resumed in 1977 until March 2005, seven states executed 22 juveniles (2 percent of the total during this period).[8] All but one of those executed was 17 years old at the time of their crime (the exception was 16 years old), and all were males. At that time 19 states (and the federal government and U.S. military) that had the death penalty did not permit it on juvenile offenders, while 12 states had a combined 71 juveniles on death row.[9] Although only a small number of juveniles have been executed since 1977, there has been a substantial amount of litigation about the constitutionality of the death penalty for juveniles.

In *Thompson v. Oklahoma* (487 U.S. 815, 1988) the Supreme Court in a 5–3 vote[11] had ruled that the execution of a youth who was 15 years old at the time that the crime was committed was cruel and unusual punishment and not permitted by the Constitution. Under the Oklahoma capital statute at the time there was no minimum age for capital punishment, making it theoretically possible for children of any age to be put to death. This feature of the Oklahoma statute was prominent in the reasoning of Justice O'Connor, who voted to join the majority and strike down the statute. If the Eighth Amendment prohibited the execution of those who were 15 years of age, what about those who were 16 or 17 at the time of their crime?

In 1989 there were two cases before the Court involving the execution of juveniles, *Stanford v. Kentucky* and *Wilkins v. Missouri* (492 U.S. 361, 109 S. Ct.). In 1981 Kevin Stanford was convicted of brutally raping and killing 20-year-old gas station attendant Baerbel Poore in Jefferson County, Kentucky. Heath Wilkins was convicted of armed robbery and murder for the killing of Nancy Allen in Avondale, Missouri in 1985. At the time he committed the murder, Stanford was 17 years and 4 months old, eligible for the death penalty under both Kentucky law and the U.S. Constitution per the *Thompson* case. Heath was 16½ at the time of his crime and also eligible for the death penalty by state law and the *Thompson* decision.

Both defendants argued to the Supreme Court that the imposition of the death penalty on those who were juveniles at the time of their offense constitutes cruel and unusual punishment prohibited by the Eighth Amendment. Stanford argued that a juvenile is anyone under the age of 18 at the time of the crime, while Wilkins argued that the bar is for those who are under the age of 17 at the time of their offense. Notice something important about these cases.

Under a "fixed" definition of the Eighth Amendment, neither Stanford nor Wilkins would be able to claim that their execution imposed a cruel and unusual punishment. That is because at the time the framers wrote the Eighth Amendment to the Constitution, the execution of those who were 16 or 17 years old at the time of their offense was not uncommon. What Stanford and Wilkins had to argue was that American society had culturally progressed (appeal to the "evolving standards of decency that mark the progress of a maturing society") to the point that it no longer found the execution of 16- and 17-year-old murderers morally acceptable.

Stanford and Wilkins made exactly that plea, arguing among other points that many states declined to impose the death penalty among those aged 16 or 17 and that even among those states that permit it, most do not actually impose it on youths that young. A majority of the Court was not convinced, however, and in a 5–4 decision it upheld the execution of those who are 16 or 17 years of age at the time of their crime.

At least at that time, then, states were not permitted to put to death someone who was 15 years of age but could do so for anyone at least 16 years old at the time of their crime. Kevin Stanford made a final appeal to the Supreme Court, arguing that the death penalty for juveniles is unconstitutional. In *In re Stanford* (537 U.S. 968, 2002), the Court refused to hear the case, leaving Stanford's pending execution intact. The decision not to hear the case was met with a strong dissent by Justice John Paul Stevens (joined by Justices Breyer, Ginsburg, and Souter), who served notice that he was more than ready to declare the execution of juveniles unconstitutional:

> The practice of executing such offenders is a relic of the past and is inconsistent with evolving standards of decency in a civilized society. We should put an end to this shameful practice. (at p. 6)

The dissent in *Stanford* clearly would indicate that by 2002 there were four justices who were ready to reexamine the issue of the constitutionality of the death penalty for juveniles (and seemingly ready to strike it down). As for Kevin Stanford, he would not be executed. On December 8, 2003 the Governor of Kentucky granted him clemency, sentencing him to a term of life in prison without parole.

Soon after *Stanford*, the movement toward the abolition of the death penalty for juveniles reached a conclusion, and the route taken was similar to that involved in the execution of the mentally retarded. In March 2005 the Supreme Court decided the case of *Roper v. Simmons* (125 C. Ct. 1183). The case involved a Missouri youth, Christopher Simmons, who was 17 at the time he committed a murder/armed robbery for which he was subsequently sentenced to death. The killing could only be described as a cruel and brutal cold-blooded murder. Simmons discussed the fact that he wanted to kill someone with two younger friends, and stated that they could get away with it because they were juveniles. At 2 A.M., Simmons and one of these friends broke into a woman's home, bound her with duct tape and took her from her home. They drove her to a state park where the two reinforced the tape bindings and threw the woman from a railroad bridge into a river below, where she drowned. The next day

Simmons bragged that he had killed a woman because "the bitch seen my face" (*Roper v. Simmons*, at p. 1188). Simmons was tried as an adult, convicted, and sentenced to death. On his initial appeal, the Missouri Supreme Court affirmed both the conviction and death sentence.

Subsequent to the Missouri Supreme Court's decision, the U.S. Supreme Court ruled in the *Atkins v. Virginia* case that the Eighth Amendment prohibited the execution of the mentally retarded because objective indicators (states moving away from the practice either by banning the execution of the mentally retarded outright or doing it sparingly) indicated that standards of decency had evolved to the point that it was no longer acceptable. With this as guidance, Simmons' attorneys filed a new appeal arguing that the logic of *Atkins* in prohibiting the execution of the mentally retarded applied to the execution of juveniles: Society no longer finds the execution of juveniles acceptable, as evidenced by the fact that most states now prohibited it. The Missouri Supreme Court agreed and overturned Simmons' death sentence and sentenced him to life without parole. On appeal by the attorney general of Missouri, the U.S. Supreme Court agreed to review this conclusion of the Missouri Supreme Court.

Similar to what it did in *Atkins*, the Court in *Roper* examined objective evidence to shed light on the issue of whether prevailing moral standards were compatible with the execution of those who were under the age of 18 at the time of their crime. Writing for the Court, Justice Kennedy concluded that the evidence suggested that most states do not tolerate the death penalty for juveniles: 30 states prohibit the execution of juveniles (12 states that are abolitionist and 18 that exclude juvenile executions by law); those states that do permit the execution of juveniles do so infrequently (since *Stanford* was decided only six states had executed juveniles, and in the past 10 years only three states); and no state that in the past has forbidden the execution of juveniles has reinstated it. The Court also examined the available medical/psychological evidence and concluded that these data seem to indicate that those under the age of 18 are cognitively immature and are significantly more rash and impulsive in their behavior and less likely to appreciate the consequences of their actions than adults. The Court also noted that in allowing the death penalty for juveniles the United States was out of step with other democratic and progressive countries of the world that have almost without exception rejected it. Taking all of these things in consideration, the Supreme Court in *Simmons* declared that the execution of anyone under the age of 18 at the time of their crime is cruel and unusual punishment and is in violation of the U.S. Constitution.

The Death Penalty for the Mentally Ill

One of the basic precepts of American justice is that offenders must be morally cognizant beings. They must be mentally able to appreciate that their conduct was against the law and be able to control that conduct. If they are not, then various determinations of "not guilty by reason of insanity" are made. A person found not guilty by reason of insanity is not judged to be "innocent" but is not guilty of a criminal offense because he or she lacks the moral culpability necessary to assign responsibility as a result of mental illness. What about someone who may have been completely sane at the time of the crime and trial but who subsequently became mentally ill before the time of execution? Can and should that person still be executed?

Another basic precept of our justice system is that those who are to be punished must be mentally cognizant of the reasons they are being punished. Having the mental capacity to appreciate their punishment is part of the notion of full moral culpability—someone who is unaware of why he or she is being punished lacks culpability. Based on this notion of full culpability, therefore, it would seem that capital offenders who are mentally ill at the time of their execution cannot be put to death. To execute someone with a diminished capacity to appreciate the reasons for his or her punishment would seem to deny the person's human dignity and thus constitute cruel and unusual punishment.

The issue of the execution of the mentally ill came to the attention of the Supreme Court in 1986 in the case of *Ford v. Wainwright* (477 U.S. 399, 1986). Alvin Ford was convicted of capital murder in Florida in 1974 and sentenced to death. During his more than 10 years on Florida's death row, however, his mental condition substantially deteriorated. He began to exhibit bizarre behavior, was delusional, and had feelings of persecution. By 1983 his delusions became so acute that he referred to himself as Pope John Paul III and believed that his friends and family were being held captive in the prison with him. When interviewed by a psychiatrist, Ford understood what the death penalty was but did not think that he could be executed because he believed that he owned the prison and controlled the governor of Florida through mental telepathy. Subsequent to this, Ford's speech became almost completely incomprehensible, using a code-like language.

Before his execution, Ford was examined by a panel of three psychiatrists appointed by the governor. After examining him for 25 minutes, each agreed that Ford was sane enough to be put to death. The governor therefore signed Ford's death warrant and an execution date was set. Ford's counsel sought a stay of his execution and an evidentiary hearing on the issue of whether the execution of the mentally ill violates the Eighth Amendment's prohibition against cruel and unusual punishment. Writing for a majority of the Court in the case, Justice Thurgood Marshall argued that executing the insane is an affront to human dignity and humanity and would further no legitimate state interest such as deterrence or retribution. As a result, the *Ford* opinion held that the Eighth Amendment's prohibition against cruel and unusual punishment precludes the state from executing an insane prisoner.

In his concurring opinion to the *Ford* decision, Justice Powell argued that the state of Florida did have a legitimate interest in executing a sane Alvin Ford and that "my point is only that if petitioner [Ford] is cured of his disease, the state is free to execute him." Justice Powell raised the interesting question of whether a state could medicate an insane inmate until he no longer manifested symptoms of insanity only to then execute him. This issue did come before the Court in *Perry v. Louisiana*, 498 U.S. 1075 (1990), but it sent the case back to Louisiana without resolving the question. The Louisiana Supreme Court, however, found compelling reason within its own constitution not to forcibly medicate a prisoner only to then execute him. Other states, such as Maryland

and South Carolina, soon adopted the Louisiana practice of not medicating mentally ill death row prisoners solely to execute them.

The Supreme Court of Arkansas, however, had a different view. Charles Singleton became mentally ill during his 24 years on Arkansas' death row and was incompetent to be executed under the *Ford* standard. Singleton was frequently treated for mental illness while on death row, sometimes voluntarily taking his medications, other times refusing. In 1997 he refused taking any more medications. After he was forced to take the drugs, Singleton's psychotic episodes were reduced and he was declared competent to be put to death. Both the Arkansas Supreme Court and a sharply divided full Eighth Circuit Federal Court of Appeals decided in favor of the state's desire to put Singleton to death. The logic of the decision was that the State of Arkansas was not medicating Singleton only for the purpose of remedying his disability so that he could be executed but that its intent was only to treat him, which had the inevitable consequence of making him competent to be executed. In a previous case, *Washington v. Harper* (494 U.S. 210, 1990), the Supreme Court had permitted the involuntary medication of mentally ill prisoners. The *Harper* case permitted forced medication when the prisoner is thought to constitute a danger to himself or to others or if the treatment is in the prisoner's own best interests. It did not, however, deal with the specific issue of whether a death row prisoner could be medicated back to mental health only to be executed. The Supreme Court refused to hear the Singleton case, and on January 6, 2004 Charles Singleton was put to death by lethal injection.

Chapter Summary

The *Furman* decision in 1972 emptied death rows across the United States and effectively struck down all existing capital statutes. The response, at least by a handful of state legislatures, was swift—new death penalty laws were passed that were hoped to be compliant with the requirements of *Furman*. Since the central defect of capital statutes identified in the *Furman* plurality was the existence of too-little-structured capital sentencing discretion, state legislative reforms of death penalty statutes tried to address this. One solution was to draw up narrowly defined categories of capital murder and make a sentence of death mandatory upon conviction of these special definitions of murder. Sentencing discretion would be handled in these "mandatory" statutes by essentially taking it away from the jury. A second solution was to continue to give the capital jury sentencing discretion but to guide or structure that discretion. These "guided discretion" statutes sought to minimize the abuses of sentencing discretion by providing the jury with lists of aggravating or mitigating factors that they were required to consider before imposing sentence.

In its review of these two types of reforms, the Supreme Court concluded that guided discretion statutes were constitutionally permissible (even in diverse form), while mandatory statutes were not. The reason mandatory capital statutes were unconstitutional, the Court said, is that they do not allow the sentencing body to fully consider all of the factors that make up the suspect's culpability—"the diverse frailties of humankind." There were two outcomes of these Supreme Court decisions in July 1976: (1) states were permitted to execute offenders again, and (2) the Court got into the business of monitoring state capital trials.

While the death penalty is constitutional today, there have been some attempts to restrict its imposition. The Supreme Court has now ruled that capital punishment is unconstitutional for those who were under the age of 18 at the time of their offense. It has also prohibited the execution of mentally retarded offenders and those who are so mentally ill that they cannot understand their impending death and its reasons. At the moment, however, the Court has not forbidden states from forcibly medicating insane prisoners until they are no longer mentally ill and then executing them.

Discussion Questions

1. What do you think the arguments would be against providing psychiatric medication to a mentally ill inmate only to "cure" him enough to be executed? What compelling state interests would there be in favor of such a practice?

2. If it is agreed that forcibly medicating a prisoner sometimes might be in his or her "best interest" (say, during a stay of execution), would it ever be in the person's "best interest" to medicate him or her in order to be mentally competent enough to be executed?

3. Do you agree with the U.S. Supreme Court's conclusion in the *Woodson* and *Roberts* cases that mandatory death penalty statutes should be forbidden? Why or why not?

4. How easy do you think it is to make a prediction of "future dangerousness"? What information do you think goes into making this determination, and how reliable is this information? With this kind of prediction, how would you know if you were wrong?

5. What evidence could you point to in order to make an argument today that the death penalty is unconstitutional because it is no longer thought to be an acceptable punishment under the "evolving standards of decency" standard of the Eighth Amendment? What evidence would you point to if you had to refute that claim?

6. Do you think there should be a general rule against the execution of juveniles, or should the issue be argued on a case-by-case basis? What are the arguments in favor of and against each approach?

7. In the *Roper v. Simmons* case, the Court alluded to the fact that many other countries have forbidden the execution of juveniles. Do you think that international law should influence death penalty practices in the United States? Why or why not?

8. In the *Gregg* cases the Supreme Court seemed to argue that death sentences had to be both consistent and individualized. Do you think there might be an inherent incompatibility between these two principles? That is, as a state tries to make its death sentences more consistent, it

starts to infringe on the necessity to provide an individualized assessment of each defendant's unique culpability.

Student Resources

A good book detailing the events of Johnny Paul Penry and the issue of mental retardation and the death penalty can be found in *The Penry Penalty: Capital Punishment and Offenders With Mental Retardation* by Emily Fabrycki (1993). For a comparable review of the issues surrounding juveniles and the death penalty, see Victor L. Streib's *Death Penalty for Juveniles* (1987). For those interested in more nuanced legal issues pertaining to the death penalty, a good source is Victor L. Streib's *Death Penalty in a Nutshell* (2005). For a good source of information on the execution of the mentally ill, see Miller and Radelet's *Executing the Mentally Ill: The Criminal Justice System and the Case of Alvin Ford*.

Endnotes

1. Even upon a conviction of a capital crime, a case may not necessarily be advanced to a penalty phase hearing. Prosecutors have the discretion not to move a case to the penalty phase if, for instance, they think they would not be able to get a death sentence from the jury.

2. While it approved of each of these three features of post-*Furman* capital statutes, the Court did not unequivocally state that any of them was required. In addition, since it approved the statutes of Georgia, Florida, and Texas that were fairly different, it was not at all clear exactly what was required for a constitutional statute except that it could not be mandatory. Weisberg (1984) probably best stated the ambiguity remaining in the wake of the *Gregg* decision: "One can say little with certainty about *Gregg v. Georgia* except that it makes a great many things constitutionally significant, but it makes nothing either constitutionally necessary or clearly constitutionally sufficient" (p. 322).

3. In writing the plurality opinion approving the Georgia statute, Justice Stewart concluded that:

   . . . the concerns expressed in *Furman* that the penalty of death not be imposed in an arbitrary or capricious manner can be met by a carefully drafted statute that ensures that the sentencing authority is given adequate information and guidance. As a general proposition these concerns are best met by a system that provides for a bifurcated proceeding at which the sentencing authority is apprised of the information relevant to the imposition of sentence and provided with standards to guide its use of the information. . . . As an important additional safeguard against arbitrariness and caprice, the Georgia statutory scheme provides for automatic appeal of all death sentences to the State's Supreme Court. (*Gregg v. Georgia*, pp. 195, 198)

   In fact, Justice Stewart was positively giddy about the procedural importance of capital sentencing standards (statutory aggravating and mitigating circumstances), noting that "[i]t is quite simply a hallmark of our legal system that juries be carefully and adequately guided in their deliberations" (*Gregg v. Georgia*, p. 193). He wrote this without commenting on the apparent contradiction between this position and the fact that he concurred with Justice Harlan's view just five years previous in *McGautha v. California* that standards for capital juries to follow were "beyond present human ability" (*McGautha v. California*, p. 204).

4. The Georgia statute requires that the state supreme court review each death sentence imposed by the trial court and determine:

   a. Whether the sentence of death was imposed under the influence of passion, prejudice, or any other arbitrary factor,

   b. Whether, in cases other than treason or aircraft hijacking, the evidence supports the jury's or judge's finding of a statutory aggravating circumstance, and

   c. Whether the sentence of death is excessive or disproportionate to the penalty imposed in similar cases, considering both the crime and the defendant. (Ga. Code. Ann. Sec. 27-2537, Supp. 1975)

5. Unlike in Georgia, the Florida statute did not specify exactly what the Florida Supreme Court should consider when it reviewed each death sentence. In its own case law, however, the Florida Supreme Court had already defined its reviewing function as including some type of comparative case review similar to that required of the Georgia Supreme Court. In *State v. Dixon* (283 So. 2d 1, 10, 1973) the Florida Supreme Court said that it would review a particular death sentence "in light of the other decisions and determine whether or not the punishment is too great."

6. In 1984 the Supreme Court would rule that the Eighth Amendment does not require proportionality review—a comparison of the sentences received among alike cases (*Pulley v. Harris*, U.S. 37 S. CT. 871, 79 L.Ed. 2d 29, 1984).

7. At the time of the *Penry* decision, only two states, Georgia and Maryland, did not by law permit the execution of the mentally retarded.

8. The states that executed juveniles between 1976 and 2005 and the number they executed are: Texas (13), Virginia (3), Oklahoma (2), South Carolina (1), Missouri (1), Florida (1), and Georgia (1). Source: Death Penalty Information Center (2005).

9. The states that had juveniles on death row as of March 2005 (and the number on death row) are: Alabama (13), Arizona (4), Florida (3), Georgia (2), Louisiana (4), Mississippi (5), Nevada (1), North Carolina (4) Pennsylvania (2), South Carolina (3), Texas (29), and Virginia (1). Source: Death Penalty Information Center (2005).

10. Justice Kennedy did not participate in the case, so there were only eight voting justices. ✦

Chapter 6

Common Justifications for the Death Penalty

In June 1991 and again in May 2003, the Gallup Organization took a public opinion poll of American attitudes toward the death penalty. Those who had stated that they generally favored the death penalty for individuals who had been convicted of murder were asked to give the reason they favored capital punishment in such cases. At each time period, the four most popular stated justifications for favoring the death penalty were (1) moral grounds—those who committed murder deserved to die because it fits the crime; (2) cost—it would save taxpayer money because it is cheaper than the alternative punishment of life imprisonment; (3) general deterrence—the threat of being executed keeps would-be murderers from committing their crime; and (4) prevention or selective incapacitation—it prevents those who have committed murder from ever killing again.

While there were other stated reasons that people supported capital punishment (biblical reasons, benefiting the family members of victims, because people cannot be rehabilitated), we think that these four are not only the most often articulated reasons but also the most compelling. In this chapter, therefore, we examine each of these justifications for the death penalty in an effort to understand why capital punishment continues to be part of the American experience of criminal justice. While we cannot provide a comprehensive treatment of religious views about the death penalty, we will conclude this chapter with a brief description of various religious perspectives on capital punishment.

Retribution: The Moral Argument for the Death Penalty

The most frequent and perhaps one of the most compelling reasons that some people think the death penalty should exist as a punishment is that they believe some offenses or offenders to be so egregious and the harm done to victims so great that the only morally fitting punishment is for the offender's own life to be taken away. In other words, capital punishment should be inflicted on some offenders because, by their own actions, they in some moral sense "deserve it." Before discussing the details of this position we think it best to narrow the discussion to the idea that death may be a deserved punishment for an offender *who has committed murder*. Although in our not too distant past death had been a permitted penalty for crimes that did not involve a homicide—kidnapping, armed robbery, and rape, for instance—we think this narrowing of the topic under discussion to murder is important for two reasons.

First, we think the most compelling philosophical argument that can be advanced that death is a morally deserved punishment is made when the offense involves the deliberate taking of the victim's life. In addition to offenses not involving a killing, this restriction would also exclude from consideration nonintentional homicides (accidents, manslaughter). The second reason is more practical. Virtually the only capital crimes today are offenses where the victim's life has been taken.[1] Although others were permitted in the past, the Supreme Court has held that the penalty of death may not be imposed in cases of the rape of an *adult* woman (*Coker v. Georgia*, 433 U.S. 584, 1977),[2] for kidnapping (*Eberheart v. Georgia*, 433 U. S. 917, 1977), or, if a murder did occur, the offender did not take, attempt to take, or intend to take the life of the victim (*Enmund v. Florida*, 458 U.S. 782, 1982).[3] For the most part, then, when people speak about an offender morally "deserving"the death penalty, they usually mean it within the context of an appropriate punishment for murder.

The argument that someone who has committed murder deserves to have his or her life taken is grounded in the philosophy of retributivism. The retributivist view of capital punishment is a nonutilitarian position. Murderers should be put to death not because it would prevent them from killing again (incapacitation), or because the fear of capital punishment would prevent someone else from committing murder (general deterrence), but simply because it is morally required. In other words, execution is the morally appropriate punishment for murder even if it prevented no other murders from taking place (and presumably even if it caused additional murders by setting the example that killing another is appropriate). Retribution does not demand that some "good" be produced from punishment other than the righting of a moral wrong. Retribution would require the punishment of someone who killed his rich aunt in order to get her fortune, even if he had no other rich aunt to kill and would not do it again, and even if because of his newfound fortune he would not commit any other crime but rather would do much good.

Kantian Retribution

The retributive position on punishment was probably most fully developed by the German philosopher Immanuel Kant (1724–1804). According to Kant, life in the state of nature (a state without government or civil authority) is precarious because we are constantly in personal danger and in danger of having our property taken. Freedom and security are advanced in civil society because, while we cannot do anything we please (we must obey the laws like everyone else), our life and property are protected (because others must also obey the laws and cannot, therefore, do anything they please). The price of having myself and my property protected is that I am under the moral obligation not to hurt others or take their property. If I do hurt another—say, by killing him—I have taken an unfair moral advantage because I receive the protection of the laws but do not give up any of my own freedom in exchange. Although I have not sacrificed my freedom (by not killing), I have made another type of sacrifice by being responsible for my action and acknowledging that because of this I should be punished for my transgression.

Punishment by civil society, therefore, is a debt that the offender both owes and consents to. In fact, we honor the dignity of the criminal in punishing him, because in punishing him we acknowledge his capacity to choose and his responsibility for his own action. Notice that in the retributive theory, punishment serves no utilitarian purpose—we do not punish to reduce crime, we punish because it is morally right to do so, even if there are no instrumental "gains" in doing it. This is required because, according to Kant, to treat human beings as a means to an end, even criminals, dishonors both their dignity and ours, and using some people (offenders) to lower the amount of crime for others is wrong. Kant's Categorical Imperative states that all human beings have dignity and that this dignity requires that they never be used as a means to another end.

While Kant's position provides us with an understanding of the *jus talionis*, or the right of retaliation, what we do not know is how much the state may punish. In understanding the amount of harm the state may inflict for the harm done by a criminal offense, Kant (1797) refers to the principle of equality and the metaphor of the scale of justice:

> What kind and what degree of punishment does public legal justice adopt as its principle and standard? None other than the principle of equality (illustrated by the pointers on the scales of justice), that is, the principle of not treating one side more favorably than the other. Accordingly, any undeserved evil that you inflict on someone else among the people is one that you do to yourself. (pp. 101–102)

The principle of equality requires that the offender be punished in an amount that is exactly proportional to the harm done by his crime. The pointer of the scale of justice cannot be allowed to tip in favor either of civil society, when too much pain is inflicted on the offender, or the offender himself, when he receives less than the harm he has inflicted on civil society. What this implies is that although civil society has the right to punish under the principle of *jus talionis*, there are moral limits on the amount that it can punish. The right to punish is, therefore, not an unlimited or unrestrained right.

Guided by the general principle of equality, how do we determine how much to punish or how much harm to inflict on an offender who has committed a crime against civil society and therefore himself? For many crimes, finding the amount of punishment that will balance the scales of justice and undo the moral wrong is difficult. With respect to the offense of murder, however, Kant (1797) is very clear that the only morally permissible punishment for murder is that the offender's own life be taken:

> If, however, he has committed a murder, he must die. In this case, there is no substitute that will satisfy the requirements of legal justice. There is no sameness of kind between death and remaining alive even under the most miserable conditions, and consequently there is also no equality between the crime and the retribution unless the criminal is judicially put to death. (p. 101)

Kant argues that murderers cannot live even under penal servitude because that is not the same as death. Only the death of the offender will remove the moral advantage taken by the murderer against his victim. The treatment of the murderer is a strict "eye for an eye, a tooth for a tooth, an arm for an arm, a life for a life" equality, what the philosopher Stephen Nathanson (1987, 2001) calls "payback" retribution: Criminals must be directly and precisely paid back for the moral wrong they have done. When the murderer is put to death by the state, justice is served (and is only then served), the moral advantage taken by the murderer is undone, and the scales of justice are rebalanced. Any other punishment for murder will not suffice.

It is important at this point to understand two things about Kantian retribution. First, while the notion of equality may require the murderer to be executed by the state, there are limits on capital punishment. For example, would retribution require that an offender who tortured his victim before killing be required to be tortured? We do not think so. In the passage from Kant quoted above, he immediately states that the murderer's death "must be kept free from all maltreatment that would make the humanity suffering in his person loathsome or abominable." Kant argues that the murderer who tortured (or raped, or bound and gagged) his victim should not be subjected to exactly the same harm. To do so, he states, would be to fail to treat the offender with dignity, and civil society would be brought down on the same odious level as the offender. The principle of human dignity, therefore, puts a limit on how an execution can be carried out. While we do not know exactly what Kant's directive demands, we do think that the admonition that the offender be "kept free from all maltreatment" would include things like torturing the offender or any other physical/psychological injury before putting the person to death.

Second, and more important, retribution is not the same thing as revenge or vengeance, nor should retributive punishment be justified on the utilitarian grounds that it serves to limit, channel, or give expression to revenge. Revenge is motivated by anger and is the desire that a private person has to inflict injury on another for real or imagined harm. For example, if someone kills a member of our family, we may want to strike the offender down by our own hands—to "give him what he has coming" or exact revenge. This action is not the same as retribution for several reasons. First, retribution is not a private act but an act on behalf of a civil society. In other words, the injury that retribution seeks to right is a harm committed against society and not any given individual. Just as civil society is injured and not an individual, it is civil society that responds to that harm through social institutions such as state-sponsored punishment. Retribution, therefore, is a function of civil society or government. Vengeance or revenge, on the other hand, is a private act of retaliation; it is an attempt to right a wrong committed against an individual by an individual.

A second and important difference between retribution and revenge is that retribution is limited by a principle of equality or proportionality that does not restrict vengeance. While civil society has a right to punish those who break its laws, it cannot inflict whatever amount of punishment it wants; retribution demands that the moral scales be balanced, implying a symmetry or proportionality between the harm done by the crime and the punishment inflicted by the sovereign. There is nothing that puts a limit on revenge, however. If someone verbally assaults my grandparents, I may extract my revenge by physically assaulting the one who insulted them. I may respond to a physical assault by killing the perpetrator. Revenge knows no limits except those placed on his actions by the avenging party.

A third difference between vengeance and retribution is that not only are there limits on the amount of punishment that may be inflicted on the offender in retribution, punishment or harm may be visited on the offender and only the offender; the state may not inflict harm on anyone else. While the state may rightfully punish an offender, because he has personal responsibility for his actions, it may not punish his family members or acquaintances. There is no such limited target in revenge. I may avenge a dishonor or harm not only by inflicting injury on the perpetrator but on any other target I deem suitable—the perpetrator's spouse, children, family, and friends. In a nutshell, vengeance or revenge is a private act that knows no limit on the amount that can be punished or the appropriate target of the punishment.

Berns' Argument

A number of moral and legal philosophers today have created retributive justifications for punishment that are compatible with the death penalty. The political philosopher Walter Berns (1979, 1991) argues a retributivist position similar to Kant's. Berns begins with the notion that human societies are moral communities whose members enjoy certain privileges and have a consequent duty to obey laws that make those privileges possible. People who break the law injure not only their victims, but all of society—the offense is against the community and its social and moral fabric (Berns 1979): "[T]he criminal . . . has injured not merely his immediate victim but the community as such . . . [h]e has called into question the very possibility of that community by suggesting that men cannot be trusted freely to respect the property, the person, and the dignity of those with whom they are associated" (p. 155). What punishment does is to reaffirm the moral community and give expression to the fact that crimes are violations of the moral fabric. Berns (1979) argues that the violation of the moral order is particularly acute in the case of murder and must be responded to with the full moral indignation of the community through the execution of the offender:

> Capital punishment serves to remind us of the majesty of the moral order that is embodied in our law and of the terrible consequences of its breach. . . .
> The criminal law must be made awful, by which I mean, awe-inspiring, or commanding profound respect or reverential fear. It must remind us of the moral order by which alone we can live as human beings, and in our day the only punishment that can do this is capital punishment. (pp. 172–173)

To a retributivist like Berns, then, because the offense of murder is the most serious harm that an offender can inflict on society, society has the obligation to reply in kind, with the most serious punishment at its disposal. The only way that the sanctity of life can be upheld, Berns (1980) argues, is by inflicting the death penalty on offenders who murder: "If human life is to be held in awe, the law forbidding the taking of it must be held in awe; and the only way it can be made awful or awe inspiring is to entitle it to inflict the penalty of death" (p. 509).

Van den Haag's Argument

Another proponent of a retributivist view of the death penalty is the late legal philosopher Ernest van den Haag (1975, 1978, 1985, 2003; van den Haag and Conrad 1983), who has written extensively about the death penalty. Van den Haag's (1983) argument in favor of capital punishment is very Kantian. He argues that the state has the right to punish in the first place because the offender in committing a crime has taken an unfair moral advantage over those who comply with the law:

> The desire to see crime punished is felt by noncriminals because they see that the criminal has pursued his interests or gratified his desires by means they, the noncriminals, have restrained themselves from using for the sake of the law and in fear of its punishments . . . the offender, unlike the nonoffender, did not play by the legal rules and took advantage of those who did. He must be deprived of his illicit advantage if others are to continue to play by the rules. His advantage must be nullified in the minds of nonoffenders by the punishment the offender suffers. (p. 30)

In terms of determining how much punishment offenders deserve, van den Haag acknowledges that it is frequently difficult in practice to comply with the principle of equality because it is hard to make the punishment fit the crime exactly. It is not possible, he concedes, to take the property from those who steal from us (they likely have little) or to rape those who have committed sexual assault. He argues (1983) that the offense of murder, however, is one where the principle of an "eye for an eye" can be nearly duplicated and should be: "[T]he *lex talionis* cannot be literally applied . . . [S]till for some crimes we can do something of the kind . . . [T]hus we may fine those whose crimes are pecuniary and execute those who murder" (p. 33). Murderers deserve the death penalty, according to van den Haag, because by violating the sense of security in a peaceful community and fostering anxiety murder is the worst crime that can be committed.

Van den Haag argues that in executing those who kill, society is reaffirming its own belief in the sanctity and importance of life and that death by execution may not at times be enough punishment because a murder harms the entire community and not just the victim. Given this focus on the "total gravity of the crime—the total injury done to the social fabric" (1985, 167), and the fact that the harm visited on the individual victim was undeserved, harm imposed on the offender must be greater than the harm or pain he has inflicted:

> If my neighbor is burglarized or robbed he is harmed. But we all must take costly precautions, and we all feel and are threatened: crime harms society as it harms victims. Hence, punishment must, whenever possible, impose pain believed to exceed the pain suffered by the individual victim of crime. (p. 167)

Other Retributivist Views

More recently, other proponents of the death penalty have appealed to similar kinds of arguments in providing a retributive justification for the death penalty. Pojman (2004), for example, asserts that some kinds of crime are so malicious (he cites the serial killings by Jeffrey Dahmer and Ted Bundy) that their perpetrators "deserve nothing less than capital punishment" (p. 56). Failure to respond in kind to those who murder, he warns, invites citizens to take the law into their own hands, thus encouraging vigilante justice. What proportional retribution does, therefore, is to affirm social order.

Judge Paul Cassell (2004) argues for a similar position. He notes that we can never really objectively verify that the death penalty is proportionate to the crime of murder—that is a moral position and "reasonable people might disagree about what constitutes fair and just punishment in particular cases" (p. 199). He does argue, however, that most state legislatures have approved capital statutes, and juries of 12 citizens do impose the death penalty on certain offenders, and we must presume that they have deemed it the morally appropriate penalty. In imposing death for the most serious crimes, Cassell argues that society is asserting the moral principle that the offender should get his just deserts and is indicating its moral condemnation of an act that not only harms individuals but threatens the safety of all, and the bonds of trust that help create social order.

Those who would argue for a retributivist justification for the death penalty make a compelling case. Confronted with the sometimes unspeakable horror that offenders inflict on their murder victims, it is difficult to argue in good faith that there are not some offenders who by their actions have in some sense forfeited their right to live with the rest of us in the human community. The retributive view is the simple one that some murders are so unconscionable, so horrific, that society must condemn them by taking the life of the offender away. As we saw in the introduction to this chapter, this uncomplicated moral view of the death penalty is supported by a large proportion of the American public and is the most frequently given reason among those who support capital punishment. The retributive justification for capital punishment does have its appeal, but things may be a little more complicated.

A retributivist view is that society has the right to execute its worst offenders, those who murder. Other philosophical positions, also based on retribution, can be constructed emphasizing that society may have the *right* to impose capital punishment but it does not have the *duty* to. That is, society does not have to impose the death penalty even though it may have the right to, that some other penalty short of the execution of the offender could still fit all the requirements of retribution. Critics of capital punishment, who also adopt a retributive view, have argued that to say that someone who has intentionally killed another deserves to be punished, and deserves the most severe punishment that society is willing to impose, is not the same thing as saying that the only punishment that may morally be imposed is death. As philosopher and death penalty opponent Hugo Bedau (2004) has pointed out, "[R]etributive considerations rightly tell us *who* deserves to be punished—it is the guilty. But it does not tell us *what* their punishment ought to be" (p. 41). These critics of the death penalty state that the whole issue of what punishment people should receive is made extremely murky by the fact that strict equality retribution is never exacted—we never destroy the property of those who vandalize, or sexually assault rapists, or beat up those who assault. The common standard for the punishment of these serious crimes is not to replicate the offense and inflict the equivalent harm on the offender but rather to demand that they lose their liberty through prison time. Why, they ask, should we then require that murderers be put to death? No, they argue, while it is clear that retribution demands some punishment be inflicted on those who murder, it is not at all clear what particular punishment must be imposed. It is with regard to what punishment should be visited on murderers that distinguishes equality retributivists who argue for "an eye for an eye" and other retributivists who argue that a sentence other than death can still provide the necessary moral balance to the murder.

Box 6.1
Closure for Victim's Family Members?

Family members of murder victims often argue that the death penalty is necessary for them to feel that justice was done, and in addition that they should be able to view the execution in order to feel "closure." *Closure* refers to a sense of finality—finality in dealing both with a senseless and tragic murder and in years-long effort to see the offender punished. Some states have "right to view" laws that allow family members of a murdered victim the right to attend the execution. Alabama, for example, allows two immediate family members to witness the execution; in Delaware only one adult member of the immediate family is permitted to attend; in Ohio no more than three people designated by the immediate family can attend. If not provided by statute, it is usually up to the prison warden where the execution takes place to determine who may be permitted to attend.

Whether or not an execution or viewing an execution produces a sense of satisfaction or closure is controversial. Some family members report that they did feel a certain sense of "justice" after witnessing the execution of their loved one's killer. Others, however, feel what can only be described as being cheated—that the killer's death provided no relief if only because it seemed an "easy" death compared to what the victim experienced. Vernon Harvey, who witnessed the execution of Robert Lee Willie in Louisiana, remarked that "they should've strapped him in that chair, counted to ten, then at the count of nine taken him out of the chair and let him sit in his cell for a day or two and then strapped him in the chair again. It was too easy for him. It went too quick" (Prejean 1994, 235). ✦

The philosopher Jeffrey Reiman (1985), for example, argues for what he calls "proportional retributivism" and distinguishes it from the "equality retributivism" of people like Kant, Berns, and van den Haag. While equality retributivism matches the principle of an eye for an eye in requiring that the punishment of an offender be in exact and equal measure to the harm the person has committed, proportional retributivism requires that serious crimes be punished only by severe punishments and that the punishment not be so lenient that it trivializes the offense. What proportional retributivism demands, then, is that the worst offenses be punished with the most severe punishment that a society deems morally appropriate, without specifying that the punishment try to replicate the harm done to the offender. In addition, however, is the requirement that the punishment for the worst crimes not trivialize the harm done by the original crime, because the moral scales must be balanced.

Reiman would argue that the execution of the murderer is not the only way that the moral scales can be balanced. He has suggested that in contemporary American society life in prison without the possibility of parole is a serious punishment that inflicts great harm on offenders and is not such an insignificant punishment that it trivializes murder. Critics might ask, "Does sentencing one who murders to life imprisonment even without parole really provide the exact equivalent as what he did to the victim, who lost his or her life?" Life in prison is clearly not an exact equivalent. However, those who argue in favor of a proportional rather than an exact retribution ask whether imprisoning a rapist for 15 or 20 years is really the equivalent harm for someone who terrorized and sexually assaulted another person? No, it is not precisely equivalent harm, Reiman would assert, but it is serious harm, and it is a punishment that is severe enough that it does not demean or do an injustice to the victim. Similarly, a sentence of life without parole is a painful punishment, likely the most painful short of the death or torture of the offender,

Bedau (2004) has also argued against the death penalty from a retributivist position. He first acknowledges that in determining the amount to punish someone who commits murder, retribution does not demand that the imposed punishment annul or morally balance the crime. No punishment can undo or annul a crime, particularly a crime such as murder—not the execution of the offender and not life imprisonment. He states that a community has a moral right to punish those who violate its laws. He further argues that given the fact that a community has a compelling interest in some goal—punishing those who commit murder, for example—a constitutional democracy that is premised on the principles of freedom and human rights is obligated to use the least restrictive means to achieve that goal.

Bedau (2004) terms this the *minimal invasion principle*. According to him, society has legitimate goals in protecting citizens against murderers and in expressing their moral condemnation against murder. Society has a right, in other words, to inflict injury and pain on offenders. It cannot, however, use any punishment at its disposal to further its legitimate goals. If it values human rights and freedom, a democratic society is required to use only as much harm or force as necessary to secure its goal—minimal invasion. It is generally agreed that putting someone to death involves substantially more invasion than life imprisonment does. The final argument is that life imprisonment without parole (LWOP) is as capable of meeting the legitimate goals of punishment as capital punishment but involves less invasion of fundamental human rights. Therefore, the death penalty is excessive and should be abolished in favor of LWOP. While this is a well-conceived argument, proponents of the death penalty might agree with Bedau that the death penalty involves more invasion than LWOP, but they might not agree that it secures the goals of punishment (protection of the public, expressing the collective abhorrence against murder) as well as capital punishment.

Some Examples

On the evening of January 16, 1974, 17-year-old Donna Marie Dixon and a friend were drinking in bars in a section of downtown Atlanta known as "the strip." In one of the bars they met Timothy McCorquodale and his friend Bonnie. Sometime after midnight Donna went to Bonnie's apartment with McCorquodale and another friend, Leroy. In the living room of the apartment McCorquodale told Donna that she was pretty, then hit her across the face. When she stood up, McCorquodale grabbed her by the blouse, ripped it off, and tied her hands behind her back. After beating her with his belt and belt buckle, McCorquodale stripped Dixon and bound her mouth with tape and a washcloth. While she was lying on the floor, McCorquodale burned Dixon with his cigarette on her breasts, thigh, and navel. He then cut her nipples with a razor blade and poured salt into the bleeding wounds. McCorquodale then lit a candle and dripped hot wax into her vagina. He and Leroy then forced Dixon to have oral sex and intercourse. Finally, McCorquodale strangled Dixon with his hands, breaking her neck. Timothy McCorquodale was convicted of the murder, rape, and torture of Donna Marie Dixon and executed by the state of Georgia on September 21, 1987.

John Arthur Spenkelink was an ex-felon traveling across the country who picked up hitchhiker Joseph J. Szymankiewicz, another ex-felon, in the Midwest. Both men were hard drinkers, and Szymankiewicz was a violent man with a vicious temper. They had checked into a Tallahasse, Florida hotel room on February 3, 1973, when Spenkelink discovered that Szymankiewicz had stolen his cash and other belongings. Spenkelink was fearful of Szymankiewicz because the latter had repeatedly forced him to perform sexual acts and had played Russian roulette with him. Spenkelink had a handgun and testified that when he confronted Szymankiewicz about the theft, they fought and the gun went off, killing Szymankiewicz. The victim had bullet wounds behind his left ear and in the back, and the state argued that he had been killed in his sleep. Spenkelink paid the motel manager for another night's lodging and fled the scene. He was later captured in California and returned to Florida, where he was convicted of capital murder. John Spenkelink was executed on May 25, 1979.

We present these two cases to provide some context for the retributive position on the death penalty. In both cases a human life was taken, but clearly they differ. The acts committed against Donna Marie Dixon by Timothy McCorquodale were horrific, and reasonable people might clearly see that someone who has committed such acts has forfeited his right to live in the human community. The murder of Joseph Szymankiewicz, though also involving the loss of an innocent human life, involved far less horror. One can understand Spenkelink's fear of Szymankiewicz and concur with his contention that the killing was in self-defense. Reasonable people might think that the loss of Szymankiewicz's life, though deeply regrettable and tragic, is not the kind of morally shocking act that would easily warrant Spenelink's execution. Others, however, would argue that Szymankiewicz's life was just as valuable as Dixon's and that the moral loss is no less deserving of the death penalty. If so, then all those convicted of capital murder should be put to death, but this does not happen. Only a minority of those convicted of a capital crime are actually sentenced to death. Does this imply that in cases where a death sentence was imposed the offenders morally deserved to die but in life-sentence cases they were not?

This is the conundrum of the retributive view of the death penalty. Both sides do offer reasonable views of the morally appropriate response to morally offensive behavior. It may be because such views are reasonable that there exists such a core group of death penalty supporters and opponents, and it may be because such views are reasonable that they are not easily reconciled.

Cost: The Financial Argument for the Death Penalty

Another justification for the death penalty is an economic one. Proponents of capital punishment have argued that it is simply too costly to support hundreds or even thousands of convicted capital offenders in prison for life terms. The burden placed on taxpayers to absorb such a cost, it is claimed, is simply too great. The cost argument must be framed carefully. The question is not whether it is more costly to provide for the lifetime incarceration of convicted capital offenders rather than executing them immediately after conviction and sentencing. No one would argue that life in prison would be cheaper than an execution immediately after trial. The correct question is whether executing someone is less costly than life imprisonment within a legal system like ours that requires careful capital trials and an adequate appeals process where potential errors could be identified and corrected. Although there have been successful attempts to shorten the legal process from sentencing to execution, it is likely that there will continue to be both an elaborate (and time-consuming and expensive) appeal of death sentences and a dedicated group of defense lawyers who will use every means at their disposal in fending off the executioner. Given the high rate of errors found by appeals courts, approximately 66 percent (Liebman et al. 2000), it does not seem a good idea to try to quicken or shorten the process any further.

In trying to determine the cost of capital punishment, we will have to acknowledge at the outset that the available information about the current cost is not extensive, nor is it precise. But we do have some data, and these data tend to indicate that a system of capital punishment may be more costly for the taxpayers to bear than one without it. In 1993 Dr. Philip Cook, a professor of public policy and economics at Duke University, published a report that compared the costs of trying and appealing death cases in North Carolina with comparable noncapital cases that resulted in a life term with parole in 20 years (Cook and Slawson 1993). They concluded that processing a capital case from trial to execution costs the citizens of North Carolina approximately $250,000 more per death penalty case. Since not every case that is prosecuted as a capital case results in an execution, however, when the comparison was made between cases that ultimately resulted in an execution and others, the extra cost to take a case all the way to execution was over $2 million per case.

In December 2003 the Legislative Post Audit Committee of the Kansas Legislature published a report on the cost of the death penalty in its state (Legislative Post Audit Committee 2003). They found that cases in which the death penalty was sought by the prosecutor and imposed (approximately $1.51 million) could cost on average about 70 percent more than a comparable noncapital murder case ($.9 million). The median cost for a death penalty case was estimated to be $1.26 million, while the median cost for a non-death case that resulted in imprisonment was only $740,000. They also reported that the trial costs in a death penalty case were 16 times greater than in non-death penalty cases, while the costs of the appeals process was 21 times greater.

In July 2004, the Tennessee comptroller of the treasury concluded a study of the costs of the death penalty in that state (Morgan 2004). This report concluded that first degree murder cases in which the prosecutor filed a notice to seek the death penalty cost the state more than cases in which the penalty was life without the possibility of parole. Contributing factors to this cost difference were the facts that trial costs in death cases were about 1.51 times higher than in LWOP cases and that appeals costs were about 10 times higher.

Other states are also beginning to realize that the costs of maintaining the death penalty can be quite high. California, for example, is planning on building a new $200 million death row at the state penitentiary in San Quentin that would house approximately 1,000 persons. As of the end of 2005, California had over 600 on its death row, more than the death rows of 25 states combined. Approximately 30 new condemned offenders are added to death row each year, with only 12 executions taking place since the state's death penalty law took effect in 1977 until the end of 2005. It has been estimated that keeping the death penalty in California will cost the taxpayers at least $114 million *a year* beyond what it would cost to house prisoners for full life terms, and trial costs for death penalty cases in Los Angles County have been estimated to be three times more than for a noncapital murder (Tempest 2005). In the state of Washington a death penalty trial takes on average five months longer than a comparable noncapital trial; appeals of non-death cases lasted two years on average and six years for the review of death penalty cases. As a result, the trial costs in a capital case were more than double that in a noncapital case (Larranaga 2004). The state of Indiana estimated that it cost its taxpayers about 37 percent more to prosecute a death penalty case than if it were prosecuted as a LWOP case (Goodpaster 2002). If Florida prosecuted its death cases as life without parole, it was estimated taxpayers would be saved about $51 million a year. With 44 executions conducted from 1976 to 2000, Florida has spent about $24 million for each execution (Date 2000).

In addition to state-level costs, individual counties also have to make large expenditures on capital cases, and to pay these costs counties are often required to cut back on other services. Baicker (2004) has estimated that over the period 1983–1999, it cost counties approximately $2 million to prosecute each death case, with expenditures of approximately $5.5 billion over a 20-year period. Funding capital cases puts an enormous strain on some counties' budgets, requiring them to either raise taxes, cut back on services, or both. Jasper County, Texas, for example, raised property taxes by 8 percent and delayed the purchase of new computers in order to pay for the capital trial of three men alleged to have killed James Byrd by dragging him behind their pickup. Baicker also found that counties that prosecute death penalty cases spend 3 percent less on law enforcement and roads. High trial costs are often cited by local prosecutors as a reason they decide not to prosecute a case as a death penalty case (Larranaga 2003).

Maintaining a *system* of capital punishment is very expensive for state and local governments. But exactly why are the costs so high? Virtually everyone who has examined this issue has come up with the same answer: At each step of the process it costs more to prosecute, defend, and appeal a death penalty case than it does a life case. Compared with a life case, in death penalty cases:

- There are far more pretrial motions filed, and more pretrial hearings to deal with these motions.
- There is more extensive investigation of the case by both the prosecution and defense.
- There are more attorneys on both the prosecution and defense sides.
- More potential jurors are selected and quizzed, so the jury selection process is longer in death cases.
- Jurors are frequently sequestered in death cases.
- There are two trials in capital cases, a trial over guilt and innocence and a penalty phase trial.
- More experts are needed at trial, including a costly mitigation investigation and mitigation experts.
- The trial itself takes longer in death cases.
- There are several rounds of appeals in both state and federal courts for death cases.

It is, then, much more expensive to try a death penalty than a non-death penalty case. Consider then that about two-thirds of all death cases are reversed for some kind of trial error, resulting in either a new guilt or penalty phase hearing, then consider that most often the retrials do not result in a death sentence, and you get some sense as to why a system of law that permits capital punishment is so expensive. Although there may be compelling reasons for maintaining the death penalty, saving taxpayer money is not likely one of the better ones.

Incapacitation: One of the Public Safety Arguments for the Death Penalty

One of the justifications for the death penalty is that it is necessary for public safety. The only sure way for society to be safe from those who have committed murder ever committing murder again is to execute them. If we do not execute them, the argument goes, they may be paroled or escape from prison and kill innocent people on the outside, or they may kill correctional personnel or other inmates while imprisoned. To save innocent lives, therefore, the convicted killer must be incapacitated, or rendered unable to offend again, and the only sure way to do this is through the death penalty.

The threat that a convicted murderer may kill again if given the opportunity is not large, but it is real. On August 6, 1966, Kenneth Allen McDuff and Roy Dale Green kidnapped at gunpoint a teenage girl and her two male friends in Guadalupe County, Texas. After killing the two males, McDuff then raped the female victim, finally choking her with a broomstick. Green turned himself into police the next day. In 1968 both boys were convicted of their crime, with Green receiving a 20-year prison sentence and McDuff receiving three death sentences. McDuff had several death warrants signed and was near execution three times before his sentence was commuted to life by the Supreme Court in *Furman v. Georgia*. After serving some 20 years on his life sentence, and because of severe overcrowding in Texas' prisons, McDuff was paroled by Texas authorities and released in October of 1989. Later that year, he was sent back to prison for parole violations but was released again in December 1990. When out this time, McDuff was involved in several abductions and murders of women, including Melissa Northrup, and the brutal kidnapping, rape, and torture of Colleen Reed. After fleeing Texas, McDuff was captured in Missouri and returned to Texas for trial. Although he was suspected of having killed as many as 15 women, he was only convicted of the murders of Melissa Northrup and Colleen Reed. He was given two death sentences and was executed by the state of Texas on November 17, 1998.

Kenneth McDuff is unusual in that he is the only person to have been sentenced to death, to be released, to commit additional murders, to be resentenced to death and finally to be executed. But his case does highlight one indisputable fact about the death penalty: Those who are executed will never commit another murder again. Whatever else can be claimed about it, the death penalty does effectively keep murderers from killing again, and it does incapacitate them better than life imprisonment. But how much better? When Kenneth McDuff had his 1968 death sentence commuted to life in prison by the *Furman* decision, Texas did not have a life without parole provision. Furthermore, McDuff's release was at the very least made easier by the fact that at the time the Texas Department of Corrections was severely overcrowded and the target of several lawsuits. Had McDuff's first death sentence been commuted to a LWOP sentence, he would not have been released to commit other murders, and he may not have been released (or at least not released as early as he was) if Texas was not under pressure to relieve inmate overcrowding in its penitentiaries. Finally, even a death sentence cannot offer a 100 percent guarantee that the condemned will not commit another crime.

On November 4, 2005, convicted murderer and death row inmate Charles Thompson escaped from custody while attending a court hearing in Harris County (Houston), Texas. Thompson managed to obtain not only civilian clothes but also an identification tag that indicated that he was a employee of the Texas attorney general's office. He was checked past security and walked out. Thompson was apprehended three days later in Louisiana. Although he was sentenced to death for the murders of his ex-girlfriend and her new boyfriend, Thompson could easily have committed murder and other crimes during his escape, before his execution could have been carried out. The

Thompson case shows that there is a risk that a convicted murderer could kill again even if sentenced to death.

Not withstanding incidents like Charles Thompson's, where death-sentenced killers escape into the community or somehow kill another inmate or a correctional officer while on death row awaiting execution, it seems to us that opponents of capital punishment would have to acknowledge that while neither punishment is capable of 100 percent incapacitation, the death penalty is more effective in preventing future crimes than life imprisonment without parole. The question that must be asked and answered is, How much more effective in incapacitating murderers is the death penalty compared to life without parole?

Although Kenneth McDuff's case is as unlikely as Charles Thompson's, those who are imprisoned after conviction of murder do sometimes kill again. Two criminologists, James Marquart and Jonathan Sorensen (1988), followed the future criminal activity of a group of offenders who were sentenced to death but whose sentences were commuted to life imprisonment by the *Furman v. Georgia* decision (see also Cheever 2006). More specifically, they compared 47 former Texas death row inmates, 28 of whom were eventually paroled and released into the community, with the parole behavior of 109 other inmates in Texas who were convicted either of murder or rape and who had served part of a life prison term before being paroled. At the time of their report only one of the *Furman* releases had committed a murder while on parole,[4] while none of the former life-sentenced parolees had. Fourteen percent of the *Furman* parolees had committed a new offense, while only 6 percent of the paroled lifers had committed a new crime when released. While it is true that the death penalty is better at incapacitating than life in prison, had it executed all 28 Furman inmates it would only have prevented one murder (two or more if McDuff is counted) and three other felonies (one rape and two burglaries). In a later paper (1989), they studied 239 convicted capital offenders from around the country who had been released from their state's death row because of the *Furman* decision. Of these 239 former death row inmates, only one had committed a murder while in the community, six had committed a murder while in prison serving their life term, and a total of only 12 new offenses were committed by these offenders over a five-year period.

Additional data support the position that while it is true that executing someone can prevent most if not all future offending, those who are convicted of serious crimes do not normally repeat their crimes. Evidence from a recent Bureau of Justice Statistics study of recidivism rates from 15 states indicates that homicide offenders represented 1.7 percent of released prisoners in 1994 (see Table 6.1). The three-year recidivism rates for homicide offenders were 40.7 percent (rearrest), 20.5 percent (reconviction), 10.8 percent (return to prison with a new sentence), and 31.4 percent (returned to prison for any reason) (Langan and Levin 2002). By any measure of recidivism, the failure rates for homicide offenders are lower than those for offenders released from prison for most other offenses. When the outcome is a return to prison with a new sentence, for example, only offenders released for nonrape sexual assaults had a lower recidivism rate (10.5 percent) than homicide offenders (10.8 percent).

Offenders in 19 other offense categories all had higher three-year recidivism rates, and most were over twice as high. When the outcome measure is rearrest, homicide offenders had the lowest recidivism rate of all 21 offense categories.

Another interesting issue raised by this report is whether homicide offenders exhibit a special tendency to commit new homicides when they return to the community. Based on the data presented in the report, the answer to this question appears to be "no" as well (see Table 6.2). Of the homicide offenders released in 1994, 1.2 percent were rearrested for a new homicide within three years of release. Only individuals released for rape (0 percent) and motor vehicle theft (1.0 percent) had a lower likelihood of being arrested for a homicide than the homicide releasees. For example, 8.5 percent of those released from prison for robbery were rearrested within three years of their release for committing a homicide (Langan and Levin 2002). Although we must keep in mind

Table 6.1 Rate of Recidivism of State Prisoners Released in 1994, by Most Serious Offense for Which Released

Most Serious Offense for Which Released	Percent of All Released Prisoners	Rearrested	Reconvicted	Returned to Prison With a New Prison Sentence	Returned to Prison With or Without a New Prison Sentence
All Released Prisoners	100%	67.5%	46.9%	25.4%	51.8%
Violent Offenses	22.5%	61.7%	39.9%	20.4%	48.8%
Homicide	1.7	40.7	20.5	10.8	31.4
Kidnapping	0.4	59.4	37.8	25.1	29.5
Rape	1.2	46.0	27.4	12.6	43.5
Other sexual assault	2.4	41.4	22.3	10.5	36.0
Robbery	9.9	70.2	46.5	25.0	54.7
Assault	6.5	65.1	44.2	21.0	51.2
Other violent	0.4	51.7	29.8	12.7	40.9
Property Offenses	33.5%	73.8%	53.4%	30.5%	56.4%
Burglary	15.2	74.0	54.2	30.8	56.1
Larceny/theft	9.7	74.6	55.7	32.6	60.0
Motor vehicle theft	3.5	78.8	54.3	31.3	59.1
Arson	0.5	57.7	41.0	20.1	38.7
Fraud	2.9	66.3	42.1	22.8	45.4
Stolen property	1.4	77.4	57.2	31.8	62.1
Other property	0.3	71.1	47.6	28.5	40.0
Drug Offenses	32.6%	66.7%	47.0%	25.2%	49.2%
Possession	7.5	67.5	46.6	23.9	42.6
Trafficking	20.2	64.2	44.0	24.8	46.1
Other/unspecified	4.9	75.5	60.5	28.8	71.8
Public Order Offenses	9.7%	62.2%	42.0%	21.6%	48.0%
Weapons	3.1	70.2	46.6	24.3	55.5
DUI	3.3	51.5	31.7	16.6	43.7
Other	3.3	65.1	48.0	24.4	43.6
Other Offenses	1.7%	64.7%	42.1%	20.7%	66.9%

Source: Langan and Levin (2002), Table 9, p. 8.

Table 6.2 Rearrest Rates of State Prisoners Released in 1994, by Most Serious Offense for Which Released and Charge at Rearrest

Percent of Prisoners Rearrested Within 3 Years of Release Whose Most Serious Offense at Time of Release Was:

Rearrest Charge Offenses	All Offenses	Violent Offense					Property Offense					Drug Offense	Public Order Offenses
		Total	Homicide	Rape	Robbery	Assault	Total	Burglary	Larceny/Theft	Motor Vehicle Theft	Fraud		
All Charges	67.5%	67.7%	40.7%	46.0%	70.2%	65.1%	73.8%	74.0%	74.6%	78.8%	66.3%	66.7%	62.2%
Violent Offenses	21.6%	27.5%	16.7%	18.6%	29.6%	31.4%	21.9%	21.9%	22.3%	26.5%	14.8%	18.4%	18.5%
Homicide	0.8	1.1	1.2	0.7	1.1	1.6	0.8	0.7	0.6	2.4	0.5	0.7	0.6
Rape	0.6	1.1	0.0	2.5	1.2	1.0	0.7	0.8	0.5	1.6	0.3	0.3	0.4
Robbery	6.2	8.5	3.4	3.9	13.4	6.1	6.3	5.9	7.3	8.4	3.3	4.9	4.6
Assault	13.7	16.4	11.9	8.7	15.1	22.0	13.7	13.8	14.4	16.1	9.0	12.4	12.1
Property Offenses	31.9%	25.5%	10.8%	14.8%	32.9%	25.6%	46.3%	45.4%	47.8%	45.7%	44.8%	24.0%	22.9%
Burglary	9.9	6.9	2.0	4.4	8.7	7.7	17.6	23.4	13.9	11.1	9.1	5.5	5.0
Larceny/theft	16.3	12.0	4.1	6.2	16.5	10.6	26.1	23.0	33.9	18.9	23.4	11.5	8.9
Motor vehicle theft	4.5	3.9	1.0	2.3	5.3	4.4	6.0	5.5	4.7	11.5	4.5	3.5	4.1
Fraud	4.7	3.2	2.1	1.8	4.0	3.2	7.1	5.1	6.8	6.6	19.0	3.1	5.1
Drug Offenses	30.3%	22.6%	13.0%	11.2%	29.4%	21.5%	27.2%	27.6%	27.1%	33.9%	18.5%	41.2%	22.1%
Public Order Offenses	28.3%	27.4%	17.7%	20.5%	29.3%	31.1%	29.2%	30.3%	25.5%	33.5%	26.3%	27.7%	31.2%
Number of Released Prisoners	272,111	61,107	4,443	3,138	26,862	17,708	91,061	41,257	26,259	9,478	7,853	88,516	26,329

Source: Langan and Levin (2002), Table 10, p. 9.

that homicide offenders released from prison are not necessarily comparable to homicide offenders entering prison and are not necessarily comparable to homicide offenders who are sentenced to death, the data do suggest that when homicide offenders are eventually released, they represent a small proportion of the total number of releasees and do not exhibit comparatively high levels of future offending or future homicide.

Those who would argue that the death penalty is better than life imprisonment at preventing new crimes on the part of the person being punished would be correct. It is extremely unlikely that, given the security precautions usually taken (the Thompson case being an exception), an offender who is sentenced to death would either kill another inmate or correctional officer while on death row or escape and kill an innocent person on the outside. The risk that someone sentenced to a life without parole term would kill another person while in prison is greater than for one sentenced to death, *but* that risk is small. We suggest that critics of the death penalty acknowledge that while there is no surefire way to prevent the victimization of the innocent, executing offenders offers greater social protection than does life imprisonment. Supporters of the death penalty, in turn, should acknowledge that while the death penalty is superior to life imprisonment in preventing new crimes and protecting the public, that superiority is slight and must be weighed against other matters, such as the risk of executing innocent people and the cost of maintaining a system of capital punishment.

General Deterrence: The Other Public Safety Argument for the Death Penalty

In addition to preventing crimes by the person actually being punished by incapacitating them, there is a second way that capital punishment can contribute to public safety: by deterring would-be murderers from taking action. The principle of general deterrence states that people are inhibited from committing crimes by the certainty, severity, and swiftness of punishment. All else being equal, a punishment that is more costly in terms of inflicting more harm is likely to be seen as more severe than another and, therefore, one more likely to be avoided by not committing the crime. Since it is generally understood that death by execution involves more pain and therefore a greater cost than life imprisonment, it is thought to deter those thinking about committing murder more effectively than life imprisonment. The general deterrence argument for capital punishment is that would-be murderers are more likely to be prevented from committing murder if they could be executed than if they could be sentenced to life in prison.

Sellin's Research

Most of the accumulated evidence about the deterrent effect of capital punishment suggests that executions are no more effective at deterring crime than conventional sentences of imprisonment are. The earliest evidence on this issue comes from work by Thorsten Sellin (1959).[5] Sellin's research strategy involved systematic comparisons of homicide rates from 1920 to 1955 between contiguous states that were similar in as many respects as possible but that also had different legal stances on the death penalty. His basic hypothesis was that if capital punishment is more effective at deterring homicide than life imprisonment, then states with capital punishment should have lower homicide rates than states with a maximum penalty of life imprisonment.

Figure 6.1 Homicide Rates per 100,000 Population For Contiguous Groups of Death Penalty (D) and Life Imprisonment (L) Cases, 1920–1955

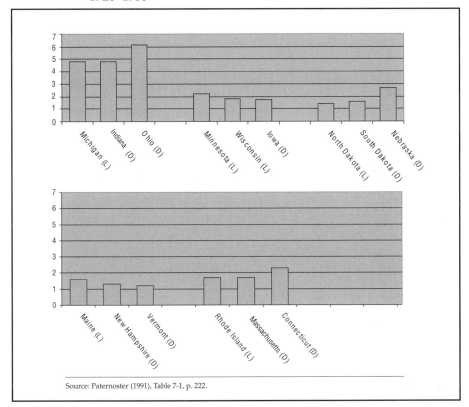

Source: Paternoster (1991), Table 7-1, p. 222.

Figure 6.1 presents a summary of Sellin's results. If capital punishment has a general deterrent effect, then the bar for death penalty states should be consistently lower than that for non-death penalty states. As you can see, homicide rates for the first set of contiguous states—Michigan (a life imprisonment state), Indiana (a death penalty state), and Ohio (a death penalty state)—did not exhibit significant variation. The two death penalty states, Indiana and Ohio, did not have lower homicide rates than the state that punished with life imprisonment. Similar statements could be made about the other comparisons in Sellin's study. Within the same geographic region, those states with the death penalty did not seem to have lower rates of homicide than presumably similar states in the same geographic area that did not. Peterson and Bailey (1988) updated this study, covering the post-*Furman v. Georgia* period of 1973–1984, comparing sets of geographically contiguous death penalty and life imprisonment states. They also found that averaged over a 12-year period, the annual homicide rate in death penalty states (8.5 homicides per 100,000 population) was actually a little *higher* than the rate in states without the death penalty (7.6 homicides per 100,000 population). Their analysis—like Sellin's—provided no evidence of reduced homicide rates in death penalty states.

The obvious problem with Sellin's strategy of matching states (which he recognized in his own work) is that we must *assume* comparability between the pairs of death penalty and life imprisonment states under examination. In other words, it is fair to ask whether the death penalty state differs in ways that make a comparison with a geographically contiguous life imprisonment state unreasonable. For example, if a death penalty state has a high homicide rate for reasons that are unrelated to the type of punishments imposed in that state and it is compared to a life imprisonment state with a low homicide rate for reasons that, too, are unrelated to the types of punishments imposed in that state, we would erroneously conclude that the death penalty actually makes the homicide problem worse—a spurious correlation. Baldus and Cole (1975) carefully explored this aspect of Sellin's analysis and compared the contiguous states on a wide variety of characteristics that might be associated with homicide rates, including the probability of apprehension and conviction, labor force participation, unemployment rate, population aged 15–24, per capita income, percent nonwhite population, per capita government expenditures, and per capita police expenditures. Baldus and Cole's study indicated that Sellin's contiguous death penalty and life imprisonment states were actually quite similar on all of these dimensions. Their finding strengthened Sellin's claim that the comparison of geographically contiguous death and life states was methodologically sound and that the substantive conclusion of the research, that capital punishment was no more effective in deterring homicide than life imprisonment, was valid.

Ehrlich's Strategy

In spite of Baldus and Cole's findings, other critics of Sellin's work concluded that the simple comparison of homicide rates between death penalty and life imprisonment states was improper. One such critic, the economist Isaac Ehrlich (1975), argued that a better strategy was to use sophisticated statistical models that mathematically considered and controlled for factors other than type of punishment in determining whether the death penalty was a more effective deterrent to murder than life imprisonment. This approach would also, he argued, allow for a consideration of the deterrent effect of the actual number of executions that have occurred rather than the fact that a state is a death penalty rather than a life imprisonment state. Rather than looking at pairs of death and life imprisonment states, Ehrlich examined the effect of the death penalty on the United States as a whole over the years 1933–1969. Although his analysis contained several factors that were thought to influence the homicide rate, such as the arrest and conviction rate for murder, labor force participation, unemployment, and the percent of the population between the ages of 14 and 24, Ehrlich's main interest was in what in called the "execution risk." The risk of execution was defined as the ratio of the number of executions in the United States for a given time period over the number of murder convictions for a given time period. If capital punishment is an effective general deterrent, higher levels of execution risk should be associated with lower homicide rates. This was exactly what Ehrlich found (1975), and publishing his work in the prestigious *American Economic Review,* he dramatically concluded that "[a]n additional execution per year over the period in question may have resulted, on average, in 7 or 8 fewer murders" (p. 414).

Ehrlich's finding that each execution in the United States may have prevented seven or eight murders was striking and generated a lot of controversy, because his was virtually the only scientific study to find such a pronounced deterrent effect for capital punishment. It also entered into the public policy debate about the death penalty. The solicitor general of the United States included a draft of Ehrlich's paper in his brief to the Supreme Court in the case of *Fowler v. North Carolina* (96 S. Ct. 3212, 1976), calling it "important empirical support for the a priori logical belief that use of the death penalty decreases the number of homicides." Ehrlich's was not, however, the only research that found evidence of a deterrent effect for executions. A student of his, Stephen Layson (1985), reported an analysis in which he concluded that each execution conducted may have prevented 18 additional homicides. Studies published after theirs seemed to confirm the finding that executions prevented homicides (Chressanthis 1989; Cloninger 1977; Cover and Thistle 1988; Yunker 1976).

Other scholars, however, found that the deterrent effect observed by Ehrlich was sensitive to the time periods and other variables included in the analysis (Passell 1975; Passell and Taylor 1977) and that his findings did not stand up to critical scrutiny. For example, there was no evidence of deterrence when the years 1962–1969 were removed from the analysis. Why would those years have such a strong influence on the results? It turns out that during that period homicide rates were increasing rather rapidly while the number of executions was dwindling to zero. The case of high homicide and few executions would give the appearance of a deterrent effect for the number of executions that occurred. Critics also claimed that Ehrlich did not include a measure of the length of prison terms for convicted murderers in his analysis, precluding a comparison of the deterrent effect of capital punishment versus a long prison sentence (Lempert 1983).

After critics took a long hard look at Ehrlich's results, it was not clear *what* the effect of executions on the homicide rate was. In an attempt to seek a resolution to this important public policy question, the National Academy of Sciences created a Panel on Deterrence and Incapacitation to, among other things, look at the relationship between capital punishment and homicides. This panel was led by Nobel prize-winning economist Lawrence Klein. Using a replica of Ehrlich's own data and after extensive analyses, Klein and colleagues (1978) came to a different conclusion: "We see too many plausible explanations for his finding a deterrent effect other than the theory that capital punishment deters murder . . . [his] results cannot be used at this time to pass judgment on the use of the death penalty" (p. 359). Using similar methods and comparable time periods, attempts to replicate Ehrlich's findings by other researchers have generally failed to find any evidence that capital punishment is a more effective deterrent than life imprisonment (Peterson and Bailey 2003).

Other Researchers

Although Ehrlich's finding of a strong deterrent effect for capital punishment was largely discredited, it spurred a great deal of additional research, and this research literature is voluminous. Other scholars began to look at the relationship between the number of executions and levels of homicide in individual states (California, Illinois, New York, North Carolina, Ohio, Oregon, and Utah) rather than for the country as a whole, and in none of these studies is there evidence that executions are a more effective deterrent than prison (Peterson and Bailey 2003). Other researchers looked at the relationship between capital punishment and the killing of police officers. Sellin (1967) found that when he compared the rate of police killings for cities in states with the death penalty it was generally no different than in cities whose state did not have the death penalty. Bailey (1982) found that neither the legal status of the death penalty (death penalty was available versus it was not available) nor the actual number of executions had any effect on the number of police killings during the period 1961–1971.

Understanding that in order for capital punishment to deter would-be offenders from committing murder they must be aware of the penalty, other researchers have examined the relationship between the amount of media publicity for executions and subsequent homicide. If capital punishment is an effective deterrent to other would-be murderers, the homicide rate should decline after well-publicized executions. One of the first to examine this issue was Dann (1935), who looked at the number of homicides that occurred in the 60 days immediately before and after five well-publicized executions (1927, 1929, 1930, 1931, and 1932). Contrary to expectations, Dann found that the number of homicides actually *increased* after each execution. Others who have looked at the issue of execution publicity have also generally found that the number of homicides slightly increases after each well-publicized execution (Graves 1956; Savitz 1958; King 1978; Bowers and Pierce 1980b; Bailey 1983).

Other researchers, however, have found some evidence of a short-term deterrent effect for execution publicity, although this evidence is far from conclusive. For example, David Phillips (1980) identified 22 murderers who were executed in London between 1864 and 1921. He then calculated the amount of publicity for each execution by counting the inches of newspaper space given to a reporting of each execution. He found that for 15 of the cases the number of homicides committed during the week of the execution was substantially below the average number of homicides and that the more newspaper space devoted to the execution, the greater the drop in homicides. Unfortunately, Phillips also found that after the initial drop in homicides during the week of the execution, there was a large increase over the next few weeks, such that "within five or six weeks of a publicized execution, the drop in homicides is canceled by an equally large rise in homicides" (p. 146).

It is possible that the various procedural reforms made to state capital punishment laws after the *Furman* decision had the effect of creating a more certain death penalty, and therefore one with greater deterrent "bite." If so, then older literature on the effect of capital punishment on state-level homicide rates might not be informative about how effective the death penalty is today in deterring homicide. Fortunately, there are numerous post-*Furman* studies of the deterrent effect of capital punishment that we can turn our attention to. For example, Cochran et al. (1994) looked at the effect on the homicide rate of Oklahoma's return to executions on September 10, 1990, when Charles Coleman was put to death. When they examined the homicide rate just before and after the Coleman execution (1989–1991) they found that the level was *higher* after the execution. When Sorensen et al. (1999) looked at the relationship between executions and monthly homicide trends for Texas during the period 1984–1997, they found that the number of executions during a given period had no effect either on the general homicide rate or the rate of felony-murders (capital murders in which murder is committed along with another felony, such as armed robbery).

Although it appeared that the scientific community had settled in on the conclusion that the death penalty is not an effective general deterrent, recent empirical work has again ignited interest and controversy, much like Ehrlich's original work in 1975. This research, too, has entered the public policy arena. Mocan and Gittings (2003) examined the relationship between over 6,000 death sentences in the United States from 1977 to 1997 and "removals" from death row (the conviction or death sentence was vacated or the commutated) on homicide. They reported that each execution from 1977 to 1997 prevented five murders, while each removal from death row produced an additional murder. Dezhbakhsh and Shepherd (2004) examined the effect of the unofficial moratorium on executions caused by the *Furman* decision and the effect when that moratorium was lifted by the *Gregg* decision. They found that consistent with a deterrent effect, the immediate effect of *Furman* was to increase homicides in states that had the death penalty, while the effect of the reintroduction in some states of the death penalty by the *Gregg* decision was a decline in the expected number of homicides.

Shepherd (2004) reported that each execution in the post-*Furman* period resulted in an average of five fewer murders and that executions not only deterred felony-type homicides but homicides committed between intimates and acquaintances. She also found that the long stays on death row before execution erodes the deterrent effect—one murder is prevented, she concluded, when the delay to execution is reduced by four and one half months. The largest deterrent effect for state executions was found by Dezhbakhsh, Rubin, and Shepherd (2003). They estimated that following resumption of capital punishment in 1977 each execution prevented approximately 18 murders. Finally, Liu (2004) found that not only did capital punishment reduce homicides, it had a deterrent effect on robbery and nonviolent crimes as well.

Other research has found additional evidence of a deterrent effect. Zimmerman (2004) found that each execution saved anywhere from 7 to 31 lives. Shepherd (2005) found that executions have a deterrent effect in some states and a brutalization effect in others and that most states do not execute enough persons to generate a credible deterrent effect. Cloninger and Marchesini (2001) examined the effect that an approximately one-year moratorium on executions in Texas had on the number of murders committed. In April 1996 the Texas Court of Criminal Appeals stopped all executions in Texas for approximately a year until it ruled on a legal issue involving limiting prisoners access to state habeas corpus petitions. Cloninger and Marchesini estimated that this moratorium resulted in an additional 18 murders being committed in the state. In a related study (2005) they examined the effect of the moratorium on executions in Illinois imposed by Governor Ryan in 2000 and his commutation of all death sentences in the state in January 2003. They estimated that the moratorium resulted in an additional 40 murders in the state compared with the United States as a whole.

Just as was the case with Isaac Ehrlich's research nearly 30 years ago, these recent findings of a nontrivial general deterrent effect for capital punishment have made their way into policy discussions, and just like his work they have been subject to intense critical review. Professor Joanna Shepherd, speaking at a hearing on H.R. 2934 before the Subcommittee on Crime, Terrorism, and Homeland Security of the House Committee on the Judiciary on April 21, 2004, stated that a "strong consensus [exists] among economists that capital punishment deters crime. . . . All of the modern economic studies in the past decade have found a deterrent effect." Professor Paul H. Rubin, in written testimony for the Senate Judiciary Committee on the Constitution, Civil Rights, and Property Rights on February 1, 2006, stated, "Recent research on the relationship between capital punishment and homicide has created a consensus among most economists who have studied the issue that capital punishment deters murder. . . . The modern refereed studies have consistently shown that capital punishment has a strong deterrent effect, with each execution deterring between 3 and 18 murders."

Not everyone who has examined these studies has been convinced that they show evidence of a general deterrent effect for the death penalty however. One recent study found no evidence of deterrence (Katz, Levitt, and Shustorovich 2003). Other studies have identified methodological flaws with existing work that, when corrected, reveal far less convincing or no evidence of deterrence with capital punishment (Berk 2005). After his extensive review of the recent studies, Berk (2005) concluded that "for the vast majority of states for the vast majority of years, there is no evidence for deterrence in these analyses" (p. 330).

In an exceptionally comprehensive and rigorous review of these recent general deterrence studies, Donohue and Wolfers (2006) found that the reported findings are fragile and either disappear or turn into "brutalization" rather than deterrent effects (executions increase homicides) when minor alterations of the data are performed. Their technical dissection of the studies is beyond the scope of this discussion, but they performed a detailed reanalysis of these studies with the original researchers' own data sets and demonstrated that with slightly different statistical assumptions or different measures of variables the evidence for deterrence disappears. They concluded that:

The estimated effects of capital punishment on homicide rates change dramatically even with small changes in econometric specifications. Aggregating over all of our estimates, it is entirely unclear even whether the preponderance of evidence suggests that the death penalty causes more or less murder. (p. 843)

Essentially, their conclusion is that the statistical evidence presented by these many recent studies is so fragile that one cannot conclude if executing people for murder makes things better (deterrence) or worse (brutalization) (see also Weisberg 2005).

The situation with respect to executions and general deterrence is now eerily reminiscent of the days of Ehrlich's research. He (and others) published sophisticated statistical studies that appeared to show nontrivial deterrent effects for capital punishment. Their studies entered public policy discussion in support of the death penalty. Subsequent researchers, however, found that the reported deterrent effects did not stand up to critical examination. When only minor variations in the data were examined, substantially different results were found. Once again, any firm conclusion about the deterrent effect of capital punishment is elusive and highly controversial.

Figure 6.2   Murder Rates for Death Penalty and Non-Death Penalty States, 1990–2004

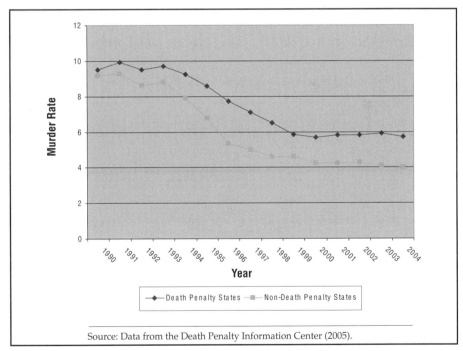

Source: Data from the Death Penalty Information Center (2005).

One interesting exercise is to go back to the old method of Thorsten Sellin and compare death penalty and non-death penalty states over time during the Modern Period to see if doing so sheds some light on the presence of general deterrence. While Sellin's simple comparative approach may not appear as methodologically sophisticated as recent econometric work, it does seem to have some strengths of its own—like clarity. In Figure 6.2 we have graphed the murder rate for two groups of states: those that had the death penalty at least on their books (even if they didn't use it or didn't use it frequently) and states that do not have the death penalty. If the possibility of execution deters homicides then the line for death penalty states should be consistently lower than that for non-death penalty states over time.[6] As you can clearly see, however, there is no evidence of any deterrent effect over time in a general comparison of death penalty and non-death penalty states. The murder rate does decline over time in death penalty states, but it declines in non-death penalty states as well. Although we would not make much of this because non-death penalty states tend to be different from death penalty states, murder rates in states without the death penalty are slightly *lower* than those in states that at least maintain the possibility of executing those convicted of murder. Although the murder rate declined for both groups of states over the period 1990–2004, it declined at a faster rate for non-death penalty states even though the number of executions increased from 23 in 1990 to 59 in 2004. Execution of murderers could not be a large factor driving down U.S. murder rates over this period, since the reduction occurred in both death penalty and non-death penalty states. Some other factors must have been operating to reduce the murder rate in both sets of states.

Figure 6.3 shows a little more refined analysis. The murder rates over the period 1990–2004 are graphed for four separate states with very different

Figure 6.3 Murder Rates for California, Michigan, Texas, New York, and the United States as a Whole, 1990–2004

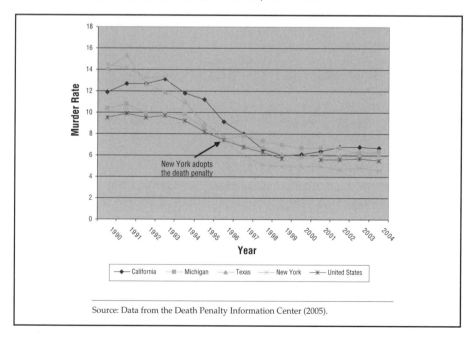

Source: Data from the Death Penalty Information Center (2005).

death penalty policies (we include U.S. murder rates as a whole for comparison). California had the death penalty over the entire period; it sentenced a lot of people to death, but it rarely executed anyone. Texas had the death penalty over the entire period, and it too sentenced a lot of people to death, but it executed many more of its convicted capital offenders. New York was an abolitionist state but adopted the death penalty in 1995 and has not yet executed anyone, while Michigan was a non-death penalty state over the entire time period. There are several things we would like to point out to you about this graph. First, notice that the trend in the murder rate over time for these four states is remarkably similar to that found in Figure 6.2. This suggests that factors that drive the murder rate over time do so for the entire country as a whole and do not affect individual states differently. Second, notice that four states with very different approaches to the death penalty have remarkable similar murder rates over time. The murder rates for Texas, which not only had the death penalty but executed a lot of offenders, maps closely to those for California, New York (which didn't have the death penalty until March 1995), and Michigan (which never had the death penalty). The similarity of these trends for states with very different approaches to the death penalty would seem to suggest that the death penalty itself is not affecting the murder rate very much. Third, in what might be seen as consistent with a deterrent effect, the murder rate for New York state declined after it adopted the death penalty in 1995. However, notice that the murder rate in New York had already been in decline before it changed its death penalty policy (it began its decline in 1993), that the decline in murder rates was greater before it adopted the death penalty than after, and that the decline coincides with declines in other states over the same period that did not alter their policy or practice with respect to the death penalty. There is not much evidence here to support the position that the death penalty is a strong general deterrent to murder.

Post-*Furman* studies of the effect of execution publicity have also not been able to identify either a strong or a consistent deterrent effect on homicide. When McFarland (1983) examined the effect of the first four executions conducted in the United States after the *Furman* decision, he found that these highly publicized executions had no effect on the homicide rate in each respective state. William Bailey (1990) conducted a more comprehensive study, examining the effect of television coverage of executions on homicides from 1976 to 1987. He reported that neither the amount nor the type ("matter of fact" versus sensational) of television coverage of an execution had any effect on the overall homicide rate in the United States over that period. Bailey (1990) also examined the effect of newspaper coverage of the Coleman execution in Oklahoma on that state's homicide rate and found that the publicity given that execution was related to *higher* levels of homicide in the state.

If you think that the empirical data with respect to the deterrent effect of capital punishment on crime is overwhelming and confusing, we would heartily agree. The only reasonable conclusion to draw is that there is no firm and consistent evidence to support the position that capital punishment is a more effective general deterrent than imprisonment to homicide. It appears that the American public is arriving at the same conclusion. According to the

Gallup Organization (Gallup 2005), when asked if they thought that the death penalty was a deterrent to murder, 62 percent of those polled in 1985 agreed that it was, but by 2004 this figure had declined to only 35 percent. Most Americans, then, do not believe that the death penalty is better at preventing homicide than a prison sentence. Furthermore, at least among those who support the death penalty the lack of any better deterrent effect is not critical. When those who already supported the death penalty for murder were asked if new scientific evidence showed that the death penalty did not deter murder would they favor or oppose capital punishment, over two-thirds (69 percent) said that they would continue to support the execution of murderers. Their support for the death penalty, therefore, did not depend on whether it is an effective deterrent to murder, but on other reasons discussed in this chapter.

Religious Positions For and Against the Death Penalty

Religious teachings are frequently called upon to provide both support for and opposition to the death penalty. Regular citizens appeal to religious precepts to support their view about the death penalty, and prosecutors and defense attorneys do as well when trying death penalty cases (Blume and Johnson 2000). If you consult religious texts, you can find support for either position. Not surprisingly, therefore, even religions with a common heritage have different positions with respect to the death penalty. Some Protestant denominations have official positions that oppose the death penalty, while others have positions that support it. Finally, conflict often occurs between the pulpit and the pew when members of religious groups do not strictly follow the position of church authorities. For example, although the Catholic Church has officially announced its opposition to the death penalty, Catholics are as likely to support the death penalty for murder as members of other religions are.

Those seeking religious support for the death penalty can find abundant evidence in the Old Testament. For example, in the book of Genesis, God announces to Noah that "whoever sheds the blood of man, by man shall his blood be shed; for God made man in his own image." Exodus 21:12 provides further proof of biblical support for the death penalty: "Whoever strikes a man so that he dies he shall be put to death." Another pronouncement about an appropriate or acceptable punishment for murder can be found in Exodus 21:22–25: "If when men come to blows, they hurt a woman who is pregnant and she suffers a miscarriage . . . should she die, you shall give life for life, eye for eye tooth for tooth, hand for hand, foot for foot, burn for burn, wound for wound, stroke for stroke." A specific command that the death penalty be used in the case of murder is found in Numbers (35:16): "the murderer shall surely be put to death." In fact, in the Torah more than 30 offenses are punishable by death under Mosaic law. It is perfectly clear, then, that those wanting to justify their position in favor of the death penalty have ample support within the Old Testament of the Bible and within the text of ancient Jewish law.[7]

Anyone adopting that position, however, would also have to contend with the issue of whether to extract the general rationale for the death penalty from the Old Testament or literally apply the death penalty according to strict biblical commands. If it is the latter, we must acknowledge that the death penalty is a permissible punishment for many other crimes besides murder:

- Following another religion (Exodus 22:20).
- Adultery (Leviticus 20:10).
- Sexual activity before marriage (Deuteronomy 22:13–21).
- Being seduced if engaged (Deuteronomy 22:23–24).
- Cursing one's parents (Exodus 21:17).
- Stubbornness and rebellion (Deuteronomy 21:18–21).
- Blasphemy (Leviticus 24:16).
- Working on Saturday (Exodus 35:2).

If we did not want to take the Bible literally but instead wanted to simply adopt the biblical command that murder be punished with death and ignore the long list of other capital offenses, there are other complexities we would have to contend with.

First, we would have to acknowledge that although Mosaic law did provide for a large number of potentially capital crimes, strict procedures were in place that substantially limited the actual use of the death penalty. For example, Mosaic law required two eyewitnesses to convict someone of a capital crime, rejected the testimony of conflicting eyewitness testimony, required eyewitnesses to warn the offender that the act he was going to commit was unlawful and could result in the punishment of death, and rejected circumstantial evidence and the confession of the accused (Douglas 2000). These strict procedural requirements meant that death sentences were rare despite the fact that capital crimes were many. Evidence of a general disinclination to apply the death penalty under ancient Hebrew law comes from a passage in the Talmud where it was agreed by several prominent rabbis that "a Sanhedrin which executes once in seven years is known as destructive" (Berg 2000, 38).

The second thing that would have to be understood by anyone wanting to cite selective passages in the Old Testament to provide support for the death penalty is that many of these passages must be interpreted in their proper historical context and might not be saying what they seem. For example, the admonition in Exodus to require "life for life, eye for eye, tooth for tooth" may also be interpreted as a desire to limit private vengeance and blood lust. It was not uncommon at the time that in seeking revenge for any number of injuries, large or small, against one of their own, family and clan members would kill all members of the injuring family or community (Berg 2000).

Third, both the Old and New Testaments offer conflicting advice about whether the death penalty is a required punishment or even the punishment that should be imposed. It is clear that the Old Testament approved of the death penalty for a wide variety of offenses. The idea that God gives civil authority the right to put criminals to death is also found in Romans (13:4) in the New Testament: "For he is a servant of God to you for good. But if you do that which is evil, be afraid, for he doesn't bear the sword in vain; for he is a servant

---

Box 6.2
Conflict Between Pulpit and Pew

With the exception of conservative Protestant denominations, the official position of mainline Protestant religions and Roman Catholicism is opposition to the death penalty. This does not square with the fact that approximately 70 percent of the United States public "approves" of the death penalty for murder. It appears as if the official position of organized Christian religion with respect to capital punishment is at odds with the personal views of many of its members. How do we explain this difference of opinion between pulpit and pew?

One explanation might be that religious denominations that officially denounce the death penalty as a matter of church policy may be reluctant to put in the effort and energy required to build support among members to oppose the death penalty. Their opposition to the death penalty, then, may be more symbolic, and organized religion has not taken the next step of being committed to teach about the abolition of capital punishment to its members. Another possibility is that the church has lost much of its influence on modern Americans compared with prior times. Fewer Americans may be relying on their faith in coming to policy decisions about moral matters such as abortion, homosexuality, and the death penalty. People today may be more likely to treat the official positions of their faith like cafeteria offerings—picking and choosing what they like, and leaving the rest behind. ✦

---

of God, an avenger for wrath to him who does evil." There is also a passage from Matthew (18:6) that could be read as supporting the death penalty (at least for child murderers): "Whosoever shall offend one of these little ones that believe in me, it is better for him that a millstone were hanged about his neck, and he were cast into the sea."

In addition to procedural restrictions on the use of the death penalty and the necessity to read scripture within its historical context, however, there are numerous passages in the Bible, particularly the New Testament, that could be seen as in opposition to capital punishment. For example, in John (8:1–11), when Jesus is brought a woman accused of adultery (a capital offense), he admonishes the accusers that "let him who is without sin cast the first stone." In the Sermon on the Mount (Matthew 5:38–39), Jesus told his followers, "You have heard that it was said, 'An eye for an eye and a tooth for a tooth.' But I say to you, Do not resist one who is evil. But if any one strikes you on the right cheek, turn to him the other also." Many have taken the God of the New Testament as a God of forgiveness and mercy in contrast to the wrathful and vengeful God of the Old Testament.

It is certainly possible, therefore, that we can find both support for and against the death penalty within the messages of the Bible. If we were to examine the formal position about the death penalty held by various religious denominations we would also get a mixed verdict—though most organized religions now seem to be opposed to the death penalty. Although it had for centuries condoned the use of capital punishment (Megivern 1997; Brugger 2003), the position of the Catholic Church today is that it opposes it as part of a "culture of death" (the Catholic Church also opposes abortion for similar reasons). In 1995 Pope John Paul II published his *Evangelium Vitae*, in which in making a general plea for the sanctity of all human life he stated that:

> There is a growing tendency, both in the Church and civil society, to demand that [the death penalty] be applied in a very limited way or even that it be abolished completely. . . . The nature and extent of the punishment must be carefully evaluated and decided upon, and ought not to go to the extreme of executing the offender except in cases of absolute necessity: in other words, when it would be possible otherwise to defend society. Today however, as a result of steady improvements in the organization of the penalty system, such cases are very rare, if not practically nonexistent.

The papacy has made good on this position, making repeated pleas to United States officials to commute death sentences to life in prison terms. The Catholic Catechism affirms the position of the *Evangelium Vitae* that the death penalty should rarely if at all be imposed:

> If . . . nonlethal means are sufficient to defend and protect people's safety form the aggressor, authority will limit itself to such means, as these are more in keeping with the concrete conditions of the common good more in conformity with the dignity of the human person. Today, in fact, as a consequence of the possibilities which the state has for effectively preventing crime, by rendering one who has committed an offense incapable of doing harm—without definitively taking away from him the possibility of redeeming himself—the cases in which the execution of the offender is an absolute necessity "are very rare, if not practically nonexistent." (Cited in Douglas, 2000, 165)

In addition to the Catholic Church, many mainline Protestant denominations have come out against the death penalty. The Episcopal Church opposes capital punishment on the grounds that "the taking of such a human life falls within the province of Almighty God and not within the right of Man. . ." (American Friends Service Committee 2006). The American Baptist Church in the U.S.A. declared that "we . . . condemn the current reinstatement of capital punishment and oppose its use under any new or old state or federal law, and call for an immediate end to planned executions throughout this country" (American Friends Service Committee 2006). The Presbyterian Church (USA) in its 197th General Assembly in 1985 "calls upon governing bodies and members to work for the abolition of the death penalty in those states which currently have capital punishment statutes, and against efforts to reinstate such statutes in those which do not" (American Friends Service Committee 2006). The American Jewish Committee joined these Christian organizations in condemning capital punishment. In its statement on capital punishment at its 66th annual meeting in 1972, it held that "the death penalty is cruel, unjust and incompatible with the dignity and self respect of man . . . [and] that the American Jewish Committee be recorded as favoring the abolition of the death penalty" (American Friends Service Committee 2006). In sum, virtually every mainline Protestant denomination, the Catholic Church, and most Jewish organizations in the United States have come out with official positions against the death penalty.

The exception to this opposition to the death penalty has come from more conservative Protestant denominations. For example, the Southern Baptist Convention in June 2000 stated that since "God authorized capital punishment for murder after the Noahic Flood, validating its legitimacy in human society . . . the messengers to the Southern Baptist Convention . . . support the fair and equitable use of capital punishment by civil magistrates as a legitimate form of punishment for those guilty of murder or treasonous acts that result in death" (Southern Baptist Convention 2006). The Lutheran Church–Missouri Synod pronounced a qualified endorsement of the death penalty. While recognizing that its members might hold a different opinion, it has resolved that "capital punishment is in accord with the Holy Scriptures and the Lutheran Confessions" (Lutheran Church–Missouri Synod 2006). It has also stated that while civil authority has the right to use capital punishment, it does not have the duty to always use it and may use some other punishment if it "would better serve society." The Orthodox Presbyterian Church believes that the Bible teaches the infallible word of God. It cites Genesis (9:6) "whoever sheds man's blood, by man his blood shall be shed" as justification for the death penalty in today's society (Douglas 2000; Orthodox Presbyterian Church 2006). Orthodox Jews break from both Conservative and Reform Judaism in supporting the death penalty, citing as authority God's command in Genesis (Union of Orthodox Jewish Congregations 2006). It also, however, recently endorsed a moratorium on all executions pending an examination of the fairness of the administration of the death penalty in states that use it.

There is also strong support for the death penalty in Islamic law. While the role of capital punishment in Islam is not influential in U.S. debates about the death penalty, most of the nations that still retain the death penalty are predominantly Islamic states (see Chapter 10). Schabas (2000) has shown that like its Christian and Jewish counterparts, Islam has progressive and conservative forms. He argues that there certainly is support for capital punishment for some crimes in the Quran. For example, according to the Quran the most severe crimes are those that are thought to threaten the very existence of Islam itself, and these are deemed to be punishable only by death. These crimes would include adultery, robbery, and apostasy (abandoning Islam). Less serious offenses are intentional crimes against the person. The principle behind punishment of these crimes is similar to the "eye for an eye" of the *lex talionis:*

> Nor take life—which Allah has made sacred—except for just cause. And if anyone is slain wrongfully, we have given his heir authority [to demand qisas or to forgive]; but let him not exceed bound in the matter of taking life, for he is helped [by the law]. (Quran 17:33)

The principle is one of giving authority to punish murder with death, but it does not demand that the only acceptable punishment for a murderer is death. This variation in Islamic law is manifested in different practices of capital punishment across Islamic states. Some countries, including Iran, Iraq, and Saudi Arabia, have executed far more offenders than others, such as Tunisia.

Chapter Summary

In this chapter we have examined four possible justifications for the existence of the death penalty: (1) the moral argument—death is morally deserved punishment for those who have taken a life; (2) the economic argument—executions save the taxpayer money; (3) the first public safety argument—the execution of the murderer keeps him from committing another crime; and (4) the second public safety argument—executions serve as an effective general deterrent by preventing would-be murderers from committing homicide. In discussing these four common justifications for the death penalty, we were led to the conclusion that they are shrouded in controversy and ambiguity. Although it may appear intuitively simple that the only morally appropriate penalty for those who kill is for their life to be taken, this simple argument quickly becomes much more complex. Determining without ambiguity how much punishment criminal offenders "morally deserve" is not always as straightforward as it appears.

The cost of maintaining the system of capital punishment that we have today, with its careful jury selection, bifurcated hearings, and lengthy appeals, may actually be substantially more than for a system that has life imprisonment without parole as its most severe sanction. The most unambiguous justification for the death penalty seems to be that it better prevents the one being punished from ever committing another crime than life in prison. While recognizing the truth of this fact, it would also have to be acknowledged that those awaiting their execution can conceivably kill while on death row or escape and kill an innocent member of the community. Finally, the argument in favor of the death penalty from the perspective of general deterrence is also intuitively appealing, although its validity remains unknown. We simply cannot say with any degree of confidence that executing people is better at deterring would-be murderers than life in prison. Like so many other elements to the death penalty, issues pertaining to its justification are always both very reasonable and greatly in dispute.

Discussion Questions

1. What role do you think religious beliefs should play in the Supreme Court's decisions in death penalty cases? Do your religious beliefs affect your view of capital punishment?

2. Based on your understanding of the evidence, do you think that capital punishment is a more effective general deterrent to murder than life imprisonment? Suppose the empirical evidence conclusively showed that capital punishment does prevent murders, but on average only one per execution. Would you favor the death penalty? Suppose the empirical evidence showed that each execution leads to an additional murder, what would think about the death penalty? Does the presence or ab-

     sence of a general deterrent effect influence your position on the death penalty?

3. Why do you think there is some controversy about the existence of a general deterrent effect for the death penalty? Why is it so difficult to find a deterrent effect that seems to stand up to critical analysis?

4. Suppose it could be shown conclusively that having the death penalty is more costly (or less costly) for taxpayers than a system of criminal justice that has only life imprisonment. Would that affect your view of the death penalty?

5. Do you think vengeance has any role to play in punishment by the state? Explain.

6. Do you think executions should be made public events again, or at least shown on television? Do you think public or televised executions would produce a deterrent effect or a brutalization effect?

7. Some states use victim impact statements that allow family members to tell the jury during the penalty phase of a capital trial the effect that the murder of their loved one has had on their life. What are the arguments for and against the use of such statements?

8. Suppose it could be shown that those convicted of murder constitute a higher risk of committing a violent crime in the future than others. Would that lead you to be in favor of executing them, or is life in prison without parole an acceptable alternative? What are the arguments on both sides of this issue?

9. How do you morally determine whether a murderer "deserves" to die? What are the moral criteria you would use in making this determination? How difficult, and how certain, do you think this determination would be?

Student Resources

     It has been argued that the death penalty should be kept because it helps family members left behind find some peace, sense of justice achieved, or closure. Like anything else about the death penalty, there are two sides to this story. Some organizations of surviving family members argue for and support the retention and use of the death penalty. A compelling tale of how family members try to make sense out of their tragic killing of their daughter, and their impassioned response to Sister Helen Prejean's book *Dead Man Walking,* is *Dead Family Talking* by D. D. Divinci.

     Some organizations of surviving family members feel strongly that the death penalty is not the solution to murder, even the murder of their loved ones. To learn more about them, go to the website of Murder Victims' Families for Human Rights at <www.murdervictimsfamilies.org/>. See also Murder Victims' Families for Reconciliation, another victims' family group opposed to the death penalty: <www.mvfr.org>. For a moving discussion of the position of family members whose loved one has been murdered, read Rachel King's

Don't Kill in Our Names: Families of Murder Victims Speak Out Against the Death Penalty and *What to Do When the Police Leave* by Bill Jenkins.

Lawyer and author Joan M. Cheever recently published a book, *Back From the Dead: One Woman's Search for the Men Who Walked Off America's Death Row* (2006). She interviewed more than 300 former prisoners who were released by the *Furman* decision, relating what happened to them when they were freed from death row. Some of them returned to crime, but all of them struggled with their lives both in and out of prison.

Seattle University has an excellent and detailed website covering religious thought on capital punishment. Find it at <www.seattleu.edu/lemlib/web_archives/DMW/religion.htm>.

Endnotes

1. There are a few exceptions. For example, some states include as a capital offense aircraft hijacking, treason, and sexual assault on a child by someone with a previous such conviction.

2. The legislatures of both South Carolina and Oklahoma, however, passed acts in 2006 that permitted the death penalty for the sexual assault of a child. Whether these acts will pass constitutional muster is not yet known.

3. In *Tison v. Arizona* (107 S. Ct. 1676, 1987) the Court held that the death penalty is permissible for an offender who did not take, intend, or attempt to take the life of another if the offender demonstrated a reckless disregard for human life and if his or her participation in the crime was major.

4. Kenneth McDuff was a former Texas death row inmate released into the community by the *Furman* decision; however, he was convicted of his murders after the Marquart and Sorensen paper was published. We also do not know if any of the former lifers who were released on parole committed a murder after their paper was published.

5. For an excellent review of the general deterrence literature on capital punishment, see Peterson and Bailey (2003).

6. This does not, of course, take into account the possible effect that the *frequency* of executions in death penalty states may make a difference for deterrence and that Figure 6.2 only examines the possibility of an execution. This is true. However, with the possible exception of one or two states, most states that have the death penalty use it so infrequently that the most likely difference is that between a state that maintains the possibility of the death penalty and one that maintains no such possibility.

7. The first five books of the Old Testament (Genesis, Exodus, Leviticus, Numbers, and Deuteronomy) make up the Pentateuch, which details the Mosaic Code. The Code provides a list of civic and religious offenses and their appropriate punishments and served as the guide for ancient Jewish law. ✦

Part III
The Administration of the Death Penalty: Issues of Race and Human Fallability

In this section of the book we discuss two features of the administration of capital punishment: (1) the fact that race (both of the offender and victim) has played and continues to play a prominent role in who gets the death penalty and who gets spared, and (2) human errors in capital cases, both deliberate and unintentional, are fairly commonplace. As we learned in Chapters 1–3, one of the inescapable facts about the death penalty is that it has been imposed more frequently on minorities and, during the Modern Period, on those who kill whites more often than those who kill blacks. In the second chapter of this section (Chapter 8) we go through the extensive evidence linking capital punishment with race at key decision-making points in the death penalty process. Since there is little quality data before 1930, we provide information on the relationship between race and capital punishment only during what we have called the Premodern and Modern periods of capital punishment. Before we discuss this empirical evidence, however, in Chapter 7 we discuss the historical context of race and the legal system.

If Chapter 8 presents evidence that "race matters" in the administration of the death penalty in America, Chapter 7 illustrates why that might be the case. Capital punishment is inextricably connected to race because the legal system and punishment have historically been connected to race. Slavery was a legal institution backed by punishment. While the Civil War ended slavery, it did not put an end to the connection between race and the law. Slave Codes, which criminalized a number of behaviors if committed by blacks, were replaced by Black Codes, which were then later replaced with so-called "Jim Crow" laws. All of these laws, and the legal sanctions that enforced them, punished not only criminal acts but violations of racial etiquette. While Chapter 8 explicitly shows the connection between race and capital punishment, Chapter 7 tries to show that this relationship did not just appear out of thin air. A history precedes the connection of race to the death penalty, and Chapter 7 reviews this historical record linking race with the operation of the legal system in general, from colonial times to the present. In making a connection between race and society in general and the workings of capital punishment, we agree with Justice Blackmun's view that "[p]erhaps it should not be surprising that the biases and prejudices that infect society generally would influence the determination of who is sentenced to death" (*Callins v. Collins*, 610 U. S. 1141, 1994).

If it's not surprising that the administration of the death penalty might be affected by the "biases and prejudices" that characterize society as a whole, it might also be reasonable to think that it is also affected by the limitations, weaknesses, and frailties of those who operate that system—human beings. Humans are not perfectly rational and perfectly moral beings, and as a result they can be affected by emotions, miscalculations, and mistakes. In his dissenting opinion in *Callins*, Justice Blackmun further characterized capital punishment as involving a "machinery of death" that is operated by human actors—defense attorneys, prosecutors, and judges. After reviewing nearly two decades of capital cases, he came to the conclusion that America's experiment with the death penalty was a failure. A failure because the law cannot guarantee that death sentences will be free of caprice, arbitrariness, racial discrimination, and mistake. While noting that the Court (with his participation) has attempted over the years to create a fair death penalty with a rigorous set of procedural requirements and rules, Justice Blackmun concluded that the effort has not brought much success: "This is not to say that the problems with the death penalty today are identical to those that were present 20 years ago. Rather, the problems that were pursued down one hole with procedural rules and verbal formulas have come to the surface somewhere else, just as virulent and pernicious as they were in their original form." This failure led Justice Blackmun, a death penalty supporter in the past, to urge the abolition of capital punishment and to state that "[f]rom this day forward, I no longer shall tinker with the machinery of death." In the final chapter of this section, Chapter 9, we show that an argument can be made that the machinery of death described by Justice Blackmun is breaking down, or at least showing considerable wear and tear. ✦

Chapter 7
Race, the Law, and Punishment

There has always been an uneasy relationship between the legal system and racial minorities in the United States, so no one should be surprised to find that race has historically been implicated in the administration of capital punishment. The uneasy relationship is that racial minorities, particularly African Americans, are often thought to be disproportionately singled out by the law and arrested, tried, convicted, and more severely punished than whites. The strong form of this claim is that the legal system is deliberately used by racial majorities to oppress racial minorities and that this oppression extends from the content of the law to the day-to-day workings of the police, the judicial system, and correctional/penal institutions. The weaker form of this claim is that although racial oppression may not be the explicit goal of the legal and criminal justice system, or the deliberate intent of its actors, racial minorities nevertheless bear the brunt of the law and the administration of the law. In other words, while the law and legal actors may not consciously intend to discriminate against racial minorities, the law still has a racially disparate impact.

The Peculiar Institution

The American colonies were settled and developed by both free people and slaves. While we often think of slavery as a Southern institution, slavery existed in early northern colonies as well. The first Dutch settlements in New Netherlands were populated by slave blacks and Creoles (Berlin 2003; Davis 2006). Without a stable crop to toil for, however, Northern slaves performed labors (tending livestock, farming, building fortifications) that did not separate them from free men and women, and many enjoyed all the amenities of life (marrying, acquiring property) that free persons enjoyed. Even at the beginning of the American Revolution there were slaves in Boston, New York, and Philadelphia and in the agricultural areas of Pennsylvania, New Jersey, and New York (Berlin 1998, 2003), and slaves made up at times between one-third and one-half of the total population.

Between the early colonial settlements and the mid-eighteenth century, Northern authorities passed legislation that restricted the freedom of blacks in a way very similar to what we will describe was occurring in the South. What happened in the North, however, that did not take place in the South was that in time whites joined with blacks in urging the end of slavery, and white farmers in the North did not reorganize their crop production system along the lines of a plantation economy. The Revolutionary War, itself driven by the goal of individual freedom and liberty, was to provide further impetus to the emancipation of slaves in the North. The process of emancipation was slow even in

Northern states, however, with slaves existing in New York and New Jersey until the mid-nineteenth century (Berlin 2003).

While slavery existed in the North, it was more firmly entrenched in the South and was protected with greater vigilance and vehemence, in large part because it became an indispensable part of the Southern plantation economy (Davis 2006). The historian Kenneth M. Stampp (1956) attributes the rise and growth of slavery in Southern agriculture not to some inevitable feature of Southern culture, politics, or economic structure but rather to the rational and conscious decision of men who realized that they could secure greater economic benefit to themselves by exploiting the labor of people they bought and owned. While purchasing the labor of others was a legitimate and available alternative to Southern planters, doing so was, according to Stampp, far more expensive, and with the importation of slaves, avoidable. The Southern agricultural economy, would, therefore, be built upon the backs of inexpensive slave labor.

The source of this cheap labor was plentiful. Although the importation of new slaves into the American colonies was widely prohibited by the later eighteenth century—Delaware prohibited the importation of new slaves in 1776, Virginia in 1778, Maryland in 1783, South Carolina in 1787, North Carolina in 1794, and Georgia in 1798—there were more than enough slaves to replenish the supply through natural reproduction. Increasing the supply of slaves after the closing of the slave trade was made easier by the ascription of black status to those born of mixed white and black blood (Davis 2006). Over time, every state legislature had some formal code or formula that defined the amount of black blood necessary to determine racial status. In Virginia, for example, a person with "one-fourth part or more of Negro blood shall be deemed a mulatto, and the word 'negro' . . . shall be construed to mean mulatto as well as negro" (Stampp 1956, 195). In addition, without exception legislatures adopted the principle of *partus sequitier ventrem*—the child inherits the condition of the mother. As a result, any child born of a slave mother, whether fathered by black or white, was a slave. As a result of this principle, slavery became an inherited characteristic.

While slaves provided a steady supply of cheap labor for the Southern economy, unlike the whites who benefited from the practice, slaves themselves were not inclined to think that their bondage was divinely inspired, natural, or for their own benefit. In other words, having slaves was only a potential solution to a labor problem for white Southern planters; slave labor had to be motivated and persuaded, and if that failed it had to be coerced. What made the motivation and control of slaves easier was the fact that slaves were considered to be the personal property of slaveholders. The transition from black servant to chattel property was a gradual one that existed in customary practices long before it did in law. Stampp (1956) has noted that both white and black bondage existed from the early days of the colonies in the form of indentured servitude. In fact, in ordinary usage the term "slave" may have referred to either white or black servants. He further argues that initially black servants were treated very much like white ones, including the fact that they were released from their servitude or indentured status after working for a term of years for their masters or if they were baptized and converted to Christianity.

It was only slowly that a distinction emerged between white and black servants, a recognition that was hastened by the Southern planters' growing need for cheap labor and the clear cultural and physical differences between white and blacks that provided a ready justification for any legal distinction. While the initial legal status of the black servant may have been unclear, what is clear is that overtime the status of the black servant deteriorated while that of the white improved. A formal (that is, legal) distinction between black and white servants did not emerge until after 1650, when statutes began to acknowledge the fact that black servants were in servitude for life, that children inherited the free/slave status of their mother, and that conversion to Christianity did not alter one's slave status. Because of the unquestioned economic benefits secured for whites by black slavery and the need to stabilize the relationship, the legal status of chattel slavery—that blacks were the private property of whites—emerged (Davis 2006).

Since slaves did not willingly adapt to their status as the purely private property of another person, a defiant position that slaveholders recognized, there had to be ways to enforce the institution of slavery. Here is where the law, both formal and informal entered. Legal statutes were constructed by slaveholders to protect their investment by providing for the disciplining of recalcitrant, disobedient, and rebellious slaves, and means were devised to enforce those statutes. Every state that was a slave state eventually adopted a formal recognition of slavery and a way to control slaves though what became known as *slave codes*.

The Slave Codes

These slave codes did a number of things that made the control over slaves less difficult. For one thing they clearly defined black servants as the chattel property of the slaveholder or master. The idea of the slave as property right was taken literally. Slaves were often included in wills along with land, horses, mules, cows and farm equipment. Slaves could be wagered at card games or horse races, and slaves and their children (both existing and as yet conceived) could and were given as gifts. The fact that the slave was taken as the legal personal property of the master meant that the slaveholder had virtually unlimited power over the slave without outside intervention. The state essentially treated the relationship between master and slave as a purely private matter. Slaveholders could, therefore, discipline and punish their slaves as they saw fit, as well as completely restrict their freedom virtually without consequence. Slaves, therefore, were legally at the mercy of their masters.[1]

While slave codes in later years did specify some limits on the master's power by regulating the hours of labor, prohibiting labor on Sunday, and preventing cruelty, slaves were mostly regulated by the rules that existed on their plantation (hours of labor, meal times, recreation, worship, care of tools), rules that were devised and enforced at the discretion of the master (Stampp 1956; Williamson 1984). The "law of the plantation" was idiosyncratic, as seen in the Louisiana Slave Code of 1806: "The master may sell him, dispose of his person, his industry, and his labor: he can do nothing, possess nothing, nor acquire anything but what must belong to his master" (Stampp 1956, 197).

Slave codes did more than define the master's property rights, they virtually regulated every aspect of the slaves' existence (Berlin 2003; Davis 2006). At the heart of every slave code were rules that enforced the manner in which slaves interacted with and behaved toward not only their master and mistress, but whites in general. For instance, although differing in precise language, all of the slave codes prescribed the demeanor and deportment of slaves toward and in the presence of whites. A slave could not talk back to a white or use abusive language. Acts of insolence or defiance were forbidden, such as a scowl, a pointed finger, rolled eyes, or even a smirk. Blacks had to move out of the way when approaching whites, take their hats off, and cast their eyes downward. The behavior of black males toward white females was even more carefully restricted. Black males were forbidden to speak or write (if they could) to white females, nor could they be found alone with them. The slave codes, then, went so far as to define what was appropriate behavior for blacks in the presence of whites and enforced a racial etiquette that unmistakably demonstrated the social inferiority of slaves.[2]

Slave codes restricted the freedoms of blacks in other ways. Slaves were forbidden to be off the plantation without a "pass" and had to show such a pass to any white man who demanded to see it. A slave without a pass and found a certain distance from their plantation was assumed to be a runaway. In many states slaves were provided with identification tags, which they were required to wear. Slaves could not live alone, outside the plantation, nor could they be out after curfew. Under many codes slaves could not smoke, play or enjoy music, or even dance. In Natchez Mississippi, all "strange slaves" had to leave the city by 4:00 in the afternoon on Sunday (Stampp, 1956). Slaves could not assemble in groups, even for the purpose of worship, nor preach to other slaves without the approval of the master or without a white person present. Slaves were forbidden to learn to read or write, and anyone teaching slaves to read or write was harshly punished. Slaves were not permitted to own weapons, musical instruments (lest they communicate behind the master's back), liquor, or even farm tools. They could not hire themselves out for work, nor work for themselves. Slaves could not marry, since marriage is a contract and all slaves were forbidden to form contracts, nor could they keep their own families together.

Violations of these codes on the part of slaves were met with a variety of responses by whites. The first line of social control was the master. To this regard, Stampp (1956) quotes a Southern judge as saying that "[t]he power of the master must be absolute, to render the submission of the slave perfect" (p. 141). We mentioned previously that under slave codes slaves as chattel property were at the disposal of their master. Slaveholders were given explicit approval to punish violations of racial etiquette and other parts of the code. Typically the punishments were physical, primarily whipping, but also included beatings and brandings. Punished slaves were also denied food and water, given barely edible "punishment food," placed in small confinement cells on the plantation or left in the hot sun staked to the ground or tied to a tree, given extra work or forced to work on Sundays, or "salted" by putting brine into whip wounds. Virtually all minor transgressions by slaves were handled by "plantation justice," and many serious offenses were as well, though it was not unusual for a slave who committed a felony to be tried by local courts. Appeals to the formal criminal justice system were not the norm, however, a point alluded to by one Southener:

> On our estates we dispose with the whole machinery of public police and public courts of justice. Thus we try, decide, and execute the sentence of *thousands of cases,* which, in other countries would go to the courts. (quoted in Ayers 1984, 135)

In addition to punishment at the hands of one's own master, communities also had responses to violations of the slave code. While other whites were not usually allowed to physically discipline someone else's slave (at least not harshly), slave patrols kept vigilance over the land. Slave patrols existed in almost every slave state, usually authorized by statute (as part of the slave code) and worked closely with the state militia (Stampp 1956; Williamson 1984). They initially consisted of groups of slaveholders themselves or their overseers who acted as watchful members of the patrol for rotating periods of time. Later, nonslaveholding whites were pressed into service on the patrols. The duty of the slave patrols was to provide surveillance, keeping a watchful eye out for trouble in a preventive strategy (checking passes, making sure there were no forbidden assemblies or dancing or drinking, and searching slave quarters) or responding reactively to trouble (such as searching for a runaway). The patrols served as police, judge, and jury and also carried out the sentence handed down by "the court." Slave patrols whipped, beat, psychologically terrorized, and lynched disobedient slaves and free blacks in an attempt to keep the racial hierarchy intact.

Criminal Codes

Slave codes were not the only legal source of control that whites had for keeping free blacks or slaves compliant and obedient. The criminal law and criminal justice system of the state were enjoined to protect the existing racial structure. Criminal codes frequently defined some kinds of conduct as illegal for blacks but not whites (reading and writing, possessing firearms, alcohol), made some acts felonies if committed by blacks but not whites, and differentially punished the criminal behavior of blacks and whites, since the crime of a slave was far more reprehensible than the crime of a free person. For example, the list of potential capital crimes for blacks far outnumbered the list for whites. In addition to murder, blacks could be put to death for attempted murder, manslaughter, rape and the attempted rape of a white woman, rebellion, arson, and robbery. An assault on a white person might also under some circumstances carry a capital penalty for slaves (Stampp 1956). For noncapital crimes the punishment for whites was likely to include imprisonment or a fine, while for blacks it was most likely to be whipping or some other physical punishment (branding or mutilation).

While most minor crimes committed by slaves were handled informally by slaveholders or slave patrols, more serious offenses such as major felonies and capital crimes were handled by the courts. These courts, however, did not exist in a social or economic vacuum. The law itself protected white interests against black, and legal procedures overwhelmingly favored whites (blacks could not serve on juries, nor could they testify against whites for example, and in a stance of racial solidarity, whites were reluctant to testify against other whites).

In sum, there was a vast set of institutions at several levels that served to keep slaves at least outwardly obedient and compliant. The highest level was the law. Slave codes gave the slave the status of chattel property and provided a way for the slaveholder and white society in general the means to regulate virtually every aspect of the behavior of slaves. The law also declared that the property right of the slaveholder was virtually absolute—the slave was required to submit to the demands of the master, and the slave codes permitted (and required) the punishment of disobedient slaves.

National law also protected the interests of whites and slaveholders. Federal troops were called on to assist in putting down slave insurrections, such as the Nat Turner rebellion in 1831. In both the Missouri Compromise of 1820 and the Compromise of 1850 Congress determined that it would not interfere with the slave trade, treating it as a local institution whose fate would be determined by the citizens of states and territories. Part of the Compromise of 1850 was the Fugitive Slave Act, under which free citizens were required to assist in the recovery and return of fugitive slaves. In 1854 the United States Supreme Court handed down its decision in the *Dred Scott* case, in which it ruled that neither free nor slave blacks could ever be considered a citizen of the United States and that contrary to the Missouri Compromise, slavery could not be excluded from any United States territory. Finally, local law and custom, including the "law of the plantation" joined state and federal efforts to keep slaves in their place, economically, politically, and socially.

Box 7.1
The *Amistad* Case

On June 28, 1839 the schooner *Amistad* left Havana, Cuba bound for another Cuban coastal town. On board the *Amistad* were five whites and 53 African slaves. The slaves had been taken from Africa in violation of an international treaty between England and Spain that forbade the importation of slaves into Spanish colonies. En route to their destination the slaves mutinied, killing the captain and a mulatto cook.

Two other crewmen were spared and were instructed by the slaves to return the ship to Africa. The crewmen slowly steered the schooner westward toward Africa during the day, but tried to speedily sail eastward at night in the hopes of landing on more hospitable shores. In August the ship anchored off the coast of Long Island and was soon boarded by the U.S. Coast Guard brig the *U.S. Washington*. The *Amistad* was towed to New London, Connecticut, where the U.S. Attorney for Connecticut, William S. Holabird, ordered a hearing.

On August 29, 1839, a hearing was held on charges of murder and piracy against the slaves. After this hearing, presiding Judge Judson referred the case to trial in federal circuit court, and the slaves were placed into custody in New Haven. Spain had been pressing the United States to return the cargo and the slaves back to Havana, and then U.S. President Martin Van Buren was sympathetic to those demands.

The trial of the Amistad's slaves concluded with the judge ruling that they were born free and kidnapped both against their will and international law. He ordered that they be returned by the Van Buren administration to Africa. The government appealed their defeat all the way to the Supreme Court, where former president then-congressman John Quincy Adams argued on behalf of the slaves. On March 9, 1841 Justice Story announced the decision of the Court: The African slaves were freemen who had been kidnapped and were entitled to their freedom. In November 1841 a ship was chartered to return the surviving Africans to Sierra Leone, their home (see Jones 1987). ✦

Clearly, then, the law and legal institutions were instrumental in supporting white interests against slaves and free blacks. National, state, territorial, and local laws, codes and ordinances protected the interests of whites and slaveholders at the expense of the interests of free and slave blacks. Moreover, as we will see, the use of the legal system to support and protect white interests against black did not end with the civil war and the passage of the Thirteenth Amendment, which abolished slavery in the United States.

Race and Legal Institutions After the Civil War

With the end of the Civil War and the defeat of Southern military forces, the now-unified United States embarked on a period of Reconstruction. For black and white Americans in the South, Reconstruction was going to be a difficult and unsettling time if for no other reason than that the Thirteenth Amendment freed several million black slaves, thereby ending, at least on its face, the absolute control of whites over blacks. Although slavery had been vanquished (at least in the law), the legal subjugation of the black population in the South did not end with the Civil War. Moreover, since the white labor pool had been decimated by years of war and blacks could no longer be forced into slave labor, and those that remained on plantations were likely reluctant to work as hard as they had, there was an acute shortage of willing and able workers in the South (Tolnay and Beck 1995).

Although they had been defeated in the war, Southern whites who had been in positions of both social and economic power were not likely to give up their legal and economic advantages easily—particularly given the almost dire economic conditions. Despite the fact that the Thirteenth Amendment had abolished slavery, powerful Southern interests, primarily agricultural interests, tried to solve their labor problems and the problem caused by blacks freed from white control by using whatever economic and political power they still possessed to ensure that they would continue to retain control over the large, but now "free" black population.

With the assassination of President Lincoln and with Congress not in session, the task of guiding Reconstruction initially fell to President Andrew Johnson. As a native Tennessean, Johnson was sympathetic to the plight of poor Southern farmers and skeptical of the role of newly freed slaves in the rebuilding of the South (Foner and Mahoney 1995). This period of Presidential

Reconstruction, as it is called, was generally lenient on the South. Johnson offered pardons to Southern whites, except wealthy planters and the leaders of the secession, and ordered that new governments be formed. The new governments, however, would consist of offices for whites only, and when they were formed, many in the old Southern white political establishment were returned to power.

The Black Codes

As evidence of the fact that little had changed since slavery and that in spite of emancipation white politicians were not ready to give up on enforced servitude for freed blacks, newly formed Southern state governments passed new laws known as *Black Codes*. These Black Codes were passed almost immediately after the Civil War; for example, Alabama, South Carolina, Louisiana, and Mississippi passed Black Codes in 1865, and by 1866 all of the former Confederate states had adopted comparable statutes. The codes defined both the legal and social status of freed blacks. They did state that former slaves had some legal rights that they previously did not enjoy, such as the rights to own property, enter into contracts including marriage contracts, and file suits. In addition, however, the Black Codes also tried to closely limit the freedom, particularly the economic freedom, of newly freed slaves and tried to reestablish the system of racial etiquette that existed under slavery. One critic of the codes noted at the time that they were attempts to "restore all of slavery but its name" (Foner 1983; Foner and Mahoney 1995). The Black Codes reflected two fears among many Southern whites: (1) that freed blacks would think of themselves and act as if they were the equal of whites, and (2) that blacks would not work unless they were forced to do so.

Some of the most important provisions of the Black Codes were the various forms of labor restrictions imposed on newly freed blacks to force them back on the plantation and to work under labor conditions that were advantageous to white planters (Nolen 1967). One of these restrictions was that freed blacks were prevented from entering certain nonagricultural occupations and trades. In South Carolina, for example, freed blacks could only secure jobs as agricultural workers or domestic servants unless they paid a hefty fee to secure a license as a skilled craftsman (Tolnay and Beck 1995). In other states, blacks were required to sign labor contracts every year that specified in detail for whom they would be working that year, the daily hours and the pay, and provided financial sanctions and physical punishments for poor performance such as insubordination, disobedience, lying, laziness, destruction of equipment, and theft. These labor contracts carried with them legal support since they generally had to be filed with the local court. Also a part of the code were new vagrancy laws. Blacks who were unemployed or who had no labor contract with a white employer could be deemed vagrants by the court. Those arrested for vagrancy were most likely fined, and those unable to pay their fine would be punished by having their labor contracted out to a local planter. Blacks arrested for other, minor offenses could also be punished by coerced contract labor. Both the vagrancy and convict-lease statutes served to provide local agricultural interests with a steady and cheap supply of labor. Unlike whites, blacks had to prove that they were either employed or self-supporting, or else the law would intervene and force them either to work or to prison. Moreover, the termination of these labor contracts before they expired was illegal for any black or mulatto.

The labor of minors was not ignored. By various apprenticeship provisions of the Black Codes, orphan black children or the children of impoverished parents who could not provide for their care became wards of the court. The court then apprenticed these children to "masters" (employers). In exchange for food, clothing, medical attention, and education in some vocational trade (which could include that of farm worker), masters had virtually complete control over the labor of the apprentice and had the authority to use corporal punishment to coerce work and enforce compliance with rules. Masters also had the authority of the legal system to pursue and punish runaway apprentices.

It was not just the labor of newly freed slaves that was regulated; indeed, as with slavery itself the Black Codes attempted to limit many of the freedoms only recently secured by emancipation. Although blacks were provided with some legal rights under the codes, they were still generally prohibited from voting, holding public office, serving on juries, or testifying in criminal and civil cases against whites. Although blacks could now enter into marriage contracts, they were strictly forbidden by law from marrying whites. Blacks could not buy, own, or carry firearms, ammunition, or in some cases even a knife. Many codes prevented blacks from owning or renting farmland, raising their own crops for sale, or residing within town or city limits. In many areas blacks were prevented from entering town without permission or without a special pass that specifically stated what business they were on and the length of the visit. Other codes required state railroads to offer separate accommodations for white and black customers (a harbinger of segregation), and educational provisions prohibited the use of public funds for black schools.

A final component of the Black Codes that is important for our concerns was the criminal justice provisions. The criminal justice system worked hand-in-hand with local white economic interests to suppress blacks. Most Southern whites believed that slavery had kept the brutal instinct of blacks in check. Without slavery these criminal instincts could be given full sway with disastrous consequences for whites and blacks (Nolen 1967). This is perhaps nowhere seen more clearly than in the preamble to the Slave Code of South Carolina, which declared in 1712 that "negroes . . . were of barbarous, wild, savage natures, and . . . wholly unqualified to be governed by the laws, customs, and practices of this province" (Stampp 1956, 11). Given the bestial nature of the black character, slaves had to governed by a special set of rules, Slave Codes, that greatly restricted their freedom and activities and provided for harsh and physical punishments for the violation of rules, even trivial transgressions.

As further proof of the fact that slavery kept the naturally lawless instincts of the black race in check was the "fact," known by most whites in the South, that black crime was on the increase since the end of the Civil War, particularly sexual crimes by black males against white women (Williamson 1984). The theme of the "regression" of blacks toward a more primitive state of nature brought on by their freedom from slavery was a common one in both the academic and lay literature of the day. Equally prominent was the fear held by whites that the "regression" of freed blacks was a direct threat to their safety as well as their dominance. Since, therefore, the lack of restraint and idleness brought on by emancipation inevitably meant vice and licentiousness among blacks, whites had to devise ways to restrict the liberty of blacks without being able to rely on slavery. The vagrancy provisions of the Black Codes nicely did this, creating a crime out of black idleness. Merely criminalizing laziness was not going to solve the problem of potential black criminality, however, since local jails were likely to reach capacity in a short time. Moreover, imprisonment by itself was not going to be much of a solution to planters' post-Civil War labor problems. Out of this twofold need to curb blacks' criminal propensities and to provide cheap labor for whites, institutions such as the convict-lease system and chain gangs developed. The Black Codes saw to it, therefore, that through coerced labor black convicts would provide some financial benefits for whites and provide at least a short-term solution to a burgeoning crime problem.

As under slavery, the criminal justice system also took a more direct role in the restriction of freed blacks in the post-Civil War period. Although not specifically mentioning race or black criminality, the Black Codes saw to it that blacks would be punished differently from whites. One way to ensure this was to give local judicial officials and juries greater discretion (Ayers 1984). Local courts could then draw from a very wide range of punishments when dispensing justice to convicted white and black defendants. A second way to differentially discipline blacks through the law was by providing for particularly severe punishments for what were commonly thought to be "black crimes," such as vagrancy, rape, arson, and burglary (Ayers 1984). There was little for blacks to do about this situation, since they were forbidden from voting (so they could not remove justices or other court officials) or serving on juries (so they could not nullify unpopular verdicts).

Radical Reconstruction

Although viewed as essential in the South for maintaining racial discipline in the absence of slavery, the Black Codes were understandably seen for what they were by Northeners, particularly Radical Republicans (those who thought that President Johnson was being far too lenient with former Confederate Southerners): a thinly veined attempt to retain slavery in only slightly altered form (see, Beck, Massey, and Tolney 1989; Tolnay, Beck, and Massey 1992). Opposition among Radical Republicans to President Johnson's approach to Reconstruction grew, and it grew more vocal as reports came out of the South about violence directed against former slaves and workers from the Freedmen's Bureau. The Freedmen's Bureau was a federal agency created in 1865 whose purpose it was to protect the legal rights of newly freed slaves, provide for the education and medical care of Southern blacks and protect their interests in their dealings with Southern employers (Foner and Mahoney 1995). Opposition to Presidential Reconstruction mounted as moderate and

Radical Republican forces in Congress united to oppose President Johnson's plan to allow former Confederate officials to take seats in Congress and lead the rebuilding of Southern governments. In addition, they passed the wide-sweeping Civil Rights Bill of 1866, which outlawed the Black Codes, defined all persons born in the United States as full U.S. citizens (in opposition to the *Dred Scott* decision), and gave blacks, both Southern and Northern, all of the civil rights enjoyed by whites (though it was silent with respect to the right to vote). President Johnson vetoed the bill, however, and conflict between him and Congress escalated.

In April 1866 Congress overrode President Johnson's veto and passed the Civil Rights Act. More than that, Congress took seriously the notion of what was at stake in the Civil War and wanted to take steps to protect the legal rights of all Americans in such a manner that they would be secure from the attempts of other presidents and Congressional majorities to take them away. Their efforts resulted in the passage of the Fourteenth Amendment to the United States Constitution in April of 1866. The Fourteenth Amendment makes many important proclamations, including the fact that all persons born in the United States are citizens of the United States, that no state can make or enforce any law that "shall abridge the privileges or immunities" of any citizen, that no state can deny any citizen of life, liberty, or property without due process of law, and that no person shall be denied "the equal protection of the laws." Essentially, the Fourteenth Amendment guaranteed equality before the law for all citizens and made it the responsibility of the federal government to protect the civil rights of all persons. Though very broad, it still left the issue of black voting rights unresolved. Not surprisingly, Southern states balked at such measures and refused to ratify the Amendment, pushing Congress to pass the Reconstruction Act of 1867, which initiated the period of more aggressive Congressional Reconstruction and stated that formerly Confederate states could only reenter the Union when they ratified the Fourteenth Amendment.

During this time, another battle was raging between Radical Republicans and Southern Democrats in Congress over the issue of black suffrage. Even after emancipation former slaves and free blacks were denied the right to vote. Together, Congressional Reconstruction and black suffrage were the two primary issues in the 1868 presidential campaign, won by Republican nominee and Civil War hero Ulysses S. Grant. With a Republican sitting in the White House, Congressional Republicans moved forward with Reconstruction and in February of 1869 approved the Fifteenth Amendment to the Constitution, which prohibited federal and state governments from depriving any citizen the right to vote on the basis of their race. It is important to note that while a victory for Radical Reconstruction, the Fifteenth Amendment removed only obvious racial restrictions on voting; it was silent with respect to other kinds of voting restrictions, such as poll taxes, literacy tests, and property requirements. It also was silent with respect to the issue of the right of women to vote!

The effect of both the Reconstruction Act of 1867 and the Fifteenth Amendment on black political participation was dramatic. For the first time African Americans voted in Southern elections and elected both black and sympathetic white officials. While nowhere did blacks control state government, they did for the first time elect numerous local and federal officials, including governors and members of both Houses of Congress. Black representation in government and black voting in state and federal elections became a new part of the Southern political landscape. Radical Reconstructionists won another victory when Congress passed the Civil Rights Act of 1875, which declared that public facilities such as streetcars, trains, hotels, restaurants, and theatres were open to all people regardless of race.

It should not be too surprising to learn that Southern whites were not likely to take these new, Radical Reconstruction-inspired changes in their life without some considerable resistance. From their point of view their livelihood and lives were being threatened, and previous means of creating social order, primarily slavery and the caste system of racial etiquette it imposed, had either dissolved or were in the process of dissolution. Most, if not all, Southern whites at the time had little faith that good things would come in the wake of black political power. In fact, they thought the South was heading toward disaster, with Southern whites among the most imperiled. Primarily this pessimism was based upon the stereotypical view that Southern whites held about blacks. We have already alluded to the fact that Southern whites firmly believed that slavery was the only thing that kept the black population from regressing into savagery. Whites generally thought blacks were biologically as well as morally inferior to whites, a belief supported by "scientific" and religious writings (see, Nolen 1967; Newby 1968).

Box 7.2
'Scientific' Evidence of African American Character

One of the rationalizations whites provided for the coercion of blacks was that because blacks were morally and biologically inferior, subjugation was for their own good. There was "scientific" evidence at the time to support such views. For example, one Virginia physician, Dr. Robert Bennett Bean (quoted in Newby 1968: 47, 52) who claimed to have scientifically studied the brains of whites and blacks concluded that :

> ...the negro brain is smaller than the Caucasian, the difference in size being represented in both gray matter (nerve cells) and white matter (nerve fibers).... The negro brain having fewer nerve cells and nerve fibers ...the possibilities of developing the negro are therefore limited, except by crossing with other races.... The Caucasian, and more particularly the Anglo Saxon, is dominant and domineering, and possessed primarily with determination, will power, self-control, self-government ... with a high development of the ethical and esthetic faculties and great reasoning powers. The negro is primarily affectionate, immensely emotional, then sensual, and under provocation, passionate. There is love of outward show, of ostentation, of approbation. He loves melody and a rude kind of poetry and sonorous language. ... They are deficient in judgment. ... They are imitative rather than original. ... There is instability of character incident to lack of self-control, especially in connection with the sexual relation. ✦

In the view of white society in the South, then, there was a literal invasion from within by newly freed blacks and their sympathizers, and given the inherently malignant (or at least impulsive) character of blacks, the previously existing social order created by whites was in jeopardy. How did Southern whites respond to this threat? Unable any longer to rely explicitly on slavery to control the black population, Southern whites sought two solutions to what they perceived to be a growing problem of social order; one set of solutions was nonviolent, while the other had a directly violent character.

The nonviolent solution to the "free black problem" was the attempt by whites to segregate white from black society and, as part of this, to disenfranchise blacks. If blacks could no longer be controlled by the institution of slavery, and if black freedom constituted a threat to white social order, then one clear solution would be to separate the races through segregation and prevent blacks from securing the political power to effect any meaningful change. What the economic system of slavery could not secure, then, legal segregation and legal disenfranchisement would.

Jim Crow Laws

The separation of the races was secured beginning in the late 1800s with the passage of state and local laws in the south that mandated racial segregation—so called *Jim Crow* laws. The term "Jim Crow" was derived from a white minstrel character popular in the 1830s who mimicked the stereotypical characteristics of blacks—he sang and danced and acted as a simple-minded buffoon. Jim Crow laws passed in the South essentially attempted to erect a racial caste system that physically separated whites from blacks. These laws required separate facilities for whites and blacks in transportation, education, housing, and other public accommodations. Signs that read "colored" and "whites only" were a constant reminder by Southern whites of the inferior social position of blacks and their second-class citizenship. Tennessee passed the first Jim Crow law in 1882, separating whites and blacks in railroad cars (Williamson 1984). Soon other Southern states adopted similar legislation that separated the races in virtually all public accommodations, including lunch counters, swimming pools, libraries, restrooms, cemeteries, water fountains, telephone booths, and hospitals. Jim Crow laws ensured that white and black children were not educated together, as Southern states built separate schools for the

---

Box 7.3
Jim Crow Laws in America

Some of the more interesting Jim Crow laws included:

- Mississippi required separate soft drink machines for blacks and whites.

- In Atlanta courtrooms blacks could not swear an oath on the same Bible as that used by white witnesses.

- In Washington, D.C. blacks could not bury their pets in the same pet cemeteries as those used by whites.

- In Alabama, white nurses could not tend to black patients.

- In Georgia, no black barber could cut the hair of a white woman.

- In Louisiana, institutions for the blind had to have separate facilities for white and black clients. ✦

races. In time, Jim Crow laws were extended to residential segregation, an already common practice in both the North and South.

These efforts by whites to form two separate societies in the South—one white and one black—were assisted by the U.S. Supreme Court in several cases that significantly eroded the legal protections that blacks had only recently won. In 1873 in the *Slaughterhouse Cases* (77 U.S. [10 Wall.] 273, 19 L.Ed. 915) the Court ruled that the Fourteenth Amendment applied only to the rights of citizens that were conferred by the federal government and not to those conferred by the states. Essentially, the Court said that there were two classes of civil rights, federal and state, and that the Fourteenth Amendment only protected the former. Persons claiming that state law discriminated against them, therefore, could not say that the behavior was unconstitutional under the Fourteenth Amendment. In 1883 in the *Civil Rights Cases* (109 U.S. 3, 3 S.Ct. 18, 27 L.Ed. 835) the Court declared that the part of the 1875 Civil Rights Act that required states to ensure equal accommodations for blacks and whites was unconstitutional. The Court held that Congress wrongly intruded into state's rights and that it could only mandate equal accommodations for federal facilities and lands. Essentially, the Court's ruling said that the Fourteenth Amendment did not prohibit *individuals* from discriminating against another on the basis of their race, opening the door for segregation in private establishments such as restaurants, movie theatres, railroad cars, and buses.

Even the practice of the complete separation of the races was given Constitutional approval by the Supreme Court. In the famous case of *Plessy v. Ferguson* (163 U.S. 537) in 1896, the Court ruled that an 1890 Louisiana law that provided separate railcar accommodations for blacks and whites was permissible provided that the accommodations were comparable. The Court's doctrine that "separate but equal" facilities and accommodations for blacks and whites did not violate the Constitution put an official seal of approval on the practice of racial segregation. In refusing to strike a blow against segregationist practices, the *Plessy* Court observed that "if one race be inferior to the other socially, the Constitution of the United States cannot put them on the same plane." In 1899 the Court further assisted the separation of the races by ruling in *Cumming v. County Board of Education* (175 U.S. 528) that separate schools for white and black children were acceptable even if the available black schools were not comparable to the white schools. For the next 60 years, blacks and whites could live in virtually separate worlds marked by explicit signs that read "whites only" and "colored," or by more implicit but older rules of racial etiquette that pushed black citizens into a separate but decidedly not equal other world.[3]

Disenfranchisement

The second type of nonviolent response of Southern states to the political and economic freedom of black citizens was disenfranchisement. In response to the Fifteenth Amendment's granting of suffrage to blacks, and the vigorous exercise of the right to vote by blacks, Southern whites almost immediately devised ways to disenfranchise black voters. Early strategies to disenfranchise blacks were crude. Whites used persuasion, fraud, intimidation, and violence to keep blacks from voting. In just a short time, however, nonviolent, and much more effective ways were devised to disqualify black voters. The specific form that disenfranchisement took varied in different states, but the intent was the same: to take away any political power that Reconstruction and Constitutional Amendments may have given the black population.

One of the most effective means of disenfranchising black voters was to have a poll tax or property requirement as a condition of the right to vote. One of the consequences of a poll tax or property requirement, however, was that it also had the effect of disenfranchising poor whites as well as blacks. While many in the South were more than willing to have white disenfranchisement as the price of keeping the vote away from blacks, not all were. As a result, many states adopted modifications of or "loopholes" to their voting requirements so that persons not able to meet one voting requirement could still vote if they met another. These modifications were designed to mitigate the impact of voting restrictions on whites.

Some states followed the lead of Mississippi, which in its 1890 Constitutional Convention instituted a poll tax requirement for voting. It also passed an article declaring that any voter must "be able to read any section of the Constitution of this State; or he shall be able to understand the same when read to him, or give a reasonable interpretation thereof" (Nolen 1967, 89). Mississippi's approach to the disenfranchisement of blacks, then, took the form of a literacy test and an understanding clause. Literacy tests were like poll taxes and property requirements in that they served to disqualify large segments of the population (white and black) from voting. The understanding clause was a loophole to resurrect the white vote. In the Mississippi literacy test, potential voters were required to demonstrate the ability to read some section of the state constitution, while the understanding clause allowed illiterate citizens to still vote provided that they could explain a section of the state constitution read to them. The "examination" was conducted by election officials who were almost always white, and it was theoretically intended to be a test of "civic intelligence" (Williamson 1984). Of course, some voters might be asked to read or understand more difficult sections of the state constitution than others, and whether or not someone "understood" a section of the Mississippi Constitution was a subjective matter to be decided by local election officials. The not surprising result was the disqualification of thousands of potential black voters, or as Nolen put it (1967) ". . . minor officials in local communities received authorization to maintain white rule by interpreting the Negro electorate out of existence" (p. 89).

Other state constitutions adopted different voting tests and requirements with the same consequence. The Louisiana Constitutional Convention of 1898 adopted what was called the "grandfather clause." Under this clause a person who could not qualify to vote under an existing test or requirement, such as a literacy test, could circumvent that if they could demonstrate some historical condition such as (1) they or an ancestor had voted before a certain date (1867 was a common cutoff year since most blacks did not have the vote then), or (2) they or an ancestor had performed some civic responsibility or had served in the military service for the state (for the Confederacy in the Civil War, for example).

Poll taxes, property ownership, and literacy tests were not the only ways in which the right to vote was taken from blacks by Southern whites. States such as Tennessee passed demanding voter registration requirements wherein citizens had to register to vote during a specified period of time long before an election. Failure to register during this time disqualified the person from voting (Williamson 1984). Polling sites, determined by white voting officials, were frequently chosen so that they were long distances away from black communities. The location of a polling place was often changed without notice, lists of registered black voters were "lost," and state statutes disqualified voters upon the conviction for minor crimes, such as petty larceny, which affected the black community far greater than the white (Nolen 1967).

The collective effect of these voting tests and requirements was to dramatically weaken black political power by taking away the capacity to elect black officials or more sympathetic white ones. There is no doubt that white disenfranchisement of black voters worked. Nolen (1967) observed that in South Carolina the number of black votes in the gubernatorial election dropped from 170,000 in 1876 to only 33,154 in 1886. The Southern historian C. Vann Woodward (1951) found that over 130,000 black citizens were registered to vote prior to Louisiana's State Constitutional Convention in 1898, but two years later the number had declined 96 percent to only 5,320. Kousser (1974) argued that the Mississippi State Constitutional Convention of 1890 had a profound effect on the number of black voters in that state. He estimated that while 29 percent of black male adults voted in the presidential election of 1888, only 2 percent did four years later, and by the 1895 election for Mississippi governor, virtually no blacks voted.

Violence Against Blacks

In response to the perceived threat of the black population brought about by Congressional Reconstruction, emancipation, and the Fifteenth Amendment, Southern whites used various nonviolent means (segregation and disenfranchisement) to reestablish both white economic and political power and cultural and social supremacy. But not all of the white response was nonviolent. The history of the South during the post-Civil War period is rife with instances of the use of violent repression by whites to enforce racial discipline. Some of this violence was sporadic, short lived, and directed by one individual against another—newly freed blacks were assaulted or even murdered for some minor insult or slight against whites. In other instances, however, the use of violence by Southern whites against the black population was more concerted, long term, and based on collective action. We will briefly discuss two prominent and related forms of white violence against blacks—violence committed by white supremacist groups such as the Ku Klux Klan and lynching.

The Ku Klux Klan (KKK) was only the best-known of several organized groups of Southern whites who used violence to re-create the system of racial discipline and white superiority that existed under slavery. Other groups included the White Brotherhood, the Pale Faces, the Invisible Empire, Constitutional Union Guard, and Knights of the White Camellia (Tolnay and Beck 1995). The Klan was founded in 1866 in Tennessee, originally as a social club, but it quickly spread to all Southern states as a group committed to violence and terrorism (Foner and Mahoney 1995). Blacks were not the sole targets of Klan violence; it was also directed against those from the North who came South to assist the black population during Reconstruction ("carpetbaggers" such as William Luke, an Irish-born schoolteacher teaching in a black school who was lynched), against Southerners who sympathized with Reconstruction and efforts to integrate blacks into Southern society ("scalawags"), and against Republicans who stood in the way of Southern Democrats who resisted Congressional Reconstruction (the Klan assassinated U.S. Congressmen and members of state legislatures and other Republican leaders) (Foner and Mahoney 1995). The majority of Klan violence and intimidation, however, was directed against blacks.

The purpose of the Klan's violent rampages was to strike fear into the hearts of blacks in the post-Reconstruction period as they were attempting to move out of slavery, economic dependence, and social servitude and were threatening the economic and political dominance of whites. Klan violence was directed against successful black farmers and shopkeepers, black teachers and politicians, and virtually any black person that would serve to further the Klan's attempt to create a rein of terror. At times Klan violence was directed at individuals such as Andrew Cathcart, a former slave in South Carolina who by 1871 had managed to accumulate 98 acres of land in York County, South Carolina. On March 11, 1871, 15 to 20 Klansmen raided the Cathcart homestead, dragged him outside, and beat him repeatedly with a gun butt (Tolnay and Beck 1995). At other times, Klan violence was more widespread. On April 13, 1873 in Colfax, Louisiana, a group of over 100 local whites, led by the parish sheriff, attacked an equal number of armed blacks. The black group was routed, but many managed to escape to the local courthouse. A mob of whites then set the courthouse on fire and began shooting those who tried to flee the burning building; those who survived were captured and later murdered. By the next day more than 200 blacks in Colfax had been killed (Tolnay and Beck 1995). That the Klan represented the majority of Southern society at the time and not just some fringe interest is evidenced by the fact that Klansmen were drawn from all sections of Southern society—rich and poor—and received both the implicit and open support of the Southern political and law enforcement establishment.

There were attempts to combat Klan activity in the South. Congress passed three Enforcement Acts in 1870 and 1871, the purpose of which was to outlaw terrorist groups and make it a federal offense to conspire to deprive another citizen of his or her civil rights. The third of these acts, the Klu Klux Klan Act, gave the president the power to use federal troops against such groups. President Grant took advantage of these powers and initiated a military campaign against the Klan that resulted in the arrest and trial of many of its leaders and the loss of much of the power it had enjoyed. Although the power of the Klan diminished slightly as a result of federal intervention, widespread violence against black citizens persisted at least until the 1930s.

Violence directed against blacks also took the form of lynchings (Brundage 1993; Tolnay and Beck 1995; Vandiver 2006). The lynching of blacks by small groups of whites or by mobs was so prevalent that Tolnay and Beck (1995) have referred to the period of Southern U.S. history between the years 1880 and 1930 as the Lynching Era. They have estimated that in the period of time between the end of Reconstruction in the South and the beginning of the Great Depression, 2,462 black men, women, and children were killed by lynch mobs, 94 percent made up of whites.[4]

We have discussed how after the Civil War white Southern society was rocked to its foundation by the emancipation of the slaves, federal Reconstruction, the extension of the right to vote for blacks, and their initial use of that right to gain some measure of political power. Blacks were also making economic progress, renting and at times buying their own land and gaining some measure of economic independence they had previously lacked. On top of this, there was at least the perception that black crime, especially black crime directed against whites, had increased substantially since emancipation, a condition whites concluded was due to the inherently savage, impulsive, and amoral character of blacks. This was the context within which whites "took the law into their own hands," using lynching to restrain black lawlessness.

But the lynching of blacks by the white population was much more than just the punishment of a particular crime or even racial slight; the purpose was to create a climate of terror so uncompromising that blacks would be forced to adopt a position of timidity and inferiority they had known (and whites had enjoyed) under slavery. One Georgia populist, Tom Watson, gave voice to this view: "In the South, we have to lynch him [blacks] occasionally, and flog him, now and then, to keep him from blaspheming the Almighty, by his conduct, on account of his smell and his color. . . . Lynch law is a good sign: it shows that a sense of justice yet lives among the people" (cited in Woodward 1963, 379).

Box 7.4
The Lynching of Leo Frank

Blacks were not the only targets of Southern lynch mobs. In 1913 Leo Frank was the 29-year-old manager of the National Pencil Company in Atlanta, Georgia. Moreover, he was a New York–born, college-educated Jew and past president of the Atlanta chapter of B'nai B'rith. On April 26, 1913, Mary Phagan, a 14-year-old laid-off employee of the pencil factory, went to the factory to get her wages. The next day her sawdust-covered body was found in the basement of the factory by the night watchman. Frank admitted to paying Mary her wages but did not know where she went after that and was the last person to admit seeing her alive. Rumors circulated that Mary Phagan had been sexually assaulted before being murdered, and other factory workers offered testimony to authorities that Frank had sexually propositioned them. Frank was arrested for the murder of Mary Phagan and was tried and convicted in less than four hours in August 1913. During the trial mobs formed outside the courtroom, and shouts of "Hang the jew" and "Kill the jew" could be heard throughout the short trial. The trial judge was so intimidated by the mob and the volatility of the situation that he barred Frank from the courtroom but did sentence him to death.

Numerous Georgia courts and the United States Supreme Court rejected Frank's appeals, but Georgia Governor Frank Slaton commuted Frank's sentence to life imprisonment. Some 5,000 Atlantans protested outside of the governor's mansion that night. On August 17, a group of about 25 to 30 men who called themselves the Knights of Mary Phagan entered the prison hospital where Frank had been recovering from an attempted killing by another inmate. They drove him more than 100 miles to Marietta, Georgia, Mary Phagan's hometown, and hung him.

Leo Frank is the only Jewish person to be lynched in the United States. The Georgia State Board of Pardons and Paroles pardoned Frank on March 11, 1986, 73 years after his lynching (see Frey and Thompson-Frey 2002). ✦

Figure 7.1 reports the number of lynchings of blacks by white mobs in 10 Southern states from 1882 to 1930 (Alabama, Arkansas, Florida, Georgia, Kentucky, Louisiana, Mississippi, North Carolina, South Carolina, and Tennessee). You can see that the lynching of blacks by white mob rule was fairly constant throughout this period, averaging about 47 lynchings per year. There were, however, periods when lynching was more prevalent. The number increased dramatically beginning in 1891 and stayed at a fairly high level for 14 years (averaging about 74 lynchings per year). With the exception of a spike in 1908, the number of executions remained fairly constant again, beginning to decline consistently in the early 1920s.

Figure 7.1   Black Victims of White Lynch Mobs in 10 Southern States, 1882–1930

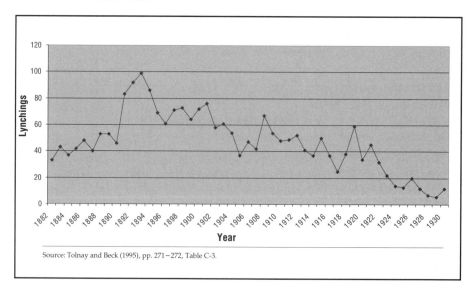

Source: Tolnay and Beck (1995), pp. 271–272, Table C-3.

In addition to providing a count of the number of lynchings that occurred over this time period, Tolnay and Beck (1995) also cataloged the stated reasons given at the time for the mob's actions. The rationales provided by lynch mobs included alleged serious criminal offending by blacks (murder, attempted murder, rape, train wrecking, kidnapping, arson, and robbery), minor criminal offending (running a bordello, stealing, peeping Tom, fraud, gambling), noncriminal acts that were perceived to be threatening by whites (voting, testifying against a white man, trying to colonize blacks, trying to vote, boasting about a riot), and noncriminal acts that were violations of previous norms of racial etiquette (arguing with a white man, being obnoxious, courting white women, demanding respect, entering a white woman's room, frightening a white woman, insulting a white person). There were, then, a wide variety of supposed reasons for whites to lynch blacks during this period. When Tolnay and Beck examined the frequency with which particular reasons for lynchings were given, they found that serious criminal offenses and violations of sexual norms were the most prevalent. In fact, in 82 percent of the lynchings the incident was triggered by a murder, rape, attempted rape, sexual or nonsexual assault, or some other violation of sexual norms (Tolnay and Beck 1995).

Based on findings such as these, some have been tempted to argue that lynchings were an attempt by Southern whites to satisfy sentiments of popular justice and retributive punishment that were being frustrated by the existing Southern criminal justice system. The purpose of lynching, it was argued, was a form of "popular justice" made necessary by the failure of the formal legal system to protect Southern white life and honor. In this view, lynching was a substitute for the formal legal punishment of blacks, which was seen by whites to be too lenient or unpredictable. Although a compelling explanation for the repeated lynching of blacks by whites, a number of facts are inconsistent with this explanation (Tolnay and Beck 1995; Vandiver 2006). First, it is difficult to argue that lynchings were the result of the perceived inability of the legal and law enforcement system to deal with black lawlessness when many lynchings occurred because mobs forcibly took their victims from the custody of legal authorities (Brundage 1993; Tolnay and Beck 1995). Brundage (1993) reported that between 1880 and 1930 in Georgia, 80 percent of the victims of mob lynchings were taken from law enforcement authorities, while 94 percent of those in Virginia were in legal custody when lynched.

Second, it would have been clear to any white Southerner that if black offenders had been turned over to the legal system rather than lynched they were not likely to be treated with any degree of leniency (Ayers 1984). The historical evidence is pretty clear that blacks were punished severely for both major and minor offenses, and the death penalty was a frequent punishment for the most serious offenses—offenses that also provided the most prevalent justification for a lynching. Tolnay and Beck (1995) report that during the period when lynchings were most frequent (1882–1930), nearly 2,000 black offenders were executed by the legal system, an average of 40 per year—and over 80 percent of those executed were black.

Third, a nontrivial number of lynchings involved not the mere death of the victim but the symbolic mutilation, burning, or torture of the body, displayed in a place that was plainly visible to the black community. James Irwin was killed by a mob in Ocilla, Georgia on January 31, 1930 for killing a white girl (Brundage 1993). The mob cut off his fingers and toes, pulled his teeth out with

---

Box 7.5
'So Long as There Is Chivalry Left in Southern Bosoms . . .'

A frequent justification for the violence of Southern lynch mobs was that the legal system acted too uncertainly and slowly. For crimes committed by whites against whites or by blacks against other blacks that belief might have been true. But for the crimes that were the target of most acts of Southern vigilante mob justice—those committed by blacks against whites—the law usually moved with lethal and certain speed. Sometimes, however, the "law" wasn't allowed to work or worked in a strange way.

On February 17, 1901 a young white woman was brutally killed with a hatchet during an attempted rape. Bloodhounds called to track the offender led authorities to the home of Fred King. King's shoes were found under the steps of the victim's house, and a bloody hatchet was found in his dresser drawer. King (along with two other suspects) was taken into custody and locked in the city jail. The next day he was taken into court escorted both by a local mob and local law enforcement authorities for trial. The "judge" in the trial was a local manufacturer. After the testimony of several witnesses, King was found guilty and was immediately hung from a tree outside the courthouse until dark, when his body was finally cut down and buried (Vandiver 2006).

After Dennis Blackwell was hung by a mob for an attempted rape in 1892, the local paper wrote, "There is no use for a man to moralize on the evil effects of lynch law . . . so long as there is chivalry left in southern bosoms the offender must pay a speedy penalty for his heinous crime" (cited in Vandiver 2006, 91). ✦

---

pliers, castrated him, and then burned him to death. A group of whites forcibly removed Albert Aiken from the county jail in Lincolnton, Georgia on May 24, 1909, took him to the scene of the crime, and lynched him. A local newspaper later reported that "the place where the negro is said to have been lynched is near the place where he committed the crime and it is supposed that the mob who took him there had it in view to let many negroes in that neighborhood see that it is time that they quieted down and stopped their efforts to ride over the farmers in that section" (Brundage 1993). The purpose of many lynchings, therefore, was not to impose a popular justice (or at least not solely to do that) but rather to make a moral and political point that white people rule and black people submit to that rule. Those who by their actions indicated that they would not abide by white rule would be severely dealt with, with the intent being to humble and terrorize not only the offender but the entire black community into submission.

Although there may be no support for the position that capital punishment was a "substitute" for lynching in the past (Vandiver 2006), there is recent evidence that the legacy of lynching and the racial animosity that drove it may have had more long-term effects. Messner, Baller, and Zevenbergen (2005) examined the relationship between Southern counties with high levels of lynching in the past and the rate of homicide in those counties today. The evidence is consistent with their position that lynchings during the "era of lynchings" provided fertile ground for a culture of violence that in turn leads to currently high levels of homicide. The legacy of lynchings, this study suggests, is a culture that tolerates a high level of violence (Nisbett and Cohen 1996). In another recent study, the sociologist David Jacobs and his colleagues (2005) found that death sentences today are higher in those states that had a high number of lynchings in the past and where minorities were viewed as a threat. Although capital punishment may not have been a substitute for lynching in the past, these two studies do find that there may be a more long-term relationship between these two forms of lethal violence.

While lynchings began to decline after the 1930s, the use of the death penalty against black offenders did not. In fact, in the next chapter we will see that historically the death penalty has been disproportionately imposed on black offenders, particularly when they have victimized whites. This chapter has presented a brief history of racial animosity in the United States to provide important context for the claim that the death penalty in the United States historically and currently has been imposed in a racially disparate manner. Those who would make this claim could point to America's history of racial conflict and the use of the law by whites in other periods (the slave codes, Black Codes, Jim Crow laws, disenfranchisement, and lynchings) to argue that the disproportionate use of the death penalty against blacks is simply another instance of racial hostility and animus by whites against blacks. In other words, in response to the question "Why would the death penalty be applied differently against blacks and whites?" one could point to a long history of the use of local, state, and federal criminal justice institutions to control the black population.

This inextricable connection between the history of racial animosity in the United States and the current imposition of the death penalty was made vivid by Justice William Brennan of the Supreme Court in his dissent in the capital punishment case of *McCleskey v. Kemp* (279, U.S. 344, 1987). In this case a majority of the Court rejected the defendant's claim that the administration of the death penalty in Georgia was tainted by racial discrimination. Justice Brennan vigorously dissented from this decision, pointing out the clear link between the past and the present:

> It has been scarcely a generation since this Court's first decision striking down racial segregation, and barely two decades since the legislative prohibition of racial discrimination in major domains of national life. These have been honorable steps, but we cannot pretend that in three decades we have completely escaped the grip of a historical legacy spanning centuries. . . . We remain imprisoned by the past as long as we deny its influence on the present.

Chapter Summary

One of the historical facts about the law and criminal punishment in the United States is that it has targeted minority groups more than whites. In the early history of our country slave codes frequently called for the use of severe punishment (including the death penalty) against slaves for serious crimes such as murder and rape, nonserious crimes such as theft and lying, and noncrimes such as learning how to read or violating racial etiquette. There was a long list of potentially capital crimes for acts committed by slaves, a much longer list than that applied to whites. While the Thirteenth Amendment gave some form of political emancipation to slaves and abolished slave codes, it did not mean that African Americans would not bear the greater brunt of the death penalty or other forms of severe punishment. Particularly in the Southern states, the post-Civil War years perhaps only increased the amount of racial tension and racial conflict as whites tried to control their newly freed black population politically, economically, and socially.

Vigilante justice in the form of the Ku Klux Klan and mob lynchings, as well as the Black Codes, kept racial discipline in place of the slave codes. In addition to controlling African Americans with direct violence, Southerners passed new laws that kept the races strictly separate. These Jim Crow laws regulated where African Americans could live, go to school, or work and other aspects of their day-to-day lives. Jim Crow laws did what the slave codes could no longer do: keep the races apart and continue the racial dominance of whites. In the next chapter we will more specifically examine the relationship between race and capital punishment in the United States.

Discussion Questions

1. Both before and after the Civil War, what different form of social control did whites use against blacks?

2. What connection (if any) do you see between the forms of social control discussed in this chapter and capital punishment?

3. Given what you know about racial conflict in the past, how do you think the death penalty would be used today as a form of "racial discipline"?

4. At the end of the chapter you read a quote from an opinion of Supreme Court Justice William Brennan that ended with the sentence "We remain imprisoned by the past as long as we deny its influence on the present." Can an understanding of the relationship between the law and race in the past provide any insight into issues today? Or is it "just history"?

5. Sometimes the death penalty is justified on the grounds that it prevents vigilante or mob justice. Do you think the prevention of vengeance by others is a legitimate justification for capital punishment?

Student Resources

Throughout this book we have emphasized other media sources as a good way to learn about capital punishment and related issues. An interesting movie that shows the racial tensions of the American South in the 1960s is *In the Heat of the Night*. This film centers on a Philadelphia police detective, Virgil Tibbs (played by Sidney Poitier), visiting a town in the rural South when he is thrust into a murder investigation. Bill Gillespie, the local and stereotypically redneck sheriff (played by Rod Steiger), is none too pleased with the expert assistance of a Northern black.

One of the best American novels is Harper Lee's (1960) Pulitzer Prize-winning *To Kill a Mockingbird*, which describes the racism and intolerance of a small town in Alabama in the 1930s through the eyes of a young girl ("Scout" Finch), whose lawyer father (Atticus) must defend a young black man (Tom Robinson) falsely accused of raping a white woman. Despite evidence indicating his innocence, an all-white jury convicts the man. A mob storms the town jail trying to get Robinson out and lynch him. Later Robinson tries to escape from the jail but is shot and killed. Another wonderful book describing racial issues in America is *The Hidden Wound* by Wendell Berry.

The Public Broadcasting System (PBS) did a superb documentary on Jim Crow laws titled *The Rise and Fall of Jim Crow: A National Struggle.* Information on Jim Crow and this documentary can be found on their website: <www.pbs.org/wnet/jimcrow/>. One of the best and most recent authoritative sources on slavery in America is David Brion Davis' *Inhuman Bondage: The Rise and Fall of Slavery in the New World* (2006).

Endnotes

1. The property rights of the slaveholder were not, however, absolute. Many state codes were like the Alabama 1852 code in that they both unambiguously defined the slaves' status as that of property and defined the slave as a person in that the law expected that masters would feed and clothe their slaves, provide for them in old age, and impose some limits on punishment (Stampp 1956; Davis 2006). Practically, however, what occurred on plantations between masters and slaves was rarely publicly visible, and masters could virtually do what they wanted with slaves. Although the law of murder did protect the slave, there are few instances in the historical record of a slaveholder being punished for killing one of his slaves.

2. Stampp (1956) quotes a North Carolina judge as noting that insolent behavior may be inferred from a variety of acts, such as "a look, the pointing of a finger, a refusal or neglect to step out of the way when a white person is seen to approach. But each of such acts violates the rule of propriety, and if tolerated, would destroy that subordination, upon which our social system rests" (pp. 207–208).

3. The hold that the "separate but equal" doctrine had over race relations in the United States did not begin to erode until the mid-1950s. Supreme Court decisions such as *Sweatt v. Painter* (1949) and *McLaurin v. Oklahoma* (1950) were crucial in getting the Court to question the *Plessy* "separate but equal" principle. It was not until the Court's historic decision in *Brown v. Board of Education* (1954), however, that *Plessy* was finally overturned.

4. Tolnay and Beck (1995) reported that 288 whites were the victims of lynchings; in all but four of these cases the perpetrators were also white. Like whites, black mobs were more likely to lynch other blacks than they were whites. Black mobs lynched 148 blacks during the period 1880–1930, but only four whites. These exceptions notwithstanding, the vast majority of the lynchings during this period were directed against blacks by groups of whites. ✦

Chapter 8

Race and Capital Punishment

In this chapter we discuss more specifically the relationship between race and capital punishment. We examine this relationship separately for two different time periods, 1930–1967 (what we have referred to as the Premodern Period) and 1976 to the present (the Modern Period). We do so because the racial forces at work during these two time periods have been somewhat different. In addition, as we saw in Chapter 2, the period 1967–1976 was a time when the death penalty was not in use in the United States because of an unofficial moratorium, and the legal landscape of capital punishment was very different after 1976.

Race and Capital Punishment: 1930–1967

The question of race and capital punishment seems like a simple one: Are racial minorities (blacks) more likely to be given the death penalty than those in the racial majority (whites)? Behind this simple question, however, is a great deal of complexity. For example, racial discrimination can manifest itself at many points in the capital punishment process: the decision of the police to define and investigate a death as a homicide, the decision of the prosecutor to charge a type of murder that can result in the death penalty (first degree) rather than a noncapital degree of murder (second degree), the decision of the jury to impose a sentence of death if the prosecutor charges a defendant with a capital murder, and the decision of a state governor to commute a death sentence or have it carried out.

There is also the thorny question of what would constitute evidence that racial discrimination was at play. We must be careful to distinguish between racial disparity, which is the disproportionate impact of a criminal penalty on a particular racial group, from racial discrimination. Not all racial disparity is due to racial discrimination. Even if, for example, all of those on death row in a given state were black, we could not automatically conclude that the imposition of the death penalty was discriminatory, though it would be racially disparate. Perhaps those on death row happened to have committed the most serious and most brutal murders, happened to have the worst criminal histories, and happened to be black. In this instance, the fact that all of the offenders on death row are black is simply coincidental with the fact that the worst offenders end up on death row and that the most serious murderers happen to be minority. Racial discrimination is at work when racial minorities are intentionally singled out for more severe sanctions from the law *because they are minorities,* not just because they commit serious offenses or have more extensive and violent criminal histories. Clearly, the role of race in the administration of capital punishment must be carefully distinguished from the role of other factors such as the seriousness of the crime and the characteristics of the offender, that may legitimately warrant the death penalty.

Let us look at some simple facts about the administration of the death penalty in the United States from 1930 to 1967. We know that approximately 3,859 executions under state and federal authority occurred in this period. Although blacks made up about 12–15 percent of the population during this period, about half of those executed for the offense of murder were black (see Figure 8.1). In comparison to their representation in the population, then, black defendants were overrepresented (by a factor of about 3 or 4) in the number of executions for murder. They were even more overrepresented in the number of executions for the offense of rape (a capital offense during this time period). Of the 455 executions for rape, 89 percent involved black or nonwhite offenders (see Figure 8.2). Further, 97 percent (443) of all of the executions for rape occurred within Southern states, and of these in 400 instances (90 percent) the person executed was black.

What we know so far is that during the period 1930–1967 about half of murder defendants who were executed were nonwhite and a vast majority of rape defendants who were executed were nonwhite. We do not know yet at what stage of the capital punishment process racial disparity shows itself, nor do we know yet whether any racial disparity that we do observe is due to racial discrimination or due to the influence of other, legally permissible factors that happen to be associated with race.

Here we need to point out that there are three sets of racial factors that are important: (1) the race of the defendant, (2) the race of the victim, and (3) the

Figure 8.1 Race of Persons Executed for Murder, 1930–1967

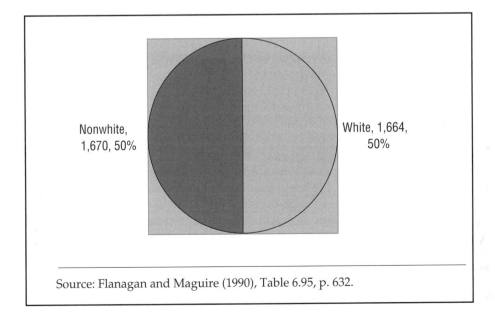

Nonwhite, 1,670, 50%

White, 1,664, 50%

Source: Flanagan and Maguire (1990), Table 6.95, p. 632.

Figure 8.2 Race of Persons Executed for Rape, 1930–1967

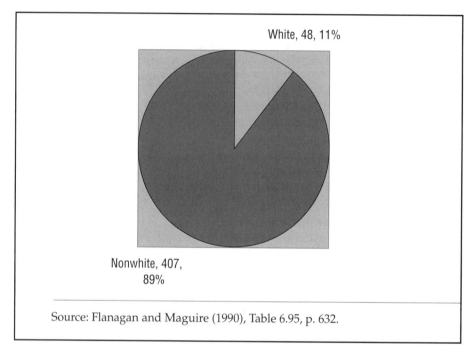

Source: Flanagan and Maguire (1990), Table 6.95, p. 632.

dynamic of the combination of the offender's and victim's races. If black defendants are singled out for the death penalty in part because they are black, if those who kill whites are singled out for the death penalty in part because they killed a white rather than a black, and if black defendants who kill white victims are singled out because in part they crossed racial lines and killed a white, racial disparity is at work. We concentrate on black offenders, white victims, and black offenders who kill white victims because the lesson of the previous chapter is that racial majorities (whites) may be inclined to use the death penalty most often against racial minorities (blacks), particularly when the minorities constitute a threat (when blacks kill whites).

In understanding the complexity of race of offender and race of victim effects, it is important to keep in mind that for both whites and blacks, homicides are much more likely to be *intra*-racial rather than *inter*-racial: When they kill, whites are more likely to kill another white and blacks are more likely to kill another black. If those who kill a white victim are more likely to be charged and convicted of a capital crime and sentenced to death than those who kill a black victim, it stands that this will more likely occur to white offenders than black offenders. We may at times find, then, that *white* offenders are more likely to be charged with a capital crime or sentenced to death. However, this finding may not be due to the fact that white offenders are discriminated against and black offenders receive more favorable treatment but rather the fact that white offenders are more likely to kill white victims and it's the white victim that is likely to land someone on death row. Black offenders may appear to receive more favorable treatment only because they more often kill black victims and the killing of a black may not be taken as seriously as the killing of white. When black offenders cross racial lines and kill a white, however, things may be different. We will turn to all of these issues now.

We have noted that there are several decision-making points in the criminal justice system where racial factors could operate. One is the decision of the prosecutor to charge a crime as a capital crime rather than a noncapital crime. During the time period we are now considering, many offenses were punishable by death, including murder, rape, and armed robbery. Of course, not every murder, rape, armed robbery, or other offense that could have resulted in the penalty of death was charged by the local prosecutor as a capital offense. Prosecutors then and now have tremendous discretion to weigh all of the facts and considerations of a case and then decide whether to pursue the death penalty for a given crime. There is the possibility, therefore, that racial factors could influence the discretion of a prosecutor in the charging of cases. And even if a prosecutor charges a crime as a capital offense, that does not mean that the death penalty will be imposed. The jury (or judge if he or she does the sentencing) has the discretion to impose a death sentence or some other noncapital sentence after convicting the defendant. It is possible that the jury could consider racial factors in exercising its discretion to sentence a defendant to death or some other penalty. Further, not all death sentences imposed by juries or judges result in a defendant actually being executed. Every state that had the death penalty during this period had some form of review by the state's chief executive—the governor. A governor could, after reviewing a case, decide that the death penalty was not called for and commute the death sentence to life or some term of prison. We will look at the operation of racial factors at each of these three critical decision points.

The Indictment and Charging Decision

In an early study of the influence of race and capital punishment, Harold Garfinkel (1949) examined the disposition of homicide indictments in 10 North Carolina counties during the period 1930–1940. At this time period only first degree murders were eligible for the death penalty, so if a prosecutor wanted to seek the death penalty for a murderer he or she had to file a first degree murder indictment rather than an indictment for some lesser degree of murder (second degree) or manslaughter. The decision to indict for first degree murder must come before the decision to actually charge a defendant with first degree murder. The data that Garfinkel assembled concerning the indictment and charging decisions are shown in Table 8.1.

Looking at the race of the offender and the race of the victim separately, Garfinkel did not find much evidence of racial disparity at the indictment and charging stages. For example, while 82 percent of white offenders were indicted for first degree murder given a homicide indictment, only a slightly higher percent (91 percent) of black offenders were indicted for first degree murder—a difference of 9 percent. Black offenders were also only slightly more likely than white offenders to be charged with first degree murder given a first degree murder indictment (59 percent versus 54 percent)—a difference

Table 8.1 Race and Number of Homicide Indictments, First Degree Murder Indictments, and First Degree Murder Charges, North Carolina, 1930–1940

	Percent Indicted for First Degree Murder Given a Homicide Indictment	Percent Charged With First Degree Murder Given First Degree Murder Indictment
Race of Offender		
White	82%	54%
Black	91	59
Race of Victim		
White	86	54
Black	90	58
Race of Offender/Race of Victim		
Black kills white	94	69
White kills white	84	44
Black kills black	91	53
White kills black	71	42

Source: Garfinkel (1949), 369–380, Table 2.

of only 5 percent. Similarly, there does not appear to be any great racial disparity when the race of the victim is considered by itself. Those who killed whites were only slightly less likely to be indicted for first degree murder than those who killed blacks (86 percent versus 90 percent), and only slightly less likely to be charged with first degree murder (54 percent versus 58 percent).

There is more evidence of disparate racial impact of North Carolina's death penalty when the race of the offender and victim are both considered. Table 8.1 shows a black offender crossing racial boundaries to kill a white was more likely to be indicted for first degree murder and more likely to be charged with first degree murder. Given a first degree murder indictment, 69 percent of black offenders who killed a white were charged with first degree murder, while only 53 percent of blacks who killed another black were charged with first degree murder. White offenders who kill white victims are only slightly more likely to be charged for first degree murder than whites who kill black victims (44 percent versus 42 percent). Even though there is some suggestion in Garfinkel's data that cross-racial slayings by blacks were treated more harshly by the legal system than other homicides, the evidence is not particularly strong. In addition, we cannot dismiss the possibility that the racial disparities observed in Table 8.1 are due to legitimate legal considerations that were not taken into account. For example, perhaps a greater percent of the homicides committed by blacks against whites resulted in a first degree murder charge because they were more aggravated than all the others—for example, more likely to have involved the commission of another felony, to have more than one victim, to have been more brutal, or to have involved any other of a number of permissible legal factors.

The Conviction and Sentencing Decision

Another set of decision-making points where racial disparity in capital punishment can be observed occurs with the decision to convict defendants of homicide and the decision to sentence them to death. When Guy Johnson (1941) examined capital punishment data in Richmond, Virginia (1930–1939) and five counties in North Carolina (1930–1940), he found that among those homicide defendants who were indicted for first degree murder, black offenders who killed white victims were more likely to be convicted of murder than any other racial combination. In fact, in Johnson's data there was only one homicide indictment for a murder committed by a white offender with a black victim, and in the North Carolina data there were only three first degree murder indictments for a white slaying a black.

In terms of racial disparity in the sentencing of defendants, Johnson's data also suggested that the race of the victim may have played a part in who was sentenced to death. He reported that almost half (45 percent) of those who killed a white in Richmond were sentenced to death, compared with only 6 percent of those who killed a black. Killers of whites, therefore, were almost eight times more likely to be sentenced to death in Richmond during this period than were killers of blacks. In North Carolina, convicted murder defendants who killed a white were almost five times more likely to receive a sentence of death than killers of blacks, and black killers who crossed racial lines and killed a white were seven times more likely to be sentenced to death than blacks who killed other blacks.

Garfinkel's (1949) data from ten North Carolina counties over the same time period confirm Johnson's results. Table 8.2 reveals some interesting and generally consistent findings about race and capital punishment. In terms of the percent convicted, white offenders were slightly more likely to be convicted of first degree murder than black defendants (14 percent versus 9 percent). Those who killed white victims were almost five times more likely to be convicted of first degree murder than those who killed blacks (24 percent versus 5 percent). There does appear to be a considerable difference in the fate of North Carolina murderers depending on the race of their victim. When the race of offender and victim are considered together, there is also evidence of disparate racial impact. A black offender who killed a white victim was almost nine times more likely to be convicted of first degree murder than one who killed another black (43 percent versus 5 percent). A white who killed a white is also more likely to be convicted of first degree murder than one who killed a black. In fact, there was no recorded case of a white offender being convicted of first degree murder for the killing of a black in Garfinkel's data.

These racial disparaties also characterize those sentenced to death given that they were charged with and convicted of first degree murder. First, notice the small percent of defendants who were sentenced to death even when they were charged with first degree murder. This suggests that a death sentence was unlikely even in the majority of first degree murder cases. Second, notice that white offenders were slightly more likely to be sentenced to death than black offenders (10 percent vs. 7 percent). This statistic is counterintuitive,

Table 8.2 Percent Convicted of First Degree Murder and Percent
Sentenced to Death in North Carolina Given a First Degree
Murder Charge, 1930–1940

	Percent Convicted	Percent Sentenced to Death
Race of Offender		
White	14%	10%
Black	9	7
Race of Victim		
White	24	18
Black	5	4
Race of Offender/Race of Victim		
Black kills white	43	37
White kills white	15	11
Black kills black	5	4
White kills black	0	0

Source: Garfinkel (1949), Tables 3 and 6.

since we would have expected any disparity to affect black offenders. Third,
notice that killers of whites were substantially more likely (over four times) to
be sentenced to death than were killers of blacks (18 percent vs. 4 percent).
Those who killed a white were almost five times more likely to be sentenced to
death than someone who killed a black. Fourth, when we consider both the offender's and victim's race we can see that blacks who killed whites were more
likely to be sentenced to death (37 percent) than any other racial combination.
Blacks who killed a white were almost nine times more likely to be sentenced
to death than those who killed another black.

Notice also that 11 percent of whites who killed a white were sentenced to
death but that no white who killed a black was ever sentenced to death. We can
now see that the reason a slightly higher percentage of white (10 percent) than
black offenders (7 percent) were sentenced to death. First, white offenders
were more likely to kill a white than a black (in 84 percent of all homicide indictments a white killed a white, while in 16 percent of the cases the victim was
black). Second, black offenders were more likely to kill a black than a white (in
92 percent of the homicide indictments for black offenders the victim was also
black). Third, those who killed whites were substantially more likely to be sentenced to death than those who killed blacks. So white offenders were slightly
more likely to be sentenced to death than black offenders because white offenders were substantially more likely to kill white victims, and killers of
white victims were at a much higher risk of a death sentence than killers of
blacks.

Both Johnson's and Garfinkel's data came from Southern states (Virginia
and North Carolina) during the 1930s and 1940s. A later study by Frank
Zimring and his colleagues (1976) examined the disposition of 204 homicide
cases reported to the Philadelphia, Pennsylvania police department in 1970.
Zimring et. al's data, then, come from a non-Southern jurisdiction and a later
time period. They found that for these 204 homicide cases a total of 245 persons
were arrested, of whom 170 were eventually convicted of some charge.

Box 8.1
The Case of Emmett Till: When Whites Killed Blacks in the South

Emmett Till was a 14-year-old black male from Chicago who in August of 1955 was visiting relatives in Mississippi. On August 24, he and some cousins were in a grocery store owned by a white couple. It is not clear exactly what happened at the store. According to the woman, Carolyn Bryant, Till grabbed her; some witnesses said he made lewd and suggestive remarks, while others said he only whistled and not at the woman, since he often whistled in order to control a speech defect. It was likely that Till whistled at Carolyn Bryant as a joke that she didn't see as funny. She immediately went to get a gun and the boys fled. The woman's husband, Roy, thought something substantial had happened and that his wife's honor needed avenging. Several nights after the incident, Bryant, his half-brother J. W. Milam, and other men kidnapped Emmett from his great uncle's home in the middle of the night, severely beat him, shot him, and dumped his body in a river. Several days later the body was found and Bryant and Milam were charged with murder.

The defense team at the trial raised the claim that Till was in fact not dead. The body taken from the river was unrecognizable, and identification was made only on the basis of a ring of Till's found on the finger of the deceased. The sheriff testified on the witness stand that it was possible that someone planted Till's ring on another body. The jury, composed of all white males, apparently agreed with that speculation. They acquitted Bryant and Milam after deliberating for only slightly longer than 60 minutes. One juror reported that it wouldn't have taken that long but the jury took a soda pop break.

In another odd twist of the case, an Alabama journalist gave Bryant and Millam $4,000 to tell their side of the case. Since they could not be prosecuted again for a crime they had already stood trial for, both men told the story of how they beat and killed Till, throwing him into the river. The story appeared in *Look* magazine on January 24, 1956. In May 2004, the U.S. Department of Justice announced that they would reopen the Till case because they had some evidence to believe that there were more than a dozen people involved in Till's murder and that some were still alive and could be prosecuted. The federal case was closed without any indictments in 2006 (see Whitfield 1988). ✦

Zimring et. al reported that 65 percent of the defendants who killed a white received a sentence of death or life imprisonment. Only 25 percent of those who killed a black received such a severe sentence. They also found that black offenders who killed a white were twice as likely as those who killed another black to receive a death or life sentence. There were only three death sentences imposed in these cases; in all of them the offender was black and the victim was white.

David Baldus and his colleagues (1990) collected detailed information on nearly 300 murder defendants in Georgia who were tried and convicted before the *Furman* decision in 1972. They gathered detailed information about each case, and with this information they were able to make an assessment as to how egregious or aggravated each homicide was. They categorized the cases into one of six levels of homicide aggravation, from the lowest to the highest. They then examined the proportion of times that defendants were sentenced to death within each level of homicide aggravation and the proportion of times defendants were sentenced to death based on their race and the race of their victim within each level of homicide aggravation. By looking at the effect of race within levels of homicide aggravation, they were able to control for many of the legally permissible factors that led to a death sentence. Any racially disparate treatment observed within a level of aggravation, therefore, was less likely to be attributed to important case characteristics and more likely due to the influence of racial factors. Table 8.3 shows the main findings from their study.

Table 8.3 Race of Victim Effects in Pre-*Furman* Georgia Capital Murder Cases by Level of Aggravation

| | | White Victim Cases | | |
Level of Aggravation	Overall Rate	Black Offender Rate	White Offender Rate	Ratio
1 (Lowest)	.02	.05	.00	—
2	.10	.10	.08	1.3
3	.20	.71	.05	14.2
4	.46	.67	.33	2.0
5	.62	1.00	.60	1.7
6 (Highest)	1.00	1.00	1.00	1.0
All cases	.15 (44/294)	.31 (24/77)	.08 (8/101)	3.9
		Black Victim Cases		
Level of Aggravation		Black Offender Rate	White Offender Rate	Ratio
1 (Lowest)		.04	.00	—
2		.11	nc*	—
3		.18	.00	—
4		.33	nc*	—
5		.20	.33	.6
6 (Highest)		1.00	nc*	—
All cases		.10 (11/105)	.10 (1/10)	1.0

*nc means that there were no cases that fell into this category.
Source: Baldus et al. (1990), p. 144, Table 27.

Notice first that juries were selective in their decision to sentence a murder defendant to death. Of 294 murder defendants, only 15 percent received a death sentence. Ignoring for a moment whom they killed, black offenders were more than twice as likely to be sentenced to death than white offenders (35/182 = .19 for black offenders; 9/111 = .08 for white offenders). Ignoring for a moment who killed them, killers of whites were almost twice as likely to be sentenced to death as were killers of blacks (32/178 = .18 for white victim cases; 12/115 = .10 for black victim cases). In these pre-*Furman* data for Georgia, then, there is evidence of racially disparate outcomes by both race of offender and race of victim. Ignoring the level of aggravation of the murder, black offenders who killed white victims were the most likely to be sentenced to death (.31), more than three times the proportion as any other offender/victim racial combination.

As we have seen in other states, white offenders who killed blacks were very unlikely to receive a death sentence for their crime. Black offenders who crossed racial boundaries and murdered a white were at greater risk of a death sentence than whites who killed a white. Inter-racial slayings for blacks were about four times more likely to result in a sentence of death than intra-racial slayings for whites (.31 versus .08). Moreover, the greater risk of a death sentence for blacks who killed whites can be seen at almost every level of aggravation. At the third level of aggravation, for example, blacks who killed whites were fourteen times more likely to be sentenced to death than whites who killed other whites. At the fourth level they were twice as likely to be sentenced to death. In fact, white offender cases were not treated the same as black offender cases until the very highest level of aggravation. Only when the murder was shockingly brutal, then, were black and white murder defendants treated equally.

Not all of the research, however, shows evidence of racial disparity. Kleck (1981) reported that during the period 1967–1978 black offenders were no more likely to be sentenced to death in the United States than white offenders. Calculating the number of death sentences per 1,000 homicide arrests, he found that the death sentencing rate was generally higher for white and not black offenders. It should be kept in mind, however, that Kleck did not consider the race of the victim, nor did he consider race of offender/victim combinations. We have seen from previous research that the race of the person slain appears to be an important factor in the imposition of capital punishment. White offenders may be at higher risk of receiving a death sentence because they are more likely than black offenders to kill white victims, and it is the killing of a white victim that substantially increases the likelihood of the death penalty.

The Commutation Decision

Not all defendants who are sentenced to death get executed. Death sentences may be commuted to a life sentence or a term of years by a governor or state board of parole and pardons. The decision to commute a death sentence involves discretion on the part of the decision maker and may, therefore, be influenced by racial factors. In an early study, Mangum (1940) reported evidence from nine states that in each a higher proportion of black than white defendants had their request for a commutation denied and were executed. For example, he found that in the state of Florida from 1928 to 1938, 56 percent of white offenders sentenced to death were actually executed while nearly 75 percent of black defendants who were sentenced to death had their death sentences carried out. Guy Johnson (1941) found that in North Carolina from 1933 to 1939, 74 percent of those who were sentenced to death for killing white victims were eventually executed, 65 percent of those who killed blacks were put to death, and 81 percent of black offenders who killed whites were executed.

Elmer Johnson (1957) conducted an extensive examination of the likelihood of execution among those sentenced to death for rape in North Carolina from 1904 to 1954. He found that 56 percent of black condemned rapists were executed, as were 43 percent of whites. He also reported that while 64 percent of those who were convicted and sentenced to death for the rape of a white woman were put to death, only 14 percent of those who were convicted for raping a black woman were executed. Similar evidence was reported by

The Administration of the Death Penalty

Partington (1965), who found that in the period 1908 to 1964 every offender executed for the crime of rape in Virginia was black, and in four other states (Louisiana, Mississippi, Oklahoma, and West Virginia) no white was ever executed for the offense of rape. Finally, Koeninger (1969) reported that there were 360 executions in Texas in 1924 to 1968 and that the governor had commuted 85 other death sentences during that time. The bulk of the governors' commutations had gone to whites; 76 percent of white condemned offenders were executed, while 99 percent of black offenders did not have their sentence commuted and were eventually executed.

In addition to Southern states, racial disparity exists in the commutation decision in other states as well. Wolfgang, Kelly, and Nolde (1962) examined the fate of 439 persons sentenced to death in Pennsylvania from 1914 to 1958. They found that black offenders who committed a felony-type murder (a murder that also involved the commission of another felony, such as murder and rape or murder during an armed robbery) were substantially less likely to have their death sentence commuted than whites (6.3 percent versus 17.4 percent)—nearly three times as many whites had their death sentences commuted as blacks.

However, not all of the evidence in the historical literature shows racial disparity in the commutation of death sentences. Bedau (1964, 1965) found that white offenders were no more likely to have their death sentences commuted than black offenders in New Jersey from 1907 to 1960 or in Oregon during the period 1903–1964. In addition, Kleck (1981) found that across the United States from 1930 to 1967 the execution rate was similar for white and black offenders; for white offenders there were 10.42 executions per 1,000 homicides while for black offenders the rate was 9.72 executions per 1,000 homicides. Kleck did report, however, that when these rates were broken down by region of the country, blacks in the South had a higher risk of execution than whites.

Collectively, these studies of the imposition of capital punishment from 1930 to 1967 suggest that race may have influenced critical decision points. Racial disparities were observed in who was indicted and charged with a capital offense, who was convicted of a capital charge, who had a death sentence imposed, and who failed to receive a commutation. While racial effects by the race of the offender are inconsistent, these early studies do seem to consistently suggest that those who victimized whites, especially if the offender happened to be black, were treated at each point of the process more severely than those who victimized blacks. It must be emphasized, however, that while the historical evidence may indicate racial disparity, the data do not speak directly to the issue of racial discrimination. That is, the majority of the studies discussed thus far do not take into account relevant legal factors, such as variations in the brutality of the crime or the criminal history of the offender. The apparent disparate impact of the death penalty on those who killed whites may have been affected by these unconsidered legitimate case characteristics. Without a careful consideration of these factors, inferring racial discrimination in the capital sentencing system is hazardous.

One of the most important studies conducted during the period 1930–1967 was undertaken by Marvin Wolfgang and Marc Riedel (1973). They collected data on over 3,000 rape convictions in 230 counties from 11 Southern states over a 20-year period. They also collected extensive information about the offender (age, employment status, criminal history), the victim (age, number of dependent children, reputation in the community), the nature of the relationship between the offender and victim (stranger, acquaintance), characteristics of the offense (use of a weapon, nature and the extent of any injuries suffered by the victim, degree of force employed by the offender), and trial characteristics (type of defense counsel, whether a defense of consensual relations was employed). Wolfgang and Riedel found that black offenders were six and one-half times more likely to be sentenced to death for rape than white offenders and that blacks who raped white women were 18 times more likely to be sentenced to death than rapists involved in all other racial combinations. They also found that if the rape was committed along with another felony (for example, armed robbery or kidnapping) defendants of both races were more likely to be sentenced to death. Black defendants were more likely to have committed an additional felony during their rape, leading Wolfgang and Riedel to speculate that this factor might account for the higher death sentencing rates for blacks.

To examine this possibility, they calculated the percent of black and white offenders sentenced to death among those who did and did not commit another felony offense. They found, however, that the racial disparity persisted. For those rapes that involved the commission of another felony, 39 percent of black offenders who raped white women were sentenced to death while only 2 percent of offenders involving all other racial combinations resulted in a death sentence. In felony-rapes, then, blacks with white victims were almost 20 times more likely to be sentenced to death than other offenders. Blacks who raped whites in nonfelony rapes were also 20 times more likely to be sentenced to death than others. The presence of another felony, then, could not account for the fact that cross-racial rapes by blacks put them at substantially greater risk for the death penalty. Moreover, when Wolfgang and Riedel considered over two dozen other possible legal factors that could account for the observed racial disparity, in no instance did the racial effect disappear. This led them (1973) to conclude that Southern rapes involving black offenders and white victims are substantially more likely to result in a death sentence than other rapes, and that this disparate treatment cannot be explained by legally relevant differences among rapes or rapists:

> All the nonracial factors in each of the states analyzed "wash out," that is, they have no bearing on the imposition of the death penalty in disproportionate numbers upon blacks. The only variable of statistical significance that remains is race. (p. 133)

In a second study, Wolfgang and Riedel (1975) examined 361 rape convictions from a sample of 25 Georgia counties over the period 1945–1965. Each rape conviction also contained detailed information about the offender, the victim, the offense, and the trial. In a statistical analysis that considered 14 legal factors simultaneously, Wolfgang and Riedel found that the *most important predictor* of who among the 361 rapists would be sentenced to death was the combination of a black offender with a white victim.

Evidence of Racially Disparate Treatment in the Courts

We have just discussed evidence leading to the suspicion that racial factors may have been at work in the administration of capital punishment in the United States from 1930 to 1967. Clearly, scholars working in the area were largely convinced that the death penalty, at least as it was applied in Southern states, was discriminatory. This was particularly likely to be the case for the offense of rape in which the offender was African American and the victim was white. Perhaps more than any other offense, cross-racial rapes violated deeply felt racial taboos (see Chapter 7). It is not surprising to learn, then, that social scientific evidence would enter the legal system to support challenges against state death penalty laws on the basis that they unfairly targeted black offenders.

One of the first times that state or federal courts reviewed social scientific evidence to support the claim that a state death penalty statute was being administered in a discriminatory manner was in the case known as the "Martinsville Seven" (Rise 1995). This case arose out of the rape of a white woman, Ruby Stroud Floyd, by seven black males in Martinsville, Virginia in 1949. All seven defendants were sentenced to death by state juries in Virginia, and lawyers working on their behalf appealed their case to both state and federal appeals courts. Part of the appeal was the use of statistical evidence to bolster the claim that Virginia's death penalty was unconstitutional because in rape cases it targeted black offenders with white victims. By today's standards this evidence was not strong, but it was the first time that any such statistical evidence was used in court to make a case of racial discrimination. The evidence presented by the defendants showed that since the state of Virginia had taken over the execution of prisoners from local jurisdictions in 1908, there had been 45 black men executed for rape but not a single white man. The racial discrimination claim and the "statistical" evidence on which it was based was not successful. The Virginia Supreme Court of Appeals rejected the argument on November 3, 1950. In a written order on January 2, 1951, the U.S. Supreme Court refused to grant *certiorari* in the case (*Hampton v. Smith*, 340 U.S. 914 No. 245 Misc., 1951). On February 2, 1951 four of the Martinsville Seven were put to death by the state of Virginia, and the remaining three followed on February 5.

One of the most publicized legal challenges against the death penalty during this period was directed against the state of Arkansas in the case of William Maxwell. He was a 24-year-old black male who was convicted of the rape of a white woman in Arkansas in 1962 and was sentenced to death for his crime. Both his conviction and his death sentence were reviewed and approved by the Arkansas Supreme Court. Maxwell sought to have his death sentence overturned and appealed in federal district court for relief. One of his claims for appeal was that the Arkansas death penalty for rape was unconstitutional because it was discriminatory in its application in violation of the equal protection clause of the Fourteenth Amendment. Maxwell's appeal claimed that the evidence he possessed showed that black defendants who raped white women in Arkansas were more frequently sentenced to death than those who raped black women.

Maxwell's initial hearing on his equal protection claim occurred on May 6, 1962 in the United States District Court, Eastern District of Arkansas (*Maxwell v. Stephens*, 229 F. Supp. 205, 1964). The "evidence" that Maxwell had to back up his claim of racial discrimination was pretty weak. His information consisted of Arkansas State Penitentiary records of executions from September 5, 1913 through October 28, 1960, and statistics from circuit court clerks, prosecuting attorneys, and the sheriffs of three Arkansas counties (Garland, Pulaski, and Jefferson) as to the number and disposition of rape prosecutions in these counties during the period 1954–1964. The evidence that Maxwell claimed proved racial discrimination was that (1) all but two of the men who had been executed for rape in Arkansas since 1912 had been black; (2) all of those executed had raped white women; and (3) in Garland, Pulaski, and Jefferson counties from 1954 to 1964 there were only three criminal charges filed for white men who raped black women, with one resulting in an acquittal and the other two resulting in reduced charges. During this same period, seven blacks were arrested for raping white women, two of whom were sentenced to death and three to life imprisonment.

The federal district court was not impressed with Maxwell's offer of proof of discrimination. The court discredited his "evidence" by noting that he had failed to consider several important legal factors that could easily account for the disparate impact of the death penalty on blacks for rape. One of these legal factors was the defense of consent. The court argued that more blacks were convicted of raping white women and were sentenced more severely because consent was not as likely in these types of rapes as in cases where a black male raped a black woman. The court also noted that an important factor that was omitted was the moral character of the victim. The court again argued that this would explain the conviction and penalty disparity against those who victimized white women, since the moral character of a white woman would be more difficult to impeach in an Arkansas court than that of a black woman. Ultimately the court concluded that Maxwell's "evidence" fell far short of what it would take to establish an equal protection violation and characterized it as "a rather naïve attempt to ascertain why a rape conviction was sought in one case and yet not in another."

Maxwell appealed the ruling against him in federal district court and the case then went to the U.S. Court of Appeals for the 8th Circuit. The Court of Appeals heard Maxwell's appeal on June 20 but again rejected his claim of a denial of equal protection. Maxwell presented no new evidence of racial discrimination in Arkansas' administration of the death penalty in rape cases, and the Court of Appeals too found the evidence lacking because the reported racial disparity was not large enough and because the court thought there were compelling and unconsidered legal factors that could account for the differences in conviction and sentencing between black and white cases. It concluded that:

These facts do not seem to us to establish a pattern or something specific or useful here, or to provide anything other than a weak basis for suspicion on the part of the defense. The figures certainly do not prove current discrimination in Arkansas. . ." (*Maxwell v. Stephens*, 348 F. 2d. 325, 1965, at 331)

After the Court of Appeals denied Maxwell relief and the U.S. Supreme Court declined to review the case, he was scheduled for execution in July 1966. The execution was stayed, however, and Maxwell entered a second round of appeals in a federal district court habeas corpus hearing (*Maxwell v. Bishop*, 257 F. Supp. 710, 1966). Among the issues raised in this new round of appeals was the earlier claim that Arkansas was discriminatory in how it imposed the death penalty in rape cases. Although the claim was old, the evidence that Maxwell presented was more substantial in this new round of appeals. This evidence was the study of the death penalty in 11 Southern states during the period 1945–1965 conducted by Wolfgang and Riedel (1973) discussed earlier. Professor Wolfgang testified at Maxwell's hearing, presenting evidence from a sample of 19 Arkansas counties (Wolfgang 1974). He testified that from 1945 to 1965 there were 55 convictions for rape in these Arkansas counties, 34 of them involving black defendants and 21 with white defendants. Of the 34 convicted black rapists, 19 were convicted of raping white women, and 9 of these (47 percent) were sentenced to death. Only 14 percent of those defendants in all other rape cases were sentenced to death. In addition, there was no case in which a white man was convicted for the rape of a black woman. Professor Wolfgang then told the court that he tried to determine whether this racial disparity was due to any legal factor such as the use of force, victim/offender relationship, or the type of weapon used. He concluded that even with legal factors considered, the race of the offender and the victim was the single most important factor in determining which Arkansas rape defendants were sentenced to death.

The federal district court rejected this evidence for two reasons. First, it said that Maxwell presented only general statistical evidence about discrimination in Arkansas courts, not evidence that he personally was the victim of racial prejudice by his jury: "Petitioner has made no effort here to show that the individual jury which tried and convicted him acted in his particular case with racial discrimination" (*Maxwell v. Bishop*, F. Supp. 710, 1966, at 719). The court seemed to be implying that general statistical evidence would fall short in establishing proof of racial discrimination and that to do so would take evidence demonstrating that a particular defendant was intentionally discriminated against by his or her jury or legal officials. The second reason the federal district court rejected Maxwell's evidence was that it thought the study by Professor Wolfgang was incomplete in that it did not consider all relevant legal variables, did not include counties from all over the state, and did not include data from the county that tried and convicted Maxwell.

The district court's denial of relief was reviewed for a second time by the 8th Circuit Court of Appeals. The opinion of this court was written by Judge (later to be U.S. Supreme Court Justice) Harry A. Blackmun. The Court of Appeals rejected Maxwell's evidence of racial discrimination for many of the same reasons the district court did: it had excluded important legal variables, the sample of counties in the data set was not sufficiently broad to be representative of Arkansas, and Wolfgang's evidence provided no proof that Maxwell himself was the subject of racially discriminatory treatment. Maxwell's case went to the U.S. Supreme Court for another review, and this time the Court granted *certiorari* in *Maxwell v. Bishop* (398 U.S. 262, 1970). It would have been interesting to see how the Supreme Court would have ruled on the issue of racial discrimination in the death penalty presented to it in the Maxwell case, but it ruled in Maxwell's favor on other grounds (that several prospective jurors were removed because they expressed general objections to the death penalty in violation of *Witherspoon v. Illinois*, 1968). The Supreme Court would one day tackle the issue of racial discrimination in the imposition of the death penalty, but that didn't happen until almost three decades after *Maxwell*.

Race and Capital Punishment, 1976 to the Present

The Supreme Court's opinion in *Furman v. Georgia* in 1972 effectively put a moratorium on the use of capital punishment. Prior to the *Furman* decision, the last execution in the United States was in June 1967. This moratorium ended on January 17, 1977, when Gary Gilmore was executed by firing squad in Utah. As we discussed in Chapter 5, in response to *Furman* state legislatures drafted new death penalty statutes that introduced legal reforms into the administration of the death penalty: (1) bifurcated hearings (a guilt and separate penalty phase), (2) the formal consideration of aggravating and mitigating factors of a crime, and (3) some form of appellate review of all death sentences.[1] Among other things, these procedural reforms promised to enhance evenhanded capital sentencing,[2] where evenhandedness meant the reduction if not the elimination of both arbitrary and capricious death sentences and the influence of race in the decision as to which capital defendants live and which die.[3]

Although post-*Furman* legal reforms in state death penalty statutes *promised* to remove any risk of discrimination, a new generation of scholars began investigating whether these new death penalty laws were actually any different from those in the past. We will examine the evidence about disparate racial impact of these new death penalty laws during the modern era of capital punishment as they operated at two stages in the process: (1) the indictment and charging stage, and (2) the conviction and sentencing stage.

The Indictment and Charging Decision

In one of the first investigations of the new post-*Furman* capital punishment statutes, Bowers and Pierce (1980a) examined the likelihood that an offender would be indicted for first degree murder once charged with homicide in Florida from 1973 to 1977. They found that black offenders charged with homicide for killing white victims were more than twice as likely to be indicted for first degree murder (thus making them eligible for the death penalty) as were black offenders who killed black victims. When they separately examined homicides that were committed with another felony (murder/rape or murder/armed robbery, for example) the disparate treatment of black killers of whites persisted—every black offender who had killed a white was indicted for first degree murder, while only 80 percent of those who killed black victims were. These results were corroborated by Radelet (1981), who studied first degree murder indictments that were handed down in 20 Florida counties during 1976 and 1977. He found that over 92 percent of homicides where a black offender killed a white victim resulted in a first degree murder indictment whereas only 70 percent of all other homicides did.

Bowers (1983) conducted a later and more sophisticated study of the capital charging process in Florida. He found that even after he considered such case characteristics as the number of offenders and victims involved in the crime, the commission of another felony, the age of the victim, the type of weapon used, and the type of attorney the defendant had, those who killed white victims (particularly if they were black) were more likely to be charged with first degree murder. In addition, Radelet and Pierce (1985) found that Florida prosecutors were more likely to "upgrade" the charge in homicides involving white victims. A prosecutor "upgrades" a homicide when he or she charges the defendant with a felony offense or some other aggravating factor in addition to murder that was not initially included in the police report. An "upgraded" homicide, therefore, is a more serious offense and is likely to be punished with a more severe sanction.

Florida is, of course, not the only state where early decision-making points in the capital punishment system may have been influenced by racial factors. Paternoster (1983; Paternoster and Kazyaka 1988) examined the role of race in the decisions of South Carolina prosecutors to charge a defendant with a capital crime. They examined approximately 1,800 homicides committed in the state over the years 1977–1981 and identified 302 as being "eligible" for the death penalty. A homicide is a potentially capital crime when the murder involves one or more "aggravating factors" listed in the state's capital punishment statute (for example, if the victim was a law enforcement or judicial officer or if the murder involved the commission of rape, armed robbery, or kidnapping). Of these 302 potentially capital crimes, local prosecutors filed a notice to seek the death penalty in only 114 (38 percent). The important question is, What factors distinguish the 114 instances where the prosecutors sought the death penalty from the 188 instances where they could have, but did not, and is race one of those factors?

These researchers first found that the decision to seek the death penalty in South Carolina was related to important case characteristics: prosecutors were substantially more likely to charge a homicide as a capital offense based on the prior violent criminal history of the defendant, the overall brutality of the murder, the number of statutory aggravating factors in the crime, the type of weapon used, and the number of felonies committed in addition to murder. Clearly, then, South Carolina prosecutors were seeking the death penalty in cases that were more aggravated than most. However, even when all of these legally relevant factors were taken into account, race still had an important role to play: killers of whites were almost twice as likely to be charged with a capital offense as killers of blacks. The most likely to have the death penalty sought against them were black offenders who killed white victims.

The authors of this study created a measure of how aggravated each homicide was, then classified the murders into one of five groups depending on the level of aggravation. In Table 8.4 we reproduce some of their results. The first thing to notice is the considerable rationality in the way that South Carolina prosecutors sought the death penalty. They were much more likely to seek a sentence of death as the homicide became more serious. Ignoring for a moment the race of the victim, prosecutors sought a death sentence in only 6 percent of the cases at the lowest level of aggravation (8/140 = .057) but in 90 percent of the cases at the highest level of aggravation (17/19). Even given the level of aggravation, however, the race of the victim still played an important role in determining which defendants were charged with a capital offense and which were not. This racially disparate impact is not characteristic of all homicides, but only those at the lower end of the aggravation scale. At the lowest two levels of aggravation, prosecutors were approximately twice as likely to seek a death sentence when a white was killed compared to black victims. At the low end of aggravation, when there was some ambiguity as to whether a murder qualified as serious enough to warrant a death sentence and the prosecutor's discretion to seek death or not was the greatest, we find evidence of racial disparity. Keep in mind that this racial difference cannot be attributable to differences in the characteristics of the murder, since this disparity for white and black victim cases occurs at a comparable level of homicide aggravation. Looking at the highest three levels of homicide aggravation, we see no evidence of prosecutorial bias by the race of the victim. When a homicide was aggravated enough to cross the third level, white victim and black victim cases were treated equally. When a homicide was egregious enough, therefore, the victim's race did not matter.

In the bottom panel of Table 8.4 the probability that the prosecutor sought the death penalty when a black offender killed a white victim is compared with cases where a black killed a black. At the lowest two levels of aggravation, again where prosecutorial discretion may have been greatest because the murder was not "shocking," the race of the victim matters. In these cases, when black offenders crossed racial lines and slew a white, South Carolina prosecutors are twice as likely to seek a death sentence than for intraracial black murders.

Vito and Keil (1988) examined the decision of the prosecutor in Kentucky to advance a first degree murder case to a penalty trial. They included in their sample all cases involving defendants convicted of first degree murder in Kentucky from 1976 to 1986 that also contained at least one statutory aggravating circumstance. These murders were "death eligible" according to the Kentucky statute, and in 104 cases the prosecutor advanced the case to a penalty trial where the jury had to decide whether the defendant was to be sentenced to death. They found that almost half of the murders where a black killed a white and nearly one-fourth of the white-on-white killings resulted in a penalty trial. In none of the 14 cases where a white killed a black did the case advance to a penalty trial, and in only 13 percent of those where a black killed another black was there a penalty phase hearing. Vito and Keil reported that these racial differences in the likelihood that a case would advance to a penalty trial persisted even when important case characteristics were considered, such as the number of aggravating circumstances present, the number of victims, and whether

Table 8.4 Race and South Carolina's Prosecutors' Decision to Seek Death by Level of Aggravation

| | Level of Aggravation of the Homicide | | | | |
| | *Lowest* | | | | *Highest* |
	1	2	3	4	5
White victim	.071	.405	.758	.895	.882
	(6/85)	(17/42)	(25/33)	(34/38)	(15/17)
Black victim	.036	.200	.833	1.00	1.00
	(2/55)	(4/20)	(5/6)	(4/4)	(2/2)
Ratio	1.97	2.02	.91	.90	.88
Black kills white	.049	.435	.867	.952	.909
	(2/41)	(10/23)	(13/15)	(20/21)	(10/11)
Black kills black	.021	.167	1.00	1.00	1.00
	(1/48)	(3/18)	(3/3)	(2/2)	(1/1)
Ratio	2.33	2.60	.867	.952	.909

Source: Paternoster and Kazyaka (1988), Table 14.

the murder was committed to "silence" the victim. In Kentucky, the victim's race mattered, at least as far as the decision to move a case through the capital sentencing system to a penalty hearing was concerned.

Not all of the evidence with respect to race and capital punishment at the indictment and charging stage is restricted to Southern states. Bienen and her colleagues (1988) conducted an extensive examination of capital sentencing in the state of New Jersey. Collecting data on 703 homicides committed during the years 1982 to 1986, they found that 404 cases were "death eligible" in that all the facts were present for the prosecutor to seek a death sentence. The death penalty was actually sought in 131 (32 percent) of these cases. They reported that after considering several kinds of aggravating and mitigating factors, relevant characteristics of the offender and victim, and trial characteristics, prosecutors were 10 times more likely to seek the death penalty when a white was killed compared to when blacks or Hispanics were victims. Black and Hispanic offenders who killed whites were twice as likely to be charged with a capital offense than those who committed intra-racial murders.

Paternoster and his colleagues (2004) conducted a study of the capital sentencing system of Maryland, examining cases from 1978 to 1999. They found that prosecutors filed a notification to seek a death sentence in about 30 percent of the cases that were eligible for the death penalty. Even when a large number of aggravating and mitigating factors were considered, prosecutors were almost twice as likely to seek a death sentence in death-eligible cases where the victim was white than when a black was murdered. Black offenders who killed white victims were about twice as likely to have the death penalty sought by the prosecutor when compared with white offenders who killed whites, and over two times more likely when compared with black offenders who killed blacks (but see Berk, Li, and Hickman 2005 for another view of these data).

In what at the time was the most comprehensive study of any state's capital sentencing system, law professor David Baldus and his colleagues (1990) examined the imposition of capital sentences in post-*Furman* Georgia. They reviewed over 2,000 homicide incidents committed in the state from 1973 to 1980 and collected information on several hundred case characteristics. They found that after controlling for these characteristics prosecutors were substantially more likely to seek a death sentence when the victim was white than if black. To better see these race effects, Baldus and his colleagues rated each homicide according to its level of aggravation, ranging from low (the least serious or egregious killings) to high (the most aggravated and brutal murders). These data are shown in Table 8.5. You can see from the overall rate of capital charging that prosecutors were more likely to charge a crime as capital when the level of aggravation was higher. Only 3 percent of cases at the lowest level of aggravation were charged as a capital crime, but all of those at the highest level of aggravation were. As was true in South Carolina, this indicates a great deal of rationality in Georgia prosecutors' decision making, as they were substantially more likely to seek a sentence of death when the case was more brutal and aggravated.

When white and black victim cases are compared at the same level of aggravation, however, there is evidence of racially disparate treatment. At the lowest level of aggravation (where only eight death requests were made), prosecutors were five times more likely to seek death in white victim than black victim cases. At the second level of aggravation prosecutors were over four times more likely to seek death if a white were killed rather than a black, and almost twice as likely to at the third level of aggravation. In fact, it is not until the fifth and sixth levels of aggravation that black victim cases are treated comparably to white victim cases. Only at the two highest levels of aggravation, then, where homicides are the most egregious, are white and black victim cases treated the same. Notice also that prosecutors sought a sentence of death

Table 8.5 Race of Victim Effects in Georgia Capital Murder Cases by Level of Aggravation: Prosecutor's Charging Decision

Level of Aggravation	Overall Rate	White Victim Rate	Black Victim Rate	Ratio
1 (Lowest)	.03	.05	.01	5.0
2	.14	.21	.05	4.2
3	.49	.56	.34	1.6
4	.86	.95	.67	1.4
5	.91	.93	.80	1.2
6 (Highest)	1.00	1.00	1.00	1.0

Source: Baldus et al. (1990), Table 36, p. 168.

nine out of 10 times in white victim cases when they reach the fourth level of aggravation. A black victim homicide case had to reach the highest level of homicide aggravation before local Georgia prosecutors sought a death sentence in such a high proportion of cases.

To be fair, not all of the more recent studies have found evidence of racial disparity in prosecutorial decision making in capital cases. In fact, the research shows that racial differences in capital charging decisions depend on the jurisdiction. In other work of Professor Baldus, in Philadelphia, Colorado, and Nebraska, prosecutors' decisions were unaffected by the race of the defendant, the race of the victim, or combinations of offender and victim's race (Baldus et al. 1998, 2002; Anderson 1991).[4] Beinan and colleagues' study (1988) study of capital sentencing in New Jersey found evidence that the victim's race mattered for the prosecutors' charging decision but not the race of the defendant. Similar prosecutorial decision making was also found in Mississippi (Berk and Lowery 1985), North Carolina (Nakell and Hardy 1987), and California (Klein and Rolph 1991). What we can conclude with some confidence is that the collective landscape of the findings regarding the role of race in the prosecutor's decision making shows that the race of the victim did generally seem to matter in this period. With only a few exceptions, prosecutors were more likely to charge a death-eligible murder as a capital crime and more likely to move a capital murder forward to a penalty hearing if the victim slain was white than if a minority. The race of the offender when considered alone did not appear to affect the decision of the prosecutor in capital cases, but black offenders who killed white victims seemed particularly at risk for adverse outcomes.

The Conviction and Sentencing Decision

Most of the recent research in this area has examined the rate at which death-eligible cases are sentenced to death. Studies have shown that only a minority of such cases actually result in a death sentence. The question is whether the decision to sentence someone to death is affected by the race of the defendant or the victim (or both). As in the case of the prosecutor's charging decision, the critical inferential task is to examine whether race matters among defendants who commit comparable kinds of crimes or, to put it differently, who are equivalent in terms of their culpability or "death worthiness." Various researchers have addressed the problem of differences in defendants' culpability in different ways.

In an early study, Bowers and Pierce (1980a) examined the probability that a defendant would receive a death sentence in several states (Florida, Georgia, and Texas). They crudely controlled for defendants' culpability by separately considering felony-type murders from nonfelony-type murders. A felony-type murder is a murder that also involves the commission of another felony offense (rape, armed robbery, kidnapping), which makes one committing it eligible for the death penalty under the laws of all death penalty states. A felony-type murder, therefore, is generally more egregious and aggravated than a nonfelony-type murder. They found that among the felony-type murders the race of the victim mattered substantially. Black offenders who killed whites in both Florida and Georgia were over seven times more likely to be sentenced to death than those who killed blacks; in Texas they were almost 10 times more likely to be sentenced to death.

In a study of 350 murder cases in Dade County (Miami), Florida, Arkin (1980) demonstrated that the presence of racial disparity may exist at one decision-making point in the capital sentencing process but not another. In examining the probability that a first degree murderer would be sentenced to death, he found that it was comparable in white and black victim cases (.167 for white victim murders and .176 for black victim murders). In looking at the decision to sentence a defendant to death in Dade County, then, it would appear that the race of the victim did not matter. However, this equality was offset by the fact that killers of whites in felony-type murder cases were more than twice as likely to be convicted of first degree murder than killers of blacks. Since a conviction for first degree murder precedes sentencing for death, a larger proportion of white victim cases advanced to the sentencing stage than black victim killings. Bowers' (1983) study of Florida homicide defendants indicted for first degree murder from 1973 to 1977 also indicated the importance of victim's race. He controlled for 10 legally relevant factors, including the existence of a felony, the number of victims and offenders, the age and sex of the victim, type of weapon used, age of the offender, and type of defense attorney. He found that even with these factors controlled defendants accused of killing whites were far more likely to be sentenced to death than those who killed blacks. Comparable results about the role of victim's race have been found in Georgia, Illinois, and five other states by Gross and Mauro (1984, 1989).

One of the most comprehensive studies of capital sentencing at the time was Baldus and colleagues' (1990) study of the Georgia capital sentencing system previously described. In addition to the decision of the prosecutor to charge a murder as a capital crime, they examined the jury's decision to impose a death sentence. As with the prosecutor's decision, they examined whether the decision to sentence a convicted murderer to death was influenced by the race of the victim. Some of their evidence is summarized in Table 8.6.

With the exception of cases at the lowest and highest levels of aggravation, Georgia offenders who killed white victims were at a higher risk of being sentenced to death than killers of blacks. As was true for prosecutors' decisions in Georgia, cases at the mid-range of aggravation seemed to be fertile ground for the exercise of disparate treatment by the race of the victim.

In a more recent study, Baldus and colleagues (1998) examined capital sentencing in the city and county of Philadelphia, Pennsylvania. They collected extensive data on nearly 700 homicides committed in that jurisdiction from 1983 to 1993. As in their Georgia study, the researchers determined the culpability level of each homicide on a scale from 1 to 6, where homicides at level 6 were the most brutal/aggravated. They then examined the effect of the race of the defendant and the race of the victim for Philadelphia jury decisions in capital cases. We summarize some of their findings in Table 8.7.

Table 8.7 clearly shows that the race of the defendant had an effect on the likelihood that the jury will impose a death sentence in Philadelphia. Juries in

Table 8.6 Race of Victim Effects in Georgia Capital Murder Cases by Level of Aggravation: Jury's Sentencing Decision

Level of Aggravation	Overall Rate	White Victim Rate	Black Victim Rate	Ratio
1 (Lowest)	.05	.04	.07	.57
2	.33	.37	.00	—
3	.71	.74	.50	1.5
4	.96	1.00	.83	1.2
5	.89	1.00	.60	1.7
6 (Highest)	1.00	1.00	1.00	1.0

Source: Baldus et al. (1990), Table 36, p. 168.

Philadelphia never imposed a death sentence against a nonblack defendant unless it was at the highest two culpability levels. At culpability level 5, black defendants were more than twice as likely to be sentenced to death as nonblack defendants, and at the highest level they were almost one and one-half times more likely. These findings for Philadelphia are remarkable in that they document the existence of *race of defendant* effects in capital sentencing after controlling for case comparability. Most studies of capital punishment have found only race of victim effects.

Baldus and his colleagues also found evidence of race of victim effects in their Philadelphia sentencing data. The bottom panel of Table 8.7 shows that overall those who killed a nonblack victim were over one and one-half times more likely to be sentenced to death by a jury than those who killed a black (.34 versus .21), and this disparity against black victims holds true at every level of the defendant's culpability. These data from Philadelphia suggest that at least in this jurisdiction the decision to sentence a defendant to death is influenced by the race of both the offender and of the victim.

Four other studies of race and capital sentencing deserve mentioning. As part of Illinois Governor George Ryan's Commission on Capital Punishment, Professors Glenn L. Pierce and Michael L. Radelet (2002) were invited to provide a statistical study of Illinois' capital sentencing patterns. They examined defendants convicted of first degree murder in Illinois who were sentenced from January 1, 1988 to December 31, 1997. There were 4,182 cases in the dataset, which included 76 cases that resulted in a sentence of death. The researchers reported that even after they considered over 20 case characteristics (number of victims, presence of a felony), the odds that a defendant would receive a death sentence were nearly 60 percent lower if he killed a black rather than a white victim.

In their study of Maryland homicide cases from 1978 to 1999, Paternoster et al. (2004) found that the probability of being sentenced to death was about twice as high for those who killed a white victim as for those who killed a black. Black offenders who crossed racial lines were particularly more likely to

Table 8.7 Race of Defendant and Race of Victim Effects in Jury Sentencing

	Race of Defendant Cases		
Culpability Level	Overall Death Sentencing Rate	Rate for Black Defendant Cases	Rate for Nonblack Defendant Cases
1 (Lowest)	.02	.03	.00
2	.00	.00	.00
3	.26	.30	.00
4	.29	.34	.00
5	.67	.72	.33
6 (Highest)	.87	.94	.67
		.32 (46/145)	.17 (5/30)
	Race of Victim Cases		
Culpability Level	Overall Death Sentencing Rate	Rate for Nonblack Defendant Cases	Rate for Black Defendant Cases
1 (Lowest)	.00	.00	.00
2	.06	.13	.00
3	.05	.08	.04
4	.52	.86	.37
5	.77	.80	.75
6 (Highest)	.87	1.00	.81
		.34 (26/77)	.21 (33/157)

Source: Baldus et al. (1998), Tables 7 and 8.

be sentenced to death: A black offender who killed a white victim was about two and one-half times more likely to be sentenced to death than a white who killed a white, and nearly three and one-half times more likely than a black who killed a black (but see Berk et al. 2005).

Examining death sentencing practices in California from 1990 to 1999, Pierce and Radelet (2005) found that even after controlling for several relevant sentencing factors, those who killed white victims were more likely to be sentenced to death than others. For example, when there were one or two aggravating circumstances present in a case, those who killed whites were about twice as likely to be sentenced to death than those who killed a nonwhite. Finally, in a study of race, gender, and capital sentencing in Colorado over the time period 1980-1999, Hindson, Potter, and Radelet (2006) found that the probability of getting a death sentence was more than four times higher for defendants who killed a white victim compared with those who killed a black. The death penalty was also a more likely sentence for those who killed white female victims compared with other gender and racial groups.

> # Box 8.2
> # Discrimination by Gender?
>
> The death penalty has historically been imposed much more frequently on men than on women. Approximately 98 percent of those put to death since 1608 have been men (Death Penalty Information Center 2006). Over the past 100 years, only 40 women have been executed in the United States, and only 11 since 1977:
>
> - **Velma Barfield** in North Carolina on November 2, 1984
> - **Karla Faye Tucker** in Texas on February 3, 1998
> - **Judy Buenoano** in Florida on March 30, 1998
> - **Betty Lou Beets** in Texas on February 24, 2000
> - **Christina Riggs** in Arkansas on May 2, 2000
> - **Wanda Jean Allen** in Oklahoma on January 11, 2001
> - **Marilyn Plantz** in Oklahoma on May 1, 2001
> - **Lois Nadean Smith** in Oklahoma on December 4, 2001
> - **Lynda Lyon Block** in Alabama on May 10, 2002
> - **Aileen Wuornos** in Florida on October 9, 2002
> - **Frances Newton** in Texas on September 14, 2005
>
> Since 1973 a total of 152 death sentences have been imposed on women, about 2 percent of the total number of death sentences handed down in that time period. About two-thirds of the women on death row are there for killing their spouse/partner or another family member. One of the reasons there have been so few women executed and so few given death sentences compared with men is that women are far less likely to commit murder than men. In 2004, for example, there were 11,392 murders committed where the gender of the arrested person was known. In 10,262 (90 percent) the offender was male.
>
> A leading expert on women and capital punishment, Professor Elizabeth Rapaport (1996) has also argued that the low number of women on death row is due to the fact that they are far less likely to commit the kinds of felony-related murders (armed robber, kidnapping, sexual assault) that make up the bulk of death cases and more likely to commit "domestic murders." In addition, we as a society also seem less willing to impose the death penalty on women than we are on men (Howarth 2002; Streib 2005). See also the American Civil Liberties Union Report, *The Forgotten Population: A Look at Death Row in the United States Through the Experiences of Women* (ACLU 2004). ✦

In sum, numerous empirical studies have been directed at the issue of racial disparity under procedurally reformed post-*Furman* death penalty statutes. While not unanimous, most have found that in terms of critical decisions in the death penalty process, killing a white victim puts a defendant at greater risk for the death penalty while killing a black victim reduces that risk. In 1990, the United States General Accounting Office (GAO), at the request of the United States Senate, published the results of its review of all the literature to date about the death penalty and racial disparity. After their evaluation of 28 studies it concluded that:

In 82 percent of the studies, race of victim was found to influence the likeli-hood of being charged with capital murder or receiving the death penalty, i.e., those who murdered whites were found to be more likely to be sen-tenced to death than those who murdered blacks. This finding was remark-ably consistent across data sets, states, data collection methods, and analytic techniques. The finding held for high, medium, and low quality studies. The race of victim influence was found at all stages of the criminal justice system process, although there were variations among studies as to whether there was a race of victim influence at specific stages. The evidence for the race of victim influence was stronger for the earlier stages of the judi-cial process (e.g., prosecutorial decision to charge defendants with a capital offense, decision to proceed to trial rather than plea bargain) than in later stages.[5] (p. 6)

The critical legal question, then, is since post-*Furman* procedural reforms promised to remedy an identified defect of previous capital statutes—that they did not result in an evenhanded imposition of the death penalty—would legal challenges be made claiming that these reformed statutes were unconstitutional because they too failed to eliminate discriminatory application of capital pun-ishment? The answer is "yes."

Post-*Furman* Evidence of Racial Discrimination in Capital Sentencing Before the Courts—*McCleskey v. Kemp*

Warren McCleskey was a black man convicted by a Georgia jury of two counts of armed robbery and one count of the murder of a white police officer in 1978. Under Georgia's new capital punishment law, the jury sentenced McCleskey to death, and his death sentence was appealed through both state and federal channels. One of the claims made by McCleskey in his appeals was that the Georgia capital sentencing system was unconstitutional because it was discriminatory in violation of both the Equal Protection Clause of the Fourteenth Amendment and the Eighth Amendment's protection against cruel and unusual punishment. McCleskey's "proof" of that claim was the study we have previously discussed by David Baldus and his colleagues of the Georgia capital sentencing system. The study presented to various appeals courts did not claim that McCleskey himself was the victim of racial discrimi-nation by the judge, prosecutor, or jury, but that the general statistical evidence of Professor Baldus indicated that Georgia murderers as a whole were the vic-tims of a discriminatory system. The Baldus study revealed that after control-ling for hundreds of case characteristics, the odds of a death sentence for those who killed white victims in Georgia were on average 4.3 times higher than for those who killed nonwhite victims. They also reported that disparities by the race of the victim existed in Fulton County, Georgia, where the jury sentenced McCleskey to death, and that the white/black victim disparity was most ap-parent for cases, like McCleskey's, that were in the middle range of defendant culpability.

McCleskey was denied relief in both state and federal appeals courts, and the U.S. Supreme Court agreed to review the case. In 1987 it released its opin-ion in *McCleskey v. Kemp* (107 S. Ct. 1756, 1987), and in a 5–4 decision upheld the lower courts' rejection of McCleskey's claim that the Georgia death sentencing system was discriminatory. In deciding that McCleskey was not entitled to relief, the Court made several observations. With respect to McCleskey's equal protection claim, the Court rejected the evidence provided by Baldus' study, noting that such general statistical evidence about the operation of Georgia's capital sentencing system cannot be the basis for an inference that McCleskey himself was deliberately discriminated against. In language reminiscent of the *Maxwell v. Bishop* decision, the Court held that "to prevail under the Equal Protection Clause, McCleskey must prove that the decision makers in his case acted with discriminatory purpose" (*McCleskey v. Kemp*, at 1766).

To be successful, then, McCleskey had to demonstrate that the prosecutors, judge, and jurors in his particular case had an intent to discriminate and acted on that intent. While agreeing that in the past the Court has accepted general statistical evidence to support a claim of purposeful discrimination, such as in employment discrimination cases, it distinguished the capital sentencing context as unique because of the many factors jurors must consider and the fact that prosecutors' and jurors' decisions would be difficult to reconstruct and explain.

In rejecting McCleskey's Eighth Amendment claim, the Court argued that the disparate racial effect observed in the Baldus study was simply not large enough to warrant questioning Georgia's capital statute, that "[a]t most, the Baldus study indicates a discrepancy that appears to correlate with race" (at 1777). In addition, the Court expressed some fear that if McCleskey prevailed there would be other claims of racial discrimination made about other penalties by other minority groups. Finally, the Court reasoned that McCleskey's evidence in the form of the Baldus study and other general statistical studies was best directed at state legislatures rather than courts. What the *McClesky* decision did, therefore, was to generally preclude the consideration *by courts* of general statistical evidence of racial discrimination in the administration of capital punishment. What it did not do, however, was to say that no evidence of racial discrimination would ever be persuasive.

Since the *McCleskey* decision was handed down, there has been at least one attempt to provide the courts with other kinds of evidence that a state's capital sentencing system is discriminatory. Earl Matthews, a South Carolina murder defendant, submitted statistical and other evidence to the South Carolina Supreme Court that the decision maker in his case, the Charleston County prosecutor, acted in a discriminatory manner (Blume, Eisenberg, and Johnson 1998). The statistical evidence indicated that since the state's new death penalty statute had taken effect in 1977, the Charleston County prosecutor had sought the death penalty in 20 cases, and in all but two of them the victim was white (the defendant was a minority in 13 of these cases). Furthermore, between 1981 and 1990 the prosecutor had sought the death penalty in 40 percent of the murder cases that involved a black offender and white victim but in only 3 percent of the cases that involved a black offender and black victim. Matthews presented corroborating evidence in the form of testimony of former employees of the prosecutor's office, one of whom said that she heard another prosecutor in the office say that a particular murder deserved less of the office's attention be-

---

Box 8.3
The *McCleskey* Decision: One Dissent and One Regret

Justice William Brennan wrote an angry dissent to the *McCleskey* decision. Recall that in the 1972 *Furman* decision Justice Brennan argued that the death penalty was unconstitutional under the Eighth Amendment's ban against cruel and unusual punishment. In his *McCleskey* dissent, Justice Brennan eloquently argued that the evidence presented by the defendant in the form of the Baldus study provided clear and convincing evidence that race matters in the Georgia capital sentencing system and that such evidence cannot be ignored:

> It is tempting to pretend that minorities on death row share a fate in no way connected to our own, that our treatment of them sounds no echoes beyond the chambers in which they die. Such an illusion is ultimately corrosive, for the reverberations of injustice are not so easily confined. "The destinies of the two races in this country are indissolubly linked together," *id.* at 560 (Harlan, J., dissenting), and the way in which we choose those who will die reveals the depth of moral commitment among the living.

> The Court's decision today will not change what attorneys in Georgia tell other Warren McCleskeys about their chances of execution. Nothing will soften the harsh message they must convey, nor alter the prospect that race undoubtedly will continue to be a topic of discussion. McCleskey's evidence will not have obtained judicial acceptance, but that will not affect what is said on death row. However many criticisms of today's decision may be rendered, these painful conversations will serve as the most eloquent dissents of all. (*McCleskey v. Kemp*, at 345)

In response to a question raised by his biographer, Justice Lewis Powell, who had voted with the majority in *McCleskey*, openly admitted that the one vote in all his years on the Supreme Court that he would like to change was his deciding vote in the 5–4 *McCleskey* decision. With respect to that vote, he confided that: "I have come to think that capital punishment should be abolished . . . it serves no useful purpose" (Jefferies 1994, 451–452). ✦

---

cause the victim was "just a little old black man" (Blume et al. 1998). Other evidence of the influence of racial discrimination came directly from the mouth of Matthews' prosecutor, who, among other things, stated that the high crime rate in South Carolina was due to the moral dissolution in the black community and gave his vocal support for flying the Confederate battle flag on top of the state capital (Blume et al. 1998). Moreover, there was no compelling reason for the prosecutor to pursue a death sentence in Matthews' case. He was 19 years old at the time of the crime, the murder resulted from a botched armed robbery when Matthews panicked, and there were no other aggravating features about the case.

In another South Carolina case, lawyers for Raymond Patterson presented statistical information that the Lexington County prosecutor's office had in the past acted in a discriminatory manner. For example, although there had been 174 murders involving black victims in the county since 1977, the prosecutor's office had not sought a single death sentence in a black victim case. Patterson's lawyers also presented evidence that the prosecutor had used his peremptory strikes to remove blacks from the jury. In Patterson's first trial, for example, peremptory strikes were used to produce an all-white jury, and this was not the first time the prosecutor's office had done this. Defense counsel also presented testimony that included racist innuendo from the prosecutor before the trial (Blume et al. 1998).

In both the Matthews and Patterson cases, therefore, there was evidence that differed in important ways from that presented to the U.S. Supreme Court in *McCleskey*. The most dramatic difference was that the evidence in both cases was directed not at statewide patterns of racial discrimination but rather racial discrimination by a single state prosecutor's office or office holder. In addition, the general statistical evidence was supplemented by other kinds of testimony, including previous actions by the prosecutor in other contexts, discriminatory practices by other members of the prosecutor's office, and the prosecutor's own race-insensitive language and behavior. In both cases, however, the evidence was ignored by the courts.

Matthews and Patterson are not the only defendants who have unsuccessfully challenged state death penalties as discriminatory. Since the *McCleskey* decision in 1987 no racial discrimination challenge based on statistical evidence has prevailed in any state court.

Chapter Summary

Since the 1930s empirical research conducted by social scientists has shown the existence of a racial imbalance in the administration of the death penalty. At several points in the administration of capital punishment, from the prosecutor's decision to seek a death sentence to the jury's decision to impose one and the state executive's decision to commute a death sentence, the literature published before 1972 has consistently shown that black offenders were treated more harshly in the criminal justice system than white offenders. In more recent decades this research has shown that the race of the offender is less important than the race of the victim: Those who kill whites are treated more harshly at virtually every stage of the process compared with those who kill nonwhites.

While the statistical evidence may seem compelling that there are traces of racial discrimination in the American capital punishment system, the Supreme Court was unconvinced. In a landmark 1984 decision, *McCleskey v. Kemp,* the Court dismissed a claim of racial discrimination made against the state of Georgia. The Court argued that general evidence of racial disparity in a state's administration of capital punishment is not sufficient to prove racial discrimination. The demanding burden of proof the Court wanted was that it be shown that officers of the state acted with discriminatory intent against a particular defendant. While the Court held out the possibility that general statistical evidence of racial disparity could be presented to state legislatures, there is little evidence to date that states that use capital punishment would ever be persuaded by such evidence.

Discussion Questions

1. In the Premodern Period of capital punishment, an overwhelming majority of the executions for the offense of rape were against black offend-

ers, and a majority of these occurred in Southern states. What social or cultural conditions do you think could have contributed to this?

2. In the *McClesky* case the Supreme Court seemed to be saying that general statistical evidence showing that the death penalty has a disparate impact by race cannot be used to make a claim of racial discrimination. Do you agree or disagree with this conclusion? Why?

3. The *McClesky* Court also said that a capital defendant must present evidence of an intent to discriminate by authorities in his or her particular case. What kind of evidence do you think this would entail? How easy would it be to get this kind of evidence? Do you think this evidentiary requirement puts an unrealistic burden on capital defendants wanting to make a claim of discrimination? What kind of evidence or proof do you think is needed to make a claim of racial discrimination in capital cases?

4. Do you think there is discrimination in the use of the death penalty against other groups in American society? Which? Do some investigation of your own to either support or refute your claim.

5. If you had been a Supreme Court Justice at the time, what would have been your decision in the *McClesky* case? Do you think McCleskey was wrongly decided? Explain.

6. In rejecting *McClesky*'s claim of racial discrimination, the majority expressed the view that if they granted this claim of racial discrimination, other claims of unequal treatment could be made—such as that capital punishment discriminates against those who are left-handed or those with red hair. Understanding as you do from the last chapter the historic role of race in the administration of the law and capital punishment, do you think this is a reasonable fear?

7. In the *Gregg* decision, the Supreme Court held the opinion that reforms made to capital punishment law would, among other things, reduce the "risk" of death sentences being influenced by race. Based on what you know, do you think state capital statutes constructed after *Furman* are any better at reducing racial disparities or racial discrimination than ones before?

8. Do you think it is possible to remove race as a factor in the imposition of the death penalty in the United States? If not, why not? If you think it is possible, what do you think has to occur (within the law, within society) for this to happen?

Student Resources

In this chapter we have concentrated on capital punishment and African Americans. If you are interested in women and the death penalty, there are a number of good sources. First, Professor Victor Streib keeps an updated report on the death penalty for females (and juveniles) at <www.law .onu.edu/faculty/streib>. Other good sources are Howarth (2002), O'Shea (1999), and Streib (2005). Information about the death penalty and Latinos can be found in

Urbina (2003). A good review of recent empirical research on race and the death penalty can be found in Baldus and Woodworth (2003) and Weisberg (2005).

Endnotes

1. For a good review of these legal reforms and their consequences, see White (1985, 1987, 1991).

2. Writing approvingly of Georgia's newly crafted capital statute, Justice Stewart in *Gregg v. Georgia* concluded that "On their face these procedures [specific jury findings as to aggravating circumstances and automatic appellate review] seem to satisfy the concerns of *Furman*" (*Gregg v. Georgia,* at 2937). In noting that *"on their face* these procedures *seem* to . . ." Justice Stewart was acknowledging that there was no evidence before the Court to indicate that procedurally reformed statutes were actually performing any better than their counterparts struck down by *Furman.*

3. A death sentence can be said to be "capricious" when there is no meaningful basis to distinguish between those sentenced to death and those sentenced to life. A capricious or arbitrary death sentence can be identified as one in which the usual sentence among comparable defendants is life. For example, if we compare the number of death sentences in a group of 50 cases that are comparable in terms of how aggravated or egregious they are and we find that only two death sentences were imposed, we can argue that since 96 percent of the time the sentence for this type of crime is not death, an imposed death sentence is arbitrary and capricious. Since the cases are comparable in terms of their level of aggravation, what meaningful basis is there to distinguish the two death sentences from the 48 life sentences? A death sentence can be said to be "discriminatory" when the decision to impose death is influenced by the race of the victim, the race of the offender, or both, and this disparate racial treatment cannot be explained by legally relevant and permissible case characteristics.

4. Race of defendant effects were, however, found in the Philadelphia data for the prosecutor's decision to waive a death sentence before trial, and race effects were found in the jury's decisions.

5. For other reviews of this literature, see Baldus and Woodworth (2003) and Weisberg (2005). ✦

Chapter 9

Problems in Administering the Death Penalty

"From this day forward I no longer shall tinker with the machinery of death. . . . I feel morally and intellectually obligated to concede that the death penalty experiment has failed."
—Justice Harry Blackmun (*Callins v. Collins*, 1994)

If we had to retain the death penalty as a viable punishment, what most of us would like is a penalty whose administration involves both fair procedures and fair outcomes. By *fair procedures* we mean that the process for imposing the death penalty would involve the provision of sufficient resources for both prosecution and defense to adequately investigate, assemble, and present their case; the use of technically competent law enforcement personnel who pursue the apprehension of the criminal, who remain unbiased in their treatment of suspects, and who show no preference for either the prosecution or defense in the investigation of the case; and the appointment of defense counsel with both the experience and legal skills to effectively defend capital cases. By *fair outcomes* we would expect the jury to always convict the guilty and acquit the innocent, and when the jury does convict the guilty to then sentence to death the offenders who in some convincing rational sense are the most morally blameworthy.

Unfortunately, like any piece of machinery run and operated by human beings, the "machinery of death" (a term used by Supreme Court Justice Harry Blackmun to describe the administration of the death penalty in the United States) is a system that contains many problems, and the product of the machinery may be what we neither expect nor want. In this chapter we discuss several problems that have arisen over the years in administering the death penalty in various states. Although it is true that some especially horrible and egregious offenders have been executed, it seems that not infrequently something has gone wrong and an innocent person has been convicted and sentenced to death. In the first section we briefly discuss the possibility that innocent persons may at some time have been wrongly executed. We then discuss people who are known as "the exonerated"—individuals who were convicted of a capital crime, were sentenced to death and spent years on death row, and then their innocence was finally revealed and they were released. Finally, we use what we know about death row exonerations to expand our discussion of the source of problems in our system of capital punishment.

The Possibly Innocent

Opponents of the death penalty (and even some supporters[1]) would argue that the worst possible mistake our criminal justice system could make would be to execute an innocent person. While the imprisonment of the innocent can later be corrected and compensation provided for lost years, a wrongly executed person obviously can never regain what has been lost. Opponents would further argue that since the system of capital punishment is administered by human beings and human beings are fallible there will inevitably be mistakes, that as a result innocent persons have surely been executed both under current statutes and at some time in the past, and that the risk of additional innocent persons being executed at some time in the future is unacceptably high. Supreme Court Justice Sandra Day O'Connor, a supporter of the death penalty, has herself remarked on this concern by observing that "If statistics are any indication, the system may well be allowing some innocent defendants to be executed" (*Baltimore Sun* 2001).

The question of whether an innocent person has ever actually been executed in America is highly controversial, and one not likely to be easily resolved. One of the problems is determining after the fact that an executed person was indeed innocent of the crime for which he or she was put to death. While there may be great doubt about a given offender's guilt during and right up to the time of execution, once an execution takes place, interest in the case and the issue of the executed person's possible innocence quickly dissipates. There have been instances in the distant past in which a person was put to death only to have another person subsequently step forward and confess to being the real killer (Banner 2002). Absent this kind of evidence (and it may not be clear even in this case since there is nothing to prevent someone from falsely claiming that they were the real killer when in fact he was not), it is not easy to make an after-the-fact determination that an innocent person has been wrongly put to death.

Interest in the wrongly executed is, of course, not new. Concern about the possibility that innocent persons have been mistakingly put to death has been raised throughout our nation's history (Bedau and Radelet 1987; Banner 2002). The fear that an innocent would inevitably be wrongly executed was part of the abolitionist movement of the mid-nineteenth century, during which time Charles Boyington was hanged by the state of Alabama in 1835 only to have the real murderer make a deathbed confession a few months later (Banner 2002). More recent interest in and controversy over the execution of the innocent began with a *Stanford Law Review* article published in 1987 by two death penalty abolitionists, Hugo Bedau and Michael Radelet, and continued in their book, *In Spite of Innocence* (Radelet, Bedau, and Putnam 1992). In their research they claimed that from 1900 to 1985 there were at least 350 instances of erroneous convictions in potentially capital cases in the United States. These convictions resulted in 139 defendants mistakenly sentenced to death and 23 innocent persons actually being executed. The vast majority (88 percent) of the death sentences imposed on those believed to have been innocent occurred before the *Gregg v. Georgia* decision in 1976 that ushered in enhanced due process protections for capital defendants. And Bedau and Radelet reported only one instance of what they determined to be an innocent person being executed since *Gregg* (James Adams, executed by Florida in 1984). This research, and the oft-mentioned claim of 23 innocent lives taken by execution, has been the empirical basis of death penalty opponents' claim that there is an unacceptably high risk that the state, in its rush to judgment, puts innocent persons to death.

The claim that innocent persons have been and are still being executed has been vigorously challenged by two legal scholars, Paul Cassell and Stephen Markman (1988). They have extensively reviewed the original Bedau and Radelet research and subsequently published their own contrary findings in a *Stanford Law Review* article. While holding open the possibility that at some point in the past an innocent person may have been executed, they found no strongly compelling evidence to suggest that in the previous 20 or 30 years anyone had been executed who was in fact innocent. They, too, examined the evidence with respect to the one case that Bedau and Radelet claimed involved the actual execution of an innocent person, James Adams. They concluded that a reasonable person could easily come to the view that Adams was in fact guilty of the crime for which he was executed.

This debate about the execution of the innocent still rages today. We take the more conservative view that there is no completely unambiguous evidence to support the claim that an innocent person has been executed during the modern era of capital punishment, but there are several "suspicious" instances in which suggest that an innocent person may have been executed but about which there may never be a resolution.

Box 9.1
DNA Tests for the Dead

Ellis Wayne Felker was convicted of the murder and sexual assault of 19-year-old Georgia college student Evelyn Joy Ludlum in 1980 and was sentenced to death. Part of the evidence in the case involved hairs found on the victim that analysts at the state crime lab said likely came from Felker. After unsuccessful appeals, Felker was electrocuted by Georgia on November 15, 1996. Felker claimed his innocence until the very end. There were other controversies in his case. For example, shortly before his execution prosecutors admitted withholding several boxes of material from the defense. Included in this material was a signed confession by another suspect and evidence that an autopsy report had been altered so that a new time of death could be established that would implicate Felker. There was also physical evidence taken that had not been subject to DNA testing. After Felker's execution, DNA tests were ordered by a Georgia judge. Sophisticated tests of the hair found on the victim could determine whether it contained Felker's DNA. These new tests proved inconclusive. Felker's case was the first time that DNA tests were used to try to determine the innocence of an already executed man. ✦

The Carlos DeLuna Case

Wanda Lopez was working alone on a February night in 1983 at a gas station on South Padre Island, Texas. Outside the station a Hispanic man asked customer George Aguirre for a ride to a nightclub. Noticing the man had a knife that he just placed into his pocket, Aquirre refused and went inside the station to warn Lopez. Lopez immediately called 911 and was told that unless the man entered the store there was nothing the police could do. Only a few minutes later the man did enter the station and Lopez called the police again, requesting assistance. A rather protracted conversation occurred between Lopez and the police dispatcher, which ended with Lopez screaming and dropping the phone. At about this time another customer, Kevan Baker, pulled into the station and got out of his car to get gas. He noticed a scuffle going on in the station between Lopez and a man. As he approached the door, the man came out, looked at Baker, said, "Don't mess with me. I've got a gun," and fled on foot. Police arrived only moments later to find Lopez dead (Possley and Mills 2006a).

Told by Baker that the assailant had fled on foot, the police conducted a search of the area. They found Carlos DeLuna 40 minutes later under a car, wearing no shirt and no shoes, with $149 in his pocket. The police put DeLuna in a patrol car and drove him back to the station where both Aguirre and Baker positively identified him as the one who had been in the station fighting with Lopez. In about two hours the crime scene was photographed, dusted for prints, and cleaned up. As they drove DeLuna to the police station that night, he told officers, "I'll help you if you help me" and "I didn't do it, but I know who did" (Possley and Mills 2006a). The day after Lopez's murder, a man found a white shirt and shoes that belonged to DeLuna. The police lab found no trace of blood on the shoes or the shirt even though the crime scene was a bloody mess. When asked why he was hiding under a truck, DeLuna said that he had seen the police cars and heard sirens when he was across the street from the gas station at a nightclub and that he ran and hid because he was on parole and didn't want any trouble.

Thinking that they had their man in DeLuna, Texas authorities charged him with armed robbery and first degree murder. A few things weren't quite right, however. First, in spite of the fact that the crime scene at the gas station was covered with blood, no blood was found on DeLuna that night nor on his shirt or shoes, which were found the following day. The crime scene blood was never tested to see whose it was (Possley and Mills 2006c). In fact there was no physical evidence linking DeLuna to the crime. Second, the aggravating circumstance in the capital case was armed robbery. Prosecutors claimed that the $149 found in DeLuna's pocket came from the cash register at the gas station. The only problem was, crime scene photos showed money on the ground covered with blood (DeLuna's money had no blood), officials for the gas station claimed that Lopez would never have had more than $100 in cash in her register, and DeLuna had cashed a paycheck of $135.49 earlier that day and $71 a week before that (DeLuna's money was found in a tight roll in his pocket and did not look like it had been quickly grabbed out of a cash register). Third,

DeLuna said that he knew who had committed the crime, Carlos Hernandez. DeLuna's attorneys passed the name of Hernandez on to prosecutors prior to the trial. Prosecutors were aware of who Hernandez was; they had investigated him before for the murder of a woman and knew that Hernandez had both a violent temper and a penchant for carrying a knife (Possley and Mills 2006b).

At DeLuna's trial, the two eyewitnesses testified against him, one saying that he saw DeLuna outside the gas station with a knife and the other that he saw DeLuna running away from the crime scene. Prosecutors ridiculed and dismissed DeLuna's claim that it was Hernandez who had killed Wanda Lopez, labeling Hernandez "a phantom" and a figment of DeLuna's imagination. The jury convicted DeLuna of murder and armed robbery and sentenced him to death in July 1983. DeLuna lost numerous rounds of state and federal appeals, and although he maintained his innocence to the end (even rejecting a plea bargain where he was offered a life sentence in exchange for a guilty plea), he was executed by lethal injection on December 7, 1989.

Two reporters for the *Chicago Tribune*, Maurice Possley and Steve Mills, picked up the case some 16 years after DeLuna's execution (Possley and Mills 2006a, 2006b, 2006c). They uncovered substantial evidence to suggest that Hernandez was the killer and that DeLuna was likely innocent. Prosecutors dismissed the claim that Hernandez was the killer and never fully investigated the lead, arguing in court that Hernandez was a "phantom." Yet in fact Carlos Hernandez was well known to police and to one of the two prosecutors on the case. He was a convicted violent felon. He was also once arrested as a suspect in the slaying of Dahlia Sauceda, who was strangled in her van with an "X" carved into her back with a knife. Police found Hernandez's fingerprints on a beer can in the van, along with a pair of his boxer shorts. Hernandez was arrested and questioned, but police let him go saying that they lacked evidence to proceed. Seven years later, a grand jury indicted him for this murder, but the charges were again dismissed. Hernandez had a long record of violent offenses, including three robberies of gas stations. In November of 1983 he was arrested for assaulting his wife with an axe handle, and he had a reputation for never being without a knife or a whetstone to sharpen it. Two months after the killing of Lopez, Hernandez was again arrested while hiding behind a convenience store—he had a knife in his pocket. When DeLuna was executed, Hernandez was on his way back to prison for 10 years for assaulting a woman with a knife, cutting her from navel to sternum. He served two years on that conviction and was released only to be arrested again in 1996 for assaulting a man; at the time he was carrying two knives. Hernandez died in prison on May 6, 1999.

After Hernandez's death in prison, reporters Possley and Mills extensively interviewed his family members and acquaintances, who seemed willing to talk only now that he was dead. They stated that Hernandez boasted that he got away with the killing of Wanda Lopez and that his "stupid tocayo" (namesake) was sent to death row for the crime. He also admitted killing Dahlia Sauced, for which he was questioned but never convicted. Nevertheless, the lead and co-prosecutor in the DeLuna case are convinced that they got the right man. One of the eyewitnesses, Kevan Baker, is, however, uncertain that he identified the right guy. He told Possley and Mills, "I wasn't all that sure, but him being Hispanic and all . . . I said, Yeah, I think it is him. The cops told me they found him hiding under a truck. That led me to believe this is probably the guy" (Possley and Mills 2006a, 2006b).

The Joseph O'Dell Case

Joseph O'Dell was convicted and sentenced to death by a Virginia court, where he, by choice, represented himself at trial.[2] In September 1986 he was convicted of the murder, rape, and sodomy of Helen Schartner on the basis of what can be characterized as circumstantial evidence: Tire tracks found on the scene were comparable to those that could have been made by O'Dell's car, bloodstains on O'Dell's clothing were found by testing to be "consistent with" the victim's, and a jailhouse "snitch" testified (but later recanted, and then recanted his recantation) that O'Dell confessed to him about the murder when they shared a jail cell.[3] O'Dell's state postconviction appeals were unsuccessful, as was his initial petition for *certiorari* to the U.S. Supreme Court. However, three members of the Court (Justices Blackmun, Stevens, and O'Connor) took the unusual position of issuing a "statement" expressing their concern over O'Dell's self-representation and his possible innocence. Justice Blackmun wrote:

> There are serious questions as to whether O'Dell committed the crime or was capable of representing himself—questions rendered all the more serious by the fact that O'Dell's life depends upon the answers. Because of the gross injustice that would result if an innocent man were sentenced to death, O'Dell's substantial federal claims can, and should, receive careful consideration from the federal court with habeas corpus jurisdiction over the case. (*O'Dell v. Thompson*, 502 U.S. 995, 1991)

Years after his trial, O'Dell had the bloodstains found on his clothing subjected to more accurate DNA tests that were not available at the time of his trial.[4] The new tests indicated that the blood on his shirt was definitely not that of the victim, while other blood found on his jacket was found to be "inconclusive." At his trial, the prosecutors had claimed that the blood on O'Dell's jacket "was consistent with" the victim's blood. With these new findings from the more sophisticated DNA tests, O'Dell sought an evidentiary hearing in state court to establish his innocence. He faced several obstacles, however. First was the fact that the DNA testing was done in 1990, some four years after O'Dell was convicted and sentenced to death, and Virginia has a "21 day rule" which states that new evidence pertaining to a defendant's innocence must be presented to the appeals court within 21 days after trial. Evidence of innocence presented after the 21 days has passed need not be heard by Virginia courts. Second, the Virginia Supreme Court refused to hear O'Dell's case because his appeals lawyers had typed "Notice of Appeal" on the title page of his brief rather than the correct heading of "Notice of Petition" (Prejean 2005).

O'Dell did get a hearing in federal district court in 1994 where he presented the new DNA evidence and an argument that his original trial court erred in not allowing him to inform the jury of Virginia's life without parole sentence. The court's decision was favorable to O'Dell on the DNA matter, but the testimony of the jailhouse snitch remained damaging. The federal judge in the case did, however, overturn O'Dell's death sentence and ordered a new sentencing hearing on the basis of the life without parole issue. This motion for a new sentencing hearing was, however, subsequently overturned by the 4th Circuit Court of Appeals and O'Dell's death sentence was reinstated, a decision upheld by the Supreme Court.

O'Dell was now headed for Virginia's death chamber. Lawyers for O'Dell then sought to have DNA tests performed on the semen samples taken in the case (the earlier DNA tests were of the blood found on O'Dell's clothing). The aggravating factor in the case was that Schartner had been raped, and if the DNA on the semen sample excluded him as the one who deposited the semen, the aggravating factor and the death sentence would disappear. Virginia prosecutors refused to turn over the semen samples, claiming that their age would preclude accurate testing, and the courts of Virginia supported this conclusion. O'Dell was then given a July 23, 1997 execution date, and an appeal to Governor George Allen to allow the DNA testing was rejected. In spite of both national and international pressure to allow the newer, more accurate DNA test results to be presented in court, the state of Virginia executed O'Dell on July 23, 1997. Subsequent to his execution, his wife sought to have the physical evidence preserved for postmortem DNA testing, but Virginia officials refused either to conduct the DNA tests themselves or to turn the evidence over to O'Dell's estate for testing, citing a need for "finality" in the case. On March 30, 2000 the evidence in the O'Dell case was destroyed by Virginia officials.

The Gary Graham Case

Another troubling case is that of Gary Graham, who was convicted of murdering Bobby Grant Lambert in the parking lot of a grocery store in Houston, Texas on May 13, 1981 (*Graham v. Johnson*, 168 F, 3d 763 767 5th Circuit, 1999). Graham, who was only 17 years old when the murder occurred, was originally arrested for other crimes and was later charged with the killing of Lambert. He was convicted of the murder primarily on the testimony of one eyewitness, Bernadine Skillern, who claimed she saw the killer's face (whom she identified as Graham) for a few seconds through her car windshield from of distance of approximately 30–40 feet. Graham did admit to being involved in a crime spree the week of the murder, during which he robbed 13 different victims.[5] In one of the armed robberies a victim was shot in the neck and seriously wounded; another was pistol whipped, and a third was hit by the car that Graham was attempting to steal from him. Graham pled guilty to 10 armed robberies but claimed that he was innocent of the murder of Bobby Lambert. Two other witnesses who worked at the grocery store where the crime occurred also said they got a good look at the killer and claimed that Graham was not that person. The testimony of these latter two witnesses was never heard by the jury, however, because Graham's court-appointed defense lawyer, Ronald Mock, never bothered to interview them and therefore never called them to testify on Graham's behalf at his trial.

Box 9.2
All That Glitters Isn't Gold

Roger Keith Coleman appeared to have been the "poster boy" of an innocent man who was executed. Two days before his execution on May 18, 1992 he was on the cover of *Time* magazine with the caption, "This Man Might Be Innocent... This Man Is Due to Die." Many things pointed toward his innocence: the DNA evidence in his case was inconclusive, police work seemed to be hasty and shoddy, he was represented by inexperienced lawyers, he had an alibi on the night of the murder that if true would have made it almost impossible for him to have committed the crime, and there was another equally or more likely suspect in the rape/murder of Wanda McCoy.

Coleman's case seemed such a pure example of an innocent man about to be executed that he was able to secure the *pro bono* services of a prestigious Washington D.C. law firm and had the backing of numerous supporters such as Centurion Ministries. Even after Coleman failed a lie detector test on the day of his execution, faith in his innocence remained firm, and he continued to unflinchingly and convincingly proclaim his innocence. As he was being strapped in Virginia's electric chair, Coleman repeated that he was innocent, and his last words were: "An innocent man is going to be murdered tonight. When my innocence is proven, I hope Americans will realize the injustice of the death penalty as all other civilized countries have."

Coleman was executed by the state of Virginia on May 20, 1992, with howls of protests about his innocence. When doubts about his guilt refused to go away, on January 5, 2006, Virginia Governor Mark R. Warner ordered new DNA testing of evidence in the case—then only the second time that DNA testing would be used when the defendant had already been executed. On January 12, 2006, those new DNA tests revealed that there was only a one in 19 million chance that the semen found on Wanda McCoy's body belonged to anybody other than Roger Keith Coleman. ✦

Other pieces of evidence pointed to Graham's possible innocence. No physical or even circumstantial evidence directly placed him at the scene of the crime. Although Graham was found with a .22 caliber pistol, Houston police firearm's experts found that the bullet that killed Lambert (a .22 caliber) was not fired from Graham's gun. Ms. Skillern also initially failed to positively identify Graham in a police photo display, but the following day in a police lineup she told police she recognized Graham from the photo she saw the day before. Lambert himself had been no stranger to legal difficulty. He was arrested in 1980 on federal drug charges and testified to a federal grand jury about his "employers." His murder in the grocery store parking lot came soon after he testified. Subsequent to Graham's conviction and death sentence, three of the jurors in his case signed an affidavit stating that had they known about the other eyewitnesses and the information they could have provided, they would not have convicted Graham. The police report that concluded the bullet that killed Lambert was not fired by Graham's gun was also not brought before the jury because of Graham's counsel's failure to interview police experts. In fact, this information was not discovered until after the trial, by other attorneys working on Graham's appeal. The key eyewitness in the case, Ms.

Skillern, however, never wavered in her belief that it was Graham whom she saw commit the murder.[6]

Most of the evidence indicating that Graham might be innocent of the Lambert killing was developed years after his initial trial, by counsel working on his second round of appeals.[7] There was a procedural bar to the presentation of this new evidence, because Texas has a rule barring a court reviewing new evidence of innocence more than 30 days after the original trial conviction and sentencing. Based on this procedural rule, the Texas Court of Criminal Appeals rejected Graham's plea for a hearing on the evidence. In 1995, the U.S. Court of Appeals for the 5th Circuit found that "there is a large body of relevant evidence that has not been presented to the state court." It did not order a new hearing because Graham had not yet exhausted his state remedies and sent the case back to Texas for an evidentiary hearing. The Texas Court of Criminal Appeals rejected the case on technical grounds. In his return to federal court seeking relief, Graham's plea for a new hearing was now blocked by the Anti-Terrorism and Effective Death Penalty Act of 1996. This act places a bar on federal habeas reconsideration of legal and factual issues previously considered and decided on by state courts. In 1996 the 5th Circuit Court of Appeals ruled, on the basis of the new Anti-Terrorism and Effective Death Penalty Act, that it could not review the case because any new evidence of innocence could not be considered if it could have been discovered at the time of the state trial. The Supreme Court refused to consider the case to stay the execution.

Although the issues of Graham's innocence were considered by state and federal courts as well as executive forums such as the Texas Board of Pardons and Paroles and the governor of Texas' consideration of executive clemency, Gary Graham was convicted, sentenced to death, and executed by the state of Texas on June 22, 2000 without ever obtaining an evidentiary hearing on all of the new evidence of possible innocence.

Box 9.3
Was an Innocent Man Executed in 1995?

One of the most difficult tasks for those trying to determine whether an innocent person has ever been executed is that once the person has been put to death, interest and effort in proving innocence wane on both the defendant's and the state's side. All this changed in July 2005 when St. Louis, Missouri circuit attorney Jennifer Joyce reopened the investigation of the murder of Quintin Moss, a 19-year-old drug dealer, on June 26, 1980 in St. Louis. Larry Griffin was convicted of Moss's murder in 1981 and maintained his innocence throughout, even when he was put to death by lethal injection on June 21, 1995.

Evidence that Griffin might have been innocent was compiled by University of Michigan law professor Samuel Gross with the assistance of the NAACP Legal Defense and Education Fund. Griffin was convicted largely on the basis of a supposed eyewitness, Robert Fitzgerald, who testified that he was 20 feet away when a car slowly drove up and gunned Moss down. He stated that Griffin was in the car with two other men. At the time, Fitzgerald was living in St. Louis while under the U.S. Department of Justice's Witness Protection Program. He was a witness in the murder of a Boston police officer and was waiting to testify in that case. Fitzgerald was no "angel"; he had prior convictions for auto theft, heroin possession, and armed robbery, and was facing felony charges for crimes committed while in St. Louis under the federal witness protection program.

A bystander, Wallace Conners, who was also shot during the murder, was never contacted by the prosecution or defense. He later told investigators that he knew Larry Griffin and that Griffin was not one of the men in the car. He also told investigators that Fitzgerald was never even at the scene of the crime. In addition, the police officer who was first on the scene has significantly changed his story. Originally, he testified that Fitzgerald was present at the crime scene, while he now claims that Fitzgerald was not there when he first arrived. Fitzgerald, who has since died, was released by St. Louis County for time served with all pending charges dropped on the day that Griffin was convicted.

This is a fascinating case in that it is the first instance where an investigation is being undertaken after the allegedly guilty person was executed. The results of this investigation undertaken by the St. Louis prosecutor will determine whether an innocent person was executed. ✦

The Exonerated

While there is no solid proof to date that Joseph O'Dell, Carlos DeLuna, Gary Graham, or any innocent person has ever been executed during the Modern Period of capital punishment, there is undisputed evidence that many innocent persons have been convicted and sentenced to death, only to later be released from death row before they could be executed. These persons are referred to as the *exonerated*. The exonerated death row inmate is a clear example of a "mistake" in our system of capital punishment. While the execution of an innocent person might arguably be the worst possible kind of mistake we could make in administering the death penalty, sentencing to death persons later found to have been innocent, persons who may have wasted years and years of their life on death row, surely is a mistake of only slightly lesser significance.

Since new state death penalty laws began to take effect in 1973 until February of 2006, 123 people in 25 states were released from death row because they were later found to have been innocent (Death Penalty Information Center 2006). This number is likely to grow higher in the time between this chapter being written and now being read—the number of death row exonerations appears to increase almost monthly. The cost for the innocent person finally released is staggering; on average, each of the 123 exonerated inmates spent more than nine years on death row before being released. Who are these exonerated inmates, and how could they have been falsely convicted and sentenced to death?

Gary Gauger

One example of the exonerated is Gary Gauger. Gauger was sentenced to death by the state of Illinois in 1994 for the murder of his parents, Ruth and Morris Gauger, on April 8, 1993 (Mills and Armstrong 1999a, 1999b, 1999c). Immediately after his parents were killed Gauger was interrogated by the police for 18 hours without food or sleep, and without the assistance of a lawyer. Law enforcement officials claimed that during the interrogation Gauger confessed to killing his parents, but Gauger himself always claimed that he made no such confession, that he only responded in conversation with the police to the hypothetical possibility that he had killed his parents during an alcoholic blackout. During the interrogation, the police told Gauger that he had failed a polygraph examination (the polygraph test was actually inconclusive) and that blood-stained clothes had been found linking him to the crime (there were no such clothes found by the police). In fact, there was no physical evidence at all linking Gauger to the crime. There was no video, audio, or written record by police of Gauger's interrogation. The police theory was that Gauger snuck up behind each of his parents, pulled their heads back by their hair, and slashed their throats. A state of Illinois forensic scientist, Lurie Lee, testified at trial that some hairs found near Ruth Gauger's body were stretched in a way consistent with the police theory but could also have gotten that shape from brushing. In addition to Gauger's allegedly incriminating statements, the police also had the testimony of a jail-house snitch, Raymond Wagner, who claimed that Gauger had repeatedly confessed to him that he had killed his parents.

On the basis of this evidence, Gauger was convicted of capital murder and sentenced to death on January 11, 1994. A year after his death sentence was imposed, the trial judge, over the strenuous objections of the prosecutor, reduced Gauger's sentence to life in prison because of mitigating factors in the case (Gauger had no real criminal record and had a history of drug and alcohol abuse). At this time Gauger's appeals case had been taken over by Northwestern University law professor Lawrence Marshall. In March 1996 the Illinois Appellate Court ruled that Gauger's confession could not be used against him in court because the police had no probable cause for arresting him. Although he was released from prison, local prosecutors continued to publicly assert that Gauger was guilty of the double killings. A federal investigation into the activities of a Wisconsin motorcycle gang, the Outlaws, however, revealed the real killers. A federal indictment against 17 members of the Outlaws included an indictment for the murders of Ruth and Morris Gauger. One Outlaw, James Schneider, pleaded guilty to acts related to the murders, and a second, Randall Miller, was convicted of murder charges in June 2000. In December 2002 Gary Gauger was pardoned by Illinois Governor George H. Ryan.

Anthony Porter

The case of Anthony Porter illustrates that it is not always the legal system that corrects its own mistake (Northwestern University Center on Wrongful Convictions 2005). On August 15, 1982 Marilyn Green and Jerry Hillard were shot to death near a public swimming pool on Chicago's South Side. William Taylor had been swimming at the time of the shooting, and although he initially stated that he had not seen the killer, after some 17 hours of police interrogation he told police that he had seen who it was who shot the two victims and that it was Anthony Porter. The police had now greatly narrowed down who the likely suspect was in the murder and may have lost interest in pursuing other leads. One of these other leads came from the mother of Marilyn Green, who told police that she thought the killer was Alstory Simon, who had been in a heated argument with Jerry Hillard over a drug deal. She also stated that both Simon and his girlfriend, Inez Jackson, were with the victims not long before the killings took place.

Porter had heard that he was a suspect in the double killing and went to the local Chicago police station to proclaim his innocence. Without any physical evidence linking him to the crime, police arrested Porter for the murders and other felonies. On the basis of the eyewitness evidence provided by William Taylor, Porter was convicted of the murders of Green and Hillard on September 8, 1983, and on the next day was sentenced to death. After an unsuccessful round of appeals in state and federal courts, his execution was set for September 23, 1998. He was within two days of being put to death when the Illinois Supreme Court stayed the execution in order to more fully examine the issue of Porter's mental competency to be executed (he had an IQ of approximately 51). Although it was legal at the time to execute the mentally retarded, the court wanted to determine whether Porter's low IQ prevented him from fully understanding why he was being executed.

During this stay of execution, Northwestern University journalism professor David Protess and his students began an independent investigation of the case. They hired a private investigator, Paul Ciolino, to follow up leads on the case. Ciolino questioned William Taylor, who told him that he was pressured by police to name Porter as the killer. Inez Jackson told Ciolino that she was present when Simon shot Green and Hillard. When Ciolino questioned Simon, he admitted the killings, saying that Hillard was killed in self-defense over a drug deal and that Marilyn Green was killed accidentally. A few days after this revelation, Porter was released from prison, and all charges against him were dropped the next month. In September 1999, Alstory Simon pleaded guilty to the Hillard and Green killings. Porter, who came within 50 hours of being put to death, had spent some 15 years in prison before being released.

Frank Lee Smith

Frank Lee Smith was convicted of the rape and murder of 8-year-old Shandra Whitehead in Florida and sentenced to death. No physical evidence linked Smith to the crime, but there were several eyewitnesses and what the state claimed was Smith's own "confession." During his interrogation of Smith, the lead police detective, Richard Scheff of the Broward County Sheriff's Office, told Smith that Shandra's brother had seen the crime occur and could identify the killer. There were no audio or video recordings of the interrogation, but Scheff's handwritten notes reported that Smith had said "No way that kid could have seen me, it was too dark." Anyone who knew Frank Lee Smith doubted the truthfulness of that statement, however, because Smith was brain damaged, was severely mentally ill, and rarely spoke with such coherence let alone articulation. In point of fact, Shandra's brother was asleep when the crime was committed and could not provide any identification of the killer. Detective Scheff's statement to Smith was a lie designed to extract an admission. Smith consistently denied ever making such a statement to Scheff.

The eyewitness evidence for the state was also shaky. Shandra's mother reported to police that she chased a man whom she found lurking around her house the night of the killing and later identified that man as Frank Lee Smith. During cross examination, however, she admitted that she did not see the man's face, only the back of his shoulders as he climbed out of a window and ran from the house. Another witness, Chiquita Lowe, reported that a "delirious" man had stopped her car near the crime scene and asked her for money. She provided a description to police of a scraggly-haired black man with a droopy eye, pockmarked face, and no eyeglasses. Smith had no droopy eye and had 20-400 vision that required him to wear "coke-bottle" thick glasses in order to see anything. Although Lowe then identified Smith as the man who asked her for money, she later said that she felt pressured by family and police to finger him. Living in the neighborhood at the time, however, was another man, Eddie Lee Mosely, who did closely fit the description given by Lowe. Mosely's picture was found by an investigator working on Smith's case years after his trial. When shown this picture, Chiquita Lowe was positive it was the man who had stopped her car and asked for money that night, and not Smith. Mosely was well known to local law enforcement officers, as he was a suspect in several sexual assaults and murders in the area, yet he apparently was never investigated as a possible suspect.

At the time that Chiquita Lowe recanted her trial testimony, Smith was under a death warrant. The Florida Supreme Court stayed the execution and ordered a hearing to examine Lowe's recanted testimony. At this hearing Detective Scheff claimed that before Smith's first trial he showed Mosley's photograph to Lowe and she still stated that Smith was the one who she saw that night. This, however, directly contradicted his own testimony at the trial that only two photo lineups were shown to Lowe, one that included Smith and one that did not. It also contradicts both his notes on the case, which made no mention of a photo of Mosely, and the recollection of the prosecutor, who stated he did not recall Mosely's photo ever being shown to any of the eyewitnesses. The judge at this hearing, however, believed Detecteive Scheff and rejected Chiquita's recantation as "not credible." The court order in fact concluded that "this court finds absolutely no credible evidence to support the defendant's claim that it was Eddie Lee Mosely who committed the murder of Shandra Whitehead" (De Vise, 2001).

Beginning in 1998 Smith's appeals lawyers pressed the state to allow new and sophisticated DNA testing of the semen found in the 8-year-old victim. Initially the state agreed to the tests, but it reneged when Chiquita Lowe's recantation was not believed and Smith's death sentence was not vacated. Smith's lawyers filed repeated motions requesting DNA testing, with the state continuing to resist those requests. Meanwhile, Smith was diagnosed with pancreatic cancer, and died on January 30, 2000, after spending more than 14 years on Florida's death row. Eleven months after Smith's death the prosecutor allowed DNA testing of the evidence and it was discovered that Smith was not the depositor of the semen. In fact, the DNA evidence implicated one Eddie Lee Mosley.

Kirk Bloodsworth

Another of the exonerated is Kirk Bloodsworth.[8] On July 25, 1984 9-year-old Dawn Hamilton was found beaten by a rock, murdered, and sexually assaulted in some woods in Baltimore County, Maryland. A composite sketch of the killer was put together by five witnesses who saw someone in the woods around the time Dawn was killed. An anonymous caller to the police stated that Bloodsworth was with the child sometime before she was killed. Another witness identified Bloodsworth from the composite sketch. At his trial, five witnesses testified that they had seen the Hamilton girl and Bloodsworth together that day. Also at trial, the police stated that during his interrogation Bloodsworth admitted that he had done something terrible that day, and that he mentioned something about a bloody rock. The police also introduced scientific evidence that linked a shoe impression found near Dawn's body with Bloodsworth. Although not brought out at the trial, the "terrible" thing that Bloodsworth said he did that day was his failure to pick up some food for his wife as he had promised, the heated argument this failure had caused, and his decision to leave home. He mentioned the bloody rock because the police had showed him one during their interrogation. It was also discovered after Bloodsworth's trial that Baltimore County prosecutors withheld evidence from his defense counsel that there was another likely suspect in the case.

Bloodsworth was convicted of the rape and murder of Dawn Hamilton and sentenced to death in March 1985. The conviction was overturned by the Maryland Court of Appeals in 1986 because the prosecution had withheld from the defense possibly exculpatory evidence (the possibility of another suspect). On retrial Bloodsworth was convicted again and sentenced this time to two consecutive life terms. During his incarceration and with the assistance of an outside religious organization (Centurion Ministries, the same organization that investigated the Roger Keith Coleman case), Bloodsworth was able to have some physical evidence reexamined with a new DNA test. This DNA testing (and independent DNA testing conducted by the FBI) indicated that Bloodsworth could not possibly have been the one who sexually assaulted Dawn Hamilton. He was finally released from prison in 1993, becoming the first death row prisoner to be released on the basis of DNA testing. In December 1994 Bloodsworth was granted a full pardon for the crime by then Governor of Maryland William Donald Schaefer. In spite of this, prosecutors in the case for years refused to acknowledge his innocence. Ten years later, the state recognized that a DNA match existed all along and that the match belonged to an inmate, Kimberly Shay Ruffner, currently confined in Maryland's prison system and whose cell was just below Bloodsworth's. In September 2003 Ruffner was finally charged with the killing of Dawn Hamilton and was ultimately sentenced to life in prison.

Rolando Cruz

Jeanine Nicarico was 10 years old on Februray 25, 1983, when she was kidnapped from her home in Naperville, Illinois, a suburb of Chicago. She was at home alone that day, down with the flu, when there was a knock on her door. When she answered it, a man said that his car had broken down and that he needed help. Jeanine said she was alone and could not open the door, whereupon the man kicked in the door and took her. She was found two days later, sodomized and killed, with a crushed skull. The crime had not been solved for several months, and police were under pressure to catch the offender. After receiving an anonymous tip, police picked up Alejandro Hernandez for questioning, and in exchange for reward money he implicated Rolando Cruz and Stephen Buckley. Rolando Cruz was then picked up for police questioning. During his interrogation, police later testified that Cruz knew facts about the crime that only the real killer would have known and that he had "visions" whose details were virtually identical to those characterizing the crime.[9] Cruz denied any knowledge of the crime and also denied making any vision statement to the police, and there was no record of the interrogation. No physical evidence linked either Cruz or Hernandez to the Hamilton murder. Nevertheless, on the basis of the alleged statements by Hernandez and Cruz, as well as the testimony of jailhouse "snitches" that Cruz admitted to killing the Hamilton girl, both were convicted of capital murder and sentenced to death on March 15, 1985. The jury could not reach a decision on Stephen Buckley, and charges against him were eventually dismissed. Just before the trial, a detective on the case abruptly resigned from the police force, claiming that prosecutors were trying to "frame" an innocent man. Then, shortly after the conviction and death sentences, a convicted murderer and sex offender, Brian Dugan, confessed that he alone killed Jeanine Nicarico and admitted to several other sex crimes and murders as well.

The Illinois Supreme Court reversed the convictions, ruling that since the statements each defendant made against the other were used as evidence, they should have been tried separately. At Cruz's second trial, where he was tried alone, prosecutors theorized that Dugan was involved in the murders along with Cruz and Hernandez but that Cruz was the one who raped Jeanine Nicarico. Cruz was again convicted of capital murder and sentenced to death a second time. In 1994 the Illinois Supreme Court reversed Cruz's second conviction, and the state prepared to try him for the third time.[10] As Cruz's third trial was about to begin, new DNA evidence on the semen found on the victim indicated that neither Cruz nor Hernandez could have raped Jeanine Nicarico. The DNA evidence did, however, point to Brian Dugan. Nevertheless, prosecutors, who knew that Dugan had admitted to the killing some 10 years before and who fought to have this evidence kept out of court because of their belief that Cruz was guilty, went ahead with the trial of Cruz. Dugan would not make a formal confession to the crime when prosecutors declined to agree that they would not seek a death sentence against him. At this third trial, a police officer admitted that he had lied under oath in relation to Cruz's supposed confession and vision statements. The state's case fell apart, and the trial judge directed a not guilty verdict. Prosecutors dropped all charges against Cruz, and he was granted a pardon in December 2002 by Illinois Governor George H. Ryan. A special prosecutor, William Kunkle, indicted four police officers and three former prosecutors in the case, charging them with perjury and obstruction of justice. All were later acquitted (Possley and Armstrong 1999a, 1999b). On November 29, 2005, more than 20 years after her murder, Brian Dugan was indicted for the killing of Jeanine Nicarico.

Ryan Matthews

Ryan Matthews was just weeks past his 17th birthday when he was arrested for the robbery and killing of convenience store owner Tommy Vanhoose in Bridge City, Louisiana, in April 1997. Someone came into Vanhoose's store and demanded money; when he refused, the robber shot and killed him. The robber then ran from the store, taking off the ski mask he had been wearing before jumping through the open window into a getaway car. There were several eye-witnesses to the crime. One saw the robber running from the store firing shots at her in her car; a second saw him from his rear view mirror. Both witnesses later identified Matthews in a police photo lineup.

Ryan Matthews and Travis Davis were stopped several hours after the crime because their car resembled the description of the robber's getaway car. Both suspects were interrogated for several hours, and after initially stating that they were not in the area at the time of the crime, Travis told police that he had been the driver of the getaway car and that Matthews had robbed the store. Matthews always maintained his innocence. No physical evidence linked either Matthews or Davis to the crime, and the gun used in the robbery was not found on them. In addition, at their trial, defense counsel presented evidence that DNA testing of the ski mask used in the robbery could not be matched with either Matthews or Davis. Further, their car could not have been the getaway car since the passenger-side window in their car that the robber supposedly jumped through was broken and could not be rolled down. Other witnesses to the crime also testified that they thought the robber was much shorter than Matthews. Nevertheless, based primarily on the testimony of the eyewitnesses, Matthews was convicted of robbery and murder and sentenced to death, while Davis was convicted of second degree murder and sentenced to life in prison. Both Matthews and Davis were borderline mentally retarded.

Not long after Vanhoose was killed, another murder occurred in approximately the same area. Rondell Love was arrested for this murder and pleaded guilty. When imprisoned, Love told other inmates that he was the one who killed Vanhoose. Matthews' appellate lawyers heard of this confession and began an investigation of Love's possible involvement in the Vanhoose murder. New DNA tests on the ski mask used in the Vanhoose killing linked Love to the crime. Matthews remained in prison for over a year when he was granted a new trial. Pending this new trial, he was released from prison on bond and on August 9, 2004, prosecutors asked that all charges against him be dropped.

A 'Broken System'

The existence of cases in which the possibly innocent have been executed or the innocent have been exonerated does not exhaust our discussion of the problems of administering a capital punishment system. Columbia University law professor James Liebman and his colleagues conducted a study in which they followed up the 5,760 death sentences imposed in the United States over the years 1973–1995 (Liebman 2000; Liebman et al. 2000, 2002; Gelman et al.

2004). They found that in 68 percent of these cases there was an error serious enough to overturn either the defendant's conviction or death sentence. This overall error rate did not include cases that may have contained an error but the reviewing court did not think that the error was serious enough that it could have changed the outcome (so-called "harmless" error). What this tells us is that there was substantial enough error in two-thirds of the death sentences imposed over this period to shake a court's confidence in the outcome. Moreover, it is not as if the errors were mere "technicalities" and the defendants were subsequently reconvicted and sentenced to death. In fact 82 percent of the defendants who were retried received a sentence of less than death, and 7 percent were found not guilty.

Professor Liebman and his colleagues identified two primary sources of the high rate of error in the capital cases that they studied: (1) incompetent lawyers for defendants, and (2) prosecutorial or police misconduct. In addition, accounts of the exonerated and defendants who have had their death sentences overturned indicate that "junk" science and the use of informant testimony (jailhouse "snitches") have also played a prominent role (Liebman 2000; Liebman et al. 2000, 2002; Gelman et al. 2004). We will examine each of these possible reasons that the administration of capital punishment may be "broken."

Ineffective or Incompetent Defense Counsel

The right to have an effective defense attorney in a death penalty case was established by the Supreme Court in *Powell v. Alabama* in 1932. In the *Powell* case seven black youths (known in history as the "Scottsboro boys" because the trial took place in Scottsboro, Alabama) were accused of assaulting two white girls on a freight train passing through Alabama. The youths, who were residents of other states, were all illiterate and poor. At their arraignment, the presiding judge appointed the entire local bar to represent the defendants, although he assigned responsibility of the case to no one lawyer, and none stepped forward to conduct the defense. On the morning of the trial a lawyer from Tennessee who was not a member of the Alabama bar indicated that he would be willing to assist a local defense lawyer should one be appointed. A member of the local bar also suggested on that morning that he might assist in the case but had made no preparations thus far. He was appointed defense counsel for the boys, and in three separate trials all defendants were convicted that same day and all were sentenced to death.

In overturning their convictions, the U.S. Supreme Court held that the fact that defense counsel was so cavalierly appointed and clearly had no time to investigate and prepare their case that the defendants could not have been adequately represented. The Court concluded that in capital cases defendants who cannot retain counsel must have it appointed by the court and that the appointment of counsel must be far in advance enough to allow for a preparation of a defense.

More than just the assistance of counsel, *Powell* requires that capital defendants are entitled to the *effective assistance* of counsel.[11] That is, the mere appointment or appearance of defense counsel in a capital case is not sufficient;

counsel must provide adequate or effective legal assistance to their client. What effective counsel does for the criminal defendant is to provide a strong counterweight of innocence and life to the case of guilty and death made by the prosecution. The defining characteristic of our adversarial legal system is that truth is best discovered when both sides have powerful champions to argue their case and that "partisan advocacy on both sides of a case will best promote the ultimate objective that the guilty be convicted and the innocent go free" (*Herring v. New York*, 422 U.S. 853, 1975). The right to the effective assistance of counsel, then, is the right for those accused of a capital crime to have counsel acting as their advocate, because only counsel-as-advocate can both present evidence favorable to the defendant and cast doubt on the prosecution's case. Ultimately, the principle behind the effective assistance of counsel requirement "is the right of the accused to require the prosecution's case to survive the crucible of meaningful adversarial testing" (*United States v. Cronic*, 466 U.S. 648, 1984). The trial of a defendant with ineffective counsel becomes "a sacrifice of unarmed prisoners to gladiators" (*U.S. ex rel. Williams v. Twomey*, 510 F.2d 634, 640, CA7, 1975).

In several subsequent decisions, the Supreme Court has provided more substance to what is required of a death penalty defense lawyer. In the case of *Strickland v. Washington* (466 U.S. 668, 1984) the Court laid out a two-pronged test for determining whether or not the counsel has been effective. The first prong of this test is that a defendant must demonstrate that the performance of counsel was deficient under "prevailing professional norms" and that the attorney's conduct "fell below an objective standard of reasonableness" (p. 688). In other words, in the world of death penalty work defense counsel is expected to do certain things by members of the profession. For example, they are supposed to conduct an examination to determine whether there are mitigating factors in favor of their client. If they fail to do so when most defense lawyers in a capital case would have, their effectiveness is called into question. The second prong of the *Strickland* test states that even if a defendant could demonstrate that the performance of defense counsel fell below some professional standard of competence, it must further show that the attorney's performance was so deficient that it prejudiced the outcome of the trial. In other words, to make a claim that counsel was ineffective, the defendant must demonstrate that had counsel performed better, he would not have been convicted or would not have been sentenced to death.

Critics of the *Strickland* decision have argued that its two-pronged test places a crippling burden of proof on the defendant and ensures that ineffective assistance of counsel claims are not provided adequate remedy. Whatever the merits of that argument, there is evidence indicating that defense counsel in capital cases all too frequently fail to provide the kind of vigorous "meaningful adversarial testing" of the evidence expected of them.

The Court went a bit further in spelling out the parameters of what defense counsel is expected to do (at a minimum) in a capital case in *Wiggins v. Smith* (539 U.S. 510, 2003). Kevin Wiggins was convicted by a jury of capital murder in Maryland in August 1989, and elected to have his sentence determined by a judge. Wiggins' two public defenders had devised a strategy for the penalty phase hearing. First, they were going to reargue the guilt phase by claiming that Wiggins was not the one who actually killed the victim. Second, they would argue for a life sentence based on any mitigating factors. The court, however, did not allow that dual strategy, and Wiggins' sentencing hearing began in October 1989. In preparation for the penalty hearing, Wiggins' defense counsel consulted the presentence report prepared for the case and records on Wiggins at the Baltimore City Department of Social Services. What counsel did not do, however, was to have a forensic social worker prepare a social history report on Wiggins, even though state funds were available to pay for it. What the social history (later done at the request of Wiggins' appeals attorneys) would have revealed was evidence of severe physical and sexual abuse of Wiggins by his mother, various foster parents, and their children. This is the kind of mitigating evidence defense counsel would have provided to the judge in recommending a life sentence. The creation of such a social history report before a sentencing hearing was common practice among death penalty lawyers at the time in the state of Maryland. The U.S. Supreme Court ruled that Wiggins' attorneys were ineffective under the two-pronged *Strickland* standard—they fell below prevailing professional standards by not requesting a social history, and the Court thought that the mitigating evidence was so compelling that had such evidence been presented it was reasonable to think that he would have been sentenced to life rather than death. The *Wiggins* Court did not question defense counsel's strategy, only that such strategy was pursued without a more detailed collection of possible mitigating evidence, evidence that was routinely collected in Maryland death penalty cases at the time.

In our discussion of several capital punishment cases in this chapter, we have gotten a hint that perhaps all too frequently defendants who are on trial for their life do not always get effective or competent lawyers to defend them. What constitutes a good death penalty lawyer? One of the most important criteria is trial experience in death penalty cases, because capital punishment law is very complex. In addition, it is important that lawyers doing death penalty cases have adequate resources to hire investigators, hire expert witnesses, and conduct forensic tests of the evidence.[12] Recall that capital trials actually involve two separate hearings, the guilt phase and the penalty phase. The penalty phase hearing is the most time-consuming and unique task required of defense counsel, because attorneys essentially have to construct a story to the jury that acknowledges that while their client is guilty of a heinous murder he has sufficient redeeming qualities that his life should be spared. During the penalty phase the defense counsel must walk a thin line between explaining why the defendant committed such a horrible deed, and should therefore not be cast out of the human community by executing him, without appearing to make excuses for the act. The penalty phase of a capital trial, therefore, is a kind of morality play in which defense counsel attempts to "humanize" the convicted offender in such a way that his otherwise malignant act is explicable, though not excusable.

One form this "humanization" takes is an attempt to strike a chord of compassion with the jury by arguing that dysfunctional and destructive events/experiences in the defendant's past deformed a normal human being. Such a humanization requires a substantial investment of time and resources on the part of the defense team. Defense counsel must have the skill, time, and resources to extensively investigate the offender's past, even going back to childhood. Relevant mitigating evidence includes information about possible physical or sexual abuse, drug or alcohol addiction, a dysfunctional childhood environment, any employment or military experience—virtually any scrap of information that would be useful in convincing a jury that the defendant is worth something in spite of the horrific act that was committed. Not all defense lawyers have the skills, time, or resources to construct effective cases to argue for their client's life.

Convicted killer Jesus Romero's attorney seemed inadequate to the task. During his penalty phase hearing, Romero's lawyer offered only the following observation as "evidence" to convince the jury that his client's life should be spared:

> *Defense Counsel:* Ladies and Gentlemen, I appreciate the time you took deliberating and the thought you put into this. I'm going to be extremely brief. I have a reputation for not being brief. Jesse, stand up. Jesse?
>
> *Defendant:* Sir?
>
> *Defense Counsel:* Stand up.
>
> [Defendant Jesus Romero rises to his feet.]
>
> *Defense Counsel:* You are an extremely intelligent jury. You've got that man's life in your hands. You can take it or not. That's all I have to say.

In trying to argue that Jesus Romero should not be executed, his defense counsel used fewer than a hundred words (*National Law Journal* 1990). He called no witnesses and provided no other evidence in mitigation of penalty than the words he spoke. It should not be too surprising, therefore, that the jury sentenced Jesus Romero to death. He was executed by the state of Texas on May 20, 1992, and his lawyer was later suspended from his law practice for reasons unrelated to his representation in the Romero case. Interestingly, the lawyer's performance in the Romero case was not found to constitute ineffective assistance of counsel under the *Strickland* standard. In fact, in reviewing the case the U.S. 5th Circuit Court of Appeals characterized Romero's counsel's behavior as a "dramatic ploy" and offered its own assessment that had the jury returned a life rather than a death sentence, counsel's acts would have been seen as a "brilliant move."

Although Romero's lawyer did not speak at great length or with great eloquence in arguing to the jury to spare his life, Romero was lucky in one respect—at least his lawyer stayed awake during his trial! Convicted Texas capital murderer Carl Johnson was not so fortunate. During his 1979 trial for armed robbery and murder Johnson's senior defense counsel, Joe Frank Cannon (Johnson's other assigned counsel was but two years out of law school and had never tried a capital case) was asleep during parts of the jury selection process and the trial itself (Dow 1996). Carl Johnson was executed in 1995. The

Johnson trial was not the first time, however, that court-appointed lawyer Cannon had fallen asleep in a death penalty case. When he was appointed by the Harris County (Houston) court to represent Calvin Burdine, Cannon was caught sleeping while the prosecution was presenting its case in the guilt/innocence phase of the trial (Bright 1999; Weinstein 2001; Prejean 2005). He failed to object when the prosecution made antihomosexual comments (Burdine is gay) and did not object when the prosecutor implied that death was the only appropriate punishment for Burdine because life in prison would not be a bad punishment for a homosexual (*Ex parte Burdine,* 1995, 456–457). At a later hearing that examined his effectiveness as Burdine's counsel, Cannon himself referred to gay men as "queers" and "fairies." At a subsequent hearing on the issue of ineffective counsel, the clerk of the court at Burdine's trial testified that Cannon "fell asleep and was asleep for long periods of time during the questioning of witnesses" (p. 457). Burdine's trial lasted only 13 hours, after which he was sentenced to death. During the penalty phase, Cannon's entire case to the jury in pleading for a life sentence was the following:

> *Cannon:* Calvin, do you want to take the stand and plead for your life?
>
> *Burdine:* No sir, they didn't listen to me the first time, I don't see . . .
>
> *The Court:* What says the Defense, gentlemen?
>
> *Cannon:* We close your honor.

Calvin Burdine was sentenced to death by this jury and had six execution dates set, all of which were stayed. In 1999 a Federal Court of Appeals vacated Burdine's death sentence and ordered the state of Texas to either retry or release him. In that decision U.S. District Judge David Hittner concluded that a sleeping lawyer was like having no lawyer at all. Texas fought the order, and although in October 2000 a three-judge panel of the U.S. Court of Appeals for the 5th Circuit overruled that decision, it was reinstated in August of the next year by the full appeals court. Texas appealed to the U.S. Supreme Court, which failed to intervene. In June 2003 Burdine pleaded guilty to murder, aggravated assault, and felony possession of a weapon in exchange for a life sentence.

Attorney John Benn represented George Edward McFarland in his 1992 Texas murder trial. The 72-year-old Benn was not court appointed but was retained by McFarland's family, although Benn had not tried a capital case in Texas in almost 20 years. Benn did little in the way of advocating for McFarland; he spent only four hours preparing for the trial, never examined the crime scene, failed to interview even a single witness, filed no motions, and visited his client only twice before trial. Benn was assisted by a court appointed lawyer, Sanford Melamed, who while he had been a practicing lawyer for 13 years had never tried a death penalty case. Melamed and Benn did not prepare McFarland's case together and apparently rarely spoke. Mr. Melamed conducted most of the trial, with Mr. Benn failing to complete many of the duties he was supposed to do. In addition, according to a *Houston Chronicle* reporter who covered the case for his newspaper, Benn was asleep during most of the trial, complete with his mouth falling open and his head snapping back occasionally (Makeig 1992). When asked by the judge if in fact he had been sleeping, the 72-year-old lawyer admitted it, with the explanation that the trial was "boring" (Makeig 1992, A35).

Judge Doug Shaver dismissed the significance of Benn's sleeping during the trial, however, noting that "the Constitution says everyone's entitled to the attorney of their choice . . . [it] doesn't say that the lawyer has to be awake." The Texas Court of Criminal Appeals didn't find anything substantially wrong with Benn's representation of McFarland either, noting that his sleeping might have been a clever tactical decision designed to elicit sympathy from the jury (*McFarland v. State*, 928 S.W. 2d 482 Tex. Crim. App., 1996, 500–505). It wasn't a clever enough tactic, however; the jury sentenced McFarland to death in August of 1992. Subsequent to McFarland's death sentence, the U.S. Court of Appeals for the 5th Circuit ruled (in Calvin Burdine's case) that a lawyer who sleeps though significant portions of the trial is constitutionally ineffective, and the same ruling might appear to hold in McFarland's case. The Texas Court of Criminal Appeals determined, however, that the *Burdine* ruling did not apply to McFarland. Although both had sleeping lawyers, the Texas high court determined that Burdine had only one attorney while McFarland had co-counsel who was awake and by their estimate served as an effective advocate. They concluded that "[a]lthough one of his attorneys slept through portions of the trial, applicant was not deprived of the assistance of counsel under the Sixth Amendment because his second attorney was present and an active advocate at all times" (*Ex parte George Edward McFarland* Case No. AP-75,044 Tex. Crim. App).

In a Georgia murder case a court-appointed lawyer presented virtually no mitigating evidence to the jury in support of a life sentence. During the penalty phase hearing, the attorney's sole reference to his client was the following:

> You have got a little ole nigger man over there that doesn't weigh over 135 pounds. He is poor and he is broke. He's got a court-appointed lawyer. . . . He is ignorant. I will venture to say that he has an IQ of not over 80. (*State v. Dungee*, 1986, 39)

Actually, had defense counsel even bothered to investigate the case he would have discovered that his client was not merely "ignorant" but mentally retarded, with an IQ of around 68. He would also have discovered that because of his grossly limited intelligence his client failed in school, could not keep even menial jobs, and was rejected from the military when he tried to enlist. As later argued in the *Wiggins* case, this is precisely the kind of mitigating evidence that a jury should hear to possibly persuade them to impose a life rather than a death sentence. In the absence of this information the jury sentenced the defendant to death.

The cases we have just outlined provide startling information about the quality of legal representation provided to some defendants who are on trial for their life. While these are truly horrific stories, perhaps they are exceptions to the rule rather than representative of the general quality of defense counsel in capital cases. Unfortunately, however, there is other evidence of a more general nature to indicate that lawyers for those accused of capital crimes are likely the least skilled of their profession. One piece of evidence comes from the study by Professor Liebman and his colleagues, who found that nearly two-thirds of all capital cases were reversed on appeal. Almost half (40 percent) of these reversals in state appeals and between 25 and 35 percent of the reversals in federal court were made on the basis of incompetent defense counsel (Gelman et al. 2004). Another study, reported in the *National Law Journal* (1990), examined the quality of defense counsel in six Southern states (selected because a majority of the death sentences imposed in the United States at the time came from these six states). This investigation revealed that lawyers who represented defendants charged with capital crimes (almost all of which were court appointed) were substantially more likely than other practicing lawyers in their state to have been disbarred, suspended from practice, or otherwise professionally disciplined (reprimanded or fined). For example, lawyers in Florida who had tried at least one death penalty case were three times more likely to have been professionally disciplined than other lawyers in the state. In Texas, death penalty lawyers were almost nine times more likely to have been sanctioned by the state bar in some way; in Georgia and Alabama they were approximately 26 times more likely, in Mississippi they were 36 times more likely, and in Louisiana death penalty lawyers were nearly 47 times more likely to have been disciplined than nondeath penalty lawyers (*National Law Journal* 1990).

In a study of 461 Texas death penalty cases conducted by the *Dallas Morning News*, it was found that about one-quarter of the inmates then on death row (more than 100) were represented by court-appointed attorneys who had been disciplined for professional misconduct, and in about half of those cases the misconduct occurred *before* the lawyer was appointed by the court to handle the capital case (Jennings et al. 2000). Even if defense attorneys have not been formally sanctioned by the bar, their performance in death cases is often abysmal. In an examination of the lawyers for the 131 persons executed in Texas when George W. Bush was governor, reporters for the *Chicago Tribune* found that in 40 cases (30 percent of all those executed) defense counsel either presented no mitigating evidence at all during the penalty phase or only one witness (Armstrong and Mills 1999a, 1999b).

In a study of legal representation in death penalty cases in the state of Washington conducted by the *Seattle Post-Intelligencer,* it was reported that in the previous 20 years less than 1 percent of the state's lawyers had been disbarred (Olsen 2001a). Among those lawyers who had tried at least one death penalty case, however, the disbarment rate was about five times higher. Among those sentenced to death in Washington state over this period 20 percent were represented by lawyers who had been or were later disbarred. All those death penalty lawyers who were disbarred had committed criminal or ethical violations, and nearly all had either addiction or mental health problems. Two were disbarred for stealing state money they were given for supposedly providing defense services in death penalty cases.

Based on the totality of the evidence we have examined, it is probably safe to say that in many instances death penalty trial lawyers do not raise rigorous defenses for their client because they are inexperienced, uninterested, incompetent, or inadequately funded. This conclusion was also reached by several U.S. Supreme Court justices. For example, in a speech to a group of lawyers in Minneapolis on July 3, 2001, Justice Sandra Day O'Connor stated that there was a large gap between the legal representation provided indigent capital defendants and those who could afford their own lawyers. She said that in Texas those who were represented by court-appointed counsel were 28 percent more likely to be convicted of a capital crime and 44 percent more likely to be sentenced to death than those who retained their own lawyers. She concluded that "[p]erhaps it's time to look at minimum standards for appointed counsel in death cases and adequate compensation for appointed counsel when they are used" (Baca 2001). In commentating about the quality of death penalty lawyers, Justice Ruth Bader Ginsburg observed, "People who are well represented at trial do not get the death penalty. . . . I have yet to see a death case among the dozens coming to the Supreme Court on eve-of-execution stay applications in which the defendant was well represented at trial" (Ginsburg 2001).

A similar concern was expressed by the primary professional organization for lawyers, the American Bar Association (ABA). The ABA has recently begun to take very seriously both the inadequacies that exist in death penalty representation in many jurisdictions and its professional obligation to do something about it. In February 2003 it approved the *Guidelines for the Appointment and Performance of Defense Counsel in Death Penalty Cases,* a document that describes the requirements for a national standard for effective representation in death penalty cases (Freedman 2003). Among the standards for effective death penalty representation are the provision of at least two defense lawyers, an investigator, and a mental health and mitigation specialist. There are also standards for workloads, training, monitoring, and compensation for those doing death penalty work, along with performance standards. The guidelines also provide standards for defense counsel to meet at each stage of a death penalty case—investigation, voir dire, trial preparation, presentence preparation, postconviction appeals, and clemency petition.

The attempt by the ABA to devise standards of experience and competence for death penalty lawyers is not simply a theoretical exercise. Numerous examples indicate that providing good lawyers for those accused of capital crimes can make a difference. We know, for instance, that a large proportion of death penalty appeals are successful because counsel at trial was found to be ineffective (Liebman 2000; Liebman et al. 2000, 2002; Gelman et al. 2004), so the provision of better-quality counsel will certainly result in fewer mistakes being made at the first trial of many of those ultimately sentenced to death. Second, the state of defense lawyering in death penalty cases is not uniformly poor. There are a number of effective defender organizations. For example, the city of Philadelphia has for more than 10 years financed the Defender Association of Philadelphia, a nonprofit corporation of lawyers assigned to provide counsel for poor residents accused of murder. Each murder defendant is assigned two lawyers, and the staff includes investigators and social workers to prepare mitigation evidence and testimony; all staff attorneys are required to have 15 years of criminal law experience. As of 2005, not one of the 994 clients of the Defender Association has been sentenced to death, even though scores of murder defendants in the city represented by appointed private counsel have been.

The state of Texas has tried to reform its defense bar in capital cases. Previously, counties without public defender systems relied on trial judges to appoint whomever they wanted as defense counsel in indigent cases. A revision of the Texas statute in 1995 now requires that appointed lawyers in capital cases be chosen from a list of "qualified" attorneys and that two lawyers be appointed. However, the prospect for substantial reform does not seem bright. For example, the statute does not set standards for capital lawyers, leaving that job for each county to determine. Lawyers have been appointed to represent capital murder defendants under this law who have been disciplined by the bar. The *Dallas Morning News* reported an instance where a judge delayed the suspension of one lawyer's license so that he could finish a death penalty case he was appointed to defend. Further, a judge seeking to appoint counsel in a death case is not required to choose a lawyer from the list (Jennings et al. 2000; Texas Defender Service 2005a). The Texas Court of Criminal Appeals has held that a judge may go off the list of qualified defense lawyers and appoint someone not on the list.

Prosecutor and Law Enforcement Misconduct

It was long ago affirmed that the function of the state in prosecuting criminals is not to win at any price, but to seek justice. Seeking justice requires a concern not only with protecting citizens from crime but also with prosecuting cases within a framework of procedural rules that require "fair play." A ruling by the 1935 U.S. Supreme Court reflects this notion of prosecutors seeking justice (rather than convictions) while also requiring fairness:

> The prosecutor's interest in a criminal prosecution is not that it shall win a case, but that justice shall be done. . . . While he may strike hard blows, he is not at liberty to strike foul ones. It is as much his duty to refrain from improper methods calculated to produce a wrongful conviction as it is to use every legitimate means to bring about a just one. (*Berger v. United States*, 295 U.S. 78, 1935)

In the performance of their duties, prosecutors and law enforcement officers can make mistakes. Police are under great pressure by the community and by their superiors to solve serious crimes, particularly the brutal crimes that are capital offenses. When they or someone else identifies a possible suspect, sometimes their vision becomes narrowed—other possible suspects are ignored and the evidence is interpreted to build a case against the identified suspect. Convinced of the guilt of a given suspect, both law enforcement and prosecution build a case from that assumption, often ignoring other, even more plausible suspects and inconsistencies in the evidence.

Rob Warden, director of the Center on Wrongful Convictions at the Northwestern University School of Law, an organization that has been involved with the exoneration of death row inmates in Illinois, expressed this situation best: "I have never seen a case where I believed the prosecutors set out to prosecute someone whom they believed to be innocent. They just get wedded to a theory and then ignore the evidence that doesn't fit" (Toobin 2005, 54). In other words, prosecutors and police do not act out of evil intent; rather, they think that they have a suspect who is himself evil and do whatever they can to demonstrate that evil. We do not, therefore, have to presume that prosecutors and law enforcement act from malignant motives, but we cannot ignore the role that these two groups of actors in the capital punishment system have in the creation of "the exonerated" or possibly innocent.

We saw this in the case of Rolando Cruz. There was a great deal of pressure for the police to solve the kidnapping, rape, and brutal murder of 10-year-old Jeanine Nicarico. Cruz and Alejandro Hernandez did not help themselves out when they implicated each other in the crime in order to get a $10,000 reward. Nevertheless, once the police thought that they "had their man," the evidence was read with Cruz's and Hernandez's guilt in mind. Police may have thought that they definitely had the killers of the little girl but also believed they lacked sufficient evidence for a conviction to stand up in court. This doubt (not that they had the right man but doubt about how strong the evidence was) may have prompted them to concoct the story that Cruz admitted to "visions" that included facts about the crime that only the true killers would have known. The prosecution was likely under equal pressure to solve the crime and bring the killers to justice. Bolstered by the confidence of the police that Cruz and Hernandez were the killers because they had "confessed," prosecutors were not inclined to waste time and resources investigating the possibility that Brian Dugan was the killer (in spite of the fact that Dugan confessed to the crime after the first trial of Cruz and Hernandez). The police story finally cracked when at Cruz's third trial one of the officers stated that he had lied about Cruz's visions and confession. Even then, the prosecutors were not willing to abandon their belief that Cruz and Hernandez were involved in the killing of little Jeanine. They developed a new theory that put Cruz and Hernandez at the scene of the murder but with Dugan committing the act of sodomy (Armstrong and Possley 1999).

The case of Ernest Willis of Texas is also illustrative of prosecutorial misconduct that can have tragic consequences. On June 11, 1986 in the West Texas oil town of Iraan there was a house fire in which two people were killed and two others, Ernest Willis and his cousin Billy, survived. Immediately, police investigation centered on Ernest because, according to them, he wasn't coughing as much as his cousin was, he seemed to be less concerned about the two women who had died in the fire, and his clothes had no evidence that he ran through the flaming house trying to rescue the others. In addition, Willis failed a polygraph test. Four months after the fire, with no other leads, police arrested Willis under the theory that he had set the blaze and that marks on the floor of the house found after the fire seemed consistent with the use of gasoline or some other fire accelerant.

While in jail awaiting trial, and during his trial, Willis was provided with powerful pain killers (he had back problems) and, without his knowledge, a heavy dose of two antipsychotic drugs (though Willis did not request them and had no prior history of mental illness). In fact, Willis was given 40 milligrams a day of Haldol when the recommended dosage for someone with acute symptoms of mental illness is 15 milligrams. It was not clear who authorized the use of the drugs, but it was not Willis, and the jail physician acknowledged that his signature was on the order for Willis to receive the drugs (Owen 2004). The effect of the drugs was profound, however. In court Willis appeared uninterested and completely unemotional, and his eyes appeared to be "bugged out" (all standard effects of antipsychotic drugs). The prosecuting attorney played on Willis' lack of emotional feeling, repeatedly referring to him as a "satanic demon" and to his "deadpan, insensitive, expressionless face." The jury believed the state's story that Willis was a remorseless, unfeeling monster and convicted him of capital murder. His appointed defense counsel appeared overwhelmed at trial; one attorney had been practicing law for less than four years and had never tried a death penalty case (Hall 2002).

Even more devastating to Willis, however, was the fact that the prosecutors failed to disclose to his defense counsel important findings in a psychological report requested by the prosecution. Under Texas law a jury must determine that a convicted capital murderer is likely to commit acts of violence in the future and thus constitutes a danger to society before it can impose a sentence of death. A major piece of evidence that the state uses in arguing for a death sentence is a psychologist's report indicating that based on his or her examination the defendant is likely to commit acts of violence in the future. The psychologist who examined Willis concluded that he was not likely to be such a danger. Although required by law, this report was not provided to the defense, and prosecutors initially denied ever having a psychologist examine Willis (Owen 2004).

Willis' out-of-state appeals lawyers working on the case had identified a new suspect, a friend of Willis, who confessed to a prison psychiatrist in 1990 that he was the one who set the house on fire that night. In June 2000, the Texas judge who heard Willis' initial case ordered a new trial based on the fact that Willis' counsel was ineffective and was not provided with the state's psychologist's report and the fact that Willis was involuntarily drugged at his own trial. In December 2002, the Texas Court of Criminal Appeals, which has the authority to grant new criminal trials in the state, did not agree with the trial court judge's order for a new hearing, and Willis remained on death row. He then sought relief in federal court, and it came. The Federal District Court for the Western District of Texas held that Willis had received an unfair trial and ordered the state of Texas to either try him again or release him. The retrial did not occur—the current district attorney where the case originated concluded that the facts of the case did not indicate that Willis was guilty. In fact, the district attorney concluded that a more careful review of the arson evidence convinced him that the fire was not deliberately started. After spending 17 years on death row for a crime he did not commit, Willis was finally released from prison on October 6, 2004.

Alan Gell was convicted of capital murder and sentenced to death in North Carolina in 1998 for the murder of Allen Ray Jenkins. The evidence against Gell consisted largely of the testimony of two teenage girls, Crystal Morris, who was a regular visitor to Jenkins' house, and Shanna Hall. Morris' account of the murder changed repeatedly, however. First she claimed to know nothing about Jenkins' murder, only that she had seen him on April 3, 1995, not long before he was killed. In her next version to local police she said that Alan Gell phoned her from jail and confessed to her of killing Jenkins. In subsequent versions to police she admitted to a role in the killing—she had distracted Jenkins while Gell murdered him for the purpose of stealing money. When interviewed by police, Gell claimed never to have met Jenkins and had never been to his house.

Crystal had reported that the killing occurred on April 3, and the murder had to have occurred that day for Gell to be the murderer, as he was either in jail or out of town with someone immediately after that day. The problem was, several people reported to police that they saw Jenkins *after* the day he was supposedly killed. Police reinterviewed these witnesses, telling them that Jenkins was murdered on April 3, and they revised their stories, claiming only that they saw Jenkins sometime in early April of that year. At least two witnesses continued to assert that they had seen Jenkins after April 3, although a police report stated that it was April 1, when they last saw him. When shown the report later, one of the witnesses claimed she never changed what she told police and that the written police report was wrong.

Gell was arrested by police for the murder of Allen Ray Jenkins on August 1, 1995. Gell spent two years in jail awaiting his murder trial, during which time he had four different lawyers. His first and second lawyers quit the case when they accepted jobs as prosecutors, and his third lawyer quit just months before the trial was to begin because she said she could not prepare for the trial and continue the divinity degree she was pursuing at Duke University. Gell's fourth lawyer, Maynard Harrell, realized that little work had been done on the case. Most important, despite an order requiring them to do so, prosecutors had not turned over to the defense evidence that there were witnesses who claimed that they had seen Jenkins after the date he had supposedly been murdered by Gell—evidence that favored Gell's innocence. Harrell filed a motion in 1998 requiring prosecutors to turn over any exculpatory evidence. In their response the prosecutors replied that there was none, that although some people who were interviewed by police thought they had seen Jenkins after April 3, they had been mistaken. At the insistence of the trial judge, however, the prosecution turned over these interviews to defense counsel. For whatever reason, however, the prosecution did not turn over to Harrell the interviews of those people who continued to assert that they either saw or spoke with Jenkins after April 3. Nor did the prosecution turn over tape recordings of their chief witness, Crystal Morris, creating a story about the Jenkins murder in a conversation with Shanna Hall.

At Gell's trial Crystal Morris testified that she saw Gell shoot Jenkins with a shotgun. It was not mentioned that in August 1997 both Morris and Shanna Hall had first degree murder charges dropped against them and both accepted guilty pleas for second degree murder. There was no physical evidence linking Gell to Jenkins' murder—no fingerprints, no DNA evidence, no footprints, no eyewitnesses saying that they had ever seen Gell at Jenkins' house. Gell's defense counsel, however, did not ask for money to hire an expert to testify as to the approximate date of Jenkins' murder, a crucial fact in the case, nor did the lawyer hire anyone to conduct ballistic tests to determine if the state's version of how the shooting occurred was credible. The jury took just over an hour to convict Gell of first degree murder, and at his penalty trail Gell continued to assert his innocence rather than ask for mercy. The jury sentenced him to death after deliberating for only two hours.

Gell's appeals lawyers began working on the case in 2000. They hired experts to determine more accurately the date of Jenkins' death. These experts concluded that Jenkins was killed on or about April 9, 1995—when Gell was in jail for auto theft. When the original medical examiner was shown this new evidence along with the testimony of witnesses who claimed to have seen Jenkins after April 3, statements the police did not give her, she concluded that Jenkins was very likely killed on April 8 or 9 and that Gell could not have been the killer. Meanwhile, Gell was on North Carolina's death row. Based on this new evidence, in 2002 a judge ordered a new trial on the basis that the prosecutors in the case had withheld crucial evidence in the case. On Februrary 18, 2004 Alan Gell was found not guilty of Jenkins' murder. Gell had spent nine years in jail or prison, four years on death row, for a crime he did not commit. After an investigation by the North Carolina State Bar, the two prosecutors in the case were formally reprimanded for their misconduct but were able to keep their license to practice law.

Texas prosecutors seemed to use a little too much zeal to convict Delma Banks, Jr., who spent more than 25 years on death row. Banks had been scheduled for execution some 15 different times, and he once came within 10 minutes of being executed before the U.S. Supreme Court granted a stay, while he was strapped to a medical gurney awaiting a lethal injection. Banks had been convicted and sentenced to death in 1980 for killing 16-year-old Richard Whitehead. At Banks' trial prosecutors used two crucial witnesses, Charles Cook and Robert Farr. Cook had presented a muddled and conflicting account of the crime when first interviewed by the police. After extensive pretrial coaching by prosecutors, Cook finally had a clear story to tell. He testified that Banks had admitted killing Whitehead and taking his car. Cook, however, perjured himself when he denied that he had spoken to anyone about his testimony or that he had been coached in his testimony by the prosecution. Cook also denied that he had received any favors in exchange for his testimony when in fact the police had dropped an arson charge. The prosecutors in the case who knew that Cook had been coached and had a charge dropped were aware that he had perjured himself with his statements but said nothing.

Robert Farr also testified for the prosecution, corroborating much of Cook's testimony. What neither the jury nor the defense were told, however, was that Farr was a paid police informant. Under discovery requirements, the prosecution was required to inform defense counsel about the coaching of Cook, the dropped charge, and Farr's being was paid for his testimony. Instead, they hid the information from defense counsel and the trial court. Years after the conviction, both Cook and Farr recanted most of their testimony, and the unethical and illegal behavior of the prosecution finally came to light. It took even more time for appeals courts to do anything about it, however. Both the Texas Court of Criminal Appeals and the 5th Federal Circuit Court of Appeals rejected Banks' claim for a new trial and essentially accepted the state's argument that Banks' defense lawyers were raising the issues too late (even though the facts were hidden from them). On February 24, 2004, the United States Supreme Court overturned Banks' death sentence and remanded the case to a lower court. In August 2004 the 5th Circuit remanded the case to the state district court to determine whether Banks deserved an entirely new trial.

In a series of investigative reports, two *Chicago Tribune* reporters, Steve Mills and Ken Armstrong, revealed evidence of systematic abuse within parts of the Chicago Police Department (Armstrong and Mills 1999a, 1999b; Mills and Armstrong 1999a, 1999b, 1999c). One murder suspect, Stanley Howard, confessed to a murder while in police custody but later claimed that he had been kicked and punched and had a plastic bag tied over his head to coerce him to confess. Howard was not the only one allegedly abused by the Chicago Police Department (CPD); an investigation conducted by the CPD itself found repeated instances of police misconduct, torture, and physical abuse. Ronald Jones confessed to a 1985 rape and murder in Chicago because he claimed he had been repeatedly beaten by the police. He was released after almost eight years on Illinois' death row when he was exonerated by DNA evidence—DNA testing that was resisted by the state.

It might be tempting to conclude from these anecdotal stories that while there are isolated instances of prosecutorial and police misconduct in capital cases, such incidents are infrequent. Unfortunately, as with incompetent defense lawyers the evidence pointing to the misconduct of prosecutors and police is more systematic. In their study of over 5,000 capital cases on appeal, James Liebman and his colleagues (Liebman 2000; Liebman et al. 2000, 2002; Gelman et al. 2004) found that at the level of state postconviction appeal, errors made by prosecutors and police were among the most common reasons a case was reversed. Prosecutors suppressing possibly exculpatory evidence alone comprised nearly 20 percent of the total number of errors. While it is true that the vast majority of prosecutors and law enforcement officials perform their jobs professionally, fairly, and with honor, the problem of misconduct by prosecutors and police in capital cases may not be rare.

Jail House Snitches and 'Junk Science'

In many of the cases of the exonerated, the prosecution's case has been bolstered by the testimony provided by jailhouse informants (or "snitches")[13] or by scientific evidence of dubious credibility. Northwestern University's Center for Wrongful Convictions has documented that an informant or snitch was used by the prosecution in the cases of 51 of the 111 persons (46 percent) exonerated of capital crimes and released from death row up to 2004 (Warden 2004). This makes "snitch cases" the leading cause of wrongful convictions in death penalty cases.

For example, Randall Dale Adams was convicted of killing a Dallas police officer during a routine traffic stop on November 28, 1976. Adams was hitchhiking when he was picked up (in a stolen car) by David Ray Harris. Adams and Harris spent the rest of the day drinking beer, smoking marijuana, and pawning things that Harris had stolen. Later that night, Harris dropped Adams off at a motel. Sometime after midnight, Dallas police pulled Harris over because he was driving without his headlights on, and when Officer Robert Wood approached the car, Harris shot him dead. Wood's partner returned fire, but Harris eluded capture. Several days later in another Texas town after Harris bragged to some friends about killing a cop, he was picked up by police for questioning. He initially denied any involvement in the crime, but after he was told that a ballistics test identified his gun as the one that killed Wood, he implicated Adams. Adams was picked up by the police, questioned, and told that Harris had "fingered" him as the killer and that Harris had passed a lie detector test while he had failed it. At Adams' trial, in addition to the testimony of Harris, prosecutors presented three other eyewitnesses who claimed to have seen Adams in the car at around the time and place Officer Wood was killed. One of these witnesses was Emily Miller. Several days after her testimony, defense counsel learned that Miller had originally told police that the person she saw in the car was either a Mexican or a light-skinned African American (Adams is white). When they sought to recall her to the witness stand, however, the prosecution falsely claimed that she had left Texas and moved to Illinois, when she had only moved to a different area of Dallas. Adams was convicted and sentenced to death. Because of an error in the trial, the Supreme Court overturned Adams' conviction and death sentence three days before he was supposed to be executed. The state of Texas did not retry Adams, however, because the governor commuted his death sentence to life in prison, where he would have stayed for the rest of his life.

A documentary filmmaker, Errol Morris, and Adams' new appeals lawyer began to discover some troubling information about the actions of the prosecution and police in the case. It turned out that robbery charges against Emily Miller's daughter were dropped when she agreed to testify against Adams. Further, during the initial investigation Officer Wood's partner that night stated under hypnosis that she did not see the killer. She testified at trial, however, that the killer's hair was the same color as Adams', and her statement under hypnosis was withheld from the defense. At a hearing to examine these issues, David Harris finally admitted to lying to the police about Adams and admitted that he alone had killed Officer Wood. On March 21, 1989, approximately 12 years after he was convicted and sentenced to death, Randall Dale Adams was released from prison.

Earlier in the chapter we discussed the case of Larry Griffin of St. Louis. Griffin, you will remember, was convicted of murdering Quinton Moss and was executed in 1995. The prosecution's case rested heavily on the testimony of Robert Fitzgerald, a convicted offender with an extensive criminal record in both St. Louis and his home state of Massachusetts. Fitzgerald was in St. Louis under the federal witness protection program. He testified that he had been at the scene of the Moss shooting and that he could identify Griffin as the killer. It is unclear how Fitzgerald came to identify Griffin. He initially claimed that he picked Griffin's picture out of a photo lineup; later he claimed that a St. Louis police detective showed him a picture that had Griffin's name on the back and asked whether this was the person who killed Moss. Although Fitzgerald had several felony charges pending in St. Louis, he was released from custody on the day that Larry Griffin was convicted of murder. No other witnesses placed Griffin at the scene of the crime nor was there any physical evidence linking him to the murder.

After Griffin's conviction Quinton Moss' sister was interviewed and she claimed that she was at the scene when the crime occurred and saw no white man there (Fitzgerald is white, and the section of St. Louis where the crime occurred is overwhelmingly African American). The first police officer at the scene, Michael Ruggeri, initially presented testimony that corroborated Fitzgerald's testimony that he was present when the crime occurred, but in an interview with lawyers from the NAACP Legal Defense Fund, he recanted that testimony. He now claims that there was no white man at the crime scene when he arrived and that Fitzgerald only showed up several minutes later and thus could not possibly have seen who did the shooting. Wallace Conners was a bystander at the time of the shooting and was shot in the same spray of bullets that killed Moss. Conners was never questioned by police, the prosecution, or the defense and was not interviewed until 2004 by the NAACP lawyers. Conners, who was 15 feet away from the car when the shots were fired, said no white man was there when Moss was killed. Fitzgerald could not be later interviewed; he died in August 2004, some nine years after Griffin was executed. The St. Louis prosecutor is reopening the Moss case.

In addition to the problem presented by the testimony of informants, the process of prosecuting death penalty cases is also tainted by bad or "junk" science. In some instances the prosecution presents evidence that is not generally

Box 9.4
Predicting Dangerousness

No discussion of junk science in capital cases would be complete without mentioning the unique condition of Texas. Under Texas law, before sentencing a convicted capital murderer to death a jury must determine that the defendant would commit violent acts in the future. The "evidence" presented to the jury by the prosecution in this matter usually comes in the form of testimony from psychiatrists. One Texas psychiatrist who has frequently testified in death cases, Dr. James Grigson, has given testimony to juries (sometimes without ever examining the defendant) that he can predict with 100 percent accuracy that the person will commit a violent crime in the future (with the implicit conclusion that to prevent this the jury should sentence the defendant to death).

The only problem is that predictions of future dangerousness by psychiatrists (by anyone!) are notoriously incorrect. Most of the available evidence seems to suggest that psychiatric predictions of dangerousness are wrong at least half of the time. The American Psychiatric Association rejects the kinds of dangerousness predictions required by the Texas statute and expelled Dr. Grigson as a member. Texas prosecutors still rely on him in death cases, however.

Texas prosecutors have other experts to call on as well. "Dr." Jean Matthews testified at Phillip Thompkins' capital trial that he was likely to constitute a danger in the future. Matthews stated that she had a Ph.D. in psychology from Florida State University and had done postdoctoral work at Harvard and the Massachusetts Institute of Technology. Thompkins was sentenced to death, and only afterward was it discovered that Matthews never attended Harvard or MIT, nor did she have a Ph.D. in psychology from Florida State University. She did, however, have a degree from FSU—in music and English (Texas Defender Service 2005a, 2005b). ✦

accepted by the scientific community as valid. Ray Krone, for example, was convicted and sentenced to death in 1992 for the murder of Phoenix, Arizona cocktail waitress Kim Ancona. Krone was convicted on circumstantial evidence, including evidence presented by the state's expert, Dr. Raymond Rawson, that bite marks found on Ancona matched teeth impressions from Krone. Krone's attorney was given only one day to prepare for the expert's testimony. There was no blood found on Krone that matched the victim, no fingerprints of his were found at the crime scene, and a witness testified that he was somewhere else at the time the crime was committed. Krone's death sentence was vacated on appeal, but he was convicted a second time and sentenced to 25 years to life. At his second trial DNA evidence indicated that saliva in a tooth impression found on the victim did not match Krone's, but the state argued that Krone was still the killer and that the saliva on the victim likely came from a glass she was carrying. Krone was finally exonerated by DNA evidence and released from Arizona prison on April 8, 2002 after spending 10 years in prison, two of them on death row. The new DNA evidence matched that of a man serving time in an Arizona prison for a child molestation charge who had been living behind the bar where Ancona was working when she was killed.

Forensic odontology (teeth mark identification) is as yet an unproven science (Wilkinson and Gerughty 1985; Seigler 1992). That is because individuals do not have unique teeth marks like they do unique fingerprints. The marks left by teeth change over time and are altered by the conditions of the skin. The American Board of Forensic Odontology, the professional organization that oversees the discipline, has urged its members to use great caution in providing testimony about bite marks. Guidelines issued by the board suggest that the word "match" not be used because it implies an accuracy that is not yet scientifically valid. The expert testimony of Dr. Rawson was also used to convict Robby Lee Tankersley of the rape and murder of a 65-year-old Yuma, Arizona woman. The state's other forensic odontist did not agree with Dr. Rawson's conclusions. Dr. Norman Sperber claimed that he could not identify any individual characteristics of the bite marks on the victim's body and was highly critical of Dr. Rawson's testimony. Tankersley was sentenced to death in 1994 by Judge Thomas Thode. Dr. Rawson had testified that bite marks on the victim clearly matched those on impressions from Tankersley's teeth. After Tankersley spent 10 years on Arizona's death row, Judge Thode finally ordered a new sentencing hearing for him.

Another shaky scientific tool that has been used to bolster the prosecution's case is hair evidence. Usually, a hair taken at the crime scene is used to provide a "match" with a hair taken from the defendant. The hairs are subject to microscopic analysis by laboratory technicians who look for similarities in color, structure, and other characteristics between the two samples. Hair, however, is not like DNA or fingerprints; it cannot be matched to a unique individual either with a known degree of probability or with scientific accuracy. In fact, one study by the federal government's Law Enforcement Assistance Administration found that hair analysis had error rates as high as 67 percent (Imwinkelried 1982; Smith and Goodman 1996; Cooley 2004). The lack of scientific merit, however, does not preclude the making of strong scientific assertions by "experts" testifying for the state. While virtually never used as the sole piece of evidence, when presented in conjunction with other prosecution evidence hair evidence may tip the balance against the defendant's innocence.

For example, Ronald Keith Williamson was convicted and sentenced to death for the rape and murder of Debbie Sue Carter in Ada, Oklahoma in 1988. The crime occurred in 1982 and remained unsolved for years. In 1987 while Williamson was in jail for passing bad checks, a woman who was also incarcerated in the jail claimed that she overheard Williamson admitting to the Carter slaying. The police also had the testimony of Glenn Gore, who claimed he saw Williamson with Carter on the night of the murder. In addition to the informant's testimony, the prosecution was aided by Oklahoma forensic scientist Melvin R. Hett, who testified that 17 hairs found at the crime scene "matched" both Williamson and a co-defendant, Dennis Fritz. A piece of information that would not come out until 2001 was that another Oklahoma State Bureau of Investigation criminalist, Susan Land, microscopically analyzed 40 hairs from the crime scene and concluded that none had come from Williamson or Fritz. This fact should have been turned over to the defense over a decade before but was not. Both men were convicted; Williamson was sentenced to death while Fritz was given a life sentence. Williamson came within five days of being executed before lawyers for the Innocence Project at the Benjamin C. Cardozo School of Law in New York arranged for DNA tests of the semen found in the murder victim. These tests showed that neither Williamson nor Fritz was the source of the semen or hair. Both were released from custody in April 1999. The DNA tests did, however, identify the source as Glenn Gore, who was subsequently convicted of Carter's murder and sentenced to death. Williamson spent 11 years in prison for the crime and died on December 4, 2004, at the age of 51.

Earlier in this chapter we discussed the case of Ernest Willis, convicted of an arson-caused murder and sentenced to death in Texas in 1987. His case involved numerous flaws in the capital punishment system; his lawyers were inexperienced and made near-fatal mistakes throughout his case, he was given large doses of antipsychotic drugs by Texas authorities without his knowledge even though he had no history of mental illness, and Texas authorities suppressed a report prepared by a state psychiatrist concluding that Willis was not likely to constitute a danger in the future. In addition, the state presented evidence that marks found on the floor of the burned down house were evidence of "pour patterns" made when a fire accelerant like gasoline had been used. Willis' pro bono appeals lawyers were successful in making a convincing case that his trial had numerous defects, and in June 2000 the Texas trial judge who first heard the case ruled that Willis deserved a new trial. The Texas Court of Criminal Appeals, however, denied this order, sending Willis back to death row. Finally, based on the same evidence a U.S. district judge ordered the state to either give Willis a new trial or release him. The state did not appeal this ruling, and the local district attorney hired a new arson expert to examine the evidence. This expert concluded that there was no evidence at all to support the charge that the fire was deliberately started. Texas declined to try Willis again, and he was released from prison on October 6, 2004, with $100 in his pocket after spending 17 years on death row.

Cameron Willingham was not as lucky as Willis. In February 2004 he was put to death by lethal injection in Texas, proclaiming his innocence. In this trial, arson investigators testified that "crazed glass"—weblike cracks on glass—at the crime scene and pour patterns on the floor indicated that a fire accelerant had been used to start the fire. Fire investigators for the state further argued that there were more than 20 indicators that the fire had been set deliberately. A jailhouse informant also testified that Willingham had confessed the crime to him. Later, a fire expert, Gerald Hurst, reexamined the state's case and found numerous errors in the investigation. A report by Hurst was attached to an appeal to the Texas Court of Criminal Appeals requesting a new hearing. Both that court and the Governor of Texas, Rick Perry, refused to reopen the case. After Willingham was executed, the *Chicago Tribune* asked Hurst and three other fire investigators to review the arson evidence presented by the state. Hurst concluded that "there's nothing to suggest to any reasonable arson investigator that this was an arson fire" (Mills and Possley 2004). Kendall Ryland, a former fire instructor at Louisiana State University, agreed, stating "it made me sick to think that this guy was executed based on this investigation. . . . They executed this guy and they've just got no idea—at least not scientifically—if he set the fire, or if the fire was even intentionally set" (Mills and Possley 2004).

In other instances the basis of the scientific proof is sound but the state's procedures in handling or investigating the evidence is poor. Sometimes this shoddy scientific work is widespread rather than isolated. For example, Earl Washington, Jr., spent 17 years in prison, nine years on Virginia's death row, and came within nine days of being executed before he was released on the basis of DNA evidence that proved his innocence. Washington, who is mentally retarded, was being interrogated by police about another crime when he was asked about the murder of Rebecca Lynn Williams. Police asked whether he'd stabbed Williams, and Washington nodded. The police then asked whether the woman was white or black and Washington said she was black. When the police informed Washington that the victim was white, he complied and stated she was white. The police also asked how many times Washington had stabbed Williams, and he replied once or twice. Rebecca Williams was stabbed 38 times. When told how many times the victim had really been stabbed, Washington again agreed. Earl Washington, Jr. "confessed" to five different crimes during his interrogations, although the confession in four of the five cases was so inconsistent with the known facts of the case that Virginia authorities acknowledged that he was likely just being led by law enforcement officers.

Although he was not a suspect when Williams was murdered and there was no physical evidence linking him to the crime, Washington was convicted in 1982 and sentenced to death. DNA from the case was tested in 1993 that cast doubt on Washington's guilt but could not completely preclude him as a suspect. In reaction to this testing, then Virginia Governor Douglas Wilder commuted Washington's death sentence to life imprisonment. Additional testing in 2000 exonerated him, however, and improper lab procedures by the Virginia Division of Forensic Science came to light including the fact that in Washington's case the lab's leading DNA analyst, Jeffrey Ban, prematurely excluded some suspects when the evidence indicated that the DNA test was inconclusive. In response to this misconduct, Virginia Governor Mark Warner ordered a review of 150 other cases where the state's crime lab did work in criminal trials. Further, on May 5, 2006, a federal jury ruled that a Virginia state police investigator had fabricated Washington's confession, and they ordered the man's estate (the investigator had died in 1996) to pay $2.25 million (Markon 2006).

Jeffrey Pierce was convicted of rape in Oklahoma in 1986 and was sentenced to 65 years in prison. Oklahoma police chemist Joyce Gilchrist placed Pierce at the scene of the rape on the basis of her microscopic analysis of hair samples taken from Pierce's head and other samples found at the victim's apartment. In a career that spanned over 20 years, Gilchrist testified for the prosecution in thousands of cases. She received favorable work reviews even after appellate courts and other forensic scientists were harshly critical of her work beginning in the mid-1980s. Her work at the Oklahoma City Police Department came under scrutiny in 1999, however, when an FBI report indicated that her analyses and conclusions could not be supported in five out of eight cases they reviewed. DNA testing in the Pierce case exonerated him, and in May of 2001 he was released from prison, where he'd spent 15 years of his life for a crime he did not commit.

Gilchrist's work has been called into question in other cases. In response to this crisis, Governor Frank Keating ordered the Oklahoma State Bureau of Investigation to review all criminal cases where she participated. Twenty-three of the cases in which Gilchrist had provided scientific testimony were death penalty cases, and in 11 of them the defendant had already been executed. Gilchrist testified that hairs found at a 1986 rape and murder belonged to Robert Miller. Miller was convicted and sentenced to death. He was exonerated and released from prison in 1998 when DNA tests determined that he was not guilty. Testing also identified the source of the semen at the crime scene as belonging to Ronald Lott, whom Gilchrist had previously dismissed as a possible suspect on the basis of her "analysis." Malcolm Rent Johnson was executed by Oklahoma on January 6, 2000. He was convicted and sentenced to death for the rape and murder of a 76-year-old woman at least in part because Gilchrist testified that Johnson's blood type matched sperm collected from items found in the victim's apartment. In a reexamination of the laboratory slides that Gilchrist had "examined," no sperm were found. Oklahoma authorities claim, however, that there was enough other evidence to prove that Johnson was the killer.

Harris County (Houston) Texas has one of the most active death penalty systems in the country. In fact, if Harris County were a state, it would have the third highest number of executions in the country since 1977, behind only the rest of Texas and Virginia. Defense counsel and other forensic scientists had been raising questions about the quality of the lab work in the Houston Police Department Crime Lab and the testimony often given in court, which has seemed particularly imbalanced in favor of the prosecution. A Houston television station began an investigative report of the lab and asked highly respected forensic scientist William C. Thompson to review the evidence and court testimony in several cases. Thompson was harshly critical of the crime lab's work, calling it "the worst laboratory work I have seen." As a result of this attention, an investigation of the lab by Texas authorities uncovered numerous problems, including evidence of "drylabbing" (falsifying results without actually testing the evidence) and evidence that most lab workers were professionally unqualified for their positions. In light of these findings, the lab work in several hundred cases was being reviewed.

Box 9.5
Developing the 'Gold Standard' for a Capital Punishment Statute

Massachusetts does not currently have the death penalty and has not executed anyone since 1947. In the spring of 2005 Republican Governor Mitt Romney introduced a bill in the Massachusetts legislature that would reinstate a death penalty in the commonwealth that he described as having so many procedural protections and safeguards that it would become the national "gold standard" for capital punishment legislation. He claimed that the bill would produce a much more limited and restricted death penalty, one that would be more fair and evenhanded in its application, and one that would, as far as humanly possible, be foolproof so that innocent persons could not be executed.

Among the many provisions of the bill was the requirement that the attorney general of the state review the decisions of local prosecutors to seek or not seek the death penalty in order to ensure a uniform application throughout the commonwealth. Capital defendants unable to afford a lawyer would have two lawyers appointed by the court to provide for their defense. These court-appointed lawyers must be capital-case qualified, which would include both extensive experience in criminal law matters and experience in a previous capital case. The state would also provide court-appointed counsel at all postconviction appeals, state and federal. During the penalty phase of the capital trial defense counsel would be permitted to speak to the limitations of the evidence in the guilt phase of the trial and appeal to any lingering doubt about the guilt of the defendant. The penalty phase jury would be required to find that there is "no doubt" about the defendant's guilt of capital murder, a higher burden of proof than guilt "beyond a reasonable doubt." The existence of any lingering doubt about the defendant's guilt could provide the grounds for the jury not to impose the death penalty.

> The statute also establishes an independent scientific review advisory committee that would review the scientific and forensic evidence in every death case to ensure its validity as well as develop standards for crime labs. The Supreme Judicial Court of the Commonwealth of Massachusetts is required to review all death sentences and has the authority to set aside either the conviction or sentence of any defendant if it determines that the death sentence was inappropriate on any basis in fact or law. The legislation also establishes a death penalty review commission to investigate any appealed or unappealed claim of substantive error.
>
> In November 2005 the Massachusetts House of Representatives rejected the proposed death penalty legislation by a vote of 100–53. A less comprehensive bill to reinstate the death penalty was voted down by the House in 2001 by a 92–60 vote. ✦

Chapter Summary

What conclusions do we draw from these stories of those sent off to death row only later to be found to have been innocent of the crimes for which they were convicted and sentenced to death? Supporters of capital punishment claim that the stories of the exonerated prove rather convincingly that since their innocence was ultimately established and they were not executed, "the system works" (Cassell 2004). The Roger Keith Coleman case adds further credibility to that interpretation. Here was a man who loudly and continuously proclaimed his innocence; the facts of the case were confusing but could reasonable be said to point to his guilt, and yet as it turned out he was guilty. Those who claim that the system works claim that the long process of appeals in death row cases is successful in separating the guilty from the innocent and that, though mistakes can be and are made, they are eventually corrected.

Not surprisingly, opponents of the death penalty have a different view. They claim that the cases of the exonerated demonstrate equally convincingly that the system of capital punishment is broken. This side contends that there are too many instances of innocent persons convicted of capital crimes who languish on death row for years and years before they are released to convince them that the system works. In addition, it is argued that the innocence of many of those eventually exonerated was not first established by the legal system but by criminal justice "outsiders," such as professors and their students. Critics also point to the reasons for improper convictions and death sentences—reliance on the testimony of jailhouse "snitches," "junk science," coercive behavior by law enforcement officers who seem too often to have decided that a suspect is guilty and then create an evidentiary case to support that, prosecutors that withhold potentially exculpatory evidence from defense counsel—to argue that they all point to serious flaws in the capital punishment system. While these kinds of corrupt practices may be an inevitable part of any criminal justice system operated by human beings, critics would argue that such practices have no place in a system that must decide so irreversible a decision as to who lives and who dies.

Discussion Questions

1. If it were found that an innocent person had been executed, do you think the death penalty should be abolished? Why or why not? If not, how

many innocent people being executed would it take for you to change your mind? Or is the number of innocents executed irrelevant? Explain.

2. Picture yourself creating a capital punishment system from scratch. All you know is that you would be subject to whatever system you build, and you do not know whether you would be rich or poor, black or white, male or female. What kinds of procedural protections would you have in place for capital defendants (knowing there's an unknown risk that you could be one), and how would your system differ from the one that currently exists?

3. Does the existence of the exonerated mean that the system of capital punishment works or that it is broken? Explain.

4. What kinds of reforms would you put in place to make sure that there is a low risk that an innocent person would be sentenced to death or executed?

5. What do you think the job of prosecutors should be in capital cases—to seek justice or to try to "win" their case and secure a conviction? What do you think should be done in order to assist prosecutors in doing their job, however you defined it?

6. If you think that the appeals process in capital cases is too long because defendants have too many ways to appeal their cases, can you anticipate what problems might arise if the appeals process were shortened too much?

7. How can we make sure that defendants who are on trial for their life are provided with quality, effective counsel? As a taxpayer, would you be willing to pay for this counsel?

8. If you support capital punishment, picture for a moment the possibility that you have been accused of committing a capital murder. Would you like to be tried by the procedures and practices that exist today? If you are opposed to capital punishment, picture for a moment the possibility that a loved one of yours has been murdered. Do you think the death penalty would help you deal with the loss? Do you think you would want the killer put to death? Do you think that the state is the proper vehicle for the expression of personal vengeance?

Student Resources

A good book that provides details of the Roger Keith Coleman case is John C. Tucker's *May God Have Mercy* (1997). Sister Helen Prejean, a Catholic nun who has ministered to death row inmates and is a staunch death penalty opponent, has written the eloquent book *The Death of Innocents*—a good book whether you oppose or support capital punishment. Other sources of information about wrongful executions in capital cases are Karen S. Miller's *Wrongful Executions and the Legitimacy of the Death Penalty* (2006) and Stanley Cohen's *The Wrong Men* (2003). If you want a detailed account of a claimed innocent man being executed, written by the lawyer who worked with him, read Michael A. Mello's *The Wrong Man: A True Story of Innocence on Death Row*. If you are interested in issues pertaining to potential innocence or the exoneration of death row and other prisoners, a number of organizations maintain websites with lots of useful information about innocence issues. Try:

1. Northwestern University School of Law's Center on Wrongful Convictions: <www.law.northwestern.edu/wrongfulconvictions/>.

2. The Innocence Project: <www.innocenceproject.org/>.

3. Cardozo Law School's innocence project: <www.cardozo.yu.edu/innocence_project/>.

Innocence projects operate in virtually every state; for an example, see the Innocence Project Northwest at <www.law.washington.edu/ipnw/>.

If you are interested in criminal forensics and the issues pertaining to scientific evidence in capital and noncapital cases, the best starting point is an article by Craig M. Cooley (2004). An excellent website that contains numerous links to useful information about criminal forensics, crime lab work, and scientific evidence in criminal cases can be found at <www.law-forensic.com/>.

Jessica Blank and Erik Jensen have written a play about six innocently convicted persons called *The Exonerated*. It is well done and worth seeing if you get the chance. It has also been made into a movie (available on DVD).

Endnotes

1. After reviewing evidence of exonerated death row inmates presented by Barry Scheck, Peter Neufeld, and Jim Dwyer in *Actual Innocence: Five Days to Execution and Other Dispatches From the Wrongly Convicted* (2000), conservative columnist George F. Will (2000) concluded that "one inescapable inference from these numbers is that some of the 620 persons executed [during the modern era of capital punishment] were innocent." Pat Robertson, head of the Christian Coalition, has also expressed a concern about the death penalty on the grounds that there is an unacceptable risk of the innocent being executed. Before leaving office, former Illinois Governor George Ryan, a longtime supporter of the death penalty when in the state legislature and who presided over an execution when governor, commuted the death sentences of 167 condemned offenders because of his concern about the risk of error in capital cases in his state.

2. O'Dell was initially appointed a public defender, Paul Ray, as his defense counsel but ultimately dismissed him after repeated disagreements. Ray was a military lawyer who concentrated on domestic cases, and according to O'Dell advised him that because the evidence seemed to point toward his guilt that O'Dell's best bet was to plead guilty by reason of temporary insanity. O'Dell continued to proclaim his innocence (Prejean 2005).

3. The O'Dell case is described in detail in the book *The Death of Innocents* (2005) by Sister Helen Prejean. She carefully outlines the ambiguous nature of the evidence against Joe O'Dell and builds a strong case for the fact that he might have been innocent of the crime for which he eventually was executed. The fact that "innocence" is an elusive issue is fully revealed when she, a clear advocate for O'Dell, described him as "a *possibly* innocent man" (italics added).

4. O'Dell's claim was that the blood found on this clothing was from a fistfight he had on the night that Helen Schartner was killed and not the blood of the victim.

5. Graham was also arrested for but not charged with the kidnapping and rape of a taxi cab driver. He abducted the woman at a gas station and raped her. He then took her to her house, where he fell asleep. The victim grabbed Graham's gun and called police, who arrested him.

6. In an affidavit filed immediately after it occurred, bailiff Larry Pollinger stated that as Graham was being led from the courtroom after being sentenced to death he said, "Next time, I'm not leaving any witnesses."

7. Graham did have an evidentiary hearing in 1988 where two witnesses gave testimony that they were with Graham at the time of Lambert's murder. These witnesses were deemed not credible by the judge.

8. Bloodsworth's story is told in *Bloodsworth: The True Story of the First Death Row Inmate Exonerated by DNA* (Junkin 2004).

9. During their interrogations, both Hernandez and Cruz were trying to implicate each other in Jeanine Nicarico's murder in order to get a $10,000 reward that was offered for information leading to the arrest and conviction of her killer.

10. In its decision, the Illinois Supreme Court held that the trial court erred in not allowing evidence pertaining to Brian Dugan's other crimes. It also held that the court erred in allowing a police dog trainer's testimony that a bloodhound had established that more than one person had been involved in the crime, contradicting Dugan's testimony that he alone killed Jeanine Nicarico. The court ruled that "testimony as to the trailing of either a man or an animal by a blood-hound should never be admitted in evidence in *any case*" (emphasis in original, *People v. Cruz*, 162 Ill. 2d 314, 1994).

11. In *McMann v. Richardson* (1970) the Supreme Court held that "It has long been recognized that the right to counsel is the right to the effective assistance of counsel."

12. See for example, Goodpaster (1986), Bright (1994, 1999), and Geimer (1995). Goodpaster has argued that in adequately preparing for the penalty phase of a capital trial defense counsel should strive to achieve four basic objectives: (1) convey to the jury that the defendant is a member of the human community who possesses redeeming attributes; (2) demonstrate that while the defendant's act may not be forgivable, it is at least understandable given the defendant's life experiences (child or sexual abuse, history of alcoholism or drug addiction, etc.); (3) attempt to put the death penalty on trial by arguing that it is an inappropriate punishment for a civilized society either generally or in the immediate case; and (4) rebut the prosecution's evidence in aggravation. See also Goodpaster (1983) and Mello (1988).

13. For a good description of the role of informants in the criminal justice system, see Warden (2004). ✦

Part IV
What's to Come of the
Death Penalty

There are a number of issues yet to be addressed about America's experience with capital punishment. One of the most important is whether there will be a death penalty in the United States in the foreseeable future. Like most of the issues we have examined about the death penalty, this is not an easy question to answer. For the most part the death penalty in America is a state rather than a federal issue. If the legislatures of Texas or California decide they want to have capital punishment, then right now they can. "Right now" is the key phrase. There are at least two ways that capital punishment can be abolished in a state.[1] One way is by popular demand. The citizens of any given death penalty state can decide that they no longer tolerate the death penalty and can put pressure on members of their state legislature to remove the authorization to use capital punishment and impose some other penalty instead, such as life imprisonment without the possibility of parole (LWOP). In the absence of popular support, a state may be compelled to abolish capital punishment by judicial order. A state supreme court or the U.S. Supreme Court could determine (for a number of reasons) that the death penalty is in violation of the state or federal constitution and could require that it be abolished.

In addressing the question about the future of the death penalty in America in this final chapter, we cover some diverse ground. In discussing the issue of popular support for the death penalty we examine some indicators of the level and strength of approval for the death penalty in the United States. We examine some of the reasons Americans say they support the death penalty when they do. We also briefly discuss international developments in the use of capital punishment and the possible relevance these developments may have for the future of the death penalty in America. We conclude with some speculation on our part about the future of the death penalty in the United States.

Endnote

1. Some states today have not abolished capital punishment de jure—that is, in the law—but have abolished it in practice, or de facto. For example, New Hampshire has been a death penalty state since 1991 but has not executed anyone or sentenced anyone to death. ✦

Chapter 10

Capital Punishment in America's Future

In this chapter we discuss what we believe to be the future of the death penalty in America. This is not an easy issue. While the death penalty has been with us since the 1600s, there have been periods when capital punishment has fallen into disuse; some states have abandoned it completely, and others use it only infrequently. Even while using the death penalty, Americans have shown themselves to be no great fans, by restricting the types of crimes subject to the death penalty, imposing it in only a minority of cases where it is possible, and wanting to ensure that the person being executed is put to death with as little pain as humanly possible. Americans do have an uneasy and ambiguous relationship with the death penalty, while at the same time seeming to show no eagerness to get rid of it completely. What does the future hold for the death penalty in America? Perhaps a logical first place to look is at American opinions about the use of capital punishment.

Public Support for the Death Penalty in the United States

There are a number of ways to gauge how much support there is for the death penalty in the United States. One of them is to look at what public opinion polls say. Figure 10.1 reports the results of more than 50 years of public opinion polling by the Gallup Organization. In these polls respondents have been asked, "Are you in favor of the death penalty for a person convicted of murder?" Figure 10.1 shows that since at least the mid-1960s a majority of the American public has expressed approval for the death penalty. This approval reached a peak in the late 1980s and early 1990s. Since 1994, when 80 percent of those polled indicated that they favored the death penalty, support has declined to about 70 percent. This decline has coincided with revelations about numerous death-sentenced defendants found to be innocent of the crimes they were convicted of and sentenced to death for. The years 2000 to 2006 saw a slight increase in support for the death penalty, from about 66 percent in 2000 to 71 percent in 2006. We will have to wait and see whether this upward trend continues and whether support for capital punishment in the United States will again reach the highs it had in the early 1990s.

Figure 10.1 indicates that a majority of Americans today are in favor of the death penalty for murderers. Even in recent years more than two-thirds of those questioned have said they support capital punishment, at least for those who commit murder. The question that Figure 10.1 addresses, however, is whether people are in favor of the death penalty, not whether they *prefer* the

Figure 10.1   Percent in Favor of the Death Penalty for Those Convicted of Murder, 1952–2005

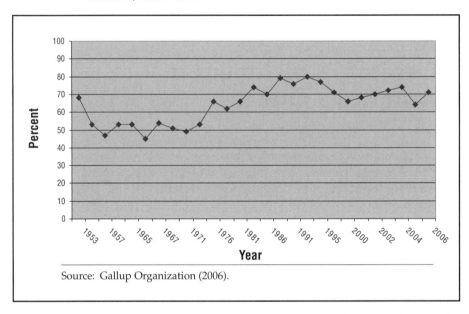

Source: Gallup Organization (2006).

death penalty for murderers compared with some other penalty. In the mid-1980s, the Gallup Organization refined its question about the death penalty and began to specify life imprisonment without parole as an alternative punishment. The question was, "If you could choose between the following two approaches [the death penalty or life imprisonment with absolutely no possibility for parole], which do you think is the better penalty for murder?" When the question is asked in this way, "support" for the death penalty declines rather dramatically. Figure 10.2 shows the percent of those polled "in favor" of the death penalty for those convicted of murder alongside the percent who reported that they would prefer the death penalty or life imprisonment without parole if given the choice.

We can now see that while a large majority of Americans consistently indicate that they generally "approve" of the death penalty for convicted murderers in the abstract (the percent indicating "approval" of the death penalty for those who murder), this percentage shrinks to a bare majority when people are asked to choose between capital punishment and life in prison without parole. Since about 2000, only slightly more than 50 percent of those polled would choose death over life imprisonment as the preferred punishment for murder. In 2004, Americans were split virtually even on the issue, with 50 percent saying they would choose the death penalty to punish murderers and 46 percent saying they would prefer life imprisonment without parole (4 percent had no opinion). In all fairness, we should add at this point that for the most part these public opinion polls do not ask about support for the death penalty in a particular case, where support might be shown to be higher. For example, approximately 80 percent of Americans polled by the Gallup Organization favored the

Figure 10.2   Percent Indicating "General Approval" of the Death Penalty (From Figure 10.1) and Percent Preferring the Death Penalty Versus Life Imprisonment

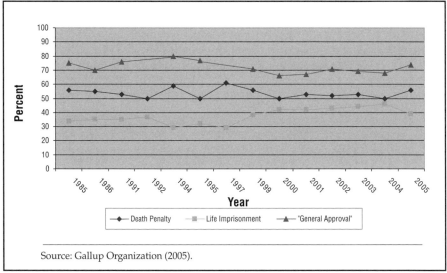

Source: Gallup Organization (2005).

execution of convicted Oklahoma City bomber Timothy McVeigh, as did more than half of those who said that they were generally opposed to the death penalty (Gallup Organization 2006). Support for the death penalty in other kinds of particularly egregious cases may also be quite high.

The perils of thinking that perhaps Americans are moving in the direction of abandoning the death penalty can be seen in the 2005 data, when public opinion had again begun to diverge. From just one year earlier, the percentage of those polled who preferred the death penalty over life imprisonment increased from 50 percent to 56 percent, while those preferring life imprisonment decreased from 46 percent to 39 percent (with 5 percent indicating no opinion). This, combined with the fact that the percentage of the public who indicated that they generally "approve" of the death penalty for those convicted of murder increased from 68 percent in 2004 to 74 percent in 2005, tends to suggest that there is no substantial disenchantment with capital punishment among the American population.

There are other indications that the public is not now tiring of the death penalty. Figure 10.3 reports the percentages of the American public saying that the death penalty is imposed "too often," "about the right amount," and "not enough." Those responding that the death penalty was being applied "too often" stayed fairly consistent at 20 percent from 2001 to 2004. This group might be thought of as "hardcore" death penalty opponents. The percent indicating that the death penalty was applied in "about the right amount" decreased from 34 percent in 2001 to only 24 percent in 2005, while the percent indicating that the death penalty was not being imposed enough increased from 38 percent in 2001 to 53 percent in 2005. Furthermore, the concern about possibly executing innocent persons, which perhaps had fueled some of the decline in support of the death penalty noted previously, may be less strong than it once was. In a Gallup Poll taken in 2003, 73 percent of those questioned said that they thought that an innocent person had been executed within the previous five years. When the identical question was asked two years later, only 59 percent thought that, a 24 percent decline.

Figure 10.3 Percent Indicating That the Death Penalty Is Imposed Too Often, About the Right Amount, and Not Enough

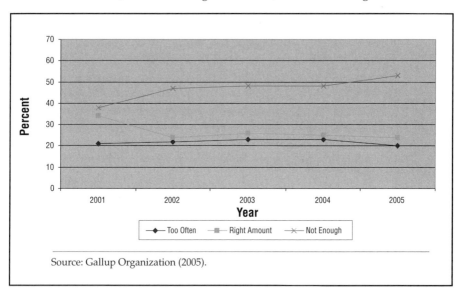

Source: Gallup Organization (2005).

Further evidence that Americans' opinion about the death penalty may be hardening can be found in other public opinion data from the Gallup Organization. As we have seen in previous chapters, for about the past 10 years over 100 cases have been brought to light in which someone on death row was exonerated and set free. In early 2000, Governor George H. Ryan of Illinois was so troubled by the administration of the death penalty in his state that in a highly publicized act he commuted all death sentences at the time to a sentence of life imprisonment (in addition to pardoning some on death row who were discovered to have been innocent). In addition, other studies have shown that the death penalty in many states may be plagued with problems of racial and geographic disparity, and newspaper and television stories have illustrated problems with state crime labs and sleeping lawyers in capital cases. This wave of "bad publicity" about the death penalty may have eroded some support in the short run, as indicated by the public opinion evidence for 2004–2005 (Figure 10.1) and 2000–2004 (Figure 10.2).

It may be, however, that the effect of this negative publicity on approval for capital punishment has run its course and might not have any long-term impact on eroding support for the death penalty. Note the upward bump in perceptions of the death penalty at the last year in Figures 10.1–10.3. In addition, most Americans continue to think that the death penalty is being applied in a fair manner, and the percent who hold this belief has been increasing over time. Figure 10.4 shows the percentage of Americans who believe that the death penalty has been fairly imposed. While in 2000 only 51 percent of those polled thought that capital punishment was fairly imposed, this figure increased to 60 percent in 2006. The percentage who thought that it was unfairly imposed declined from 41 percent in 2000 to 35 percent in 2006.

Part of this increase in the perception of a "fair" death penalty may be the fact that fewer Americans believe that an innocent person has been executed. When the Gallup Organization asked respondents in 2003 whether they thought that an innocent person had been executed in the previous five years, a large majority (73 percent) said "yes." When asked the identical question in 2005, only 59 percent agreed.

Figure 10.4 Percent Stating That They Think the Death Penalty Is Fairly/Unfairly Imposed in the U.S., 2000–2006

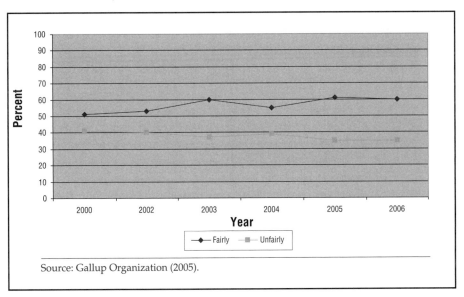

Source: Gallup Organization (2005).

What is also clear is that the upward swing in support for the death penalty observed in 2005 is not due to the fact that citizens think that capital punishment is a better deterrent to murder than life imprisonment. Figure 10.5 shows that the percentage of the American public who think that the death penalty deters murder *decreased* from 62 percent of those polled in 1985 to only 35 percent of those polled in 2004. What has not changed is the percentage of Americans in favor of the death penalty for retributive reasons (see Chapter 6 for a discussion of retribution and the death penalty). Figure 10.6 shows the percentage of Americans who said they supported the death penalty for murder because it "fits the crime" in some sense or "they deserve it." For more than 10 years approximately half of supporters of the death penalty have indicated that their approval was based on the grounds that murderers deserve to be put to death. There are, then, fairly strong and persistent moral grounds for supporting the death penalty among those who believe in it. We would also add that there seem to be strong moral grounds among those who oppose it. When those who do not support the death penalty were asked why they do not support it, nearly half said that it was "wrong to take a life."

Figure 10.5 Percent Indicating That the Death Penalty Is a Deterrent to Murder, 1985–2004

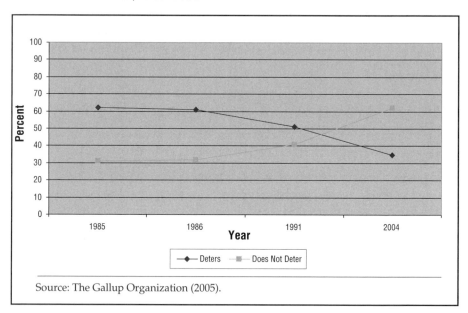

Source: The Gallup Organization (2005).

Figure 10.6 Percent Indicating They Approve of the Death Penalty Because Murderers Deserve It or It Fits the Crime, 1991–2003

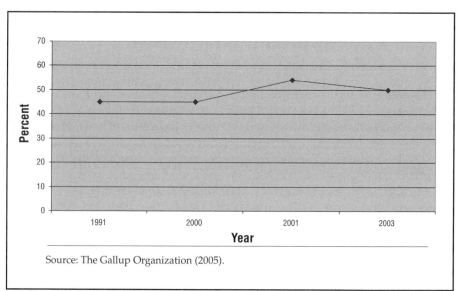

Source: The Gallup Organization (2005).

Box 10.1
Would Death Penalty Opponents Approve of the Execution of 'Moral Monsters'?

A question that opponents of the death penalty are frequently asked is whether they oppose the use of capital punishment in all cases or if there are exceptions for truly horrible offenders—so-called "moral monsters" who have committed shockingly brutal crimes. Some examples:

Timothy McVeigh: McVeigh planted a truck bomb outside the Alfred P. Murrah Federal Building in Oklahoma City on April 19, 1995. When the homemade bomb exploded, it tore off an entire side of the building. One hundred and sixty-eight people inside were killed, including children in a day care center. McVeigh called the deaths of the children "collateral damage" in his private war against the United States government. He was executed by the federal government on June 11, 2001.

John Wayne Gacy: Gacy was a Chicago-area small businessman who liked to perform as a clown at children's hospitals. During a three-year period Gacy drugged, sexually assaulted, and killed more than 30 young men, burying their remains under his house. He later admitted to police that he began dumping his victim's bodies into a nearby river because he was running out of space under the house and was getting a bad back digging all the graves. Gacy was executed by the state of Illinois on May 10, 1994.

Theodore "Ted" Bundy: Bundy had been a boy scout, a law student, and an assistant director of the Seattle Crime Prevention Advisory Committee. During the 1970s, however, he went on a crime spree. He would befriend young women with his good looks and charm only to brutalize them sexually before killing them. He confessed to more than 20 murders and may have been responsible for killing anywhere from 30 to 100 young women. Bundy was executed on January 24, 1989, in Florida.

Is the death penalty an appropriate punishment for these and other "moral monsters"? ✦

Americans seem to be deeply and about evenly divided about whether they think the death penalty is the best sanction for the crime of murder. There appear to be large groups of both strong supporters and strong opponents of the death penalty who base their position on moral grounds—what they feel to be the "right" or "most deserved" punishment. There is a smaller group among the population who express general support for the death penalty in the abstract as a punishment for murder but who find life in prison without parole a preferred alternative. A large proportion of the population would also approve of the death penalty for particularly egregious offenders such as convicted Oklahoma City bomber Timothy McVeigh, who in a single act of domestic terrorism killed 168 men, women, and children. What also seems equally clear to us is that there does not seem to be an overwhelming trend within the American populace to reject the death penalty. If opponents of capital punishment would like to see it abolished, it seems unlikely to be based on popular revolt—particularly in the most active death penalty states.

At this point it might be instructive to briefly examine the position of the international community regarding the death penalty. Do most other countries retain the death penalty as a punishment for criminal acts? If so, how often is capital punishment carried out, and for what kind of crimes? The study of the international view of capital punishment is valuable in its own right, but it also has practical utility. Recall in Chapter 4 that the meaning of the Eighth Amendment's prohibition against cruel and unusual punishment is not fixed in time but changes, reflecting "the evolving standards of decency that mark the progress of a maturing society." In a long line of Eighth Amendment cases, the Supreme Court has looked at what other countries were doing to help it gauge whether a penalty is to be considered cruel and unusual.[1] It has also conducted such a comparative analysis in death penalty cases. For example, in a footnote of his opinion for a majority of the Court in *Atkins v. Virginia*, Justice Stevens argued that in addition to the reluctance of state legislatures to impose the death penalty on the mentally retarded, "within the world community, the imposition of the death penalty for crimes committed by mentally retarded offenders is overwhelmingly disapproved" (*Atkins v. Virginia*, 122 S. Ct. 2242, 2002, at 2249, n21).[2] In the Court's opinion in *Roper v. Simmons* that struck down the death penalty for juveniles, Justice Kennedy observed that "the United States is the only country in the world that continues to give official sanction to the juvenile death penalty" (543 U.S., 551, 2005 at 575). We think it is of great value, therefore, to briefly examine beliefs about the death penalty in the "world community."[3]

The Death Penalty in Other Countries

The practice of the death penalty elsewhere in the world may be relevant not in the sense that the United States is required to blindly follow criminal justice practices in other countries but in the more subtle sense that practices in other countries can help inform the U.S. Supreme Court as to whether there is an evolving consensus that civilized nations have rejected some forms of punishment as cruel or barbaric. Clearly, international experiences are not the only indicator of what constitutes a civilized punishment, or even the most important, but they may provide one piece of information.

Figure 10.7 shows the number of countries in the world that have abolished the death penalty for all crimes (abolitionist-strict); those that have abandoned it for ordinary crimes but not for a few strictly specified extraordinary crimes such as treason (abolitionist-ordinary); those that have abolished the death penalty in practice in that, although they continue to maintain the death penalty by law, they have not executed an offender in 10 years or more (abolitionist-practice); and those countries that retain the death penalty (retention). There are more strictly abolitionist counties (86) than retentionist countries (73), and more countries have abolished capital punishment in some form (123) than have retained the death penalty for ordinary criminal offenses like murder (73). Moreover, not all countries that have retained the death penalty impose it with the same frequency. Amnesty International has estimated that approximately 2,148 executions occurred worldwide in 2005, in 22 different countries (Amnesty International 2005). About 94 percent of these executions took place in only four countries (China, Iran, Saudi Arabia, and the United States) with about 82 percent occurring in China alone (some 1,170 executions).

It is probably not true that the world has completely abandoned the death penalty. It is, however, fair to say that Western democratic countries have turned away from capital punishment and that there is likely a worldwide

Figure 10.7 Number of Countries That Have Abolished the Death Penalty in Some Form or Have Retained It, 2006

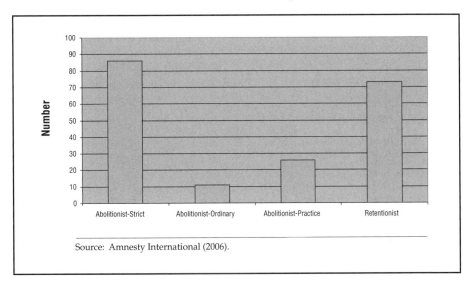

Source: Amnesty International (2006).

trend away from it. The list of strictly abolitionist countries include Belgium, Denmark, France, Germany, Ireland, Italy, the Netherlands, Norway, Spain, Sweden, Switzerland, and the United Kingdom, countries that the United States would likely consider its democratic "peers." Countries that retain the death penalty are more likely to be Islamic countries or those with weak human rights records. In addition to the number of countries that have abolished the death penalty, therefore, it is also important to look at which countries have rejected it and which continue to use it (see Table 10.1). Evidence that the world community as a whole may be moving away from the death penalty can be seen

Box 10.2
The Death Penalty in China

China is the leading death penalty country, executing more people than any other country in the world. In fact, it may execute more people annually than all other countries combined. Amnesty International estimates that at least 1,770 persons were executed in China in 2005. This is just a guess, and the real number is unknown. In March 2004, according to Amnesty International, a senior Chinese legislator stated that his country likely puts to death approximately 10,000 of its citizens a year. This may be true since the Chinese criminal justice system is shrouded in secrecy and there are scores of capital offenses in China. Not only are many violent crimes such as murder and rape capital offenses, but property crimes such as corruption, tax fraud, breaking into cars, embezzlement, and producing counterfeit currency are capital offenses.

Chinese capital defendants enjoy virtually none of the procedural projections afforded those on trial for their life in America. Moreover, torture and coerced confessions are commonplace. Capital punishment in China is usually imposed with a single bullet to the head, although death by lethal injection is becoming more prevalent. ✦

Table 10.1 Some Examples of Countries That Have Abolished the Death
Penalty and Those That Have Retained It

Abolitionist Countries		Retentionist Countries	
Australia	Ireland	Afghanistan	Japan
Austria	Italy	Belarus	Pakistan
Belgium	Netherlands	China	Palestinian Authority
Canada	New Zealand	Congo	Philippines
Denmark	Norway	Cuba	Saudi Arabia
Finland	Sweden	Egypt	Somalia
France	Switzerland	Iran	Syria
Germany	United Kingdom	Iraq	Uganda

in Figure 10.8, which indicates that the number of abolitionist countries has increased steadily over the past 20 years, and in fact has nearly doubled.

Other evidence that many nations do not regard the death penalty as an
acceptable sanction for most criminal offenses can be seen in various protocols
and international treaties. Article 6 of the United Nations International Covenant on Civil and Political Rights urges member states to abolish the death
penalty or to restrict its use to the most serious of crimes and bans its use
against juveniles, while Optional Protocol 2 abolishes it entirely (Schabas

Figure 10.8 Number of Countries That Have Abolished the Death Penalty
by Law or in Practice, 1984–2005

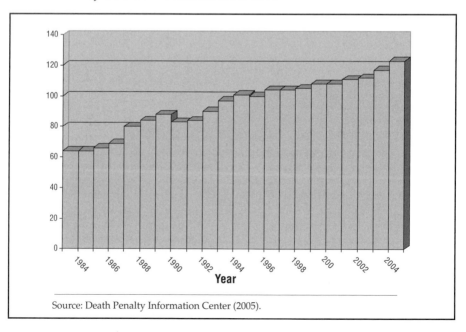

Source: Death Penalty Information Center (2005).

2002; Wilson 2003). All members of the European Union have abolished the death penalty and abolition is a requirement for those wishing to join both the EU and the Council of Europe. Protocol 13 of the European Convention of Human Rights bans the death penalty in all circumstances, even in time of war. These protocols are only binding on signatories, however, and nothing in international law explicitly forbids the death penalty.

International tribunals created by the United Nations to try war criminals from the conflict in the former Yugoslavia—crimes including the most serious against humanity—have barred the death penalty for those convicted. The International Criminal Court, which was created by the U.N. in 2002 and is a permanent court to prosecute individuals for war crimes, genocide, and other crimes against humanity, also prohibits the death penalty. In 1990, the Organization of American States, made up of countries in the Western Hemisphere including the United States, adopted the Protocol to the American Convention on Human Rights to Abolish the Death Penalty. Article 1 of this protocol urges member states to abolish the death penalty and urges those who retain it not to impose it.

Box 10.3
Out of Step With the International Community?

Until 2002 the United States was one of only a handful of countries that permitted the execution of mentally retarded persons. In a 2001 *amici curiae* (friend of the Court) brief to the Supreme Court in *McCarver v. North Carolina*, nine former U.S. diplomats argued that this practice is "manifestly inconsistent with evolving international standards of decency" and that the continued execution of the mentally retarded by the United States would "strain diplomatic relations with close American allies, provide ammunition to countries with demonstrably worse human rights records, increase U.S. diplomatic isolation, and impair the United States foreign policy interests." In June 2002 the Supreme Court struck down as "cruel and unusual" punishment the execution of mentally retarded persons in *Atkins v. Virginia*. ✦

Because of the clash between the use of capital punishment in the United States and these international agreements and treaties that attempt to abolish it, the United States has come into conflict with other nations over the death penalty with respect to the execution in the United States of foreign nationals and the extradition of suspected offenders from other countries to U.S. states that impose the death penalty. In 1989 the European Court of Human Rights blocked the extradition of German citizen Jens Soering from the United Kingdom to Virginia to face murder charges and a possible death sentence under Virginia law (Hood 2002). The basis of the court's decision was that it believed the conditions on Virginia's death row to be so deplorable that they amounted to degrading and inhumane treatment (Hood 2002). Soering was extradited to Virginia only after the European Court was given assurances that he would not be sentenced to death.

In 2001 the Canadian Supreme Court ruled against the justice minister of Canada's failure to seek assurances from the state of Washington not to impose the death penalty on Canadian citizen Glen Burns before extraditing him. This marked a change in the Canadian Supreme Court's previous position on extradition to American death penalty states. In the Burns case it argued that the new position was warranted in part because of what it called a growing rejection of the death penalty in the world (Wilson 2003). Burns and a co-defendant, Atif Rafay, were not extradited until Washington authorities stated that they would not seek the death penalty against the two. Some European countries have even indicated that they would not extradite terrorist suspects to the United States and would not cooperate in terrorist investigations with the United States because of the possibility of a federal death penalty (Amnesty International 2001; Hood 2002; Death Penalty Information Center 2005).

Conflict has occurred between the United States and other countries because U.S. states have, in violation of international law, denied foreign nationals arrested for crimes, including capital crimes, the right to communicate with the consulate of their country. Under Article 36 1(b) of the 1963 Vienna Convention on Consular Relations, an agreement initially advocated by the United States in order to protect American citizens traveling abroad and ratified by the United States without reservation in 1969, local authorities are required to inform all detained foreigners "without delay" of their right to communicate with their consulate. Further, at the request of the detained foreigner, local authorities must notify the consulate "without delay" and grant the consulate access to the detainee. This is a nontrivial set of rights, because consulates can provide substantial assistance, even legal assistance, to detained citizens. In 1997, the state of Texas executed a Mexican national, Tristan Montoya, who without the assistance of counsel signed a murder confession written in English—a language he could neither speak nor read (Amnesty International 2005). Amnesty International has reported that out of a total of 160 death sentences imposed in the United States on foreign nationals since 1975, full compliance with the requirements of Article 36 has occurred in only seven cases.

Instead of prompt notification, detained foreigners have not been notified of their right to consular access until weeks, or months after their detention. Some have gone even longer—German citizens Karl and Walter LeGrand were not even notified by Arizona authorities of their right to have access to the German consulate even though the authorities knew that the brothers were German citizens (Wilson 2003). They were convicted in Arizona of murder and armed robbery and sentenced to death. While on death row, the LeGrands found out about consular access on their own and more than 15 years after their arrest. They appealed their conviction on the grounds that they had been denied their right to consular access and that, had they had such access, they would have been able to mount a more effective defense. Their appeal was denied by all federal courts on the procedural grounds that issues cannot be raised in federal court unless they are first raised in state court (the doctrine of procedural default). Karl LaGrand was executed on February 24, 1999.

On behalf of Walter LaGrand, German authorities then took their case against the United States to the International Court of Justice (ICJ). With a provisional ruling, the ICJ granted Germany's request to halt the execution of

Walter LaGrand at least until it could make a decision on the merits of the case. Germany took this "provisional measure" to the U.S. Supreme Court for enforcement. The Supreme Court ruled against Germany on all issues and refused to grant a stay of LeGrand's execution. Although the Arizona clemency board recommended to the governor that LeGrand's execution be stayed pending resolution of the ICJ issues, he ignored the recommendation, and Walter LeGrand was executed on March 3, 1999. Germany returned to the International Court of Justice, alleging that the United States had violated international law. On June 27, 2001, the ICJ ruled that the United States had violated the tenets of the Vienna Convention requiring consular access and that it had acted unlawfully in ignoring its provisional decision to stay the execution of Walter LeGrand pending a final resolution of the legal matters. In response, the United States promised future compliance with Article 36 of the Vienna Convention regarding detained foreign nationals' right to communicate with the embassy (Hood 2002).

As of May 2006, there were 120 foreign nationals from 32 countries on death rows across the United States (Death Penalty Information Center 2005). The largest number of these foreign nationals, about half (52), were from Mexico. For example, 18-year-old Jose Medellin was arrested on June 29, 1993 for the rape and murder of two girls in Houston, Texas. Medellin informed arresting authorities that he was a Mexican citizen and not a U.S. citizen, but he was never advised of his right to have communication with the Mexican consulate. Medellin was convicted of murder and sentenced to death. In April 1997, after the Texas Court of Criminal Appeals had denied his direct appeal, the Mexican consulate first learned, through correspondence from Medellin himself, that he was a detained Mexican citizen and on death row. The Mexican consulate began assisting Medellin and in subsequent appeals argued that the death sentence should be vacated because Texas had been in violation of Article 36 of the Vienna Convention. Mexico argued in its briefs that it would have provided Medellin with immediate legal assistance had it known of his status as a Mexican citizen. Each appeal was denied. Mexican authorities then took its case to the International Court of Justice, alleging violation of Article 36 on behalf of Medellin and some 53 other Mexican nationals on death rows across the United States.

In March 2004, by a vote of 14-1, the ICJ held that the United States was in violation of Article 36 in 51 of the 54 cases, including Medellin's. It argued that the convictions and sentences in all cases ought to be vacated and the defendants granted new trials. In subsequent appeals to state and federal courts, Medellin argued that his rights to consular access had been denied, but in each case the procedural default claim that Medellin failed to raise the issue at trial was upheld. On December 10, 2004 the Supreme Court granted *cert* in the case, and oral arguments were heard on March 28, 2005. In February 2005 President George Bush issued an executive order for state courts to abide by the ruling of the International Court of Justice and review the cases of the affected Mexican nationals. The Supreme Court then dismissed Medellin's appeal as "improvidently granted" pending further examination of the case by Texas. This executive order would seem to have mended some diplomatic fences. However, on

March 7, 2005 Bush's secretary of state, Condoleezza Rice, informed the United Nations that the United States was withdrawing from the Optional Protocol to the Vienna Convention of Consular Rights.

It should be noted here that although many Western democratic countries have abolished the death penalty, the abolition may have occurred *in spite of* and not because of public opinion about the matter. For example, although Great Britain does not have the death penalty and in fact abolished it in 1965, a majority of the public was in favor of capital punishment when it was abolished, and a public opinion poll taken 10 years later indicated that 82 percent wanted the death penalty reinstated (Zimring 2003). A Gallup Poll taken in England in 2003 indicated that 55 percent of those surveyed were in favor of the death penalty for those convicted of murder (Death Penalty Information Center 2005). When Germany abolished the death penalty, 74 percent of its public were in favor of capital punishment and only 21 percent wanted abolition (Noelle and Neumann 1967). A majority of the French also supported the death penalty when it was abolished by a left-of-center government in 1981 (Marshall 2000; Steiker 2002). In fact, at the time capital punishment was abolished in many European countries the level of public support for the death penalty was high, and it did not decline until *after* abolition. The abolition of the death penalty in Europe was, therefore, not conducted by national governments on behalf of a public that demanded the end of capital punishment. On the contrary, it could be argued that the abolition of capital punishment came about as a result of antidemocratic processes, with governments acting in spite of relatively strong public sentiment that the death penalty remain (Marshall 2000; Zimring and Hawkins 1986; Zimring 2003).

It would appear that whatever the trend has been in the international community, the United States has been relatively unaffected by any worldwide movement to abolish the death penalty. States that currently have and impose the death penalty (primarily Southern and western states) have historically been relatively active death penalty states, while those that have abolished it today are states that have been long-term abolitionist or have had the death penalty "on the books" but have never imposed it with any frequency (Iowa, Maine, Michigan, Minnesota, Vermont, West Virginia, Wisconsin). In between are the large majority of states, which in the past and currently have death penalty statutes but do not execute offenders with any degree of regularity.

Given the facts that most democratic countries have abandoned the death penalty, that there are visible problems with the way the death penalty has been administered (innocence, racial disparity), that questions exist over the humaneness of the most recent method of executing offenders, and that we have doubts about how cost effective it is, is there likely to be a movement toward abolition in America's future?

Predictions About the Future of the Death Penalty in America

In the 1972 case *Furman v. Georgia*, the Supreme Court struck down existing death penalty statutes as "cruel and unusual," resulting in the vacating of over 625 death sentences to life imprisonment. When the decision was made, death penalty supporter Lt. Governor Lester Maddox of Georgia called it "a license for anarchy, rape, and murder," while opponent Jack Greenberg, a lawyer who worked on the case for the NAACP Legal Defense Fund, predicted that "there will no longer be any more capital punishment in the United States" (Meltsner 1973, 291). While Greenberg's prediction might have been more likely than Maddox's, both turned out to be false. There was no increase in violent offending or lawlessness in the wake of *Furman,* and within four years states were back sentencing offenders to death under procedurally reformed death penalty statutes.

Today, the death penalty in America seems almost as popular as it always has been. A large majority of the public report that they "favor" the death penalty for those who commit murder; a smaller majority seem to prefer the death penalty over life imprisonment; in spite of obvious problems in its administration a majority of the public still believe that the death penalty is being imposed either just enough or not enough; and most think it is being fairly imposed and not likely inflicted on the truly innocent. While some states have been abolitionist for a long period of their history (Maine, Vermont, Michigan, Wisconsin, Minnesota, Hawaii), most other states have maintained the death penalty in some form for a long time, even if they infrequently use it.

In addition to fairly consistent (and possibly increasing) public support for the death penalty in many if not all states, the number of death sentences imposed by juries, though declining over time, is still quite high. Even though the number of death sentences imposed dropped dramatically from 1994 to 2005, there were still over 125 new death sentences handed down by state and federal courts in 2005 (Death Penalty Information Center 2005).

Despite what seems to be evidence that the death penalty shows no sign of disappearing, many opponents argue that capital punishment will be abolished in the United States at some time in the not-too-distant future. Radelet and Borg (2000) and Stephen Bright (2004), for example, each strident critics of capital punishment, have written that they foresee the end of capital punishment. Radelet and Borg (2000) point to several pieces of evidence to lead them to their prediction of a gradual abolition of the death penalty: (1) the adoption of lethal injection as the preferred method of execution speaks to an uneasiness with the death penalty and indicates that even those in favor of the death penalty see a limit on retribution (the electric chair inflicts too much suffering); (2) public opinion polls taken in the late 1990s indicated the beginning of a disenchantment with the death penalty in the United States, as a lower percentage indicated general support for the death penalty and many preferred life in prison without parole; and (3) there is a general worldwide decline in the use of capital punishment. Taking this evidence as a whole, Radelet and Borg (2000) drew the conclusion that "[f]or those who oppose the death penalty, the long-term forecast should fuel optimism" (p. 57).

In an essay titled, "Why the United States Will Join the Rest of the World in Abandoning Capital Punishment," death penalty lawyer and critic Stephen Bright (2004) argues that it is "inevitable" that the United States will abolish the death penalty. His reasons include what Bright takes as the "realities" of capital punishment: the facts that the death penalty undermines the moral authority of the United States in international affairs, that it is unfairly imposed against the poor and racial minorities, and that it results in the conviction and possible execution of innocent persons. Bright argues that when Americans are fully aware of the realities of the way the death penalty is administered in the United States, they will abandon it as they have other uncivilized punishments of the past.

One of the "deans" of death penalty scholarship, Frank Zimring (2003), also sees an America without the death penalty in the future, but not without some concerted action on the part of those who wish to see it abolished. Zimring has developed a long-term political/moral/cultural strategy that includes a program of creating public debate and discourse about the death penalty and the many problems in administering it, a program that would weaken support for capital punishment among those whose support is "soft" and increase the resolve of those who are opposed to it. In each of these instances the author is convinced that the death penalty will at some point in the near future be abandoned in America as a legitimate sanction by state and local government.

Our own view about the future of the death penalty in America is decidedly more pessimistic than those just expressed. We think that there are more than enough signs to indicate that the death penalty is going to be with us for a long time. To be sure, we are not saying that the United States will be executing large numbers of offenders at a level approximating what we saw in the 1930s and 1940s. No, part of the future of the death penalty in America is that it will continue because it will continue to be infrequently used. While some states may abolish capital punishment within a few decades, our view is that those that do will not be among the currently active execution states and that all Southern states (where the lion's share of executions occur) will retain it. Why are we so pessimistic?

First, there is the issue of public opinion. Measured a number of different ways, public support for the death penalty remains not only fairly high, but consistent as well. Figure 10.1 indicated that general approval for the death penalty has hovered near 70 percent since at least 1980. While there was some decline for a few years, approval has never dropped below 60 percent and it increased somewhat from 2004 to 2005. Whether this is going to be a general trend upward to 75–80 percent approval we do not know, but general support for the death penalty among the public has been amazingly high and consistent. What has also been consistent is the fact that when asked, a majority of the public seem to prefer the death penalty to life imprisonment without parole. Figure 10.2 indicated that while general support for the death penalty declines when LWOP is included as an alternative, a majority of the public still favor death over life, and from 2004 to 2005 this majority increased. What is remarkable, and a testimony to the resilience of this support for the death penalty, is that disapproval for the death penalty did not really substantially increase in the wake of what might be thought of as "scandals" such as the coming to light of widespread police and prosecutor misconduct in Illinois, official and unofficial moratoriums on the death penalty in some states in order to study its fairness, the publicizing of sleeping lawyers in death penalty cases, and the exoneration of over 100 former death row inmates. While the decade from

1990 to 2000 revealed profound problems with the way the death penalty was being administered, these revelations did not really translate into a dramatic decline in general support among the American public for it. As we have noted, it may be that the death penalty has "weathered the storm" of its most recent scandals, and public support may recover over the next few years.

Nor are we optimistic that the international movement toward abolition will have any appreciable effect on the future of the death penalty in the United States. While there has been a steady increase in the number of abolitionist-in-some-form countries, this movement has been mainly driven by political rather than social or cultural changes. We have discussed the fact that the European Union and Council of Europe have passed a number of treaties requiring members *and those wishing to become members* to abandon the death penalty. A large number of Eastern European countries have recently abolished the death penalty either completely (Bulgaria, Czech Republic, Croatia, Hungary, Lithuania, Poland, Slovak Republic, Ukraine, Yugoslavia) or for ordinary crimes (Bosnia-Herzegovina, Estonia, Hungary, Turkey) in order to make it more likely that they could join the European Union, the Council of Europe, or the North Atlantic Treaty Organization (NATO). It is not likely that these abolitionist events, driven as they were by political expediency rather than any widespread cultural or social movement, will have any impact on abolition in the United States.

A second obstacle in the way of any profound impact of international abolition on the death penalty in the United States is the fact that for the most part capital punishment is a business of the states and not the national government, and most states are isolated from and immune to international pressure. Capital punishment will be with us (or at least some of us) for a while, then, because of federalism—the separation of federal and state powers—which may be the most influential impediment to abolition. The vast majority of both death sentences and executions in the United States are conducted by states rather than the federal government. We doubt that either individual countries alone or countries working in organized concert (for example, the European Union) will have the kind of impact on the abolition of the death penalty in Texas, Virginia, or other states that it has had on other European countries. This feeling was perhaps best expressed by John B. Holmes, Jr., the district attorney of Harris County, Texas, which has put more people on death row than any other jurisdiction in the country: "When one of the national television news programs was pushing me about why we sent so many people to death row, I told the anchor that it's nobody's business but Texans', I said, I don't give a flip how you all feel about it" (Gwynne 2002).

There was a time when it was the United States that was leading the movement away from the death penalty. In the mid-1960s, when much of Europe still retained and used the death penalty, the United States had virtually stopped. Figure 10.9 shows the annual number of executions in the United States from 1972 (when *Furman* was decided) until 2006, along with the years when European countries were abolishing the death penalty. It shows that American practices with respect to the death penalty were consistent with those of its European allies until 1976, when capital punishment was reestablished in many states de jure and by the 1980s when executions resumed with greater frequency. At the time of the *Furman* decision, then, in 1972 America was more abolitionist than most of Europe (and most of the world). Had *Furman* been decided more forcefully and by a less divisive Supreme Court, capital punishment might have been abolished in the United States. By 1976, however, with the decision of *Gregg v. Georgia* and its companion cases, the Court appeared to adopt the position that it was going to regulate the states' use of the death penalty rather than forbid it (see also, Steiker and Steiker 1995).

Our own prediction is that the death penalty will continue to be available

Figure 10.9 Number of Executions in the U.S. and Years When European Countries Abolished It, 1972–2006

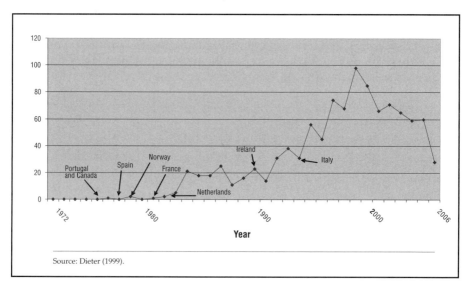

Source: Dieter (1999).

in a majority of U.S. states in the foreseeable future. If past is prologue, most states will have the death penalty as a sanction for the most serious crimes, but it will be mostly "on the books" and not be imposed frequently; a handful of states will be active execution states but even within those active states most of the death penalty business (death sentences and executions) will be generated by a smaller number of jurisdictions within those active states; and while there will continue to be problems raised in the future about the death penalty in terms of how fairly it is being implemented, how costly it is, whether it deters, or whether innocent people are being put to death, it will remain a constant feature of the American criminal justice system. In fact, to the extent that the number of executions remains low and the province of only a few active states and a few jurisdictions in those states, there will not be a great deal of action toward abolishing the death penalty. There may be movement toward "refining" some features of capital punishment similar to what has occurred in the past—new and "more humane" methods of execution, a narrowing of the kinds of crimes eligible for the death penalty, procedural reforms such as enhanced standards for counsel in death penalty cases or additional funding for the defense of capital cases—and some states (those that only infrequently used the death penalty and were close to abolition anyway) may temporarily abandon capital punishment in favor of life without parole. In short, we think there will be additional "tinkering with the machinery of death" but no widespread abandonment of the practice. What we see, therefore, is that as a country, our experience with the death penalty will continue well into the future.

What About Life Without the Possibility of Parole?

One alternative to the death penalty that has been frequently discussed in policy debates is life without the possibility of parole (LWOP). Currently, 37 of the 38 jurisdictions that have the death penalty also provide the option of a sentence of life without parole. New Mexico is the only death penalty state that does not have LWOP as a possible penalty. Of the 12 states that do not have the death penalty, 11 provide for the penalty of life without parole (Alaska does not). At least in the eyes of the public, LWOP is a viable alternative to the death penalty. Figure 10.2 indicated that while 50 percent of the public seemed to prefer the death penalty for those who have committed murder, almost as many (46 percent) preferred life imprisonment as the appropriate punishment. It is not clear, however, that LWOP will ever completely replace the death penalty. States that use capital punishment frequently (Texas, Virginia) have also allowed convicted capital offenders to be sent to prison for life, but death sentences have continued there and in other states. With about 60 percent of the public also believing that death is a "morally acceptable" punishment for murder (Gallup Organization 2006), the number of death sentences is not likely to dramatically decline soon. This brings up an interesting question: Why hasn't the availability of a life without parole sentence eliminated the need for the death penalty? The answer to this question, though admittedly conjectural, converges with the central issue in this final chapter, the future of the death penalty in America.

LWOP serves many of the functions of capital punishment. It promises to protect the public by keeping murderers behind bars for the rest of their life. Because those doing life terms can theoretically escape and commit another crime, or can commit criminal acts behind bars, LWOP is not as effective as the death penalty at incapacitating murderers, but it's close. While not as good as capital punishment at preventing future crimes by murderers, it is better in another way: LWOP would ensure that no innocent person is ever executed. While errors could occur and an innocent person could be convicted and sentenced to life in prison, this error could be later corrected. This situation is not possible if a person is executed and later found to be innocent. Finally, life in prison without the possibility of parole is a serious punishment. As the most serious punishment short of executing someone, it is a severe enough sanction to honor the moral wrong caused by a murder. In other words, while short of a death sentence, life without parole is still a painful punishment that does not trivialize the criminal act committed.

But here is the catch. While LWOP is a serious punishment *it is not death*. The offender sentenced to life without parole still has life, while the murder victim does not. However serious and painful a life without parole sentence is, and virtually all parties to the debate agree that LWOP is a severe punishment, it still lets the offender live. For those who believe in a strict notion of retribution—"an eye for an eye, a tooth for a tooth"—even life in prison will not suffice. For perhaps a majority (but a bare majority) of Americans (see Figure 10.8) death is the morally appropriate punishment for those who murder. For these, LWOP will not provide the level of punishment morally required for a murder. The central issue, then, is the strength of the moral or retributive requirement that murder be punished by the death of the murderer.

Because the death penalty is largely an issue of federalism, what states are doing is critical. We know that the death penalty is used far more frequently in Southern (and Western) states than anywhere else in the country. The "American" death penalty is really a "Southern" death penalty. We know also that support for the death penalty is higher in the South than in other regions. In 2005, 68 percent of polled Southerners reported that they were in favor of the death penalty for those who commit murder, compared with 65 percent in the west, 64 percent in the midwest, and only 59 percent in the east (Gallup Organization 2005). More Southerners also believe in the "fairness" of the death penalty. When asked if they thought the death penalty was being fairly applied in the country, 64 percent of those in the South said "yes," compared with 53 percent in the east, 52 percent in the midwest, and 48 percent in the west (Gallup Organization 2005). There is also evidence to support the position that Southern conservatism and religious fundamentalism is positively related to the death penalty—those with very conservative political views and religiously fundamentalist views are more inclined than others to support punitive and retributive punishment, including capital punishment (Grasmick et al. 1992, 1993; Grasmick, Bursick, and Blackwell 1993; Nisbett and Dov 1996; Borg 1997; Britt 1998; Baumer, Messner, and Rosenfeld 2003; Stack 2003; Unnever and Cullen 2006). So there is a population in the Southern "Bible Belt" with conservative political views and fundamentalist religious/moral views that incline them to support more punitive and retributive criminal justice policies such as capital punishment (Zimring and Hawkins 1986). For persons with such retributive views, the punishment of life imprisonment without parole is a morally insufficient punishment for those who commit murder. The Bible Belt is then translated into the "Death Belt." Added to this is the fact that politicians (and elected state judges and prosecutors are politicians) can appeal to these populist sentiments, as seen in the comments made by Harris County, Texas District Attorney John B. Holmes, Jr., it becomes reasonable to think that there will continue to be pockets of strong support for capital punishment, particularly in the South. This support, along with federalism, will ensure the existence and perhaps the health of the death penalty in America for years to come.

Chapter Summary

Public support for the death penalty is consistently high when expressed as general "approval" for its use as a punishment for those convicted of murder. Although the strength of the support has varied, being as high as 80 percent in 1994 and as low as 45 percent in 1966, during the Modern Period of capital punishment it has never dropped below 60 percent. Approval of the death penalty for those who commit murder does not mean that people strongly prefer capital punishment to an alternative sanction such as life in prison without the possibility of parole. In fact, when asked which penalty for murderers they prefer, barely more than half of Americans say that they prefer death to life in prison. In recent years highly publicized cases of innocent people being mistakenly sentenced to death and questions by many governors of whether they should impose a moratorium on executions may have temporarily weakened public support for capital punishment. It remains to be seen whether or not such negative publicity or any new events will continue to weaken support for the death penalty or whether support will rebound.

The United States is the only Western democracy to currently use the death penalty. All European countries have abolished it and require abolition of the death penalty for entry into the European Union and Council of Europe. Many of those countries that do use capital punishment have histories of authoritarian government and a neglect of if not outright hostility toward human rights. Although there may be some reforms of the death penalty, it is a punishment that has been with us since colonial times, and it shows no sign of disappearing in the near future.

Discussion Questions

1. What do you see as the future of capital punishment in the United States?

2. Do you think that lethal injection will be declared an unconstitutional form of punishment? Why or why not? If you think it will be declared unconstitutional, what do you think will replace it?

3. Does the fact that no Western European country imposes the death penalty affect your own opinion about it? Why or why not?

4. Should the United States or European Union use its economic power (trade embargos, and so on) to force China to abolish capital punishment or at least bring it in line with Western European legal standards?

5. What are the arguments for and against abolishing the death penalty in the United States and replacing it with life without parole? What would be gained and what would be lost?

Student Resources

If you are interested in the issue of public opinion and the death penalty, consult the following sources:

Death Penalty Information Center: <www.deathpenaltyinfo.org/>.

The Gallup Polling Organization: <www.gallup.com/>.

The National Opinion Research Center: <www.norc.uchicago.edu/>.

For information about the death penalty internationally (albeit with an antideath penalty spin), visit the website of Amnesty International: <www.amnesty.org/>.

An interesting account of life in prison is given by James A, Paluch, Jr., in *A Life for a Life* (2004). Mr. Paluch, who is serving a life sentence without parole in

Pennsylvania for first degree murder, gives a vivid picture of what serving a life sentence in prison means.

Endnotes

1. For example, in rejecting the penalty of denaturalization in *Trop v. Dulles* (356 U.S. 86, 1958) the Court stated that "The civilized nations of the world are in virtually unanimity that statelessness is not to be imposed as punishment for crime" (at 100).

2. Earlier, in the case of *Thompson v. Oklahoma* (487 U.S. 815, 1988) Justice Stevens writing for a plurality of the Court argued that states cannot execute any person who was under the age of 16 at the time of the offense. In support he noted that a ban on executing those under 16 is supported by "other nations that share our Anglo-American heritage, and by the leading members of the Western European community" (at p. 830).

3. Not all would agree that what the other countries of the world have to say about the death penalty is relevant for Americans. Justice Scalia, in his dissent in *Atkins*, sharply rebuked the Court for looking at capital punishment practices in other countries: "Equally irrelevant are the practices of the 'world community,' whose notions of justice are thankfully not always those of our people" (at p. 2264). He again chided the Court for in part relying on international practices in striking down the juvenile death penalty in *Roper* saying that "Because I do not believe that the meaning of our Eighth Amendment, any more than the meaning of other provisions of our Constitution, should be determined by the subjective views of five members of this Court and like-minded foreigners, I dissent" (at p. 608). ✦

About the Authors

Ray Paternoster is professor in the Department of Criminology and Criminal Justice at the University of Maryland. He has conducted studies of the capital sentencing systems of both South Carolina and Maryland, juror attitudes in capital cases, and is currently involved in a study of the effect of victim impact evidence in capital cases. He is the author of a previous book on the death penalty, *Capital Punishment in America*. In addition to issues related to capital punishment, Ray is interested in criminological theory, offender decision making, and quantitative methods.

Robert Brame is an associate professor in the Department of Criminology and Criminal Justice at the University of South Carolina. He received his M.S. in Criminal Justice from the University of North Carolina at Charlotte and his Ph.D. in Criminology and Criminal Justice from the University of Maryland. His current research emphasizes capital punishment, continuity and cessation of offending, collateral consequences of a criminal record, estimation of treatment effects in observational data, and law enforcement responses to domestic violence.

Sarah Bacon is an assistant professor in the College of Criminology and Criminal Justice at Florida State University. She earned her Ph.D. in criminology from the University of Maryland in 2006. In addition to her research on the death penalty, she conducts research on life-course and developmental theories of offending behavior, desistance from crime, testing criminological theory, and offender re-entry. ✦

References

Alotta, Robert I. (1989). *War Justice: Union Army Executions*. Shippensburg, PA: White Mane Publishing.

American Civil Liberties Union (2004). *The Forgotten Population: A Look at Death Row in the United States Through the Experiences of Women*. Available online at <www.afsc.org/forgotten-population>.

American Friends Service Committee (2006). *The Death Penalty: The Religious Community Calls for Abolition*. Available at <www.deathpenaltyreligious.org/resources>.

American Medical Association (2006). *Code of Medical Ethics*. Available at <http://ama-assn.org/>.

Amnesty International (2001). *United States of America No Return to Execution—The US Death Penalty as a Barrier to Extradition*. London: Amnesty International Publications.

——. (2004). *Executed According to Law? The Death Penalty in China*. London: Amnesty International Publications.

——. (2005). *Amnesty International Report— 2005: The State Of the World's Human Rights*. London: Amnesty International Publications.

——. (2006). <http://web.amnesty.org/pages/deathpenalty-index-eng>.

Anderson, Scott (1991). As Flies to Wanton Boys: Death Eligible Defendants in Georgia and Colorado. *Trial Talk* 40: 9–16.

Armstrong, Ken and Steve Mills (1999a). The Failure of the Death Penalty in Illinois. Part 1: Death Row Justice Derailed. *Chicago Tribune* November 14.

——. (1999b). The Failure of the Death Penalty in Illinois. Part 2: Inept Defense Cloud Verdict. *Chicago Tribune*, November 15.

Armstrong, Ken and Maurice Possley (1999) Trial and Error. Part 1: Verdict: Dishonor. *Chicago Tribune*, January 10.

Ayers, Edward L. (1984). *Vengeance and Justice: Crime and Punishment in the 19th-Century American South*. New York: Oxford University Press.

Baca, Maria Elena (2001). Sandra Day O'Connor Speaks in Minneapolis. *Minneapolis Star Tribune*, July 23.

Baicker, Katherine (2004). The Budgetary Repercussions of Capital Convictions. *Advances in Economic Analysis and Policy*, Volume 4, Issue 1, Article 6.

Bailey, William C. (1982). Capital Punishment and Lethal Assaults Against Police. *Criminology* 19:608–625.

——. (1983). Disaggregation in Deterrence and Death Penalty Research: The Case of Murder in Chicago. *Journal of Criminal Law and Criminology* 74:827–859.

——. (1990). Murder, Capital Punishment, and Television: Execution Publicity and Homicide Rates. *American Sociological Review* 55:628–633.

Baldus, David C. and James W. Cole (1975). Statistical Evidence on the Deterrent Effect of Capital Punishment: A Comparison of the Work of Thorsten Sellin and Isaac Ehrlich on the Deterrent Effect of Capital Punishment. *Yale Law Journal* 85: 170–186.

Baldus, David C. and George G. Woodworth (2003). Race Discrimination in the Administration of the Death Penalty: An Overview of the Empirical Evidence with Special Emphasis on the Post-1990 Research. *Criminal Law Bulletin* 39: 194–227.

Baldus, David C., George G. Woodworth, Catherine M. Grosso, and Aaron M. Christ (2002). Arbitrariness and Discrimination in the Application of the Death Penalty: A Legal and Empirical Analysis of the Nebraska Experience (1973–1999). *Nebraska Law Review* 81:194–227.

Baldus, David C., George G. Woodworth, and Charles A. Pulaski, Jr. (1990). *Equal Justice and the Death Penalty*. Boston: Northeastern University Press.

Baldus, David C., George G. Woodworth, David Zuckerman, and Neil A. Weiner (1998). Racial Discrimination and the Death Penalty in the Post-*Furman* Era: An Empirical and Legal Overview, With Recent Findings From Philadelphia. *Cornell Law Review* 83:1638–1770.

Baltimore Sun (2001). "Justice O'Connor Expresses New Doubts About Fairness of Capital Punishment," *Baltimore Sun,* July 4.

Banner, Stuart (2002). *The Death Penalty: An American History*. Cambridge: Harvard University Press.

Baumer, Eric D., Steven F. Messner, and Richard Rosenfeld (2003). Explaining Spatial Variation in Support for Capital Punishment: A Multilevel Analysis *American Journal of Sociology* 108:844–875.

Beck, E. M., James L. Massey, and Stewart E. Tolnay (1989). The Gallows, the Mob, and the Vote: Legal Sanctioning of Blacks in North Carolina and Georgia, 1882–1930. *Law and Society Review* 23:317–331.

Bedau, Hugo A. (1964). Death Sentences in New Jersey 1907–1969. *Rutgers Law Review* 19:1–64.

———. (1965). Capital Punishment in Oregon 1903–1964. *Oregon Law Review* 45:1–39.

———. (1982) *The Death Penalty in America* (3rd Edition). New York: Oxford University Press.

———. (2004). An Abolitionist's Survey of the Death Penalty in America Today. Pp. 15–50, In Hugo A. Bedau and Paul G. Cassell (Eds.), *Debating the Death Penalty*. New York: Oxford University Press.

Bedau, Hugo A. and Michael Radelet (1987). Miscarriages of Justice in Potentially Capital Cases. *Stanford Law Review* 40:21–179.

Berg, Thomas C. (2000). Religious Conservatives and the Death Penalty. *William and Mary Bill of Rights Journal* 9:31–60.

Berger, Raoul (1982). *Death Penalties: The Supreme Court's Obstacle Course*. Cambridge, MA: Harvard University Press.

Berk, Richard (2005). New Claims About Executions and General Deterrence: Déjà Vu All Over Again. *Journal of Empirical Legal Studies* 2:303–330.

Berk, Richard, Azusa Li, and Laura J. Hickman (2005). Statistical Difficulties in Determining the Role of Race in Capital Cases: A Re-Analysis of Data from the State of Maryland. *Journal of Quantitative Criminology* 21:365–390.

Berk, Richard and Joseph Lowery (1985). *Factors Affecting Death Penalty Decisions in Mississippi*. Unpublished manuscript.

Berlin, Ira (1998). *Many Thousands Gone: The First Two Centuries of Slavery in North America*. Cambridge, MA: Harvard University Press.

———. (2003). *Generations of Captivity: A History of African-American Slaves*. Cambridge, MA: Harvard University Press.

Berns, Walter (1980). Defending the Death Penalty. *Crime and Delinquency* 26:503–511.

———. (1987). *For Capital Punishment.* New York: Basic Books.

———. (1991). *For Capital Punishment* (2nd Edition). Lanham, MD: University Press of America.

Berry, Wendell. (1989). *The Hidden Wound.* New York: North Point Press.

Bienen, Leigh B., Neil A. Weiner, Deborah W. Denno, Paul D. Allison, and D. L. Mills (1988) The Reimposition of Capital Punishment in New Jersey: The Role of Prosecutorial Discretion. *Rutgers Law Review* 41:27–372.

Blume, John H. and Sheri Lynn Johnson (2000). Don't Take His Eye, Don't Take His Tooth, and Don't Cast the First Stone: Limiting Religious Arguments in Capital Cases. *William and Mary Bill of Rights Journal* 9: 61–104.

Blume, John H., Theodore Eisenberg, and Sheri Lynn Johnson. (1998). Post-*McCleskey* Racial Discrimination Claims in Capital Cases. *Cornell Law Review* 83:1771–1810.

Borg, Marian J. (1997). The Southern Subculture of Punitiveness? Regional Variation in Support for Capital Punishment. *Journal of Research in Crime and Delinquency* 34:25–46.

Borg, Marian J. and Michael L. Radelet (2004). On Botched Executions. Pp. 143–168 in Peter Hodgkinson and William A. Schabas (Eds.), *Capital Punishment: Strategies for Abolition.* Cambridge, UK: Cambridge University Press.

Bowers, William J. and Glenn L. Pierce (1980a). Arbitrariness and Discrimination Under Post-*Furman* Capital Statutes. *Crime and Delinquency* 26:563–575.

———. (1980b). Deterrence or Brutalization: What Is the Effect of Executions? *Crime and Delinquency* 26:453–484.

Bowers, William J. (1983). The Pervasiveness of Arbitrariness and Discrimination Under Post-*Furman* Capital Statutes. *Journal of Criminal Law and Criminology* 74:1067–1100.

Bragg, Rick (2000). Florida Inmate Claims Abuse in Execution. *New York Times,* June 9, at A14.

Brands, H. W. (2005). *Andrew Jackson: His Life and Times.* New York: Doubleday.

Bright, Steven B. (1994). Counsel for the Poor: The Death Penalty Not for the Worst Crime, But for the Worst Lawyer. *Yale Law Journal* 103:1835—1883.

———. (1999). Neither Equal Nor Just: The Rationing and Denial of Legal Services to the Poor When Life and Liberty are at Stake. *New York University School of Law Annual Survey of American Law* 1997: 783–836.

———. (2004). Why the United States Will Join the Rest of the World in Abandoning Capital Punishment. Pp. 152–182, in Hugo A. Bedau and Paul G. Cassell (Eds.), *Debating the Death Penalty.* New York: Oxford University Press.

Britt, Chester. L. (1998). Race, Religion, and Support for the Death Penalty: A Research Note. *Justice Quarterly* 15:175–191.

Brugger, E. Christian (2003). *Capital Punishment and Roman Catholic Moral Tradition.* Notre Dame, IN: University of Notre Dame Press.

Brundage, W. Fitzhugh (1993). *Lynching in the New South.* Urbana: University of Illinois Press.

Cassell, Paul G. (2004). In Defense of the Death Penalty. Pp. 183–217 in Hugo A. Bedau and Paul G. Cassell (Eds.), *Debating the Death Penalty.* New York: Oxford University Press.

Cassell, Paul G. and Stephen J. Markman (1988). Protecting the Innocent: A Response to the Bedau-Radelelt Study. *Stanford Law Review* 41:121-160.

Cheever, Joan M. (2006). *Back from the Dead: One Woman's Search for the Men Who Walked Off America's Death Row.* New York: John Wiley.

Chressanthis, George A. (1989). Capital Punishment and the Deterrent Effect Revisited: Recent Time-Series Econometric Evidence. *Journal of Behavioral Economics* 18:

Cloninger, Dale O. (1977). Death and the Death Penalty: A Cross-Sectional Analysis. *Journal of Behavioral Economics* 6:87–106.

Cloninger, Dale O. and Roberto Marchesini (2001). Execution and Deterrence: A Quasi-Controlled Group Experiment. *Journal of Applied Economics* 33: 569–576.

———. (2005). Execution Moratoriums, Commutations and Deterrence: The Case of Illinois. *Journal of Applied Economics.* 38: 967–973.

Cochran, John K., Mitchell B. Chamlin, and Mark Seth (1994). Deterrence or Brutalization?: An Impact Assessment of Oklahoma's Return to Capital Punishment. *Criminology* 32:107–134.

Cohen, Stanley (2003). *The Wrong Men: America's Epidemic of Wrongful Death Row Convictions.* New York: Carroll and Graf Publishers.

Cook, Rhonda (2001). Gang Leader Executed by Injection Death Comes 25 Years After Boy, 11, Slain. *Atlanta Journal Constitution* Nov. 7, p. B1.

Cook, Philip J. and Donna B. Slawson (1993). *The Costs of Processing Murder Cases in North Carolina.* Durham, NC: Terry Sanford Institute of Public Policy, Duke University.

Cooley, Craig M. (2004). Reforming the Forensic Science Community to Avert the Ultimate Injustice. *Stanford Law and Policy Review* 15: 381–441.

Cover, James P. and Paul D. Thistle (1988). Time Series, Homicide, and the Deterrent Effect of Capital Punishment. *Southern Economic Journal* 54:615–622.

Dann, Robert H. (1935). The Deterrent Effect of Capital Punishment. *Friends Social Service Series* 29:1–20.

Date, Shirish V. (2000). The High Price of Killing Killers. *Palm Beach Post,* January 4, at 1A.

Davis, David Brion (2006). *Inhuman Bondage: The Rise and Fall of Slavery in the New World.* New York: Oxford University Press.

Davis, Burke (1988). *The Civil War: Strange and Fascinating Facts.* New York: Random House.

Death Penalty Information Center (2005). Available at: <http://www.death penaltyinfo.org>.

Deathpenaltyreligious.org (2006). <http://www.deathpenaltyreligious.org/education/statements>.

Denno, Deborah W. (1994). Is Electrocution an Unconstitutional Method of Execution? The Engineering of Death Over the Century. *William and Mary Law Review* 35:591–692.

———. (1997). Getting to Death: Are Executions Constitutional? *Iowa Law Review* 82:319–464.

———. (2003). Lethally Humane? The Evolution of Execution Methods in the United States. Pp. 693–762, in James R. Acker, Robert M. Bohm, and Charles S. Lanier (Eds.), *America's Experiment With Capital Punishment.* Durham, NC: Carolina Academic Press.

DeVise, Daniel (2001). For 14 Years, Justice Failed a Man Condemned to Die. *Miami Herald,* June 25.

Dezhbakhsh, Hashem and Joanna Shepherd (2004). The Deterrent Effect of Capital Punishment: Evidence from a "Judicial Experiment." *Emory University Law and Economics Research Paper Series,* Paper No. 04–04.

Dezhbakhsh, Hashem, Paul H. Rubin, and Joanna Shepherd (2003). Does Capital Punishment Have a Deterrent Effect? New Evidence From Post-Moratorium Panel Data. *American Law and Economics Review* 5:344–376.

Dieter, Richard C. (1999). International Perspectives on the Death Penalty: A Costly Isolation for the U.S. Report for the Death Penalty Information Center. Available online at: <http://deathpenaltyinfo.org>.

Divinci, D. D. (2005). *Dead Family Walking: The Bourque Family Story of Dead Man Walking*. New Iberia, LA: Goldlamp Publishing.

Donohue, John J. and Justin Wolfers (2006). Uses and Abuses of Empirical Evidence in the Death Penalty Debate. *Stanford Law Review* 58:791–846.

Douglas, Davison M. (2000). God and the Executioner: The Influence of Western Religion on the Death Penalty. *William and Mary Bill of Rights Journal* 9:137–170.

Dow, David R. (1996). The State, the Death Penalty and Carl Johnson. *Boston University Law Review* 37:691–711.

Duff, Charles (2001). *Handbook on Hanging*. New York: New York Review of Books.

Edds, Margaret (2003). *An Expendable Man: The Near-Execution of Earl Washington Jr.* New York: New York University Press.

Ehrlich, Isaac (1975). The Deterrent Effect of Capital Punishment: A Question of Life and Death. *American Economic Review* 65:397–417.

Espy, M. Watt and John O. Smykla (2002). *Executions in the United States, 1608–1987: The Espy File* [machine-readable data file]. John O. Smykla (producer), Tuscaloosa, Alabama. Inter-university Consortium for Political and Social Research (distributor), Ann Arbor, MI.

Essig, Mark (2003). *Edison and the Electric Chair: A Story of Light and Death*. New York: Walker Publishing.

Fabrycki, Emily (1993). *The Penry Penalty: Capital Punishment and Offenders with Mental Retardation*. Lanham, MD: University Press of America.

Fagan, Jeffrey, Franklin E. Zimring, and Amanda Geller (2006). Capital Punishment and Capital Murder: Market Share and the Deterrent Effects of the Death Penalty. *Texas Law Review* 84:1803–1867.

Fischer, David H. (1989) *Albion's Seed: Four British Folkways in America*. New York: Oxford University Press.

Flanagan, T. J. and K. Maguire (1990). *Sourcebook of Criminal Justice Statistics*. Washington, DC: U.S. Department of Justice, Bureau of Justice Statistics.

Foner, Eric (1983). *Nothing But Freedom: Emancipation and Its Legacy*. Baton Rouge: Louisiana State University Press.

Foner, Eric and Olivia Mahoney (1995). *America's Reconstruction: People and Politics After the Civil War*. New York: HarperCollins.

Freedman, Eric M. (2001). Earl Washington's Ordeal. *Hofstra Law Review* 29:1089–1112.

———. (2003). Add Resources and Apply Them Systematically: Governments' Responsibilities Under the Revised ABS Capital Defense Representation Guidelines. *Hofstra Law Review* 31:1097–1104.

Frey, Robert S. and Nancy Thompson-Frey (2002). *The Silent and the Damned: The Murder of Mary Phagan and the Lynching of Leo Frank*. Lanham, MD: Rowman and Littlefield.

Gallup Orgaization (2005). <http://poll.gallup.com>.

———. (2006). <http://poll.gallup.com>.

Garfinkel, Harold (1949). Research Note on Inter- and Intra-Racial Homicides. *Social Forces* 27:369–380.

Geimer, William (1995). A Decade of Strickland's Tin Horn: Doctrinal and Practical Undermining of the Right to Counsel. *William and Mary Bill of Rights Journal* 4:91–178.

Gelman, Andrew, James S. Liebman, Valerie West, and Alexander Kiss (2004). A Broken System: The Persistent Pattern of Reversals of Death Sentences in the United States. *Journal of Empirical Legal Studies* 1:209–261.

Ginsburg, Ruth Bader (2001). In Pursuit of the Public Good: Lawyers Who Care. Joseph L. Rauh Lecture. David A. Clarke School of Law, University of the District of Columbia. April 9, 2001.

Goodpaster, Gary (1983). The Trial for Life: Effective Assistance of Counsel in Death Penalty Cases. *New York University Law Review* 52:299–362.

——. (1986). The Adversary System, Advocacy and the Effective Assistance of Counsel in Criminal Cases. *New York University Review of Law and Social Change* 14:59–92.

——. (2002). Cost Comparison Between a Death Penalty Case and a Case Where the Charge and Conviction Is Life Without Parole. Pp. 122A–122FF in *The Application of Indiana's Capital Sentencing Law*. Indianapolis: Indiana Criminal Justice Institute.

Gottlieb, Gerald (1961). Testing the Death Penalty. *Southern California Law Review* 34:268–281.

Grasmick, Harold G., Robert J. Bursik, Jr., and Brenda S. Blackwell. (1993). Religious Beliefs and Public Support for the Death Penalty for Juveniles and Adults. *Journal of Crime and Justice* 16:59–86.

Grasmick, Harold G., Elizabeth Davenport, Mitchell B. Chamlin, and Robert J. Bursik, Jr.. (1992). Protestant Fundamentalism and the Retributivist Doctrine of Punishment. *Criminology* 30:21–45.

Grasmick, Harold G., John K. Cochran, Robert J. Bursik Jr., and M'Lou Kimpel (1993b). Religion, Punitive Justice, and Support for the Death Penalty. *Justice Quarterly* 10:289–313.

Graves, W. F. (1956). A Doctor Looks at Capital Punishment. *Medical Arts and Sciences* 10:137–141.

Gross, Samuel R. and Richard Mauro (1984). Patterns of Death: An Analysis of Racial Disparities in Capital Sentencing and Homicide Victimization. *Stanford Law Review* 37:27–153.

——. (1989). *Death and Discrimination: Racial Disparities in Capital Sentencing.* Boston: Northeastern University Press.

Gwynne, S. C. (2002). Dealing out Death. *Texas Monthly,* July.

Hall, Michael (2002). Death Isn't Fair. *Texas Monthly,* December.

Halttunen, Karen (1998). *Murder Most Foul: The Killer and the American Gothic Imagination.* Cambridge: MA: Harvard University Press.

Hearn, Daniel Allen (1999). *Legal Executions in New England, 1623–1960.* Jefferson, NC: McFarland and Compnay.

Hindson, Stephanie, Hillary Potter and Michael L. Radelet (2006). Race, Gender, Region and Death Sentencing in Colorado, 1980–1999. *University of Colorado Law Review* 77: 549–594.

Hindus, Michael S. (1980). *Prison and Plantation: Crime, Justice, and Authority in Massachusetts and South Carolina, 1767–1878.* Chapel Hill: University of North Carolina Press.

Hood, Roger (2002). *The Death Penalty: A Worldwide Perspective.* New York: Oxford University Press.

Howarth, Joan W. (2002). Executing White Masculinities: Learning From Karla Fay Tucker. *Oregon Law Review* 81:183–229.

Hughes, Rupert (1927). *George Washington, Volume II.* New York: Morrow.

Huie, William Bradford (1954). *The Execution of Private Slovik.* Yardly, PA: Westholme Publishing.

Imwinkelried, Edward J. (1982). Forensic Hair Analysis: The Case Against Under-employment of Scientific Evidence. *Washington and Lee Law Review* 39:41–67.

Jacobs, David, Jason T. Carmichael, and Stephanie L. Kent (2005). Vigilantism, Current Racial Threat, and Death Sentences. *American Sociological Review* 70: 656–677.

Jefferies, John C. (1994). *Justice Lewis F. Powell, Jr.: A Biography.* New York: Charles Scribner and Sons.

Jennings, Diane, Dan Malone, Steve McGonigle, and Pete Slover (2000). Quality of Justice: Defense Called Lacking for Death Row Indigents. *The Dallas Morning News.* September 10.

Johnson, Elmer H. (1957). Selective Factors in Capital Punishment. *Social Forces* 36:165–169.

Johnson, Guy (1941). The Negro and Crime. *Annals of the American Academy of Political and Social Science.* 217:93–104.

Jenkins, Bill (2001). *What To Do When the Police Leave.* Richmond, VA: WBJ Press.

Jones, Howard (1987). *Mutiny on the Amistad: The Saga of a Slave Revolt and Its Impact on American Abolition, Law, and Diplomacy.* New York: Oxford University Press.

Junkin, Tim (2004). *Bloodsworth: The True Story of the First Death Row Inmate Exonerated by DNA.* Chapel Hill, NC: Algonquin Books.

Kant, Immanual ([1797] 1965). *The Metaphysical Elements of Justice.* Indianapolis: Bobbs-Merrill.

Katz, Lawrence, Steven D. Levitt, and Ellen Shustorovich (2003). Prison Conditions, Capital Punishment, and Deterrence. *American Law and Economics Review* 5:318–343.

Keedy, E. R. (1949). The Early History of Murder and Manslaughter. *University of Pennsylvania Law Review* 97:759–777.

King, D. R. (1978). The Brutalization Effect: Execution Publicity and the Incidence of Homicide in South Carolina. *Social Forces* 57: 683–687.

King, Rachel (2003). *Don't Kill in Our Names: Families of Murder Victims Speak Out Against the Death Penalty.* Piscataway, NJ: Rutgers University Press.

Kleck, Gary (1981). Racial Discrimination in Criminal Sentencing: A Critical Evaluation of the Evidence With Additional Evidence of the Death Penalty. *American Sociological Review* 46:783–805.

Klein, Lawrence R., Brian E. Forst, and Victor Filatov (1978). The Deterrent Effect of Capital Punishment: An Assessment of the Estimates. In A. Blumstein, J. Cohen, and D. Nagin (Eds.), *Deterrence and Incapacitation: Estimating the Effects of Criminal Sanctions on Crime Rates.* Washington, D.C.: National Academy Press.

Klein, Stephen P. and John E. Rolph (1991). Relationship of Offender and Victim Race to Death Penalty Sentences in California. *Jurimetrics* 32:33–48.

Koeninger, Rupert C. (1969). Capital Punishment in Texas 1924–1968. *Crime and Delinquency* 15:132–142.

Koniaris, Leonidas G., Teresa A. Zimmers, David A. Lubarsky, and Jonathan P. Sheldon. (2005). Inadequate Anaesthesia in Lethal Injection for Execution. *The Lancet* 65:1412–1414.

Kousser, J. Morgan (1974). *The Shaping of Southern Politics: Suffrage Restriction and the Establishment of the One-Party South.* New Haven: Yale University Press.

Langan, Patrick A. and David J. Levin (2002). *Recidivism of Prisoners Released in 1994.* Bureau of Justice Statistics Special Report. U.S. Department of Justice, Office of Justice Programs.

Larranaga, Mark A. (2003). *Where Are We Heading? Current Trends of Washington's Death Penalty.* Seattle: Washington Death Penalty Assistance Center.

———. (2004). *Washington's Death Penalty System: A Review of the Costs, Length, and Results of Capital Cases in Washington State.* Seattle: Washington Death Penalty Assistance Center.

Layson, Stephen K. (1985). Homicide and Deterrence: A Reexamination of U.S. Time-Series Evidence. *Southern Economic Journal* 52:68–89.

Legislative Post Audit Committee (2003). *Costs Incurred for Death Penalty Cases: A K-Goal Audit of the Department of Corrections.* Legislative Division of Post Audit, Legislature of Kansas.

Lempert, Richard (1983). The Effect of Executions on Homicides: A New Look in an Old Light. *Crime and Delinquency* 29:88–115.

Liebman, James S. (2000). The Overproduction of Death. *Columbia Law Review* 100: 2030–2156.

Liebman, James S., Jeffrey Fagan, Valerie West, and J. Lloyd (2000). Capital Attrition: Error Rates in Capital Cases, 1973-1995. *Texas Law Review* 78:1839–1865.

Liebman, James S., Jeffrey Fagan, Valerie West, Andrew Gelman, Garth Davies and Alexander Kiss (2002). *A Broken System Part II: Why There Is So Much Error in Capital Cases and What Can Be Done About It.* Columbia University School of Law.

Liu, Zhiqiang (2004). Capital Punishment and the Deterrence Hypothesis: Some New Insights and Empirical Evidence. *Eastern Economic Journal* 30:237–258.

Long, Phil and Steve Brousquet (2000). Execution of Slayer Goes Wrong; Delay, Bitter Tirade Precede His Death. *Miami Herald,* June 8.

Lutheran Church-Missouri Synod (2006). Report on Capital Punishment. Available at <http://www.lcms.org>.

Makeig, John (1992). Asleep on the Job: Trial Boring, Lawyer Said. *Houston Chronicle,* August 14.

Markon, Jerry (2006). Wrongfull Jailed Man Wins Suit. *Washington Post,* (Metro Section) May 6.

Markman, Stephen J. and Paul G. Cassell (1988). Protecting the Innocent: A Response to the Bedau-Radelet Study. *Stanford Law Review* 41:121–160.

Marquart, James and Jonathan Sorensen (1988). Institutional and Post-release Behavior of *Furman*-Commuted Inmates in Texas. *Criminology* 26:677–693.

———. (1989). A National Study of the *Furman*-Commuted Inmates: Assessing the Threat to Society From Capital Offenders. *Loyola of Los Angeles Law Review* 23:5–28.

Masur, Louis P. (1989). *Rites of Execution.* New York: Oxford University Press.

Meltsner, Michael (1973). *Cruel and Unusual: The Supreme Court and Capital Punishment.* New York: Random House.

Mangum, C. S. (1940). *The Legal Status of the Negro.* Chapel Hill: University of North Carolina Press.

Marshall, Micah (2000). Death in Venice: Europe's Death Penalty Elitism. *New Republic,* July 31.

McFarland, Sam G. (1983). Is Capital Punishment a Short-Term Deterrent to Homicide? A Study of the Effects of Four Recent Executions. *Journal of Criminal Law and Criminology* 74:1014–1030.

Megivern, James J. (1997). *The Death Penalty: An Historical and Theological Survey.* Mahway, NJ: Paulist Press.

Mello, Michael A. (1988). Facing Death Alone: The Post-Conviction Attorney Crisis on Death Row. *American University Law Review* 7:513–607.

———. (2001). *The Wrong Man: A True Story of Innocence on Death Row.* Minneapolis: University of Minnesota Press.

Meltsner, Michael (1973). *Cruel and Unusual: The Supreme Court and Capital Punishment.* New York: Random House.

Messner, Steven F., Robert D. Baller, and Matthew P. Zevenbergen. (2005). The Legacy of Lynching and Southern Homicide. *American Sociological Review* 70: 633–655.

Miller, A. S. and J. H. Bowman (1988). *Death by Installments: The Ordeal of Willie Francis.* Westport, CT: Greenwood Press.

Miller, Karen S. (2006). *Wrongful Executions and the Legitimacy of the Death Penalty.* New York: LFB Scholarly Publishing.

Miller, Kent S. and Michael L. Radelet (1993). *Executing the Mentally Ill: The Criminal Justice System and the Case of Alvin Ford.* Newbury Park, CA: Sage Publications.

Mills, Steve and Ken Armstrong (1999a) The Failure of the Death Penalty in Illinois. Part 3: The Jailhouse Informant. *Chicago Tribune,* November 16.

———. (1999b). The Failure of the Death Penalty in Illinois. Part 4: A Tortured Path to Death Row. *Chicago Tribune,* November 17.

———. (1999c). The Failure of the Death Penalty in Illinois. Part 5: Convicted by a Hair. *Chicago Tribune,* November 18.

Mills, Steve and Maurice Possley (2004). Texas Man Executed on Disproved Forensics. *Chicago Tribune,* December 9.

Mocan, H. Naci and R. Kaj Gittings (2003). Getting Off Death Row: Commuted Sentences and the Deterrent Effect of Capital Punishment. *Journal of Law and Economics* 453:453–478.

Moran, Richard (2002). *Executioner's Current: Thomas Edison, George Westinghouse, and the Invention of the Electric Chair.* New York: Alfred A. Knopf.

Morgan, John G. (2004). *Tennessee's Death Penalty: Costs and Consequences.* State of Tennessee, Comptroller of the Treausury.

Nakell, Barry and Kenneth A. Hardy (1987). *The Arbitrariness of the Death Penalty.* Philadelphia: Temple University Press.

Nathanson, Stephen (1987). *An Eye for an Eye? The Morality of Punishing by Death.* Totowa, NJ: Rowman and Littlefield.

———. (2001). *An Eye for an Eye? The Morality of Punishing by Death* (2nd Edition). Lanham, MD: Rowman and Littlefield.

National Law Journal (1990). *Fatal Defense, Death Row Defense: Lawyers in Trouble.* June 11.

Newby, I. A. (1968). *The Development of Segregationist Thought.* Homewood, IL: Dorsey Press.

Nisbett, Richard E. and Dov Cohen (1996). *Culture of Honor: The Psychology of Violence in the South.* Boulder, CO: Westview Press.

Noelle, Elisabeth and Erich Peter Neumann (1967). *The Germans: Public Opinion Polls 1947–1966.* Allensbach, Bonn: Verlag für Demoskopie.

Nolen, Claude H. (1967). *The Negro's Image in the South.* Lexington: University of Kentucky Press.

Northwestern University Center on Wrongful Convictions (2005). <http://www.law.northwestern.edu/wrongfulconvictions/>.

Oberer, Walter E. (1961). Does Disqualification of Jurors for Scruples Against Capital Punishment Constitute Denial of Fair Trial on Issue of Guilt? *Texas Law Review* 39: 545–567.

Oberly, James W. *Executions in the United States, 1608–1991: The Espy File.* Inter-University Consortium for Political and Social Research. Ann Arbor: University of Michigan.

Orthodox Presbyterian Church (2006). Position on capital punishment available at: <http://www.opc.org/>.

Olsen, Lise (2001). Uncertain Justice. *Seattle Post-Intellingencer Reporter*, August 6.

——. (2001). Defense for Capital Crimes Often Done on the Cheap. *Seattle Post-Intellingencer Reporter*, August 8.

O'Shea, Kathleen (1999). *Women and the Death Penalty in the United States, 1900–1998.* Westport, CT: Praeger Publishers.

Owen Robert C. (2004). Zen and the Art of Exoneration. *Texas Observer*, November 5.

Paluch, James A. Jr. (2004). *A Life for a Life.* Los Angeles: Roxbury.

Partington, D. C. (1965). The Incidence of the Death Penalty for Rape in Virginia. *Washington and Lee Law Review* 22:43–75.

Passell, Peter (1975). The Deterrent Effect of Capital Punishment: A Statistical Test. *Stanford Law Review* 28:61–80.

Passell, Peter and John B. Taylor (1977). The Deterrent Effect of Capital Punishment: Another View. *American Economic Review* 67:445–451.

Paternoster, Raymond (1983). Race of Victim and Location of Crime: The Decision to Seek the Death Penalty in South Carolina. *Journal of Criminal Law and Criminology* 74:754–785.

——. (1988). The Administration of the Death Penalty in South Carolina: Experiences Over the First Few Years. *University of South Carolina Law Review* 39:245–414.

——. (1991). *Capital Punishment in America.* New York: Macmillan.

Paternoster, Raymond, Robert Brame, Sarah Bacon and Andrew Ditchfield (2004). Justice by Geography and Race: The Administration of the Death Penalty in Maryland, 1978–1999. *Margins: Maryland's Journal on Race, Religion, Gender and Class* 4:1–97.

Peterson, Ruth D. and William C. Bailey (1988). Murder and Capital Punishment in the Evolving Context of the Post-*Furman* Era. *Social Forces* 66:774–807.

——. (2003). Is Capital Punishment an Effective Deterrent for Murder? An Examination of Social Science Research. Pp. 251–282 in James R. Acker, Robert M. Bohm, and Charles S. Lanier (Eds.), *America's Experiment With the Death Penalty.* Durham, NC: Carolina Academic Press.

Phillips, David P. (1980). The Deterrent Effect of Capital Punishment: New Evidence on an Old Controversy. *American Journal of Sociology* 88:165–167.

Pierce, Glenn L. and Michael L. Radelet (2002). Race, Religion, and Death Sentencing in Illinois, 1988–1997. *Oregon Law Review* 81:39–96.

——. (2005). The Impact of Legally Inappropriate Factors on Death Sentencing for California Homicides, 1990–1999. *Santa Clara Law Review* 46:1–47.

Pojman, Louis P. (2004). Why the Death Penalty Is Morally Permissible. Pp. 51–75 in Hugo A. Bedau and Paul G. Cassell (Eds.), *Debating the Death Penalty.* New York: Oxford University Press.

Possley, Maurice and Ken Armstrong (1999a). Trial and Error. Part 2: The Flip Side of a Fair Trial. *Chicago Tribune*, January 11.

——. (1999b). Trial and Error. Part 3: Prosecution on Trial in DuPage. *Chicago Tribune*, January 12.

Possley, Maurice and Steve Mills (2006a). "I Didn't Do It. But I Know Who Did." *Chicago Tribune,* June 24.

———. (2006b). Phantom or Killer. *Chicago Tribune,* June 26.

———. (2006c). The Secret That Wasn't. *Chicago Tribune,* June 27.

Prejean, Helen (1994). *Dead Man Walking.* New York: Vintage.

———. (2005). *The Death of Innocence: An Eyewitness Account of Wrongful Executions.* New York: Random House.

Radelet, Michael L. (2003). Post-*Furman* Botched Executions. Unpublished manuscript available at <http://www.deathpenaltyinfo.org>.

———. (1981). Racial Characteristics and the Imposition of the Death Penalty. *American Sociological Review* 46:918–927.

Radelet, Michael L. and Glenn L. Pierce (1985). Race and Prosecutorial Discretion in Homicide Cases. *Law and Society Review* 19:587–621.

Radelet, Michael, Hugo A. Bedau, and Constance E. Putnam (1992). *In Spite of Innocence.* Boston: Northeastern University Press.

Radelet, Michael and Marian J. Borg (2000). The Changing Nature of Death Penalty Debates. *Annual Review of Sociology* 26:43–61.

Radzinowicz, Leon (1948). *A History of English Criminal Law, Vol. 1.* London: Stevens and Sons.

Rapaport, Elizabeth (1996). Capital Murder, Gender, and the Domestic Discount. *Southern Methodist Law Review* 49:1507–1548.

Reiman, Jeffrey H. (1985). Justice, Civilization, and the Death Penalty: Answering van den Haag. *Philosophy and Public Affairs.* 14:115–148.

Report of the Commission to Investigate and Report the Most Humane and Practical Method of Carrying Into Effect the Sentence of Death in Capital Cases (1888). Albany: The Argus Company.

Ressig, Mark (2003). *Edison and the Electric Chair: A Story of Light and Death.* New York: Walker Publishing.

Rise, Eric W. (1995). *The Martinsville Seven: Race, Rape, and Capital Punishment.* Charlottesville: University Press of Virginia.

Roach, Marilynne K. (2004). *The Salem Witch Trials: A Day by Day Chronicle of a Community Under Siege.* Lanham, MD: Taylor Trade Publishing.

Savitz, Leonard (1958). A Study in Capital Punishment. *Journal of Criminal Law, Criminology, and Police Science* 49:338–341.

Schabas, William A. (2000). Islam and the Death Penalty. *William and Mary Bill of Rights Journal* 9:223–236.

Schabas, W. A. (2002). *The Abolition of the Death Penalty in International Law* (3rd Edition). New York: Cambridge University Press.

Scheck, Barry, Peter Neufeld, and James Dwyer (2000). *Actual Innocence.* New York: Doubleday.

Schwarz, Philip J. (1988) *Twice Condemned: Slaves and the Criminal Laws of Virginia, 1705–1865.* Baton Rouge, LA: Louisiana State University Press.

Sellin, Thorsten (1959). *The Death Penalty.* Philadelphia: The American Law Institute.

———. (1967). *Capital Punishment.* New York: Harper and Row.

Shepherd, Johanna M. (2004). Murders of Passion, Execution Delays and the Deterrence of Capital Punishment. *Journal of Legal Studies* 33: 283–321.

———. (2005). Deterrence Versus Brutalization: Capital Punishment's Differing Impacts Among States. *Michigan Law Review* 104: 203–255.

Smith, Clive A. S. and Patrick D. Goodman (1996). Forensic Hair Comparison Analysis: Nineteenth Century Science or Twentieth Century Snake Oil. *Columbia Human Rights Law Review* 27:227–279.

Sorensen, Jon, Robert Wrinkle, Victoria Brewer, and John Marquart (1999). Capital Punishment and Deterrence: Examining the Effect of Executions on Murder in Texas. *Crime and Delinquency* 45:481–493.

Southern Baptist Convention (2006). SBC Resolution on Capital Punishment June 2000. Available at http://www.sbc.net/resolutions.

Stack, Steven. (2003). Authoritarianism and Support for the Death Penalty: A Multivariate Analysis. *Sociological Focus* 36:333–352.

Stampp, Kenneth M. (1956). *The Peculiar Institution.* New York: Alfred A. Knopf.

Steiker, Carol S. (2002). Capital Punishment and American Exceptionalism. *Oregon Law Review* 81:97–125.

Steiker, Carol S. and Jordan M. Steiker (1995). Sober Second Thoughts: Reflections of Two Decades of Constitutional Regulation of Capital Punishment. *Harvard Law Review* 109: 355–438.

Streib, Victor L. (1987). *Death Penalty for Juveniles.* Bloomington: Indiana University Press.

——. (2005). *Death Penalty in a Nutshell.* St. Paul, MN: West.

Teeters, Negley K. (1963). *Scaffolds and Chair.* Philadelphia: Temple University Press.

Tempest, Rone (2005). Death Row Means a Long Life. *Los Angeles Times,* March 6.

Texas Defender Service (2005a). *A State of Denial: Texas Justice and the Death Penalty.* Austin: Texas Defender Service.

——. (2005b). *Deadly Speculation: Misleading Texas Capital Juries With False Predictions of Future Dangerousness.* Austin: Texas Defender Service. Available at: <www. texasdefender.org/publications>.

Tofte, Sarah (2006). So Long As They Die: Lethal Injections in the United States. Human Rights Watch Report available at <http://www.hrw.org/>.

Tolnay, Stewart E. and E. M. Beck (1995). *A Festival of Violence: An Analysis of Southern Lynchings, 1982–1930.* Urbana: University of Illinois Press.

Tolnay, Stewart E. and E. M. Beck, and James L. Massey (1992). Black Competition and White Vengeance: Legal Execution of Blacks as Social Control in the American South, 1890 to 1929. *Social Science Quarterly* 73:627–644.

Toobin, Jeffrey (2005). Killer Instincts. *The New Yorker.* January 17, 2005.

Tucker John C. (1997). *May God Have Mercy.* New York: W.W. Norton.

United States General Accounting Office (1990). *Death Penalty Sentencing: Research Indicates Pattern of Racial Disparities.* Washington, DC, U.S. General Accouting Office. Report available at <http://archive.gao.gov>.

Unnever, James D. and Francis T. Cullen (2006). Christian Fundamentalism and Support for Capital Punishment. *Journal of Research in Crime and Delinquency* 43:169–197.

Urbina, Martin G. (2003). *Capital Punishment and Latino Offenders: Racial and Ethnic Differences in Death Sentences.* New York: LFB Scholarly Publishing.

Union of Orthodox Jewish Congregations (2006). Union of Orthodox Jewish Congregations Endorses Death Penalty Moratorium. Available at <http://www.ou.org/public/statements/2000/nate19.htm>.

van den Haag, Ernest (1975). *Punishing Criminals: Concerning a Very Old and Painful Question.* New York: Basic Books.

——. (1978). In Defense of the Death Penalty: A Legal-Practical-Moral Analysis. *Criminal Law Bulletin* 14:51–68.

———. (1985). Refuting Reiman and Nathanson. *Philosophy and Public Affairs* 14:165–176.

———. (2003). Justice, Deterrence and the Death Penalty. Pp. 233–249 in James R. Acker, Robert M. Bohm, and Charles S. Lanier (Eds.), *America's Experiment With the Death Penalty.* Durham, NC: Carolina Academic Press.

Van den Haag, Ernest and John P. Conrad (1983). *The Death Penalty: A Debate.* New York: Plenum Press.

Vandiver, Margaret (2006). *Lethal Punishment: Lynchings and Legal Executions in the South.* Piscataway, NJ: Rutgers University Press.

Vito, Gennaro and Thomas J. Keil (1988). Capital Sentencing in Kentucky. *Journal of Criminal Law and Criminology* 79:483–503.

Warden, Rob (2004). *The Snitch System: How Snitch Testimony Sent Randy Steidl and Other Innocent Americans to Death Row.* Center of Wrongful Convictions. Northwestern University School of Law. Available online at <www. law.northwestern.edu/wrongfulconvictions>.

Weigler, S. (1992). Bite Mark Evidence: Forensic Odontology and the Law. *Health Matrix: Journal of Law and Medicine* 2:303–323.

Weinstein, Henry (2001). Attorney's Dozing at Center of Texas Murder Case Challenge: Defendant Facing the Death Penalty Contends That His Lawyer in 1984 Trial Was No More Than a Potted Plant. *Los Angeles Times,* January 23.

Weisberg, Robert (1984). Deregulating Death. In P. B. Kurland, G. Casper, and J. J. Hutchinson, *The Supreme Court Review 1983.* Chicago: University of Illinois Press.

———. (2005). The Death Penalty Meets Social Science: Deterrence and Jury Behavior Under New Scrutiny. *Annual Review of Law and Social Science* 1:151–170.

White, Welsh S. (1985). *Life in the Balance: Procedural Safeguards in Capital Cases.* Ann Arbor: University of Michigan Press.

———. (1987). *The Death Penalty in the Eighties: An Examination of the Modern System of Capital Punishment.* Ann Arbor: University of Michigan Press.

———. (1991). *The Death Penalty in the Nineties: An Examination of the Modern System of Capital Punishment.* Ann Arbor: University of Michigan Press.

Whitfield, Stephen J. (1988). *A Death in the Delta: The Story of Emmett Till.* New York: Free Press.

Wilkinson, Allen P. and Ronald M. Gerughty (1985). Bite Mark Evidence: Its Admissibility Is Hard to Swallow. *Washington State University Law Review* 12:519–542.

Will, George (2000). Innocent on Death Row. *Washington Post,* April 6.

Willimason, Joel (1984). *The Crucible of Race.* New York: Oxford University Press.

Wilson, Richard J. (2003). The Influence of International Law and Practice on the Death Penalty in the United States. Pp. 147–164 in James R. Acker, Robert M. Bohm, and Charles S. Lanier (Eds.), *America's Experience With Capital Punishment.* Durham, NC: Carolina Academic Press.

Wolfgang, Marvin E. (1974). The Criminologist in Court. *Journal of Criminal Law and Criminology* 65:244–247.

Wolfgang, Marvin E. and Marc Riedel (1973). Race, Judicial Discretion, and the Death Penalty. *The Annals* 407:119–133.

———. (1975). Rape, Race, and the Death Penalty in Georgia. *American Journal of Orthopsychiatry* 45:658–668.

Wolfgang, Marvin E., Arlene Kelly, and Hans C. Nolde (1962). Comparison of the Executed and the Commuted Among Admissions to Death Row. *Journal of Criminal Law, Criminology, and Police Science* 53:301–311.

Woodward, C. Vann (1951). *Origins of the New South, 1877–1913*. Baton Rouge: Louisiana State University Press.

——. (1963). *Tom Watson: Agrarian Rebel*. New York: Oxford University Press.

Yunker, J. A. (1976). Is the Death Penalty a Deterrent to Homicide: Some Time-Series Evidence. *Journal of Behavioral Economics* 5:1–32.

Zimring, Franklin E. (2003). *The Contradictions of American Capital Punishment*. New York: Oxford University Press.

Zimring, Franklin, Joel Eigen, and Shula O'Malley (1976). Punishing Homicide in Philadelphia: Perspectives on the Death Penalty. *University of Chicago Law Review* 43:227–252.

Zimring, Franklin E. and Gordon Hawkins (1986). *Capital Punishment and the American Agenda*. New York: Cambridge University Press.

Zimmerman, Paul R. (2004). State Executions, Deterrence, and the Incidence of Murder. *Journal of Applied Economics* 7:163–193. ✦

Case Index

Name Index

Subject Index

Southern colonies plantation economy, 5, 6, 13, 21, 160, 161
Southern states
  executions from 1930 to 1967, 30
  Premodern Period, 36–37
  whites killing blacks in the South, 191
Special groups of people in capital punishment, 108–17
Standardless juries, 85, 87–89, 90–94
Stanford Law Review articles on innocent persons executed, 216, 217
State boards of parole and pardons, commutations, 193
State of nature, 122
State rather than federal issue, 258, 275, 278
Statelessness, 280n1
States
  capital crimes listed for Modern Period, 44–45
  executing juveniles, 120n8
  jurisdiction of, 3, 21–22, 35–37
  with juveniles on death row, 120n9
  methods of execution by in Modern Period, 54
  number of executions by in Modern Period, 52
  prohibiting execution of juveniles, 115
  prohibiting execution of the mentally retarded, 109, 111
  and United States Supreme Court, 18, 77
  with and without the death penalty in Modern Period, 41
Stealing hogs, horses, money, or tobacco, 6
Strangulation, 15
Suffocation, 58
Symbolic benefit of capital punishment, 5, 12, 20, 25n2, 25n7

Talmud, 149
Ten-year moratorium on death penalty, 3–4, 38, 40, 70
  end of, 27
  legal challenges leading to, 29
  and Modern Period, 74
Tennessee
  cost of capital punishment, 132
  cost of death penalty, 132
  mandatory death statute, 28
Terrorism, 68
  domestic, 265
  racial, 176, 180
  suspects in, 270
Texas
  capital punishment in, 277
  capital punishment used frequently, 277
  executing a Mexican national, 270
  and George W. Bush, 3
  Harris County (Houston), 251, 275, 278
  Houston Police Department Crime Lab, 251
  ineffective defense counsel, 235–36, 239
  jail house snitches, 245

"junk science," 246–47, 248–49, 251
lethal injection, 56, 57
mentally retarded, 109–10, 111–12
murder rates for 1990–2004, 146–47
numbers of executions in, xv, 48, 50
one-year moratorium on executions, 144
possible innocence, 218–20, 221–23
prosecutor and law enforcement misconduct, 240–42, 243–44
prosecutors in, xiii–xiv
"quasi-mandatory" statute, 105–6
statutes approved, 119n2
within-state variation, 64
Thirteenth Amendment, 166
Three-drug "cocktail" in lethal injection, 57, 58, 59
Time magazine, 222
To Kill a Mockingbird (Lee), 182–83
Torah, 148
Torture, 77, 79, 179, 267
Treason, 5, 42, 155n1
Trials
  bench versus jury, 101
  bifurcated, 83, 100, 104–5, 108, 199
  bifurcated capital trials (*McGautha v. California*), 85–89
  death qualifying juries, 82–83
  guilt/innocence phase, 67, 83, 100
  penalty phase, 67, 83, 86, 100, 101, 102, 119n1, 255n12
  see also Juries

Uniform Code of Military Justice, 69
United Nations and execution of juveniles, 268
United Nations International Covenant of Civil and Political Rights, 268
United States Census Bureau, "death by execution" in *Mortality Statistics,* 3, 27
United States Constitution
  approval of state death penalty statutes, 4, 40, 45, 74
  death penalty constitutionality, 82–85
  Eighth Amendment, 18, 29, 34, 37, 40, 59, 90, 209, 266
  executions of juveniles, 115
  Fifteenth Amendment, 170
  Fifth Amendment, 78, 79, 96n1
  Founding Fathers of, 76, 77
  Fourteenth Amendment, 18, 19, 87, 89, 90, 170, 196, 209
  framer's intent theory, 76, 79, 80
  lethal injection constitutionality, 59
  method of imposing death, 76–79
  methods of capital punishment and the Eighth Amendment, 74
  new theory of Eighth Amendment, 80–82, 266
  theories about what the Eighth Amendment prohibits, 79–82
  Thirteenth Amendment, 166